Is Your God Big Enough? Close Enough? You Enough?

"This book is magnificent. Smith, in clear contemporary yet biblically grounded language, explains the spiritual essence of Jesus' teaching, and therefore of Christianity, better than any writer I have ever read. He shows us how to relate to God in three very distinctive ways—to the Supreme Creator of multi-universes seen and unseen, to the intimate friend Jesus described at the Last Supper, and to our own deepest and highest self, the God within us all. I recommend this book to every Christian and to all spiritual seekers."

—Jim Marion, author of *Putting on the Mind of Christ: The Inner Work of Christian Spirituality*

"This book is a spiritual jewel. Smith's impressive erudition, combined with a lifetime of deep spiritual experience, provide profound and useful guidance for each reader's personal journey, convincingly demonstrates what it means to feel the presence of God. This delightful book is both theologically sophisticated and pragmatically accessible. I highly recommend this important contribution to evolutionary spirituality."

—Steve McIntosh, author of *The Presence of the Infinite, Evolution's Purpose*, and *Integral Consciousness*

"This is the most important book I have read in the last 15 years. For those who desire a deeper and richer understanding of Jesus, this book is a feast. It is a new wineskin, which represents an ever more divine level of consciousness capable of bringing together the body of Christ in a way that nothing else can."

—James P. Danaher, Ph.D., Head, Department of Philosophy, Nyack College, and author of *Philosophical Imagination*

"This book brings together a rich tapestry of science and spirituality in a way that is accessible to a world seeking light. One can read it over and over again, finding new insights each time. May this book touch your life and transform your vision of God who dwells in the heart of the cosmos as the fullness of love."

—Ilia Delio, OSF, Chair of Theology, Villanova University

"Smith is ahead of the curve theologically with his wise combination of modern mysticism, biblical literacy, religious inclusivity, knowledge of integral studies, depth and breadth of reading, and practical application. He makes so much that passes for modern theology seem timid and constrained. Read this book to get ahead of that curve yourself. He pushes the mind and the heart where they want to go but are afraid to become free enough to soar. And in doing so he shows the way to a depth of spirituality we never thought was there."

—Robert N. Minor, Ph.D., Professor Emeritus of Religious Studies, University of Kansas and author of *When Religion Is an Addiction*

"To tackle the concept of the Trinity is a daunting task for any theologian or scholar. Paul Smith, however, does it with relish, vigor, and a creative spirit. He has given thoughtful Christians a new prism by which to reflect upon the partial truths we have about God and about ourselves. In this carefully researched and readable work, he writes to always engage the mind and heart for a more authentic experience with God. Because of this dual purpose, readers will reap both academic and spiritual benefits."

—David May, Ph.D., Professor of New Testament, Central Baptist Theological Seminary, Shawnee, Kansas

"In this timely and important book, Smith goes beyond others by leading the reader through reflection and practice all the while answering the big questions through the examples of Jesus, the great mystics, scripture, and the author's own experience. A must read for anyone ready to experience God the way that Jesus did."

—Adam Luedtke Ph.D., Founder of Transformative Life Contemplative Monastic Spiritual Center

"If you think the Trinity is a topic for stodgy theologians who smoke pipes in leather chairs in wood-paneled rooms, Paul Smith challenges you to think again. The Trinity, Smith claims, leads to daring and bold experiences. *Mystical* experiences. This is not a book for the dispassionate or detached. Paul Smith is out to awaken you. Be careful! His latest book ignites passion and practice."

—Jack Levison, W.J.A. Power Chair of Old Testament Interpretation and Biblical Hebrew, Perkins School of Theology, Southern Methodist University, and author of *Filled with the Spirit* and *Fresh Air: The Holy Spirit for an Inspired Life*

Is Your God Big Enough?
Close Enough?
You Enough?

Jesus and the Three Faces of God

Is Your God
Big Enough?
Close Enough?
You Enough?

Jesus and the Three Faces of God

Paul R. Smith

PARAGON HOUSE
St. Paul, Minnesota

First Edition 2017

Published in the United States by

Paragon House

www.paragonhouse.com

Copyright © 2017 by Paul Smith

Credits on page viii.

Library of Congress Cataloging-in-Publication Data

Names: Smith, Paul R., 1937- author.
Title: Is your God big enough, close enough, you enough? : Jesus and the
   three faces of God / by Paul R. Smith.
Description: St. Paul, Minnesota : Paragon House, 2017.
Identifiers: LCCN 2017010538 | ISBN 9781557789310 (pbk. : alk. paper)
Subjects: LCSH: God (Christianity) | Trinity. | Spirituality--Christianity.
Classification: LCC BT103 .S595 2017 | DDC 231--dc23 LC record
   available at https://lccn.loc.gov/2017010538

The paper used in this publication meets the minimum requirements of American National Standard for Information Sciences—Permanence of Paper for Printed Library Materials, ANSI standard Z39.48-1992.

Manufactured in the United States of America

10 9 8 7 6 5 4 3 2 1

For current information about all releases from Paragon House, visit the website at http://www.paragonhouse.com

Dedication

This book is dedicated to Ken Wilber who gave me a contemporary model of the spiritual life by his life and a relevant path to get there by his integral map.

Credits

Contents Overview

Dedication . . . . *vii*

Credits . . . . *viii*

Foreword by Richard Rohr. . . . .*xix*

Introduction 1

PART ONE
Is Your God Big Enough?
Opening our mind to Trinity beyond us

CHAPTER 1
Beyond "the Father" to the Wonder of Infinite Being 31

CHAPTER 2
Beyond "the Son" to the Glory of the Cosmic Christ. 47

CHAPTER 3
Beyond "the Spirit" to the Marvel of Infinite Consciousness 69

PART TWO
Is Your God Close Enough?
Opening our heart to Trinity beside us

CHAPTER 4
God Beside Us as Father-Mother .103

CHAPTER 5
Why I Still Talk to Jesus 117

CHAPTER 6
Is Anybody Really There? 149

CHAPTER 7
God, Jesus, and Gender 165

CHAPTER 8
The Closeness of God as Spirit. 175

PART THREE
Is Your God You Enough?
Opening our identity to Trinity being us

CHAPTER 9
The Spectrum of Spirit as Consciousness 213

CHAPTER 10
The Record of Awakened Consciousness (in the Bible) 225

CHAPTER 11
The Reality of Awakened Consciousness. 245

CHAPTER 12
The Results of Awakened Consciousness 269

CHAPTER 13
The Bliss of Transcendent Consciousness 287

CHAPTER 14
The Peace of Oneness Consciousness 313

CHAPTER 15
The Moses and Elijah Phenomenon 339

CHAPTER 16
The Unknown God of Today. .357

Afterword by Ken Wilber 361

Appendix: What Every Body Can Say. 381

Bibliography 391

Index 405

Detailed Contents

Dedication . . . . *vii*

Credits . . . . *viii*

Illustrations . . . . *xvii*

Foreword by Richard Rohr . . . .*xix*

Introduction 1

God in three persons, 2; The classical Trinity, 4; Trinity—Breakthrough or breakdown?, 5; Looking at Trinity's "God in three persons" through the lens of The Three Faces of God, 7; Twelve words that changed my mind and heart about God, 8; We learned this in elementary school, 9; The three basic perspectives on everything, 9; Jesus embraced all three perspectives with God, 9; The three–dimensional God of Jesus, 10; From traditional Trinity to the nine–dimensional "Expanded" Trinity, 11; The faces of God, 11; Why we need a God that is big enough, close enough, and you enough, 15; Healing the Western Soul, 18; Did Jesus really say that?, 20; Going beyond textual certainty, 20; The risen Jesus also taught the early Christians, 23; Reading our Bible the same way Jesus did his, 24; A dynamic system, 25; The Nine Pictures of the Expanded Trinity, 25; Summary of The Three Faces of God, 25; Questions for Reflection and Group Discussion, 26; Practices, 26

PART ONE
Is Your God Big Enough?
Opening our mind to Trinity beyond us

Are you in touch with the Infinite?, 29; The presence of the Infinite in the finite, 30

CHAPTER 1

Beyond "the Father" to the Wonder of Infinite Being 31

Is your God as big as the God of Jesus?, 32; The I AM God of Jesus, 33; God as Infinite Being, 34; Why did Moses need a name?, 35; The Awesome Wonder of Infinite Being, 36; God beyond Being, 37; God as Being Itself is echoed down through the ages, 38; An important qualification, 40; The Incredible Unbearable Love-Drenched Radiance of Being, 41; Jesus and the transpersonal Great I AM, 41; Imaging Infinite Being, 42; Is your

God big enough to encompass everything we know about the universe?, 43; How do you know if your God is big enough?, 43; Summary of Is Your God Big Enough?, 44; Question for Reflection and Group Discussion, 44; Practices, 45

CHAPTER 2
Beyond "the Son" to the Glory of the Cosmic Christ. 47

Jesus becomes Christ the Messiah, 47; Jesus becomes the risen Jesus, not the Cosmic Christ, 48; Christ the Messiah becomes Christ the Cosmic Christ, 49; The Cosmic Christ, 50; Who and what is the Cosmic Christ?, 50; A stunning description of the Cosmic Christ, 51; Eight observations about the Cosmic Christ., 60; Summary of Is Your Jesus Big Enough, 66; Questions for Reflection and Group Discussion, 67; Practices, 68

CHAPTER 3
Beyond "the Spirit" to the Marvel of Infinite Consciousness 69

What is spirit?, 69; A Detective Story: Solving the Mystery of Spirit, 70; Spirit in awakened form in the heroes of the Old Testament is different from spirit as life in everyone, 76; Awakened, intensified spirit becomes dominant in the New Testament, 77; The divine side of divine-human spirit as consciousness in fifteen sentences, 87; Does God know your name?, 88; A diagram of Trinity Beyond Us, 89; Summary of Is Your God as Spirit Big Enough?, 91; Questions for Reflection and Group Discussion, 92; Practices, 93

PART TWO
Is Your God Close Enough?
Opening our heart to Trinity beside us

How do you know your God is close enough?, 96; What others have said about falling in love with God, 98; Questions for Reflection and Group Discussion, 100; Practice, 100

CHAPTER 4
God Beside Us as Father-Mother .103

What's in a name?, 103; My first naming of God/She was "Heavenly Father", 104; My second naming of God/She was "Father-Mother" in my teaching and writing, 105; Why did Jesus call God Father but not Mother?, 108; A parable of life after birth, 109; My third naming of God/She was "Daddy," for my own healing, 111; The sacrament of naming, 111; Debate over "Daddy", 112; Summary of God Beside Us As Father-Mother, 114; Questions for Reflection and Group Discussion, 114; Practices, 115

CHAPTER 5

Why I Still Talk to Jesus 117

A transforming friendship with Jesus, 117; Others have spoken about this transforming friendship with Jesus, 118; The challenge of devotion to Jesus for thoughtful people today, 121; Is talking to Jesus talking to God?, 125; What does Jesus' kind of friendship look like?, 127; Devotion to Jesus among the first Christians, 128; Various branches of Christianity respond differently to friendship with Jesus, 132; Whom do you admire?, 134; The chair, 135; Sitting with Jesus, 136; One person's experience in Sitting with Jesus, 141; Summary of Why I Still Talk to Jesus, 145; Questions for Reflection and Group Discussion, 145; Practices, 146

CHAPTER 6

Is Anybody Really There? 149

What is real and how do we know?, 150; Evidence for the reality of a personal Divine Other, 155; Summary of Is Anybody Really There?, 162; Questions for Reflection and Discussion, 163; Practices, 163

CHAPTER 7

God, Jesus, and Gender 165

God's wonderful plan of diversity, 165; Mary carries Good News not only with Jesus but with gender healing, 166; The spiritual body of Jesus is beyond ordinary limits, including gender, 168; The New Testament feminine image of Jesus as Sophia, the wisdom of God, 170; When we pray, 171; Summary of God, Jesus, and Gender, 172; Questions for Reflection and Group Discussion, 173; Practices, 173

CHAPTER 8

The Closeness of God as Spirit. 175

Getting personal with personalization, 175; Spirit "with you and in you", 176; The lively biblical language of other forms of spirit's personal presence, 177; Spirit and wine, 178; Summary of The Closeness of God as Spirit, 178; Questions for Reflection and Discussion, 179; Practice, 179

PART THREE
Is Your God You Enough?
Opening our identity to Trinity being us

We are God become flesh, 184; God being us, 185; Jesus said that you are a god, 186; Divinity runs in the family, 187; What does being a god mean?, 188; What being a god does *not* mean, 188; How it works, 189;

God and Jesus are linked together, 191; God being us is both in process and yet already a present reality, 192; We will become gods in the future, 192; Others down through the ages who say that we are gods in the making, 193; On the other hand, the Bible claims we are *already* gods, 196; Others who say that we are already gods, 203; Why Christians often resist embracing their divinity, 207; Becoming what we already are, 207; Why it is important to know that your God is you enough, 209; How do you know your God is you enough?, 209; Summary of Part Three: Is Your God You Enough?, 210; Questions for Reflection and Group Discussion, 210; Practices, 211

CHAPTER 9

The Spectrum of Spirit as Consciousness 213

Consciousness in the Bible has four primary expressions, 214; Four introductory points about spirit, 214; The human side of divine-human consciousness in ten sentences, 215; Consciousness is more than just awareness, 216; The Apostle Paul writes about consciousness, 217; The spectrum of consciousness in four modes, 218; Summary of The Spectrum of Spirit as Consciousness, 223; Questions for Reflection and Group Discussion, 223; Practices, 224

CHAPTER 10

The Record of Awakened Consciousness (in the Bible) 225

Do we read the Bible through the glasses of doctrine or experience?, 226; The best beliefs are beneficial and beautiful, 228; The drama of awakened mystical consciousness in the Old Testament, 228; Awakened spirit-breath in the Hebrew scriptures, 229; A new era of awakened consciousness is predicted for all humankind, 231; Jesus and numinous consciousness for all, 232; Jesus, the mystic with a social and political agenda, 233; The activation of higher consciousness, 234; Activation of numinous awakening continues, 235; What is "tongues"?, 235; What is prophecy?, 237; Channeling, 237; Christianity began in a blaze of awakened consciousness, 238; Psychedelic visions in Revelation, 238; More paranormal phenomena, 239; They had never seen spirit-breath like this!, 240; The first Christians began their Christian lives with mystical experience, 241; Jesus leaves, and mystical spirit-breath comes, 242; Summary of The Record of Awakened Consciousness (in the Bible), 243; Questions for Reflection and Discussion, 243

CHAPTER 11

The Reality of Awakened Consciousness. 245

My journey, 249; All spiritual paths are explorations of awakened consciousness, 250; What happened to all these mystical dimensions?, 252;

Awakened consciousness can be intentionally turned off, 253; Demythologizing the Bible, 254; My journey, 255; Scientists point to the reality of the mystical, 257; Research into the paranormal, 260; Religions neglect awakened mystical consciousness, 262; Seven qualities of authentic mystical experiences, 263; Summary of The Reality of Awakened Consciousness, 265; Questions for Reflections and Discussion, 266; Practices, 266

CHAPTER 12

The Results of Awakened Consciousness 269

Four factors in biblical spiritual experiences, 275; Paul, the consummate Christian mystic, was also a passionate, intellectual activist, 275; Paul's numinous, awakened consciousness events, 277; Ananias, the quiet ministry of an "in the background" mystic, 278; Fourteen Transforming Results of Mystical Experience, 279; Summary of The Results of Awakened Consciousness, 284; Questions for Reflection and Group Discussion, 285; Practices, 285

CHAPTER 13

The Bliss of Transcendent Consciousness 287

Will the Real Me please stand up?, 287; Our poor, trashed ego, 288; Four Stages in Moving to the Real You, 288; Stage One to the Real You: Become a Somebody, 288; Stage Two to the Real You: Become a Nobody, 288; Stage Three to becoming the Real You: Begin to Embody (God), 293; Stage Four to the Real You: Become Everybody!, 308; Summary of The Bliss of Transcendent Consciousness, 309; Questions for Reflection and Discussion, 309; Practices, 310

CHAPTER 14

The Peace of Oneness Consciousness 313

The nondual consciousness of the Reign of God, 313; This is the main point of Jesus' teachings, 314; The Reign of God is Oneness Consciousness, 316; Do we lose our unique identity in oneness?, 317; Jesus, nonduality in sandals, 318; Single-seeing the gleam in your eye, 319; My "dimming" experience, 321; That strange word "nonduality", 322; Oneness consciousness as One Mind, 323; Oneness as Quantum Consciousness, 324; Separateness is an illusion, 326; How does Oneness consciousness feel?, 328; The Jesus Path of Heart-Centered, Devotional, Nonduality, 331; Summary of The Peace of Oneness Consciousness, 332; Questions for Reflection and Discussion, 332; Practices, 332; A diagram of Trinity Being Us, 333; The Transfiguration by Raphael (painted 1516-1520), 338

CHAPTER 15

The Moses and Elijah Phenomenon 339

Jesus with three close friends, two dead guys, and one sick boy, 339; A living picture of the Reign of God, 339; Jesus in distress, 340; Four pictures of the Reign of God coming in power, 341; Picture One: Three friends from his journey through life, 341; Picture Two: Two friends from the other side, 342; The Moses and Elijah phenomenon, 343; After Death Communication, 344; C. S. Lewis does a Moses and Elijah, 346; Medical anthropology weighs in, 347; Picture Three: The Ultimate Reassuring Voice, 348; Picture Four: A friend in need, 348; At home with four kinds of relationships, 349; When the saints go marching in, 350; My journey with Jesus and the saints, 351; Summary of The Moses and Elijah Phenomenon: A living picture of the Reign of God, 353; Questions for Reflection and Group Discussion, 354; Practices, 354

CHAPTER 16

The Unknown God of Today. .357

The religion of today, 358; The religion of the future, 359; Final Summary, 359

Afterword by Ken Wilber *361*

A Knower (or Who) x a Knowing (or How) x a Known (or What), 370

Appendix: What Every Body Can Say. *381*
Signing the Three Faces of God

What every body can say, 381; Devotion in Motion, 382; God beyond me, 383; God beside me, 384; God being me, 384; Alone or together, moving towards a full spectrum God, 385; The Sign of the Cross and the Three Faces of God, 386; Questions for Reflection and Group Discussion, 387; Practices, 388

Bibliography *391*

Index *405*

Illustrations

Trinity Beyond Us 90
Trinity Beside Us. 180
Trinity Being Us 337
The Transfiguration by Raphael 338

Foreword by Richard Rohr

We all need to *de-center* our own self and small perspective, or we cannot even imagine or get anywhere close to the Big Picture that Jesus calls "the Reign of God." We all seek that "Big Picture" in one way or another, through science, theology, or culture.

One of Jesus' most consistent themes is the need to "die to the self to find the self." I suspect that most Christians do not actively disobey this rather clear teaching, as they just do not know what it means—so they innocently forget it. It just sounds like gobbledygook! Or they interpret it as being humble now and then, or perhaps being generous to others.

Both of these are surely good directions, but you have before you now a very practical guide on how you can get to a very big picture of yourself, and also get yourself out of the way—and recognize a more humble self that comes to compassion almost naturally.

You are about to be the beneficiary of a most subtle understanding of what Jesus himself talked about when he spoke of at least four different kinds of soil (Matt. 13:4-23), and how seed would react very differently in each different soil. Today, we would recognize Jesus as a very advanced "developmental psychologist." He even presents his "soil theory" at the very beginning of a whole string of parables, as if they might be the interpretive key for understanding all of his wisdom. In other words, he gave us a rather sophisticated epistemology and psychology ("how do you know what you think you know") before he ventured into any metaphysics or theology ("what is it that you are trying to know").

Some theorists in our times said there were as many as six kinds of developmental soil, some seven, some eight, and some even more. But the amazing thing is that the general trajectory was always rather similar or at least highly complementary. All of these agreed that there is a meaning and direction to human growth. I will not give that to you here, because Paul Smith is about to do it much better, but I do want to say this much in this short foreword. Once you talk about growth you are directly talking about always-losing-a-self-to-find-a-self. To turn eight, you have to give up seven. To go to high school, you have to give up middle school. To get married you have to give up being Mom and Dad's little darling, so you can be someone else's little darling. And believe it or not, some people never fully make that leap, and of course the marriage does not work. They remain narcissists at that little child level.

We all have training and absolute insistence on *letting go* from our very birth, if we are honest; but a lot of us do not seem to accept the invitations into a bigger future that are always being given. In fact, Christians have often been adamant protectors of the past and the status quo, wanting "old time religion" with no validation from Jesus whatsoever, whose very starting words are "change!" (Mark 1:15, Matt. 4:17). Their "old time religion" is apparently not as old as Jesus, but usually trapped inside their own recent tribalism. You see, the ego hates change, because it always demands dying to the old self. And there is only one thing more dangerous than the individual ego—and that is the collective, group ego. Few can move beyond both their personal and their group ego without major conversion. This is what Smith offers you here.

We now have a very compelling and truly helpful—and well examined—way for each of us to de-center ourselves, and to situate ourselves outside of our own group, our own culture, and our own limited time. Some have also called it Spiral Dynamics, some call it Integral Theory, and most know nothing about it. Even though our own USA Diplomatic Core believes it to be "essential information."

We are now overwhelmed by the all-pervasive culture wars, the rapid rate of change, the globalization of knowledge at every level—which is either paralyzing us, making us angry and sometimes mentally or emotionally ill, but surely making many of us long for some meaningful pattern, a pattern that really explains and satisfies the seeking mind, and is true to our own observations. The human soul cannot live without meaning, just as the body cannot live without food. We all want some good, healthy seed to be planted in what we hope is our own good soil. I promise you this book is very good seed, and here you will have some criteria by which to test the quality and depth of your own soil.

I have taught this schema to five years of students here in our Living School for Action and Contemplation, although not nearly as wisely as you are about to be taught. Our cohort of 220 students each year are intelligent and faithful believers from all over the English-speaking world who are eager to grow as Christian leaders and thinkers and servants—without going to a seminary or taking formal university classes—although some do that, too.

I have never had a single student resist or oppose this wisdom. It explains so much. It is not ideology from above, but accurate description from below. I have never had one think that it lessened their faith or their love of God, Christ, their neighbor, or the church. In fact, it gave them a whole new entranceway into a compassionate understanding of the forces and changes that have brought us to this moment of time, with all its complexity. God is so very, very patient. It is we who are not.

You have in your hands a book that will be at the top of my recommended reading list for all of my students: Paul Smith's *Is Your God Big Enough? Close Enough? You Enough: Jesus and the Three Faces of God*. Please trust me as I tell you to trust the wisdom you are about to uncover here. It will make you a lot bigger too! Without you, God *will not*—for some strange reason. Without you, God *cannot*—for another reason I will never understand.

—Fr. Richard Rohr, O.F.M.
Center for Action and Contemplation
Albuquerque, New Mexico,
May 2017

Introduction

The Three Faces of God

Five travelers who had been seeking God for some time found themselves lodging one evening in the same place. They introduced themselves to one another as they sat in the lobby in front of the warmth of a huge rustic fireplace. The first traveler said, "I am seeking the Creative Principle of the universe, an Infinite Mind. I'm a spiritual person but not a religious one." When asked, "Where is God right now?" This traveler opened his hands upwards and said, "Beyond me."

The second traveler said "I have found something different. I feel God is a Presence that is close to me. God is with me all the time, like an intimate friend." When asked, "Where is God right now?" she said, "Right here beside me," placing her hands together in prayer.

The third traveler said, "I have arrived at another conclusion. I have found that God is within. God is my deepest Inner Self. I am a part of God." When asked, "Where is God?" he said, "In here, being me," hugging his arms and hands over his heart.

A fourth traveler, knowledgeable about these three entirely different claims about Ultimate Reality, said, "I have decided to give up trying to find God anywhere. If wise and sincere people like you three can't agree, then it seems to me that none of you are right. God is nowhere."

The fifth traveler remained silent for a moment. Then she said, "I have also explored various paths. They have often seemed to be incompatible and irreconcilable with one another. She looked at the fourth traveler and said, "However, I have come to a different conclusion than you have. I don't believe that if these three others here can't agree, then they are all wrong. Instead, I think they are all right, including you!" Looking at everyone, she said, "God is *beyond us,* and ultimately nowhere. God is also *beside us* as our dearest friend, and God is also in us, *being us,* as our deepest Self."

I have come to believe and experience what this last seeker discovered. Each of these seekers has found a part of the truth. When we put them together, we have a fuller truth. Why do I think this? Two reasons: First, the wisest person I have ever known, Jesus, had a three-dimensional relationship with God. He embraced a big God, a close God, and a you God—all three in a seamless, integrated whole. Each of these three faces of God has a crucial and quite different part of the truth. And second, as a follower of Jesus, I experience these same three faces of God in my life.

By whatever name, God is big enough to be beyond us. Ultimately, this face of God is nothing and nowhere. If this dimension of God was something and somewhere, God would be limited by space and time.[1] However, you can't just say *one* thing about God. You must always say several things about God to get the fullest picture. God is also close enough to be beside us as a transforming friend. God is also you and me enough to be our divine, deepest Self. Each of these Three Faces of God is true and real. Better yet, each of these can be personally experienced.

God in three persons

I was at a conference where I was speaking about Jesus' experience

---

1. Christian philosopher Paul Tillich called the God who is nothing and nowhere the "God beyond God" and "God above God." This is the face of God in the unmanifest realm beyond creation. This is God beyond mere existence, and transcends all religions, words, and descriptions, including this one.

of God. A man came up to me and said: "I hear you are going to talk about the Trinity." I replied, "Yes, but I'm going to look at the Trinity in a different way." He continued in an incredulous voice, saying, "Just don't tell us again that God is two men and a bird!" I laughed and said, "I guess when you put it like that, I certainly hope not!"

Behind his humor was a serious question. Because of traditional language and classical religious art, many people picture the "God in three persons" of the Trinity as an old guy, a young man, and a dove. When Michelangelo painted God by picturing an old man, he was just doing what our religious language told him to do—God is like a father who has an adult son. Of course, these are just artists' pictures, but they carry powerful messages in their images. We have done the same thing with Jesus. We have limited him to the historical person of Jesus and, perhaps, someone risen from the dead. Is that all there is to Jesus? How about spirit?[2] Spirit is relegated by some artists to looking like a dove, an image from Jesus' baptism. Of course, we all know that spirit is more than that, and theologians explore something of a God who is more than all of these. But that thinking has not reached many folks. The traditional Trinitarian shorthand of "God the Father, Son, and Spirit" came out of centuries of serious reflection about Jesus and God. However, too often, these images and language, as commonly perceived, hide the profound depth that is held within and behind that often-repeated phrase, "Father, Son, and Spirit."

For centuries theologians have pondered, writing millions of words about what this "Trinity" means. I have researched more of those ideas than I ever planned to over the years. A frustrated theologian was once reported to have said, "You must believe in the Trinity to be called orthodox, but if you try to define it, you'll be called a heretic." Yes, I've been called a heretic. Another jokingly said that Saint Augustine stated that anyone who denies the Trinity loses

2. In Chapter 3, I explain why I do not usually capitalize "spirit" unless included in the traditional three-part wording of the Trinity as "God the Father, Son, and Spirit."

their salvation, but anyone who tries to understand it loses their mind. I'd like not to lose my mind, but it seems to me that *there is a bigger, closer, and more human trinity behind each of the faces of the classical Trinity than Christians commonly think.*

The classical Trinity

We instinctively look for patterns to help us reflect about life. In the fourth and fifth centuries, church leaders formally recognized an emerging pattern at that time about God that was called "God in three persons." They worked out a complicated version of it that went something like "God is one being made up of three distinct persons who exist in equal essence and eternal communion as the Father, Son, and Holy Spirit." It was a foundational and initial way to capture the first Christians' three different experiences of God as "Father, Son, and Spirit."

• "Father" was the name that Jesus called the transcendent God of Abraham, Isaac, and Jacob. Rabbi Alon Goshen-Gottstein, founder and director of The Elijah Interfaith Institute, points out that the occasional use of "Father" for God in the Old Testament is generally a metaphor and not a proper name for God. It is rather one of many titles by which Jews speak of and to God. He says that in Christianity fatherhood is taken in a more literal and substantive sense, making for a more metaphysical rather than metaphorical interpretation.

The rabbi says, "Jesus spoke of God as Father when he turned to God in prayer and when he made God's presence a center point of his teaching. It is likely that we have here a product of his personal consciousness, as it encountered God and experienced God in the form of Father... What for others was metaphorical was experienced by him as fully real and immediate."[3]

---

3. Alon Goshen-Gottstein, "God the Father in Rabbinic Judaism and Christianity: Transformed Background or Common Ground?" *Journal of Ecumenical Studies*, 38:4, Spring 2001.

• The "Son," Jesus himself, became a close face of God for the first Christians. In the Gospels of Mathew, Mark, and Luke, Jesus acted like God. In the Gospels of John and Thomas, Jesus talked like God. Pointing back to this and believing "God has made this Jesus, whom you crucified, both Lord and Christ" (Acts 2:36), the first Christians soon came to honor and worship Jesus in the same way they honored and worshiped God.

• The "Spirit" or the divine life force was seen as the breath of life in every person alive in the Old Testament. In the New Testament, spirit becomes the intensified divine energy field that awakens us to new life, elevating us beyond everyday consciousness to experience within ourselves direct contact with and union with God.

Trinity—Breakthrough or breakdown?

Originally the idea of the Trinity, framed in terms of Greek philosophical thought, was a vital breakthrough in understanding God sixteen centuries ago. This has valiantly served as an anchor down through the history of theological turmoil and disputes. However, I believe that today the common Christian picturing and understanding God as the Trinity of Father, Son, and Spirit is a breakdown, not a breakthrough. The words "Father, Son, and Spirit" don't do justice to the fuller meaning hidden behind them. Now, rather than a way to display God, they distort the God that Jesus experienced and taught about, as well as the God and Cosmic Christ that Paul opened for us as the risen Jesus continued to teach him.

The language of the classical Trinity limits the Three Faces of God that Jesus taught and modeled. The naming of "Father, Son, and Spirit" can appear one-dimensional in that all of these names are about second person relationship. As crucial as this intimate dimension is, does God only appear as a personal relationship? Is there a God beyond this? So far beyond us that it pushes our minds beyond mere words. Is God not only intimate but infinite, too? And then is there a God closer to us than three personal relationships? So close as to actually *be* us? Is God not only intimate, infinite, but also inner in ways we have not unfolded?

Even the Trinity as three relationships is not always an actual personal reality in the lives of those who believe it to be true. Even though it is framed as a relational concept of three "persons" one can relate to, many Christians do not seem to experience God in this intimate way. The understanding of God as a loving relationship is central to Christianity, but the concept is meant to be experienced as a living, warm, close reality for us, just as it was for Jesus.[4]

The traditional language of "Father, Son, and Spirit" as well as Christianity in general appears quite patriarchal in our gender consciousness society. Must God look like a "he," a male parent, a male King and a male Lord? Even the word "God" has come to mean a male god. If we mean a feminine god, then we must use "goddess."

The traditional Trinity, although insightfully seeing God/She[5] as a relational community of three "persons" loving one another, appears as a limited, closed system. It became a picture of a God of three internal relationships that leave us out. Father, Son, and Spirit are having a great time loving one another, and we get to watch and be grateful. It reverses the whole movement of our direct participation in God that Jesus dramatically presented. We are not just observers of the divine nature but, as the writer of 2 Peter points out, we are "participants in the divine nature" (1:4).

As vital as God up close is, God is also infinitely bigger than three personal relationships. Trinity, as traditionally framed, not only

---

4. Richard Rohr's *The Divine Dance* is an insightful exploration of Trinity that includes us in God's warm embrace.

5. I sometimes use "God/She" to remind us that God, as a word standing by itself, in our culture is a masculine word. Since God is beyond gender but includes both male and female, I use God/She as a balanced, "made in the image of God, male and female" compound noun-pronoun. See Chapter 4 for more on the naming of God.

seems to leave us out, it also leaves out the rest of the universe as something entirely separate from God. The word "Father" does not even hint at the face of God that is so far beyond us that it does not even exist in time and space, which would make God finite.

The Trinitarian Father, Son, and Spirit do describe something of the face of God close to us in the Christian tradition. And I want to feature it in a deeply experienced way. But let's also value God who is beyond us and God who is within us. I offer a way in this book to move from obscuring to revealing God that honors both the traditional Trinity and all the other faces of God hidden within and behind it.

Looking at Trinity's "God in three persons" through the lens of The Three Faces of God

In this book we will look beyond what the traditional words "Father, Son, and Spirit" seem to imply to many today, to find a much bigger God, a far closer God, and a substantially more "you" God, all hidden behind the words of the Trinity. I have previously called this the Infinite Face of God, the Intimate Face of God, and the Inner Face of God.[6] The title of this book implies a Big Face of God, a Close Face of God, and a You Face of God, which is another naming. Here I will introduce one more naming of these Three Faces of God which I call God-beyond-us, God-beside-us, and God-being-us. These three dimensions of God are the lens through which we will be looking at the three "persons" of God found in the traditional Trinity.

This is not a mere play on words or making minor changes in perceptions about the common impressions that the oft-repeated "God the Father, Son, and Spirit" give about what and who God is. *I am after a major change in both common perceptions and in the way theologians and scholars view the Ultimate Reality and Mystery that we call God.*

---

6. Paul R. Smith, *Integral Christianity: The Spirit's Call to Evolve*, (St. Paul, Minnesota, Paragon House, 2011), 167-198.

I am a lifelong follower of Jesus, grounded in the scholarship and experience of the Christian tradition, and a mystic who is open to learning from all loving spiritual paths. I want to share with you the culmination of my life-long search for a path to experiencing God that has liberated me in new and deeper ways.

Twelve words that changed my mind and heart about God

Fifteen years ago I found the dense and delightful writings of Ken Wilber, to whom this book is dedicated. He is a writer on transpersonal psychology[7] and his own integral theory. The most widely translated academic writer in America, with 25 books translated into some 30 foreign languages, his goal is to integrate all the essential knowledge, traditions, practices, and experiences available to human beings.[8] In Ken's writings I found a map for my spiritual life, and in his life, I found a model for my spiritual practice. Although he is a practicing Buddhist, his map and model serve well for any spiritual path, even a Baptist like me! In his book *Integral Spirituality*, he opened up the idea of what he calls the "Three Faces of Spirit." I consider this the greatest breakthrough in understanding and experiencing God since the formulation of the Trinity in the fourth century. I embraced this as a beautiful way to integrate what had seemed impossible to put together before. With this in mind, I discovered a simple pattern in Jesus' life that I had not seen before. It can be summed it up in twelve simple words:

Jesus talked about God, to God, and as God. We can too!

---

7. "Transpersonal psychology is the study of humanity's highest potential, and with the recognition, understanding, and realization of unitive, spiritual, and transcendent states of consciousness" (*Journal of Transpersonal Psychology,*1992:91, Lajoie and Shapiro).

8. If you are not familiar with Wilber's work, I recommend starting with *The Integral Vision, The Simple Feeling of Being,* and *Grace and Grit.* My book, *Integral Christianity,* is an easy way to see a Christian version of some of his key points.

We learned this in elementary school

Talking *about*, *to*, and *as* someone or situation are the three basic perspectives in life we all learned in elementary school, even if we didn't realize it. Our teachers called it third, second and first person perspectives. For instance, I can *talk about* a friend in third person, using "he, she, it" language saying, "He's a good guy." I can *talk to* my friend in second person, using "you" language saying, "Hey, you have sure been busy with your new job." I can *talk as* my friend in first person, using "I" language, saying, "I can feel your happiness!"

The three basic perspectives on everything

These three perspectives of third person "about," second person "to," and first person "as," when focused on any situation, give us three very difference experiences of that situation. This can be observed in my three perspectives on this book. I can talk *about* this book in third person "IT" space, describing it as a book *about* us and God. I have often seemed to talk *to* it while writing it, in second person "YOU" space. "I'm going to get you shaped the way I want even if it takes me another year!" Finally, it is obviously in a first person "I" space since I am writing *as* me and my viewpoint. All three perspectives together give a fuller picture of my view of this book.

Jesus embraced all three perspectives with God

Early in his life, as all Jewish children did, Jesus learned to *talk about* a big God in third person IT space language of "he, she, it," the awesome God of Abraham and Moses. In Jesus' culture this was always "he" language: "He is kind to the ungrateful and wicked" (Luke 6:35).

Then, at some point in his early life, Jesus began to call God "his Father." Luke records Jesus, as a preteen, staying in Jerusalem after his parents had left to return home. He was in the temple courts listening to the teachers there and asking questions. When his parents returned to find him, the boy Jesus said, "Why were you looking for me? Didn't you know that I must be in my Father's house?" (Luke 2:49). Jesus not only talked about God as his Father but he *talked to* this God in a close and intimate way, calling God by the same name of love and respect all Jewish children and adults called their fathers, *Abba*. "He said, '*Abba*, Father, for you all things are possible; remove this cup from me; yet, not what I want, but what you want'" (Mark 14:36 NRSV). Here he was using the second person "you" of YOU space language and perspective.

As he continued to grow and began to find his calling in life, he saw himself, at times, *talking as* God in the first person "I" space language. He seemed to know that he was acting and speaking on behalf of God in the world. The symbols of God's presence with the Jewish people were the Torah and the Temple. Jesus saw himself as replacing them both, acting on God's behalf: "One that is greater than the temple is here" (Matt. 12:6). "You have heard it said [in the Torah], 'An eye for an eye' [Deut. 19:21] . . . but I say to you . . . love your enemies" (Matt. 5:38, 44).

This book is about the big God Jesus *talked about*, the close God Jesus *talked to*, and the inner "you" God that Jesus *talked as*. It's also about his invitation to us to go on that same journey with him.

The three–dimensional God of Jesus

Many people in the world today admire Jesus. They find Jesus' wisdom and penetrating critique of the religious, social, and political world of his day relevant to our day. They respect his willingness to live and die for his liberating beliefs. However, sometimes these same people ignore or dismiss Jesus' own understanding and experience of God. They seem to think he was both brilliant and delusional. Any reading of the life and teaching of Jesus shows that he believed the source of his wisdom and liberating acts came from his deep multi-dimensional relationship with God. In this book I want to explore this three-dimensional God of Jesus.

From traditional Trinity to the nine–dimensional "Expanded" Trinity

The traditional naming of God/She, the mystery of Ultimate Reality, as the classical Trinity of Father, Son, and Spirit is a basic truth in Christian history. It is not going away even if this naming disguises or hides other more expanded Christian understandings of God. So I want to open it up to a new framing. This framework is composed of the three basic perspectives of "about," "to," and "as." *I want to look at the traditional Trinity through the lens of the three basic perspectives in life.* The will give us what I call the *Expanded Trinity*. The Expanded Trinity gives us a "God the Father" that is beyond us, beside us, and being us. It opens us up to a "God the Son" who is beyond us, beside us, and being us. Finally, it transforms our identity with "God the Spirit" beyond us, beside us, and being us. Seeing these nine faces gives us an astonishingly enlarged picture and experience of God.

Theologians, biblical scholars, and mystics are often aware of some of this "Expanded Trinity," but it can be hidden behind their dense theological or mystical language. Looking at the traditional Trinity of Father, Son, and Spirit through the lens from an "IT" space, a "YOU" space, and an "I" space reveals a bigger, closer, and more human God than we have perhaps recognized. I frame it here with these three questions: Is your God big enough? Close enough? You enough? Just as Jesus used stories and metaphors to talk about God, I offer the three metaphors of big, close, and you as a way to go deeper into knowing God as revealed in Jesus.

The faces of God

The classical Trinity is most simply stated in terms of "one God in three persons." The Greek word for persons here is *hypostases*, meaning individual existence as a person or persona. Its meaning has gone through a complicated history, and all meanings have their limitations for what is mystically beyond description. Some prefer terms like "mode of being,"[9] or "distinct manner of subsisting."[10] However, instead of "persons" I like to use another Greek word for "person" that we find in the New Testament which is *prosopon*.

Prosopon also means "person" in the sense of a face or appearance. It originally came from the Greek theater in which actors on a stage wore masks to reveal their character and emotional state to the audience. Church leaders in the fourth century used this word in the Greek philosophical sense to talk about God. I continue this use of "face" to show how Jesus talked about, to, and as God. The Bible sometimes speaks of the "face of God" as the writers tried to metaphorically convey the idea of meaningful and intimate communication with God. Metaphors are a wonderful way to speak about God that describe but do not define. Here are three examples:

"In this way, God would speak to Moses *face to face*, as *friends* would speak to one another" (Ex. 33:11, italics mine).

"May God's *face* shine upon you, and give you peace" (Num. 6:25-26).

"For God has shined in our hearts in the *face (prosopon)* of Jesus Christ" (2 Cor. 4:6).

Ultimately there are an infinite number of faces of God which Catherine Keller, contemporary Christian theologian and Professor of Constructive Theology, beautifully calls "the breaking up of the face of God across an endless cosmic surface of faces."[11]

I call the Infinite, Intimate, and Inner faces of God "The Three Faces of God." I also call these three faces "God-beyond-us, God-beside-

9. Karl Barth, *The Doctrine of the Word of God: Church Dogmatics*, vol. I/1. G. Bromiley, trans. (Edinburgh: T & T Clark, 1975), 355-359.

10. Karl Rahner, *The Trinity*, trans, J. Donceel, (New York: Crossroad Publishing Company, 1997), 104-113.

11. Catherine Keller, *Cloud of the Impossible: Negative Theology and Planetary Entanglement* (Insurrections: Critical Studies in Religion, Politics, and Culture), (New York: Columbia University Press, 2015), 113.

us, and God-being-us." These are the topics of the three parts of this book which I briefly introduce here.

Part One
*Jesus talked **about** the Infinite Face of God, the wondrous God **beyond him***

Scholars agree that whenever Jesus talked about God/She, he was ultimately referring to the awesome creator God of his spiritual tradition, the God of Abraham, Isaac, and Jacob. This God was the source of all that is and life itself. Jesus did not spend much time in abstract philosophical ideas about God. But it was clear that the God he referred to, even as *Abba*, was the One who declared the divine name to Moses as "I AM." As we shall see, this is best understood, to the extent it can be understood, as existence or being itself. When 1 John 4:12 declares "No one has ever seen God," the writer was pointing out that God cannot be contained in any image, vision, thought, or concept. This is the infinite, transcendent God who is beyond our ability to "see." This is *God beyond us*.

Part Two
*Jesus talked **to** the Intimate Face of God, the warm God **beside him***

In addition to talking about the Infinite Face of God, Jesus also talked about a God who was so close and caring that he called this face of God by the name "*Abba*," the same warm name of respect and love that all Jewish children and adults called their fathers. However, Jesus did much more than talk *about* this close, Intimate Face of God. His life was animated by actually talking *to* God in this cherished and familiar personal way. Jesus not only practiced this, but he invited his friends to do the same. He invited them, and us, to talk *to* the warm *God beside us*.

A note on the male "God-language" of the Bible

While his own Jewish religion at times used the word "father" for

God, Jesus made it his primary name for God/She. He even used the word "*abba*" of his native Aramaic language for father which resembles our intimate fatherly names such as "Papa," "Dad" and "Daddy." *However, Jesus' naming of God as "father" was not pointing to gender, but to the caring love of a parent.* The sense of the word "father" in Jesus day was of the corporate personality of the family and included mother legally and socially in a way that is not true today in our gender conscious world. Lest we forget that difference, I usually translate "father" in the New Testament when referring to God/She as "father-mother." The Inclusive New Testament from Oxford University Press does this, also. See Chapter 4 for more on father-mother and God/She.

Part Three
*Jesus talked **as** the Inner Face of God,*
*the within God **being him***

Finally, Jesus talked about God as if he himself was divine. He so identified with the great I AM of Moses that in the Gospels of Mathew, Mark, and Luke, he referred to himself acting as God and on behalf of God in the world. In the Gospels of John and Thomas he saw himself speaking as God/She. Jesus said, "Before Abraham was, I am" (John 8:58). He proclaimed, "I am the light that is over all things. I am the all. From me all came forth, and to me all attained." (Gospel of Thomas,77). This was the God who was his deepest self.

This is the God that is also ultimately our deepest and most authentic self. So this God *beyond* us and *beside* us also has a face that acts and speaks *within* us *as* us. This is not the surface us, the ego us, the constructed self. This is the deep us, the real us, the divine self, the presence of the infinite in the finite.[12]

Many Christians are comfortable with "in" language about God and

---

12. "The presence of the infinite in the finite" is Steve McIntosh's striking phrase in his insightful book on the integration of theism and nonduality, *The Presence of the Infinite: The Spiritual Experience of Beauty, Truth, and Goodness.*

themselves. We talk about God being "in" us, Jesus coming to live "in" us, and the spirit dwelling "in" us. That is true, but it is a partial truth. There is a more radical truth. This more revolutionary truth has to do with *how* God is in us. Is God in us as a visitor who drops in and out? Is God an outside presence come to live inside of us? Is God in us as another being? Or is God in us AS us?

This is the divine image in which we are already made. This is the human face of the divine that we can see most easily in Jesus. When we can see it in Jesus, then we can begin to realize that he is showing us our true identity, too. We are living with a mistaken identity. He wants us to discover our real one! The real "us" is one with God like Jesus was one with God. This is the face of God that is revealed *as* us deep within. We can then see that we, too, are divinity in human form, called to act as the voice, heart, hands, and feet of God in the world today. This is the face of God who is not beyond us or close to us, but rather God/She within us *as* our very inner being. This is *God being us*!

Why we need a God that is big enough, close enough, and you enough

We need a God big enough for our minds

We need a God big enough to expand and challenge our minds and then to push us beyond our thinking. Many people seem to have a "sort of" big God. Sometimes God is a cosmic-sized, kindly version of Santa Claus living somewhere "up there." Or God is the "man upstairs," meaning a gigantic man living up in the heavens. Or God is like a cosmic watchmaker who has intricately fashioned the universe, flung it into the cosmos, and is now sitting back watching everything that happens. These versions of a big god are not nearly big enough for the modern, thinking, and reflecting creatures we have become. We are incurably curious about the world which, due to the miracle of modern science and astronomy, has become an incredibly big world. We are so hungry for knowing about things that we have created vast fields of knowing such as science, mathematics, physics, business, culture, literature, psychology, anthropology, philosophy, spirituality, and the list goes on. Thinking and pondering about these things allows us to go big.

If we cannot reflect *about* God in *big* enough ways, then that God will not stand up against other, more attractive, but lesser gods in our world. As Rabbi Jonathan Sacks says, "The truth is that not all the great religions and not all the great leaders of the religions are fully adapted to living in a world of complexity and diversity. And the face religion is showing the world today is not a smiling one."[13] Traditional religions are not only not smiling at the world today, they are often not even looking at the world.

Many thinking people reject the God of Christianity because that God is not big enough for this modern world of billions of galaxies whirling in dark matter, quarks, and bosons. The marvels of science seem to answer our questions even if they have no answers about meaning and purpose. We need a God that is big enough to embrace science and then go beyond it to what science cannot answer.

We need a God close enough for our hearts

We are relating creatures. Lots of animals run in packs or have some form of social relationships in their groups. But we human beings are communal beings at our very core. We are born needing at least one other person, and all our lives we need others to not only survive but to thrive. Loved ones and friends are important to us as human beings. Loneliness is universally considered an undesirable condition. Close relationships are what make us human.

A God who is relatable is crucial to us as communal creatures. If your God is not close enough, then that God will not be profoundly transforming in your life. We are formed and transformed by our relationships. Not having a relationship with the divine source that is Ultimate Reality leaves one alone and unloved by the cosmos.

---

13. Rabbi Jonathan Sacks, *The Christian Century*, November 25, 2015, 9.

These widely embraced words, although often wrongly attributed to Albert Einstein, stand alone in their wisdom:

> I think the most important question facing humanity is, "Is the universe a friendly place?" This is the first and most basic question all people must answer for themselves.[14]

We only experience the universe as friendly if we know it as a friend. Jesus gives us a God who is just such a friend.

Then there are those people who don't find Christianity meaningful because the Jesus they hear about in the Gospels, while heroic and attractive in some ways, does not seem very real or interesting in today's world. This stained-glass Jesus does not have anything to do with them and their everyday lives. Jesus may be divine but that divinity is not close enough to them to make any real difference. Jesus may have called his first followers his friends, but he does not seem to be a friend to many of his followers today. Many people have a schizophrenic, bi-polar God who sometimes loves us and sometimes plans to toss us into a burning hell forever if we don't do the right thing. They fervently believe in this God, yet remain unchanged because of these distancing beliefs. Being in a relationship with a God who has a borderline personality disorder does not invite closeness!

Yet, the writers of the New Testament reported that Jesus talked to God like he was talking to his closest and most valued friend. And he taught his followers to do the same. Was this wise man deluded about being close to God? I think not.

We need a God "us" enough to be our deepest self-identity

Are we just animals with a more developed consciousness? Are we passing creatures in the long history and future of evolution? Or, are we eternal souls, Star People, the Infinite present in finite human form? I have come to believe that we have an eternal inner identity

---

14. Albert Einstein, "Is the Universe Friendly?" http://www.awakin.org/read/view.php?tid=797#sthash.8Gln900H.dpuf.

that shapes everything we do and become. We have a rich inner world of experiences, identity, personal history, hopes, and dreams that make us uniquely us. If we are divine creatures made in the image of God, then we must know that all the richness and depth of Ultimate Reality is deep within us. Knowing our deepest, eternal self is crucial as evolving human beings.

If God is you enough as revealed in your most transcendent consciousness, then you will be liberated enough to live as the New Human, the fully human, fully divine person. The people who can change the world are people who know who they are. No problem can be solved from the same level of consciousness that created it. So we must be people of a higher consciousness—people who are not afraid of their divine identity.

Jesus was all about God/She being in him and him being in us (John 17:21). But there are many questions about what that means: What did one of the New Testament writers mean when he wrote that we are "all partakers of the divine nature" (2 Pet. 1:4)? Was Jesus the only "partaker of the divine nature"? Was he one of a kind, the only fully divine and fully human to ever live? Or was he essentially the prototype, the model for all of us who are also human and divine? Was he the exception or the example? Is it possible that deep inside you are more like God than you thought?

Many Christians keep trying to make Christianity work in their lives. But who or whatever "Father, Son, and Spirit" are does not appear to relate to who they are deep inside. They may believe they are made in the image of God but that has little to do with the image they have of themselves, the reality of their inner life. If you resonate with this, then perhaps you are ready to find a God who is you enough.

Healing the Western Soul

We Westerners often have another problem with our spiritual path. It is a unique problem for the spiritual seeker with a Western mind and soul raised in traditional Christianity. Many of us began our spiritual journey in a traditional version of the Christian religion. Coming into a more modern or progressive way of viewing the world often brings a challenge to our traditional religion. What do we do with those spiritual experiences and Bible stories that come from our youth that were perhaps meaningful at one time? They seldom find any affirmation by our progressive peers. Instead, they are diminished or even dismissed by others relegating them to immaturity or fantasy based on biblical myths, rejecting them because they don't have a place for them any longer.

Judith Miller, professor of developmental psychology at Columbia University, in her insightful book, *Healing the Western Soul: A Spiritual Homecoming for Today's Seekers,* has found that many Westerners have lost their traditional spiritual anchors.[15] They are now searching to find them in other religions, spiritual paths, or their own mixture of various beliefs and practices. She found that healing comes when people reclaim and transform their original traditional anchors. She says that our healing must take place in the tradition we were first at home in, not in later ones we have found useful but that lack the power to evoke profound spiritual experiences and articulate deep understandings. When our deep wounds are healed and we find our authentic spiritual grounding, we can then benefit from exploring other traditions and spiritual paths.

This is just what I have found in my spiritual journey. Beginning as a conservative Southern Baptist, I sensed there was more than I was being taught. I explored and pushed my way through limiting and abusive rules and theology for fifty years. At each turn I found a more liberating Jesus and a more loving God. At one point I realized I was so delighted and fulfilled with following Jesus that I had no need to stop being a Christian. It was then I began drinking from the riches of other traditions while delighting in my own.

---

15. Judith Miller, *Healing the Western Soul: A Spiritual Homecoming for Today's Seekers,* (St. Paul: Paragon House, 2015).

In one sense this book is a way of doing that for those who come from the Western soul shaped by Christianity, even if they eventually find that the Christian path no longer fits for them. When we find a way to embrace rather than dismiss our own early, meaningful, spiritual experiences, we can continue our spiritual journey with a healed and grounded mind, heart, and soul. We can understand the Bible in a larger framework and can recover its wisdom. Finding a God/She who big enough, close enough, and you enough is a way to reclaim our early authentic spiritual experiences and then move on to deeper, expanded ones in a more integrated way. An integral view includes the best of traditional Christianity, transcends the worst, and is open to the ever new.

Did Jesus really say that?

There is one more introductory issue to address before we delve into our three questions. I will be quoting words attributed to Jesus from the four biblical Gospels and the Gospel of Thomas. Thoughtful people often ask, "Did Jesus really say that or are these words simply put into his mouth by overzealous followers?"

When one enters the modern era we become aware of the application of the historical-critical method in attempting to determine what Jesus really said. This can lead to a crises of faith and almost always to a broadening of one's perspective. Many are aware of the much-publicized Jesus Seminar viewpoints, but have not kept up with more recent scholarly opinion which seems to leave many of the Seminar's conclusions suspect. When one enters the progressive postmodern culture, the exploration of other religions shows they all face a similar problem with texts. There is an inability to bring modern standards of authentication and certainty into their sacred texts.

Going beyond textual certainty

As we continue to evolve, we learn to value the truths found in all the world's great religious traditions which transcend our desire for textual certainty. The Jesus Seminar may have inadvertently promoted a kind of fundamentalism in its search for certainty. I have heard more than one seminarian say, "At last we can finally know what Jesus really said!" That sounds like the fundamentalist claim that "Jesus said it, I believe it, and that settles it." While it may be interesting to explore this, *there is no way to absolutely know for sure* who said what in any ancient document, including the Bible.

Instead, at a spiritually mature level, we begin to rely upon our own inner discernment about the truth of what is being communicated rather than the text's precise provenance. *To search for the historical Jesus to the point of certainty is beyond our scholarship. Rather we must ask what is the spiritual truth we find in the records from those closest to him in history.*

It has been broadly assumed that the more metaphysical statements in the Gospel of John indicate the divinity of Jesus more so than passages in the other three Gospels. Recent scholarship has shown this not to be true. The question of whether Jesus said or did something or it was attributed to him later is especially relevant in referring to Jesus as divine. There is a change in the belief and practice of his followers that can be observed in the accounts narrating events before the resurrection and those after. Immediately following the resurrection, the worship of Jesus as divine exploded onto the scene. This points back to Jesus' own mission and self-understanding. N. T. Wright, a leading New Testament scholar and retired Anglican bishop, writes:

> The Temple in Jerusalem was the center of Jewish spiritual life and was the dwelling place of Israel's God in the midst of God's people. It represented sacrifices which assured fellowship with God and forgiveness of sins. Jesus acted as a one-man substitute for the Temple, offering forgiveness and fellowship with God in place of the Temple. The Torah was also an incarnational symbol of God in their midst. Jesus saw himself as the new Torah-giver. Jesus believed that he was called to do and be the things which only God did in Israel's religious tradition.

Let me be clear, also, what I am not saying. I do not think Jesus "knew he was God" in the same sense that one knows one is tired or happy, male or female. He did not sit back and say to himself "Well I never! I'm the second person of the Trinity!" Rather, as part of his human vocation grasped in faith, sustained in prayer, tested in confrontation, agonized over in further prayer and doubt, and implemented in action, he believed he had to do and be, for Israel and the world, that which according to scripture only YHWH himself could do and be.[16]

Placing Jesus' divinity first in his vocation before we get to the more metaphysical statements in the Gospels of John and Thomas and Paul's letters about his divinity helps us get the sense of Jesus' words and actions on behalf of God more clearly.

The first followers of Jesus saw and heard these words and actions of Jesus in taking divine authority over the Temple and Torah. Then, rather as the commonly assumed view of Jesus' divinity evolving over a long period of time, we see that it occurred as a remarkable and rapid, almost volcanic eruption within ten or twenty years after the crucifixion in a world without rapid transportation, radio, TV, phones, or the internet. That world relied upon the latest traveler to bring news from afar. Worship of Jesus as divine in a way similar to God is the most notable theological and worship practice feature of early Christianity. Paul's conversion a few years after the crucifixion was based on a radical change in his view of who Jesus was. This view of a divine Jesus was already in place among Christians, perhaps within a few years after the crucifixion.[17]

---

16. N. T. Wright, "Jesus' Self-Understanding," in *The Incarnation*, ed. S. T. Davis, (Oxford: D. Kendall, G. O'Collins, 2002), 47–61. The name YHWH is composed of four Hebrew letters called the "Tetragrammaton" and transliterated as Yahweh, which people commonly call "The Lord" or "God."

17. See Larry Hurtado, *How on Earth Did Jesus Become a God?* (Grand Rapids: Wm. B. Eerdmans Publishing, 2005).

Even Jesus' crucifixion was a result of his political, social, and theological actions and speech which claimed divine authority. Politically, his claims to bring in a new kingdom would provoke revolutionary activity. Socially, he challenged the traditional family by calling his family those who followed God's will which defied the whole system of who was in and who was out. He confronted the theological symbols of Israel's identity, Temple and Torah, by bringing their authority to himself. He claimed to bring in a new "Kingdom" of God redefining what that Kingdom was. It was based on love, not violence. Rather than a King, it had a self-giving *Abba*, a fatherly/motherly figure. At his trial he placed himself alongside the God of Israel (John 18:36-38).

The early Christians put Jesus' actions on behalf of God and his speech on behalf of God together and concluded that he was a breakthrough revelation of God. Their response was so transforming that the monotheistic Jews were convinced that God wanted them to offer Jesus the same devotion they offered God. This was a revolutionary break with the past.

The risen Jesus also taught the early Christians

A critical factor in considering the authenticity of the words of Jesus in the Gospels is that some of them, especially in the Gospel of John and the Gospel of Thomas, may not be ones that Jesus spoke during the time of his brief physical ministry. Rather, they may be ones revealed by Jesus to his friends after his resurrection. His words to these friends from his spiritual presence were just as real and true as those that came from his physical presence. They were quickly incorporated into their narratives of Jesus' life and teaching. He said that he had more to teach them (John 16:12) and here was some of the more. Paul expressly said he received words from the risen Jesus and had passed them on (Gal. 1:11-12; 2 Cor. 5:1-12). The Gospel of John was written thirty or forty years after the other three biblical gospels. This means the writer, or writers, had a chance to reflect more on Jesus life and teaching as well as to listen to Jesus himself continue to teach them. They not only listened to the risen Jesus but collected what others had heard from Jesus and wove it all together into a spiritual masterpiece.

Therefore, I do not attach primary importance to attempts to differentiate between what may be Jesus' words in his physical body and what may be the words of the risen Jesus coming through those who were closest to him in history. They knew him best both in terms of historical proximity and in the intense altered states of consciousness that the early Christians such as Paul experienced in encountering the risen Jesus. Therefore I have no difficulty believing that the words and actions of Jesus in the Gospels could be authentic representations of what Jesus said and did.

This is not to say we should take every word in these gospels, letters, or any other writings as what Jesus did and said, or would have. What is critical for me is discerning whether the words look, sound, and feel like the Jesus I know and experience. Do these words reflect the deep reality of inner spiritual experience, rather than the standards of modern journalism? Do these words reflect truth about our lives, rather than certainty about who first said them?

Reading our Bible the same way Jesus did his

How did Jesus read his Bible, the Hebrew scriptures? Did he think it was all to be embraced as truth for all time? Here is what Jesus did with his Hebrew Bible: He embraced some parts, he ignored some parts, and he rejected some parts! He specifically rejected any words about a supposed vengeful God who hates some people and will punish them forever. Jesus taught that we should love our enemies, not hate them. If we assume that God practiced what Jesus preached, then God does not hate or punish anyone, but only forgives and loves. And God, like Jesus, does not believe even enemies should be punished, but rather should be loved. *Therefore, I embrace some parts of my Bible, ignore some parts, and reject some parts based on whether they seem to be Christ-like or not.*

In addition, we must face the challenge of translating ancient Hebrew and Greek into contemporary English. I primarily quote from *The Inclusive Bible* in this book. This is the first egalitarian translation of the entire Bible into English and came from the efforts of a large group of Catholic priests to whom I am greatly indebted. I sometimes use other translations, including my own.

A dynamic system

Who or what is God? If you need more than one answer to that, you are on the right track! What I am proposing as a big enough, close enough, you enough God may seem to some like a contrived framework that squeezes everything into one convenient pattern. However, for me and others who embrace it, this is a dynamic system which engages every part of me with every part of reality.

The Nine Pictures of the Expanded Trinity

Looking at the traditional Trinity of "Father, Son, and Spirit" through the lens of the Three Faces of God-beyond-us, beside-us, and being-us *reveals three sets of three, a big set, a close set, and a you set.* In the following chapters we will explore each of these nine depictions of God contained in the full spectrum of this Expanded Trinity and how they can change our understanding and experience of God.

Summary of The Three Faces of God

• The common naming and understanding of the classical Trinity of God the Father, Son, and Spirit distorts or hides the reality behind each of them.

• The twelve words about Jesus that changed my mind and heart about God are: *Jesus talked about God, to God, and as God. So can you!*

• In this book we will look at the classical Trinity through the lens of these three basic perspectives on everything in life—third person "about," second person "to," and first person "as."

• Applying these three basic perspectives to God results in God-beyond-us, beside-us, and being-us.

• Our mind needs a God who is big enough. Our heart needs a God who is close enough. And our inner identity needs a God who is "us" enough.

• The Western soul needs to find healing from the wounds of traditional Christianity from a new view of Christianity that allows such healing to take place.

• We can interpret the Bible based on Jesus' own scriptural interpretive model of embracing, ignoring, and rejecting.

Questions for Reflection and Group Discussion

1. What is your initial response to the pattern of Jesus talking about God, to God, and as God?

2. Which one do you most favor at this point in your life? Why?

3. Which do you least favor? Why?

4. Has your "Western soul" needed any healing from previous religious wounding such as liberation from abusive images of God as exclusively male, angry, punishing, or rejecting? Where are you in that process right now?

5. How comfortable are you with the author's position on the reliability of many, but not all, of Jesus' words recorded in the four Gospel and the Gospel of Thomas coming from either the historical Jesus or the risen Jesus through the first Christians?

6. Where are you with the author's idea of accepting, ignoring, and rejecting parts of the Bible? What passages do you reject?

Practices

1. I have found three primary practices or doors that open us to experiencing God in the ways we long for and that Jesus showed us

were our birthright. Up to this point I have called them talking about God, talking to God, and talking as God. Now I want to introduce the names I use for these three practices that are both more accurate and easily remembered. They are:

REFLECTING ABOUT GOD

RELATING TO GOD

RESTING AS GOD

This introductory chapter is reflecting about God and this book. Therefore, rather than a call to relating prayer or resting meditation, it is a call to reflective thinking. One easy way of reflecting as you read this book is to underline or mark those parts that resonate with you. Go back and mark up those parts in this book or highlight in the Kindle edition if you have not already done so. *An unmarked book is an undigested book!* The parts you mark will be easily available for further reflection and discussion with others.

2. You can find books and websites for further reflection in the Bibliography. The Integral Life website, www.Integrallife.com, is enormous and contains not only some of my work but hundreds of fascinating explorations and resources from experts in many fields that will enrich your life.

3. Close your session with this signing of Three Faces of God exercise (next page) explained in the Appendix. If by yourself, use the first line in each segment. The second line is for a group practice.

"God beyond me, in whom I live and move, and have my being."

("God beyond us, in whom we live and move, and have our being.")

"God beside me, you are always with me."

("God beside us, you are always with us.")

"God being me, I am the light of the world."

("God being us, we are the light of the world.")

"God beyond me."

PART ONE

Is Your God Big Enough?
Opening our mind to Trinity beyond us

Are you in touch with the Infinite?

The infinite is not just an abstraction unrelated to real life. Carl Jung (1875–1961), influential Swiss psychiatrist and psychotherapist and founder of analytical psychology, explored the depths of our human experience. He wrote about what he considered the critical question for humanity. Here are his words from a time of masculine-oriented language:

> The decisive question for a man is: is he related to something infinite or not? That is the telling question of his life. Only if we know that the thing which truly matters is the infinite can we avoid fixing our interest upon futilities, and upon all kinds of goals which are not of real importance. . . . If we understand and feel that here in this life we already have a link with the infinite, desires and attitudes change. In the final analysis, we count for something only because of the essential we embody, and if we do not embody that, life is wasted.

The feeling for the infinite, however, can be attained only if we are bounded to the utmost. The greatest limitation for man is the "self"; it is manifested in the experience: "I am only that!" Only consciousness of our narrow confinement in the self forms the link to the limitlessness of the unconscious. In such awareness we experience ourselves concurrently as limited and eternal, as both the one and the other. . . . we possess also the capacity for becoming conscious of the infinite. But only then![1]

The presence of the Infinite in the finite

The Jesus path offers the presence of Infinite in the One Jesus talked about and called his and our heavenly father-mother. In addition, the early church looked at Jesus' life and teaching and came to believe that God/She told them to see Jesus himself as the presence of the infinite in the finite. Then the Apostle Paul was taught by Jesus to expand Jesus as the Messiah to Jesus as the Cosmic Christ, the blueprint and Christian symbol of the whole of both finite and infinite reality. Finally, the early Christians began to see spirit as the presence of the infinite in the finite within and as us. However, none of this is immediately apparent in the Trinitarian words, "Father, Son, and Spirit." In this first of the three parts of this book I want to make visible the Infinite God behind the "Father," the Cosmic Christ behind Jesus, and Infinite Consciousness behind "Spirit."

In Part One, let's set our imaginations free to *reflect about* a Trinitarian God who is big enough for our minds. We begin with looking behind Jesus' parental imaging and experience of his *Abba* God for the One who is big enough to be called "Infinite."

---

1. C. G. Jung, *Memories, Dreams, Reflections*, (New York: Vintage Books, 1963), 325.

"God beyond me."

CHAPTER 1

Beyond "the Father" to the Wonder of Infinite Being

Philosophers have wrestled with big ideas about a big God for centuries. Early on they searched for metaphors and descriptions that were big enough to get at that which cannot be measured. Here is a beautiful, often quoted expression from Hermes Trismegistus whom Augustine and others called a "wise pagan prophet who foresaw the coming of Christianity."

> "God is an infinite sphere, the center of which is every-where, the circumference nowhere."[1]

Trappist monk and priest and one of the architects of a contemporary method of contemplative prayer called Centering Prayer, Father

---

1. James D. Heiser, *Prisci Theologi and the Hermetic Reformation in the Fifteenth Century* (Malone, Texas: Repristination Press, 2011). This was repeated in several forms including one by Alain of Lille, twelfth-century French theologian and poet, "God is an intelligible sphere, whose center is everywhere, and whose circumference is nowhere."

Thomas Keating, puts it in a charming way with, "God loves to be everywhere all at once."[2]

These are big ways to reflect about God. However, for most Christians, the "thinking" definition of God is the Trinity, "God, the Father, Son, and Spirit." While pointing to a truth, it is a partial truth. It is not the whole story according to the Bible, theologians, scientists, and mystics. The constant repetition of the words of this traditional phrase can reduce our reflecting about God, and for some, diminish it to an old guy, a young guy, and a bird!

Is your God as big as the God of Jesus?

Christian scholars and mystics agree that the awesome God of Abraham, Isaac, Jacob, and Moses was behind whatever terminology or story about God/She that Jesus was using at any given moment. Jesus recited the Shema daily as a good Jew, "Hear, O Israel, the Lord is our God, the Lord is one." He would have learned about the Jewish view of God at his village school until the age of twelve and after that at the local synagogue. He knew the Hebrew language of the Hebrew scriptures and the Aramaic language in which religious discussions were held. It was also the custom of the time for young adults to attach themselves to a local teacher or sage. John the Baptist may have been one of those for Jesus. Jesus knew and probably memorized passages from the Hebrew scriptures such as:

> For YHWH[3] is a great God,
>   the great ruler above all gods.
> O God, in your hands are the depths of the earth;
>   the mountain peaks are yours also.
> Yours is the sea, for you made it,
>   the dry land as well for your hands formed it.

---

2. https://integrallife.com/future-christianity/becoming-nothing.

3. YHWH is four letters of the Hebrew alphabet translated into Latin letters, one of the Hebrew names for God used in the Bible.

> Come, let us bow down in worship,
> let us kneel before YHWH, our Maker!
> (Psalm 95:3-6)

This is the God Jesus was talking about even as he was adding an intimate dimension of parental love and care as he walked and talked with this God. Jesus' challenge was to take the big "how great are you" God of his religion and let others see that this God was also close, caring, and relatable not only to him but everyone. However, he never diminished the glory and greatness of this God to call God his *Abba*.

The Jewish view of God that Jesus was taught to reflect and talk about was based on a few basic ideas. There is only one God and the universe owes its existence to this one God who created heaven and earth. God is the source of life itself. We are God's children created in God's likeness and image, and we are to worship only this God and no one or nothing else. God has no beginning and no end, living and reigning forever. This was an awesome, transcendent, big God!

The I AM God of Jesus

The mighty God of Israel that every Jewish child learned about was a God who was primarily defined by divine action, not by abstract or metaphysical reflection. God was the one who created, who intervened in history, who did things that revealed the divine character. There was one staggering, profound exception to this action type of description of God in the scriptures of Judaism. Perhaps that is why it was considered the most important passage in the Torah for understanding the name of God. Jesus would have known it very well. It is found in the second book of the Hebrew Torah and the Christian Bible, Exodus, where God tells Moses to go to Egypt and to bring the people of Israel out of captivity. Moses, in one of the most famous verses in the Bible, says to God:

> When I go to the people of Israel and say to them, "The God of your ancestors has sent me to you," and they

ask me, "What is this god's name?" what am I to say to them?" God replied, "I AM THAT I AM. This is what you will tell the Israelites: 'I AM has sent me to you'" (Ex. 3:13-14).

God as Infinite Being

The phrase "I AM THAT I AM" derives from the 1st-person form of the verb "I will be." This can be most simply understood to mean that God is pure existence or being. Let's call this Infinite Being or Being Itself.[4] The passage continues:

> God also said to Moses, "Say this to the people of Israel, 'YHWH, the I AM, the God of your ancestors, the God of Sarah and Abraham, Rebecca and Isaac, of Leah and Rachael and Jacob, has sent me to you': this is my Name you are to remember for all generations. (Ex. 3:15)

The letters YHWH significantly mean "to be" or "I am." They also stand for the divine Hebrew name. They are usually translated as LORD and spelled with capital letters in our Bibles. This is also a linguistic connection with the name "LORD" to infinite being itself.[5]

The name YHWH or LORD and God's own self-naming of "I AM" both give us an early and profound understanding of God. The Jewish God of Jesus was very, very big. So big that God might be called simply Existence, or Being, or Infinite Being.

What if God/She had answered: "I am the voice of the god who lives on this mountain?" Or "I am the god who is first among all the gods." Or "I am the god who orders you to kill your enemies." It

4. Popular, readable explanations of this can be found at http://www.hebrew4christians.com/Names_of_G-d/YHVH/yhvh.html and http://en.wikipedia.org/wiki/I_Am_that_I_Am.

5. *A Hebrew and English Lexicon of the Old Testament*, ed. Brown, Driver, and Briggs, (Peabody, Massachusetts: Hendrickson, 1994).

can be confusing because those very images of God show up as the biblical record continues. Is God a giant being who is both kind and vengeful? Or is God Being Itself? The dominating image of God in the Old Testament is of a giant, super-powerful, invisible male figure who is loving and compassionate at times and also vengeful and angry at times. These are the kinds of things that *a* being does rather than Being Itself. Therefore it is even more profound that so early in the history of the Jewish people, they have a passage in their sacred books where God identifies as *Being Itself* rather than as *a being*.

Why did Moses need a name?

Names are shortcuts for distinguishing things. You could go through life talking about your small wireless electronic device for storing and processing data, typically in binary form, according to instructions given to it in a variable program and used to communicate with others over a radio frequency carrier while the user is moving within a telephone service area using a cellular network architecture. Or you could just call it your cell phone.

However, names are often more than shortcuts. What's in a name? W. H. Auden says, "Proper names are poetry in the raw. Like all poetry they are untranslatable."[6] American novelist and poet Erica Jong says, "To name oneself is the first act of both the poet and the revolutionary."[7] The name Moses received from God, I AM THAT I AM, is both poetry and revolutionary!

Notice how uncomfortable we get when a baby is born and the parents refuse to name it for some time. Why are we uncomfortable? Because to name something is to give it importance in our lives. Our minds need a name so we can talk and think about that which is named. It is impossible to think without language. Our hearts need a name so we can love what is named.

---

6. W. H. Auden, *A Certain World: A Commonplace Book*, (New York: Viking Press, 1970), 22.

7. http://nameberry.com/nametalk/threads/139856-Favorite-Quotes-about-Names.

Naming something is also dangerous. British-Indian novelist and essayist Salman Rushdie writes, "Names, once they are in common use, quickly become mere sounds, their etymology being buried, like so many of the earth's marvels, beneath the dust of habit."[8] Unfortunately "God" is just such an easily buried name. However, it seems to me that the name I AM or Infinite Being defies burial much less easily.

The Awesome Wonder of Infinite Being

We don't know what to do with the infinite. That's as it should be. The infinite is always beyond us. However, we may get a sense of the wonder of infinity by looking up at the night sky away from city lights. Seeing some of the five thousand stars visible to the human eye, you wonder how many stars there are. When does star-filled space end? This has fascinated dreamers, philosophers, poets, and scientists throughout the centuries. There are an estimated 300 septillion (that's a 3 followed by 23 zeros) stars in just the known, observable universe shining in the vast dark canvas of space.[9] Yet God is bigger in dimensions that are beyond time and space.

Quite often in this book I quote from the writings of Raimon Panikkar (1918–2010) who was a Roman Catholic priest, prominent scholar, and professor of philosophy at the University of Madrid. His embrace of Hindu scriptures and Buddhism made him an influential voice for promoting dialogue among the world's religions. Panikkar writes, "The conception of God has always been intimately connected with the reigning worldview of a particular epoch. Cosmology was part of theology as long as the cosmos was believed to be God's creation, the Divine intrinsically related to the

8. Salman Rushdie, *The Satanic Verses*, (New York: Vintage Press, 1989). http://m. csmonitor.com/index.php/Books/2013/0618/Salman-Rushdie-10-quotes-on-his-birthday/Naming-things.

9. http://www.huffingtonpost.com/2010/12/01/number-of-stars-in-universe_ n_790563.html

universe."[10] The church and Christians need to see God through the eyes of a new cosmology, and that cosmology is quite remarkable in its ability to expand our understanding of God if we will but manage to keep God and cosmology together which Christianity unequivocally states they are.

In a 2014 news release, speaking of the results of the physicists of the University of California, Berkeley mapping 1.3 million galaxies down to about 1 percent accuracy, physicist David Schlegel said, "It's likely the universe extends forever in space and will go on forever in time. Our results are consistent with an infinite universe."[11] Globally recognized ecumenical teacher of the universal awakening within Christian mysticism, Franciscan friar, and Roman Catholic priest Richard Rohr comments, "If humankind could have known God without the world, God would never have created the world. . . . Creation is God's first, oldest and clearest Bible."[12] Creation itself declares an infinite God.

God beyond Being

We must also point out that God is bigger than Being, and more than Being. We simply don't have words or concepts for that. Famous, outspoken German Catholic theologian and mystic Meister Eckhart (1260–1328) was addressing this when he said, "I pray God to rid me of God."[13] That sounds like nonsense unless you realize he is

---

10. Raimon Panikkar, *The Rhythm of Being: The Gifford Lectures.* (Maryknoll, New York, Orbis Books, 2009), 41. Panikkar famously said, "I left Europe (for India) as a Christian, I discovered I was a Hindu and returned as a Buddhist without ever having ceased to be a Christian." (http://www.raimonpanikkar.it/contents.asp?L=2&H=34&P=&ie=).

11. http://www.isciencetimes.com/articles/6651/20140109/universe-measured-perfect-accuracy-infinite-flat-eternal.htm.

12. http://www.huffingtonpost.com/fr-richard-rohr/the-great-chain-of-being_b_829255.html and http://myemail.constantcontact.com/Richard-Rohr-s-Meditation--Meister-Eckhart--Part-I.html?soid=1103098668616&aid=-xhq5KjhO-g.

13. Meister Eckhart, *Breakthrough: Meister Eckhart's Creation Spirituality in New*

trying to get past the smallness of concepts about God. Eckhart was pointing to a God that is beyond our understanding. God cannot be contained in a word or concept. We must continually let go of our small ideas of God so we can come closer to divine reality. He called this "God beyond God."[14] As early Christian theologian and philosopher whose writings influenced the development of Western Christianity and Western philosophy, Augustine (354–430), said, "If you comprehend it, it is not God."[15]

Having affirmed that God is beyond all our ideas, we still must go ahead and talk and reflect about God because we are humans with highly evolved minds and increasingly sophisticated language. This is the dilemma Moses faced. He was having a transcendent conversation with an even more transcendent God that did not lend itself to descriptions or words. Yet, he knew he had to communicate to others this very conversation, and he needed a name to identify this god among all the other gods being worshiped in his day. So God supplied Moses with a name that described God/She in a way that was profoundly distinct from all the other gods of that day. If we need a word to describe this big face of God, and I believe we do, I find that "I AM" or "Infinite Being" inches closer to the Great Mystery (which is another name that helps in some ways, also).

God as Being Itself is echoed down through the ages

Here are some of the influential thinkers who have understood God as Being throughout Christian history:

Translation, Intro. and Commentaries by Matthew Fox (New York: Image Books, 1991), 45.

14. Bernard McGinn, "The God beyond God: Theology and Mysticism in the Thought of Meister Eckhart." *The Journal of Religion*, Vol. 61, No. 1. (Jan., 1981), 1-19.

15. Augustine's Sermon 15, On the New Testament, http://www.newadvent.org/fathers/1603.htm.

- Augustine (354–430), in his *Confessions,* says that God is equated with being.[16]

- Medieval Catholic scholastic theologian and philosopher St. Bonaventure (1221–1274) said, "God is Being Itself."[17]

- Thirteenth-century Catholic philosopher and theologian John Duns Scotus (1266–1308) says that the concept of "infinite being" is the simplest concept available to us for understanding God.[18]

- Meister Eckhart (1260–1328) often wrote, "God is being." Everywhere in his Latin and German works he repeats this proposition, "God is pure being. . . . God and being are the same. . . . Being is God's first name. . . . Whether we ask what God is or who God is, the answer is always—being."[19]

- Christian existentialist philosopher and theologian Paul Tillich (1886–1965), widely regarded as one of the most influential Christian theologians of the twentieth century, famously affirmed that God does not exist, meaning God does not exist as a being but as Being Itself. He explains it this way:

> The being of God is being-itself. The being of God cannot be understood as the existence of a being alongside others or above others. . . . Whenever infinite or unconditional power and meaning are attributed to the highest being, it has ceased to be a being and has become being-itself. . . God is being itself, not a being.[20]

16. *Sanford Encyclopedia of Philosophy*, Augustine, *Confessions,* VII.x.16, revised 2010, http://plato.stanford.edu/entries/augustine/.

17. http://www.eckharttolle.com/article/Spirituality-And-The-Christian-Tradition/.

18. http://plato.stanford.edu/entries/duns-scotus/.

19. Mary Elizabeth Funke, Meister Eckhart, Meister (1916). *Meister Eckhart* (Kindle Locations 436-442).

20. Paul Tillich, *Systematic Theology*, Vol. 1. (Chicago: University of Chicago Press, 1951), 205, 235, 237.

• Prominent and prolific contemporary religious historian Karen Armstrong says, "God is not the supreme spirit. God is not the supreme being. God is not a being at all. God is being itself. It is wrong even to think that God exists, because our notion of existence is far too limited to apply to God. When we're talking about God, we're talking about a different mode of reality."[21]

• Presbyterian scholar Eugene Peterson, in his popular *The Message— The Bible in Contemporary Language,* eloquently paraphrases John 4:24 as, "God is sheer being itself–Spirit. Those who worship him must do it out of their very being, their spirits, their true selves, in adoration."

• Contemporary Eastern Orthodox theologian David Bentley Hart says, "God, in short, is not a being but is at once 'beyond being' (in the sense that he transcends the totality of existing things) and also absolute 'Being itself' (in the sense that he is the source and ground of all things)."[22]

• Raimon Panikkar, after a detailed study in his book *The Rhythm of Being,* concludes that the "Ground of all existences is both Being *and* God."[23] By Being he means an idea of God arrived at by reflection. By God he means a theistic Someone we relate to. Panikkar affirms not only a God who is big enough, the topic here, but a God who is close enough, which we explore in Part Two.

An important qualification

I differ with one aspect of many of the previous statements (as they stand, without qualification) except for the last one by Raimon Panikkar who points out both God as Being and God as a theistic Someone. To *only* say, "God is Being" is a *partial* truth which we can

---

21. Karen Armstrong lectures and interviews, http://thesethingsinside.wordpress.com/2013/01/08/karen-armstrong-lectures-and-interviews/.

22. David Bentley Hart, *The Experience of God,* (New Haven and London: Yale University Press 2013), 109.

23. Panikkar, *The Rhythm of Being,* 55 (italics his.) He also understands our inherent divinity which is discussed in Part Three.

reflect about. God is also a spiritual Presence or Someone that we can *relate to.* And God is also within us, as us, that which we can *rest* in as our own Universal Identity. I am emphasizing again that what I find most helpful is to always keep in mind the three dimensions or faces of God. I think we are closer to more truth when we say, or think, something like "*One Face of God* is The Infinite Face of God which can be described as God is Being Itself." This is not a minor point since my primary thesis is that most Christians have a one or two-dimensional God, and not a three-dimensional God of Three Faces. This includes those Christians who seem to embrace the classical Trinity but limit each of the "Father, Son, and Spirit" to one dimension.

The Incredible Unbearable Love-Drenched Radiance of Being

Being Itself is not just some abstract idea removed from real life. Infinite Being is not divine goo that has no life or consciousness. Being Itself is that which creates life, love, and consciousness because it holds these qualities in unmanifest form within its formlessness. Being is greater than life itself. It is the Creator and Container of life. God's Being is also our being. We can experience this directly as we will explore in Part III. We can rest in God's being. Being is not passive, empty, or static. Perhaps every time we speak of God's Being and our Being we should call it something like, "The Incredible Unbearable Love-Drenched Radiance of Being."

Jesus and the transpersonal Great I AM

This profound Jewish understanding of God as I AMness opens Jesus' statements about God in a radical way. I AM is not a concept. It is beyond conceptualization. I AM is not a substance. It is not matter. I AM is not a person. It is not personal or impersonal. Rather, it is transpersonal. I recently heard a man who had come through a life-threatening experience say, "I guess the Man Upstairs was looking out for me on this one." This is the God we are called to leave behind because "he" is much too small to be the God that Jesus spoke about. The Big Man Up There needs to be replaced by Infinite God Everywhere!

Jesus said, "God sends the sun and rain on the just and unjust" (Matt. 5:45). By "God" did Jesus mean some divine superman living in the sky that controls the weather sending one kind of weather here and another there? Or perhaps he had in mind that out of the I AM God of Moses, Being Itself, comes all of creation which includes rain and the sunshine. This is the "natural" process of earth's weather systems and patterns and climate changes that is "beingness" manifest as the weather—sunshine, rain, hot or cold.

When I read Jesus' statement, "Consider the birds of the air. Your Father-Mother cares for you more than them" (Matt. 6:26), here is what I hear: The Great I AM of Moses that is Infinite Being Itself pours into creation as ever-evolving love. We are "cared for more" as human beings because we have evolved beyond the birds of the air enough to be aware of, receive, and embrace that divine care.

Imaging Infinite Being

Full color images for many of the abstract concepts that I use in my talks and for this book are available at www.revpaulmsith.com. You may want to refer to them as you read each chapter. Psychospiritually active images can open us up to the mystical through pictures rather than words.

You can find there images of vast, outer space—a metaphor for the life, love, and light of Infinite Being. The Apostle Paul pointed out that the natural world reveals God in his letter to the Romans, saying, "Though invisible to the human eye, God's eternal power and divinity have been seen since the creation of the universe, understood and clearly visible in all of nature" (Rom. 1:20). Images from the Hubble Space Telescope sing of the infinite, divine, vastness of the mystery of Ultimate Reality.

Of course, all symbols have their limitations. The Hubble Space telescope's awesome images of outer space may give us a sense of the vast spaciousness of Infinite Being. What they do not communicate is that Infinite Being as space metaphor is *empty space*. I try to get at that on my website by imagining of outer space being *pulled back* to reveal that which is not a "something" but that which is beyond time and space in the metaphor of an empty dark hole.

Is your God big enough to encompass everything we know about the universe?

I said at the beginning of Part One, that you can know if your God is big enough if that God at least encompasses what we know about the universe today. We think of creation in terms of the Big Bang and almost 14 billion years of ongoing evolution which is still going on. We talk about space that stretches and wraps, dark matter, quarks, and God particles.

Astronomer and cosmologist Carl Sagan said,

> How is it that hardly any major religion has looked at science and concluded, "This is better than we thought! The universe is much bigger than our prophets said, grander, more subtle, more elegant. God must be even greater than we dreamed." A religion, old or new, that stressed the magnificence of the universe as revealed by modern science might be able to draw forth reserves of reverence and awe hardly tapped by the conventional faiths. Sooner or later, such a religion will emerge.[24]

That religion is emerging now, and we are exploring one expression of it here.

How do you know if your God is big enough?

1. You know your God is big enough if your God at least encompasses what we know about the universe today.

---

24. Carl Sagan. *Pale Blue Dot: A Vision of the Human Future in Space* (New York: Random House Publishing, 1994), 50.

2. You know your God is big enough if you can't wrap your mind around that God, but you can wrap your life around that God.

3. You know your God is big enough if you think it is reasonable to believe in that God enough for your heart to love that God. The heart cannot embrace what the mind rejects.

4. You know your God is big enough if that God is as big as the God Jesus knew and talked about.

5. You know your God is big enough if your imagination soars to new levels when reflecting about God in the healing and further evolution of this world.

Summary of Is Your God Big Enough?

•   Behind the face of God that was the intimate *Abba* God of Jesus is the awesome face of the I AM God of Moses.

•   The I AM God of Moses is not *a* being but *Being Itself*.

•   God-Beyond-Us is ultimately even beyond Being.

•   Being Itself is that which creates life, love, and consciousness because it holds these qualities in unmanifest form within its formlessness.

Question for Reflection and Group Discussion

1. Which one of the five travelers most expresses where you are? God beyond, God beside, God within, no God anywhere, or an integrated view of beyond, beside, and being us.

2. Which one represents the place where you are currently the least comfortable?

3. How realistic does integrating all three faces of God in your life seem to you at this point? In the Christian world?

4. In speaking about symbols and not concepts, what symbols of God are meaningful to you?

5. What resources such as websites, articles, books, and CDs has your group found helpful to enlarge their thinking about God?

6. When and where have you experienced awe and joy in nature, music, the arts, or other channels for the beauty and awesomeness of our divine life to come forth?

Practices

1. In "Nine Ways Not To Talk About God" Raimon Panikkar says that we should always begin talking about God with silence.[25] Begin this discussion alone or in a group with a minute or two of silence.

2. One of the best ways to reflect about God for those who enjoy reading is to read the books, articles, and websites of those with whom you resonate. I draw upon such spiritual thinkers as Cynthia Bourgeault, Ilia Delio, David Bentley Hart, Jim Marion, Steve McIntosh, Raimon Panikkar, Richard Rohr, and Ken Wilber. You can find others by asking your friends what they have found helpful.

3. Look at yourself in a mirror and sense that you live, and move, and have your being in God who is Being Itself.

4. Look at another person and sense that they, too, live and move and have their being in divine Being Itself.

5. Whenever you see a beautiful mountain, an awesome tree or flower, notice that it is existing in God as Infinite Being.

6. When you think "Infinite Being" think "no substance or material or energetic form." Just rest in the simple feeling of being.

7. Infinite Being is the I AM of every person. Say "I am" out loud while allowing yourself to feel the personal and transpersonal dimensions of this simple statement of being. It is both the simple feeling of being you have right now and the Infinite Face of God

---

25. Raimon Panikkar, "Nine Way Not to Talk About God," http://dimensionesperanza.it/english-articles/item/6187-nine-ways-not-to-talk-about-god-raimon-panikkar.html.

totally beyond you. Allow yourself to hold both of these senses with as little conceptualizing as you can. Just feel it rather than think it. When I do this, I feel both awe and my own intense presence.

8. Writer and blogger Tom Rapsas says,

> It's a thought worth entertaining for a moment. If God really is "being itself," then God exists right here, right now. God can be found in the space between your eyes and the computer screen in front of you. In the air you're inhaling and exhaling. In the thoughts that are entering your mind at this very moment. . . . God resides not on a throne up in the heavens, but in a place much closer to our hearts, right here on Earth.[26]

9. Close with this most simple form of signing the Three Faces of God.

 "God beyond me (us)."

 "God beside me (us)."

 "God being me (us)."

26. http://findingtheinnerway.com/2009/11/17/is-god-a-being-or-being-itself/.

"God beyond me."

CHAPTER 2

Beyond "the Son" to the Glory of the Cosmic Christ

"the glory of God in the face of Jesus Christ" (2 Cor. 4:6)

The word "Christ" can be a challenge to understand because it has a changing meaning in the Bible. It finds its fullest meaning in the writing of Apostle Paul. I have found that if my readers keep the following foundational, cosmic idea in mind while reading this chapter, everything here will make more sense:

Christ is the Christian symbol for everything— all that has ever existed and is happening everywhere and all the time—held in seamless Oneness. Christ is all of reality seen without any separation.

I use the term "Cosmic" Christ to signify this "all-ness." What follows is how this idea developed in the Bible and its many facets. Keep this understanding in mind as you read.

Jesus becomes Christ the Messiah

Many people think that if Jesus would walk into their church on some Sunday morning he might introduce himself by saying, "Hello, my name is Jesus Christ." But that's one thing he would not do. He might say something like, "Hello, my name is Jesus of Nazareth." He would not add "Christ" because that was not his last name or part of his name at all. The early Christians believed it was a title given to Jesus by God.

In ancient Greek Christ, *christos*, simply meant "anointed." In Judaism it came to mean the Messiah, the spirit-anointed one for whom the people of Israel were waiting to bring liberation. It then became a title with a specific and limited meaning which was applied to Jesus in the Gospels.[1] Jesus, conscious of his vocation, framed the title "Messiah" quite differently from all popular expectations, one in which he was acting and speaking on behalf of the God of Israel in bringing liberation to all people. Saying "I believe in Jesus Christ" means you have two quite different but intimately connected beliefs—one about his name as a person in history, the other about his historical and cosmic purpose.

Jesus becomes the risen Jesus, not the Cosmic Christ

Many theologians make the mistake of equating the risen Jesus with Christ the Messiah. The risen Jesus was simply the risen Jesus who then morphed into the Cosmic Christ in Paul's magnificent vision of the whole of reality. Some assume that whenever Jesus appears in non-physical form after his death, he must be the (Cosmic) Christ that is beyond history. That is simply wrong because it does not square with the experiences of the early Christians with the risen Jesus as the Jesus they knew personally in physical form, now in non-physical energetic form. This is not the transpersonal symbol named Christ, although they are connected. The risen Jesus is simply and gloriously that—the risen Jesus. When the Apostle Paul talked to the risen Jesus (Acts 9:5; 18:9; 22:8; 22:17; 26:15; 2 Cor. 12:1; Gal. 1:11-12) he was talking to the historical person named Jesus now present in a spiritual body. When Paul was talking about Christ, he was not talking personally about or to Jesus but about the glorious

---

1. N. T. Wright, *The New Testament and the People of God*, (Minneapolis: Fortress Press, 1992), xiv.

Cosmic Christ, who, as we shall see next, is the blueprint and symbol for the whole of reality. The Cosmic Christ includes and is intimately connected to Jesus, but goes infinitely beyond Jesus to encompass all of reality without separation.

Christ the Messiah becomes Christ the Cosmic Christ

Teilhard de Chardin (1881–1955) was an influential French philosopher and Jesuit priest who trained as a paleontologist and geologist. He asked this important question referring to Jesus as the Jewish Messiah: "Is the Christ of the Gospels, imagined and loved within the dimensions of a Mediterranean world, capable of still embracing and still forming the center of our prodigiously expanded universe?"[2]

There were several different versions of the Messiah in the Jewish tradition. Jesus redefined all of them, and after the resurrection the meaning of "Christ" as Messiah continued to leave the understanding as Messiah of the Jewish nation and further evolved into a new and radically cosmic dimension. This can be confusing since the Apostle Paul so associates Jesus with the Cosmic Christ that he often refers to both simply as "Christ" in his writings, although there are significant exceptions.[3] The answer to Teilhard's question is to point to the Cosmic Christ as described by Paul and others down through the centuries. Paul's use of the title "Christ" reflects a sweeping expansion of the understanding of Jesus that is vastly bigger than history.

---

2. Teilhard de Chardin, *The Divine Milieu*, (New York: Harper & Row, 1960), 46.

3. There are significant exceptions to Paul calling Jesus "Christ" because the historical Jesus in his spiritual body Jesus continued to appear to Paul. In Paul's first encounter with Jesus he addresses him as "Lord." Ananias is instructed in a vision by Jesus to go to Paul and tell him that the same "Lord Jesus" who appeared to Paul also appeared to Ananias. Jesus, named as such, then appears to Paul in a vision to reassure him in Act 18:9-10. Paul refers to Jesus as the Christ when, in the language of devotion, he writes "that at the name of Jesus every knee will bend in heaven and earth and under the earth and every tongue will confess that Jesus Christ is Lord" (Phil 2:10-11).

The Cosmic Christ

When you look *beyond* both the historical Jesus and the risen Jesus who is still with us now in a non-physical energetic body, you find the Cosmic Christ. The historical Jesus was a conscious, divine, physical, human being. The risen Jesus was and is Jesus himself with us now in his energetic spiritual body and personality. The Cosmic Christ looks like a cosmic scale Jesus—infinite consciousness, infinite divinity, and the whole physical universe rolled up into one seamless package of infinite being and finite becoming—all of reality without separation. While "cosmic" and "Christ" are not placed next to each other in the New Testament, they are certainly present in the New Testament descriptions of Christ.

Who and what is the Cosmic Christ?

I went through four stages in thinking about the following passages. As a university student and active in my church, these passages, when read or talked about in church, seemed like meaningless, grandiose preacher talk. Then in seminary they were just texts in Greek that I had to translate to pass my biblical languages courses. Gradually they became inspiring, pointing to something beyond me. That phase lasted forty years because I was so emotionally limited and therefore challenged in my ability to have and recognize spiritual experiences. Then, fifteen years ago, they started to become descriptions of a glowing reality that I was experiencing in my head and heart. I am so grateful for this. Here are some of the exciting meanings they have for me now, experienced in my mind, heart, body.

"I am the light of the world" (John 8:12). Jesus was speaking here not as the human personality Jesus but as the Cosmic Christ. The word "world" here is *cosmos* (κόσμου) in Greek and is a reference to the whole universe.[4] We can read it as, "Jesus said, 'I am the light of the cosmos.'" If the cosmos is infinite, that's a really big light!

---

4. *Theological Dictionary of the New Testament*, Vol. III, ed. Gerhard Friedrich, ed. and trans. Geoffrey Bromiley (Grand Rapids: Wm. B. Eerdmans, 1971), 894.

"The word became flesh and lived among us" (John 1:14). The Cosmic Christ is the colossal Word ("Logos") that became flesh, shouting there is no division between the natural and the supernatural, the divine and the human. They are different aspects of the same reality.

"Christ is the radiance of God's glory and the exact representation of God's very being, upholding the universe by a powerful word" (Heb. 1:3). Christ not only perfectly represents God, but holds the entire universe in place.

"And the same one who descended is the one who ascended higher than all the heavens, in order to fill the entire universe" (Eph. 4:10). Christ, as Jesus, took form to fill a human body. Then Jesus took cosmic form as Christ to fill the universe. Christ not only fills everywhere but *is* the everywhere.

"I am the light that is over all things. I am the all: from me all came forth, and to me all attained. Split a piece of wood; I am there. Lift up the stone, and you will find me there" (Gospel of Thomas, Saying 77). Nothing can be more cosmic than "the all." Jesus as the Cosmic Christ is not only everywhere, and is the everywhere, but is also *the source* of everywhere.

A stunning description of the Cosmic Christ (from Colossians)

Christ is the image of the invisible God,
the firstborn over all creation.
For in Christ all things in heaven and earth were created:
things visible and invisible . . .
All things have been created by Christ and for Christ.
Christ is before all things, and in Christ all things hold
together . . .
The beginning and first born from the dead,
So that Christ might have first place in everything.
For in Christ all the fullness of God was pleased to dwell,

(Abbreviated as TDNT in all following.)

And through Christ God was pleased to reconcile to Godself all things (Col. 1:15-19).

Here is how I understand each part of this passage:

• *"Christ is the image of the invisible God."*

Who or what is Christ? Christians usually think of this passage as referring to the historical Jesus which it certainly includes. However, Christ is much "bigger" than Jesus. If Jesus is the image of God in the humanity of flesh, then Christ is that same image of God in the totality of all that is—divine, human, and material reality.[5]

In Christ we see that God is not separate from material things including our bodies and the earth. Colossians 1:15 does not say Christ *contains* the image of the invisible God. Rather, Christ *is* that image. In Genesis 1:27, the human being does not *contain* the image of God but rather *is* the image of God. In John's Gospel the Word *became* flesh, not the Word came *into* flesh. Colossians 2:9 makes this startling claim, "For in Christ the whole fullness of divinity dwells bodily." Yes, bodily. As Jorge Ferrer, scholar, theorist, and leader in the field of Transpersonal Psychology,[6] says, "Embodied spirituality regards the body as subject, as the home of the complete human being, as a source of spiritual insight, as a microcosm of the universe and the Mystery, and as pivotal for enduring spiritual transformation."[7] Christ signals the end to the dichotomy between matter and spirit—there is nothing the matter with matter!

---

5. This is the theme of Raimon Panikkar's brilliant *Christophany: The Fullness of Man.*

6. *Journal of Transpersonal Psychology* describes transpersonal psychology as "the study of humanity's highest potential, and with the recognition, understanding, and realization of unitive, spiritual, and transcendent states of consciousness" (Lajoie and Shapiro, 1992:91). https://en.m.wikipedia.org/wiki/Religious_experience#Hinduism.

7. Ann Gleig and Nicholas G. Boeving, "Spiritual Democracy: Beyond Consciousness and Culture" review of *The Participatory Turn: Spirituality, Mysticism, Religious Studies,* edited by Jorge N. Ferrer and Jacob H. Sherman, State University

• *"The firstborn over all creation."*

The new creation story is the Big Bang. God/She is not sitting back away from creation in order not to be burned or harmed. No way! God is in the very middle of the Big Bang as creator creating. God does not invade from outer space. Rather, God is present in the depths of the cosmos and of the human heart calling us to see Christ—that is, to recognize the love-filled nonseparablity of all reality which Christians call the Reign (or Kingdom) of God.

Let me pause to refer to my use of the phrase "Reign of God" rather than "Kingdom of God" which is used by traditional translations of the Bible. The phrase Kingdom of God (Βασιλεία του Θεού) was a meaningful term in ancient times and can certainly be translated this way. However, today, most of us do not live in an ancient or medieval kingdom ruled by a male king. The word Kingdom today is both antiquated and patriarchal. It implies that the sovereign must be male and not female. This is why I translate Βασιλεία του Θεού as the Reign of God which fits both ancient and contemporary meanings without linguistically signaling that men should be in charge and not women.

At the moment God decided to emerge in the Big Bang, Christ was first to emerge. According to Big Bang cosmology, the prevailing scientific model, our universe was created 13.8 billion years ago. From a spiritual perspective, this was the first manifestation of the Cosmic Christ in our universe. Within this Big Bang was the pattern for all that was and is being created. To use Richard Rohr's brilliant term, Christ was the "blueprint" for all creation. Christ was "born," or incarnated at the moment of the Big Bang when formless Infinite Being took form in the creation of the cosmic blueprint. The Cosmic Blueprint was birthed from Being Itself. Christ was the first *transpersonal* manifestation of Being Itself as evolutionary love. Billions of years later Jesus was to be the breakthrough *personal* manifestation of that transpersonal, evolutionary love which was first born into creation as Christ.

Christ as the Blueprint was the design plan, the precise instructions, or pattern for all that followed. Scientists tell us that even the slightest variation from this incredible blueprint would have meant that the universe would not have evolved the way it has and we would not have evolved as conscious human beings. The cosmological understanding of science helps us understand the *material* process that led to the creation and evolution of the universe. The cosmological understanding of the Cosmic Christ helps us understand the *spiritual* meaning of the process of creation and evolution of the universe.

• *"For in Christ all things in heaven and earth were created."*

If God is Being Itself, then how did creation come about? How did a speck of infinitely compressed matter evolve to roses, giraffes, and the wonder of consciousness in human beings? Christians understand that it was through the Cosmic Christ who was and is the plan, the vehicle, and the purpose of all created things.

The Cosmic Christ is the cosmic matrix, the living web of love from which all things emerge.

Christ is Infinite Being in action—creating, shaping, and loving all things. The phrase "all things" (τὰ πάντα) is repeated six times in this passage. It is an almost technical phrase in the Greek language of antiquity, meaning all of reality.[8]

Paul and others saw Jesus as Christ in cosmic terms. How could God who was the pure being of "I AM" do all this creating? It was through this face of the creating God called "Christ." This was not the Messiah of the Jews. This was a manifest dimension of the formless I AM God of Abraham, Isaac, and Jacob. Christ is the designer, architect, blueprint, and construction manager of the entire cosmos!

• *"Things visible and invisible . . ."*

---

8. Curtis Vaughan, *Ephesians* (Nashville: Convention Press, 1963), 26.

Some of creation is visible to us in material physical form. Some is visible through scientific instruments and exploration. Some remains invisible in basic, ordinary consciousness but becomes visible in higher consciousness, such as energy fields, visions, and spiritual beings. Some are eternally "invisible" as Divine Being and Consciousness, which holds the visible in its own unseen existence. But even more, beyond blueprint and architect, now Christ has become "the symbol for the whole of reality" to use Raimon Panikkar's comprehensive phrase.[9] Christ is the Christian icon or likeness of "the all" that Thomas calls all of reality (Gospel of Thomas, Saying 77). The whole of reality consists of three intertwined centers: (1) material reality (visible to the ordinary eye), (2) invisible divine reality (increasingly visible to the awakened eye), and (3) human reality (the eye that does the seeing). These three comprise one seamless, nonseparate whole.

One result of seeing Christ as the creator of all things, visible and invisible, was the rejection of the Platonic idea that the material world was evil. Jesus reaffirmed the Hebrew idea that the created world was good. Then he also reaffirmed his religion's view that every human being carried the image of God and took it to new levels by reaffirming that every human was the light of the world, even though clouded over by a bushel basket of ego. When he announced his own light-bearing reality in, "I am the light of the cosmos" (John 8:12), he was proclaiming that he was the prototype for all of humankind. As the breakthrough model, he demonstrated the capacity of all human beings to reveal their own inner light-bearing reality. That's why Jesus, the Light of the Cosmos, shouted back at us, "YOU are the Light of the Cosmos" (Matt. 5:14)! He was declaring to that very cosmos that a new breakthrough had occurred in letting the light of love shine in a material reality greatly in need of it.

• *"Christ is before all things and in Christ all things hold together."*

Christ is the cosmic face of God by which all things are connected

---

9. Raimon Panikkar, *Christophany: The Fullness of Man*, (Maryknoll: Orbis, 2004), 144.

and held together in oneness. Christ is the cosmic pattern that holds everything together. Christ, as the symbol for the whole of reality, holds all things together within the infinite space of Infinite Being. Christ, as the blueprint and pattern that comes first, holds everything together from the very beginning, making it all work. Christ is the web of life pervading all creation, holding it all together in the cosmic force field of ever-creating love.

This web of life and love:

1. Connects us with the divine spiritual realm seen through the mystics' awakened and transcendent eye.

2. Connects the consciousness of everyone and everything. It is symbolized in our day through the eye of the Internet which connects individuals, institutions, nations and, increasingly, most information about the world, around the world.

3. Interconnects all the parts of the material realm with all the other parts seen through the scientist's eye of quantum physics. Fritjof Capra is an American physicist and writer on quantum physics and the parallels between modern science and mysticism. He says:

> A careful analysis of the process of observation in atomic physics has shown that the subatomic particles have no meaning as isolated entities, but can only be understood as interconnections between the preparation of an experiment and the subsequent measurement. Quantum theory thus reveals a basic oneness of the universe. It shows that we cannot decompose the world into independently existing smallest units. As we penetrate into matter, nature does not show us any isolated "basic building blocks," but rather appears as a complicated web of relations between the various parts of the whole.[10]

Capra says that we are finding that all the systems and various fields

---

10. Fritjof Capra, *The Tao of Physics*, (Boulder: Shambhala, 2010), 78.

we humans study, from quantum physics to ecology to mathematics, are themselves interconnected in what can be called the unified theory of living systems.[11] Christians already have a name for this unified theory—the Cosmic Christ!

4. Ultimately this web of love and life unites all three dimensions of reality: the divine spiritual realm, the human consciousness realm, and the material physical realm. Christians call this web by the name of Christ, the Cosmic Christ.

Jon Kabat-Zinn, Professor of Medicine Emeritus and creator of the Stress Reduction Clinic and the Center for Mindfulness at the University of Massachusetts Medical School, says, "To drop into being means to recognize your interconnectedness with all life, and with being itself. Your very nature is being part of larger and larger spheres of wholeness."[12]

Scottish-American naturalist John Muir (1838 –1914) said, "When we try to pick out anything by itself, we find it hitched to everything else in the Universe."[13] Such is Christ as the "holding together" (Col. 1:17) or union of human consciousness, divine being, and the mater-ial universe. Christians first see this in the historical Jesus who is the union of human consciousness, divine being, and a material body. Then Jesus is "cosmologized" as the reality of the Cosmic Christ— the union of cosmic infinite being, cosmic infinite consciousness, and the material cosmos itself which may also be infinite.

• *"For in Christ all the fullness of God was pleased to dwell."*

The Face of God that is Jesus contains the fullness of God in one body. This is not "all of God" in the sense that there is nothing left

---

11. See *The Web of Life: A New Scientific Understanding of Living Systems* by Fritjof Capra, (New York: Anchor, 1997).

12. http://www.brainyquote.com/quotes/keywords/interconnectedness.html.

13. John Muir, *My First Summer in the Sierra* (San Francisco: Sierra Club Books, 1988), 110.

of God outside of Jesus. This "fullness" is in the sense of a holon,[14] something that is simultaneously a whole and a part. Rumi put it in poetic form when he said, "You are not a drop in the ocean. You are the entire ocean in a drop." Of course we know there is the ocean as well as the drop, but the drop really does contain the entire ocean in some sense. Christ is not a holon but the whole, the source of all holonic parts.

• *"The beginning and first born from the dead."*

Christ is forever connected to but not identical with Jesus. Christ is the transpersonal form of the personal Jesus. The humanity of Jesus points us to the inner transpersonal dimensions of the Cosmic Christ. Jesus is the "beginning" or the prototype for Christians and others, the first evolutionary breakthrough model of what the Superhuman, the consciously divine human, looked like.

• *"So that Christ might have first place in everything."*

Christ, as the whole of reality, is the meeting of humanity, divinity, and matter. This meeting of loving unity must come first so that everything else makes sense beyond the rational. That is, it makes transrational sense. This is what Jesus called the Reign of God. He said to put the Reign of God in first place (Matt. 6:33) since this is simply recognizing what is already the nondual reality that is the way things are.[15] This was Jesus' way of saying that the Cosmic Christ has first place as the nondual Oneness that is everything. When we see reality first from this place, suddenly everything has its place. There is no paradox, no duality, no piece that does not fit. Literally, everything fits if we acknowledge that Christ is "first place in everything."

---

14. The word "holon" was coined by Arthur Koestler in his book *The Ghost in the Machine* (New York, Penguin, 1990), 48.

15. Nondual means "not two" or "one undivided without a second." It is a term and concept used in some religious and spiritual thought, both Eastern and modern Western spirituality. See Chapter 14 for a fuller exploration of nonduality.

• *"Through Christ God was pleased to reconcile to Godself all things."*

"All things," or reality, has never been separated in any way from God or any of the divine faces. However, it appears that way to the distorted dualistic eye of humankind. Therefore from the perspective of humankind, it must be reconciled. Jesus saw everything as already reconciled and called that vision the Reign of God. He proclaimed unrepentant sinners as forgiven because he saw them this way and knew they were already reconciled to God. He loved and embraced the outcast because he saw they were already loved and embraced by God.

The reconciled nature of everything is made known and visible in Jesus' reconciling life and death. Love drives evolution to create more and more consciousness of the connectedness and oneness of all creation. Humankind is now consciousness conscious of itself—and becoming more and more conscious as we continue to evolve. What do we become more and more conscious of at ever higher levels of awareness? We become aware that there is no separation between us and God, us and one another, and us and creation. Humanity, divinity, and creation are already in perfect harmony and union. Those that see this then work to let that become a manifest reality (reconciled) in the world of form.

Mary Evelyn Tucker, Senior Lecturer and Research Scholar at Yale University, and Brian Swimme, professor at the California Institute of Integral Studies teaching evolutionary cosmology, say, "If scientific cosmology gives us an understanding of the origins and unfolding of the universe, philosophical reflection on scientific cosmology gives us a sense of our place in the universe."[16] The Christ is a biblical as well as a philosophical reflection on scientific cosmology and can give us an even more complete sense of our place in the universe.

In summary, Christ is the blueprint and Christian symbol for the

---

16. *Moral Ground: Ethical Action for a Planet in Peril*, Kathleen Dean Moore and Michael P. Nelson, eds. (San Antonio: Trinity University Press, 2011), 348.

whole of reality without separation. By the whole of reality, I mean (a) spiritual or divine reality, (b) human reality or consciousness, and (c) material or physical reality.

Eight observations about the Cosmic Christ.[17]

1. God is still creating through Christ

Christ is not only the Christian symbol of the whole of reality as it is, Christ is also the symbol of the whole of reality as it is becoming— the icon of the future. As the conscious edge of creation, we humans are dynamic partners in the continuing creation along with the divine mystery. As Ilia Delio, Chair in Theology at Villanova University and Franciscan Sister, says, "We humans are evolution made conscious; hence, our choices for and in the world shape the future of the world."[18]

2. The Cosmic Christ is the ultimate morphogenetic field

Rupert Sheldrake is a biologist, researcher, and author who is best known for his hypothesis of morphic fields and morphic resonance, which leads to a vision of a living, developing universe with its own inherent memory. He worked in developmental biology at Cambridge University, where he was a Fellow of Clare College. He writes:

> Morphic fields organize atoms, molecules, crystals, organelles, cells, tissues, organs, organisms, societies, ecosystems, planetary systems, solar systems, and galaxies. In other words, they organize systems at all levels of complexity, and are the basis for the wholeness that we observe in nature, which is more than the sum of the parts.[19]

---

17. I am indebted to Raimon Panikkar's *Christophany* for much of this way of framing the word Christ.

18. Ilia Delio, *From Teilhard to Omega: Co-creating an Unfinished Universe*, (NY: Orbis 2014), 47.

19. http://www.sheldrake.org/about-rupert-sheldrake/frequently-asked-questions.

Basically, morphogenetic fields as theorized by Rupert Sheldrake are "self-organizing wholes."[20] A morphogenetic field is the non-physical blueprint that gives birth to forms. These fields appear to be available throughout time and space without any loss of intensity after they have been created.

This resembles the way the Apostle Paul describes Christ, only in modern scientific terms. As the ultimate morphogenetic field, Christ is the non-physical blueprint that gives birth to all the forms of the universe. Christ is the self-organizing Whole that is the master blueprint for the universe.

Sheldrake links his theory of morphic fields with the idea of an extended nonlocal mind, or what I call infinite consciousness. He believes these mental fields can extend over large distances, and that there is a "medium of connection" in these mental fields through which prayer works. He contends that a mental field is a series of connections between us and people, animals, places, etc., that we know and care about. Morphic fields must have a link between the sender and recipient in prayer. A mental field cannot simply spread without direction, whether in terms of recipient or locale. In some way the person praying must know or know of the recipient. He says that this provides some other approaches besides religious ones to non-religious prayer.[21]

3. The Cosmic Christ is Love

Jesus, and therefore all of us, are the individualized form of the creative loving Face of God. The Cosmic Christ beyond Jesus is the transpersonal creative loving Face of God that creates all things and in whom all things hold together. This Cosmic Christ is the creating, loving aspect of Pure Being within us and *as* us and in all creation. Franciscan theologian Zachary Hayes says, "When God's Word,

---

20. http://www.sheldrake.org/research/morphic-resonance/introduction.

21. Beatrix Murrel, Stoa del Sol, http://www.bizint.com/stoa_del_sol/imaginal/imaginal_nj2.html.

Love aware of itself, comes pouring into nothingness, the universe happens."[22]

Simone Weil (1909 –1943), French philosopher, Christian mystic, and political activist said, "The beauty of the world is Christ's tender smile for us, coming through matter."[23] The transpersonal, evolutionary love of the Christ, the "Cosmic Person," to use Ilia Delio's grand phrase, is the primary quality of creation.[24] This transpersonal love, exquisitely personalized in Jesus, fills the universe. Paul is certain that, "neither death, nor life, nor angels, nor rulers, nor things present, nor things to come, nor powers, nor height, nor depth, nor anything else in all creation, will be able to separate us from the love of God in Christ Jesus our Sovereign" (Rom. 8:38-39).

4. The Christian recognizes Christ in and through Jesus

Jesus was a living, audio-visual demonstration of this oneness of all of reality in history. In Jesus, the human and divine, the finite and the infinite meet. The material and the spiritual, time and eternity are not separated. Jesus reduces to nothing the distance between heaven and earth. He eliminates the perceived space between God and humankind. He does away with the idea that the material and the spiritual are separate. He does all of this without losing the polarity of any of these which is the essence of nonduality.

Albert Einstein wrote a letter to a distraught father who had lost his young son and had asked him for some comforting words. Einstein wrote:

> A human being is a part of the whole, called by us "Universe," a part limited in time and space. He

---

22. http://www.spiritualtreasureman.com/cosmic-christ/.

23. Simone Weil, trans. Emma Craufurd, *Waiting on God* (New York: Routledge, 1951), p. 60.

24. Ilia Delio, *The Unbearable Wholeness of Being*, (Maryknoll: Orbis, 2013), 122.

experiences himself, his thoughts and feelings as something separate from the rest—a kind of optical delusion of his consciousness. The striving to free oneself from this delusion is the one issue of true religion. Not to nourish it but to try to overcome it is the way to reach the attainable measure of peace of mind.[25]

Unfortunately, Einstein could not offer a way for this grieving father to access this connectedness to the "Universe." Christians see that connection in the beauty and love of the Cosmic Christ which is made real for us in the transforming companionship of the ever-present Jesus.

5. Christ, while connected to the historical Jesus for Christians, transcends Jesus

Recognizing the polarity between Christ and Jesus allows us to recognize Jesus as fully and personally present with us now as he was to the early Christians when he walked the earth in a physical body and after his death when he returned to them in a spiritual body. Then the symbol of Christ can fully expand beyond Jesus to its mystical union of transcendence and immanence in divine, human, and material realities. The Cosmic Christ includes and transcends Jesus. This counters the tendency among both Christians and others to use the words Jesus and Christ interchangeably.

6. Christ is the personal center of existence that holds all creation together both in relationship and nondual unity

Physical evidence of the function of the Cosmic Christ is found in the physicists' scientific exploration of the inherent connectedness of all things. The Cosmic Christ is the personal center of existence that holds all creation together in seamless relationship. If creation is personal, it should not be difficult to think of God/She as personal—

---

25. http://www.lettersofnote.com/2011/11/delusion.html.

manifesting in Jesus as well as in our consciousness and beingness. Christ personalizes and animates everything.

St. Bonaventure (1221–1274) was an Italian medieval Franciscan, scholastic theologian, and philosopher. Believing that Christ has something in common with all creatures, he wrote, "With the stone he shares existence; with plants he shares life; with animals he shares sensation; and with angels he shares intelligence. Thus all things are transformed in Christ since in his human nature he embraces something of every creature in himself when he is transfigured."[26]

7. The Cosmic Christ and the religions of the world

Some Christians make a point of not using Christian terminology in writing about spirituality. They do this to affirm that all loving spiritual paths make authentic contributions to the whole and that Christianity does not have an exclusive corner on truth. Perhaps they sometimes also do this with the aim of melding all religions together into one universal path. However, I take a different direction. I use specifically Christian terminology to explain my understanding of Christianity. I am also clear that other traditions can be authentic spiritual paths. My using Christian naming and categories affirms the use of each tradition's terminology in describing its own path. For me to stop using Christian terminology subtly implies that Buddhists and others should not use their unique terminology either. This diminishes each tradition rather than building on it and encouraging it to have the most evolved understanding. I agree with Jorge Ferrer who says, "If we try to unify the faiths of the world into one religion, we will also lose many of the qualities and richness of each particular tradition. Therefore, I feel it is better, in spite of the many quarrels in the name of religion, to maintain a variety of religious traditions."[27]

The Gospel of John that says Jesus is the light of all people (1:4). If

26. Sermo I, Dom II, in Quad. IX, 215–19.

27. Jorge Ferrer, *Revisioning Transpersonal Theory: A Participatory Vision of Human Spirituality*, (New York: State University of New York Press, 2001), 41.

that is true, and I believe it is, that obviously means this light is called by names other than Jesus for some and understood differently by others who have different religious images. It is also understood by using very different concepts which may not sound at all similar. If anything applies to all people it obviously must take into account the quite different ways various people view the world and interpret it. This could mean that no religions are true, or that all of them are true for their particular audience. I advocate the latter and that is why I am confident about the Jesus path as an ontologically rich source of reality.

Christ is the universal symbol for Christians of divine-human unity, the human face of God and the divine face of humankind, God being us. Christianity approaches Christ in a particular and unique way, informed by its own history and spiritual evolution. But Christ vastly transcends Christianity. Panikkar calls the name "Christ" the "Supername," in line with St. Paul's "name above every name" (Phil. 2:9), because "it is a name that can and must assume other names, like Rama or Krishna or Ishvara."[28]

8. The second coming of the Cosmic Christ

The first coming of the Cosmic Christ occurred at the Big Bang as the blueprint of the cosmos that is the Cosmic Christ emerging into manifest reality.

Then came Jesus, who was the personification and prototype of the Cosmic Christ in relatable, lovable, knowable, flesh and blood. The second coming of Jesus occurs when anyone opens to love. God is love. "Everyone who loves has been born of God" (1 John 4:7).

The Second Coming of the Cosmic Christ is different from the second coming of Jesus. The more nondual, unitive consciousness inhabits humankind, the more the Cosmic Christ has returned and the more heaven and earth have become one.

---

28. http://diversejourneys.com/?tag=raimon-panikkar.

The second coming of Christ is the Christian way of speaking about Cosmic Christ as unity consciousness coming more and more into humankind's consciousness in spiritual evolution. This is an authentic spiritual creation which did not exist before in our awareness and is increasingly manifest today as we each participate in our own evolution of consciousness. Every step of awakening you and I take is a step toward the second coming of Christ into the world. Imagine that!

The higher the consciousness the greater the degree of inclusion, unity, and the more the second coming of the Cosmic Christ becomes a reality.

Any movement toward removing what separates us increases compassion and love—and is a move towards the second coming of the Cosmic Christ. The first coming was in creation. The second coming will be the reuniting of creation, God, and human consciousness in the manifest world without division or separation.

We are heading for new heaven and a new earth in the poetic metaphors of Revelation.

> Then I saw a new heaven and a new earth, for the first heaven and the first earth, had passed away, and the sea was no more. I saw the holy city, the new Jerusalem, coming down heaven from God, prepared as a bride and bridegroom adorned for each other. And I heard a loud voice from the throne saying, "See, the home of God is among mortals. God will dwell with them, and they will be God's people, and God will indeed be with them. God will wipe every tear from their eyes. Death will be no more; mourning and crying and pain will be no more, for the first things have passed away."
>
> (Rev. 21:1-4 *NRSV* IV)

Summary of Is Your Jesus Big Enough

• Jesus becomes the Messiah, and the Messiah becomes the Cosmic Christ.

• The Cosmic Christ is the Christian symbol for the whole of reality without separation.

• God is still creating through the Cosmic Christ which is the ultimate morphogenetic field.

• The Cosmic Christ is love which Christians recognize through Jesus.

• The Cosmic Christ includes and transcends Jesus.

• The Cosmic Christ is the personal center of existence that holds all creation together in relationship and unity.

• The Cosmic Christ transcends Christianity and finds truth in all loving spiritual paths.

• The literal Second Coming of Christ is the emergence of union with God and one another, by whatever name, in the consciousness of the people of the world.

Questions for Reflection and Group Discussion

1. On a scale of one (little) to ten (much), how did you resonate with the idea of the Cosmic Christ?

2. Did anything new to your thinking make sense that you marked in your book or device? Is there anything about the term "Christ" that you understand differently now?

3. Do you find any practical consequences for seeing the Cosmic Christ beyond Jesus as the symbol for all of reality in seamless unity?

4. Close your group discussion with one person or the group reading this prayer from Ephesian 3:17-19:

> And I pray that you, being rooted and established in love, may have power, together with all the saints, to grasp how wide and long and high and deep is the love of Christ, and to know this love that surpasses knowledge–that you may be filled to the measure of all the fullness of God.

Practices

1. *"Reflection about"* is the primary practice here in Part One. Suggested books for reading for those who like to think deeply are *Integral Consciousness and the Future of Evolution: How the Integral Worldview Is Transforming Politics, Culture and Spirituality* by Steve McIntosh and *A New Earth* by Eckhart Tolle.

2. Later, in Part Three, we explore the experience of the Cosmic Christ within as Oneness Consciousness. However, you can begin at any time to sink into the reality of no separation between us and God, us and one another, and us and the universe. Go inside yourself and begin to rest in as much of that oneness with God, people, and nature as you can.

3. Close with signing this Three Faces of God benediction.

 "God beyond me, in whom I live and move, and have my being."

("God beyond us, in whom we live and move, and have our being.")

 "God beside me, you are always with me."

("God beside us, you are always with us.")

 "God being me, I am the light of the world."

("God being us, we are the light of the world.")

"God beyond me."

CHAPTER 3

Beyond "the Spirit" to the Marvel of Infinite Consciousness

Halloween is coming up as I write this and the ghosts and spirits will be coming out in full costume as we play with the Celtic origins of Halloween. The Celts believed the spirits of the dead roamed the streets and villages at night. Since not all spirits were thought to be friendly, gifts and treats were left out to temper their anger and ensure that next year's crops would be plentiful. This custom evolved into trick-or-treating. Down through the centuries that sounded to some folks like the way God acts, too. Is God a ghost, a sometimes loving, sometimes wrathful spirit who needs the gift of blood to stop being angry at us? Older translations of the Bible talked about God the spirit as the "holy ghost" until scholars in the 18th century made the change to "holy spirit" because of the connotations of the word "ghost." But the idea of God's spirit as a "ghost" still hangs around.

What is spirit?

In an astonishingly revealing statement, the Gospel of John records Jesus saying, "God is spirit, and those who worship God must worship in spirit and truth" (John 4:24). The Bible talks about "spirit" and "holy spirit" over six hundred times and Jesus takes it to a new level. Right away we can see that spirit has something to do with God ("God is spirit") and something to do with us (we must "worship in spirit and truth"). In this chapter we will explore the first half ("God is spirit"), the divine dimension of spirit. Then we will take the last six chapters to explore the second half of this revealing sentence ("worship in spirit and truth"), the human dimension of spirit.

What is spirit? If God/She is "spirit" and we should worship in "spirit," then spirit is certainly important. Traditional Christianity says "spirit" is the third person of the Trinity. That is a foundational theological formulation of the experience of the early Christians phrased in a fourth and fifth-century Greek philosophical context. But what is God's spirit understood with our minds and felt with our hearts that connects with us where we live in real life?

A major theme in this book is the bold idea that a Christian, biblical, and mystical understanding of spirit is best found in the one word "consciousness." There is nothing closer to us than consciousness. At the same time, there is nothing harder to explain. Consciousness, like quantum physics, is one of the few incredibly important things about life and reality which we have only just begun to explore. I arrived at seeing spirit as consciousness by two pathways. First, I decided to take the biblical accounts seriously when describing the arrival and effects of "spirit" in today's language. Second, I began to explore the phenomena I had experienced in myself and observed in others down through the years associated with God's spirit and my spirit to see if I could make sense of it in today's understanding of consciousness. I share this in later chapters. First is the story of my journey through the Bible in getting a better grasp on spirit—so spirit could get a better grasp on me.

A Detective Story: Solving the Mystery of Spirit

Okay, that's an exaggeration. I don't really *solve* the mystery of spirit, but I do think I have moved closer to what spirit is and how spirit works in the biblical accounts and our lives. In terms of the focus of this chapter on infinite spirit, I discovered something I had not seen for most of my religious and scholarly life:

Spirit is Infinite Consciousness present in and as the consciousness of finite humankind

It took six clues or discoveries for me to move from a traditional theological understanding of spirit as "the third person of the Trinity" to a "down where I live" experienced understanding of divine spirit as divine-human consciousness. Here are the six consecutive discoveries that led me to these conclusions as I explored the Bible, the writings of mystics and scientists, and my own evolving mystical consciousness.

Clue #1: God is spirit – infinite spirit

The first thing I noticed was that Jesus did not say God is *a* spirit but "God is spirit" (John 4:24). This is like our discussion in Chapter One about whether God is *a* being or being itself. I have already pointed out that the I AM face of God is not *a* divine being but is more expansively thought about as Being itself. Likewise, the Infinite Face of God is not *a* spirit. This dimension of God can be more helpfully thought about as spirit itself. The Psalmist asks, "Where can I go from your spirit? Where can I flee from your presence?" (Psalm 139:7). In Jeremiah 23:24 God declares, "Do I not fill heaven and earth?" The infinite spirit of God is everywhere and is associated with God's conscious presence. In all the ventures of life, "even though I walk through the darkest valley, I fear no evil; for you are with me" (Psalm 23:4). Since we are talking about "everywhere," it appears that spirit itself is big, infinitely big. So let's identify this divine "everywhere" spirit as infinite spirit.

Clue #2: Spirit is both divine and human

Next I decided to go back to the beginning of everything in the opening scene in the Bible. In dramatic story-telling, "the earth was a formless void and darkness covered the face of the deep, while spirit (*rûach*) of God swept over the face of the waters" (Gen 1:2). One of our problems with understanding spirit in the Bible is that we must use translations from the Hebrew and Greek. No translation can catch the rich and nuanced mixtures of meanings of the word "spirit" in Hebrew. In my Hebrew studies in seminary I found that the word "spirit" here, *rûach* in Hebrew, amazingly means not only "spirit" but "breath," "wind," and even, at times, "mind," "ecstatic state," and "symbol of life."[29]

Translators must choose whether they will use spirit, breath, wind, or other meanings based on the context and their interpretation of which meaning is most likely. For instance, in Ezekiel 37 we see all three different translations of the same word: "I will put my spirit (*rûach*) within you and you shall live. . . Come from the four winds (*rûach*). . . and breath (*rûach*) came into them" (Ezekiel 37:6, 9, 10). We see how mysteriously nuanced the one word *rûach* is as our life force, wind, and breath.

In describing Joshua in Deuteronomy, The New International Version says, "Joshua was filled with the spirit" (Deut. 34:9). The footnote reads, "Or Spirit." The translators, as they saw it, had to decide whether Joshua was filled with the life force of awakened human consciousness (spirit) or the divine spirit of God (Spirit). In most places the translators seem to believe they had to determine whether to call this God's spirit or human spirit because their theological view was that it could not be both. The normal reader doesn't realize all the theologizing going on behind the translation of "spirit" that reflects the translator's beliefs. An integrated view sees spirit as both divine and human to avoid a false dichotomy between human and divine spirit.

In classical Greek classes at my alma mater, Washington University in St. Louis, and in my biblical Greek studies later at Midwestern Baptist Theological Seminary in Kansas City I learned that *pneuma*

---

29. *Brown-Driver-Briggs Hebrew and English Lexicon*, Unabridged, Electronic Database, http://biblehub.com/hebrew/7307.htm.

(πνεῦμα) is the Greek word for spirit. It is found 362 times in the New Testament and corresponds to the Hebrew *rûach* in the Old Testament. Amazingly, like *rûach*, *pneuma* can also mean spirit, breath, or wind.

The divine spirit is also the human spirit

But wait, I found out that there is even more mixing and blending. *Rûach* and *pneuma* can also mean both divine and human spirit or breath. God creates the first human being by starting with dust, dirt, or clay (depending on the translation) from the ground formed into a body or "earth creature" as the *Inclusive Bible* translates it. "So YHWH fashioned an earth creature from the clay of the earth." But that earth creature was not yet a living person. God then "blew into its nostrils the breath (*niš·maṯ*) of life. And the earth creature became a living being" (Gen. 2:7 IB). *Niš·maṯ* is another Hebrew word that can also mean divine or human breath, a living person, and spirit. Human life is created when spirit is breathed!

Next I moved to the dramatic scene of Noah and the flood. It's a mirror image of retelling the creation story, only now the "breath of life" becomes the "spirit of life." As the flood continued, "All that had the breath (*niš·maṯ*) of the spirit (*rûach*) of life that were on dry land died" (Gen. 7:22). This word "breath" is also "spirit (*rûach*) of life." In Hebrew, spirit is the inner nature of God and the principle which gives life to the human body.[30] All of this continues the great mixing of divine and human spirit, life, and breath in the Hebrew Scriptures. Job says "as long as my breath (*niš·maṯ*) is in me and the spirit (*rûach*) of God is in my nostrils" (Job 27:3). And again, "The spirit (*rûach)* of God has made me and the breath [from *niš·maṯ*] of the Almighty gives me life" (Job 33:4). Spirit as the breath of all human life and spirit as the breath of God are melded together. My friend Jack Levison is W. J. A. Power Chair of Old Testament Interpretation and Biblical Hebrew at Perkins School of Theology,

---

30. TDNT, VI, 364.

Southern Methodist University, and author of over a dozen books. Jack writes, "The *rûach*, the spirit-breath, is an amazing amalgamation of human breath and divine spirit—all of this a gift of God."[31]

We can readily make the connection between the divine spirit and our very life in other passages such as Ezekiel 36:7. God says, "I will put my spirit (*rûach*) within you and you shall live." This rich and nuanced connection of divine and human spirit with divine and human breath in the one word "*rûach*" is so lost in the usual translation that Levison renders *rûach* as "spirit-breath" to signify the mingling of divine, human, spirit, and breath all in this one word. The divine spirit and breath become the human spirit-breath even while remaining the divine spirit-breath.

You and I are individualized expressions of this single, indivisible, infinite, universal divine spirit. The human spirit is a holy spirit!

Holy Spirit or holy spirit?

Notice that I do not capitalize "holy spirit." The term "holy spirit" may look strange since it is normally capitalized as is usually done for names referring to God. However, I have adopted a practice of not normally capitalizing the word spirit when it refers to God in translating biblical passages or in my writing except when I am quoting someone who uses the upper case for spirit. I also use the upper case when referring to the classical Trinitarian formula of God the Father, Son, and Spirit.

The early copies of the Greek New Testament were written in all uppercase letters with no spaces and, at first, with no punctuation like this: ALLCAPITALLETTERSANDNOPUNCTUATION. Aren't you glad our writing style has changed! The Greek alphabet did not have punctuation until at least the second century, and there were no lowercase letters until much later. Later copies and translations

31. Jack Levison, *Fresh Air: The Holy Spirit for an Inspired Life*, (Brewster, Massachusetts: Paraclete Press, 2012), 35.

began adding our kind of case, sentence, and punctuation. Scholars add these things to their translations of the New Testament texts based on their theology and what seems reasonable to them. My theology is the basis for my choosing *not* to capitalize spirit.

Levison points out that the reason he does not capitalize the word "spirit" is to maintain its biblical use for both divine and human spirit, divine and human breath. He says, "I am not refusing to acknowledge the role of holy spirit in the Trinity or the personhood of the spirit. I am simply avoiding a false dichotomy between the human and divine spirit."[32] As we shall see next, there is no distance or separation between God's spirit and our spirit. We will explore this again more fully in Part Three about Trinity being us.

Clue #3: Spirit is given to all living persons

As I read the following biblical passages, I could only conclude that divine spirit-breath is given to everyone.

• "In God's hand is the life of every living thing and the spirit (*rûach*) of every human being" (Job 12:10). Spirit is in every living person.

• Speaking of his life itself, Job phrased it, "as long as my breath (*niš·ma̱t*) is in me and the spirit (*rûach*) of God is in my nostrils" (Job 27:3). The breath in everyone is spirit-breath. Spirit-breath is not just given to Christians or even human beings, but to all the living.

• "The earth is full of your creatures . . . When you hide your face, they are dismayed; when you take away their breath (*rûach*), they die and return to their dust" (Psalm 104:24, 29). If your spirit leaves your body, your body dies and returns to the earth. Spirit-breath is in all living creatures.

• "The spirit-breath (*rûach*) of God has made me and the spirit-breath (*niš·ma̱t*) of the Almighty gives me life" (Job 33:4). Every human being is right now breathing not just air, but God's spirit-

---

32. Levison, *Fresh Air*, 17.

breath. Every time you breathe you are a living demonstration that divine–human breath is your very life and the life of all humankind.

Reformer, Roman Catholic saint, and priest, St. John of the Cross (1542–1591) said, "One should not think it impossible that the soul be capable of so sublime an activity as this breathing in God, through participation as God breathes in her."[33] Take a breath of divine-spirit right now!

In Luke 8:55, Jesus raised a little girl from the dead, and the Bible says, "Her spirit (*pneuma*) returned, and at once she stood up...." Spirit is that which makes the human being a living person. When Jesus was dying on the cross, he "gave up his spirit" (*pneuma*), (Matt. 27:50) and died because "the body without the spirit (*pneuma*) is dead" (James 2:26).

Spirit in awakened form in the heroes of the Old Testament is different from spirit as life in everyone

I saw that "spirit" in the Old Testament is the divine spirit of God breathed as life into every human being. However, there were instances where spirit did more than just make a body alive. Something more than basic, ordinary life and awareness took place. I call this something more, "awakened spirit-breath" here and "awakened consciousness" later on. Here are some of the many examples.

• When Samuel anointed David to be king over Israel, "the spirit of the Lord *came mightily* upon him from that day forward" (1 Sam. 16:13, italics mine).

• The young Samson "grew and . . . the spirit of the Lord began *to stir* in him" (Judges 13:24-25, italics mine). Later, as a young man, "the spirit of the Lord *rushed* on him and he tore the lion apart barehanded" (Judges 14:6, italics mine).

---

33. St. John of the Cross, "The Spiritual Canticle," stanza 39, commentary, no. 4, in *The Collected Works of St. John of the Cross*, trans. Kieran Kavanaugh, O.C.D. and Otilio Rodriguez, O.C.D. (ICS Publications, Institute of Carmelite Studies, 1973), 558.

• Next Samson was bound by ropes and "the spirit of the Lord rushed on him" and he escaped the ropes and "killed a thousand men with the jawbone of a donkey" (15:14-15). Egad, Samson became an early James Bond with a jawbone instead of a gun!

• Spirit was not limited to massive force but included higher intelligence and delicate craftsmanship: "I have called by name Bezalel . . . and I have filled him with the spirit of God, with ability and intelligence, with knowledge and all craftsmanship, to devise artistic designs, to work in gold, silver, and bronze" (Ex. 31:2-4).

I knew from the rest of the Hebrew scriptures that all these people as living persons already had divine spirit-breath, so what was this "came mightily, stirring, rushing, filling" spirit-breath business? Evidently it was a stronger, more intensified version of spirit-breath. It seems that the divine-human spirit-breath we all have by virtue of being alive is different from the spirit-breath that stirs and rushes so mightily. This was not just basic spirit or life force, but elevated or super life force. It was awakened, intensified spirit-breath.

Awakened, intensified spirit becomes dominant in the New Testament

When the prophet Joel announced that spirit was to be poured out on everyone, he was speaking of this awakened and elevated consciousness, saying:

> I will pour out my spirit on all flesh;
> your sons and your daughters shall prophesy,
> your elders shall dream dreams,
> and your young people shall see visions.
>
> (Joel 2:28)

Peter quotes this passage from Joel at Pentecost as an explanation of what was happening. Spirit-breath was being poured out on the followers of Jesus in this intensified level. The awakened spirit that came to a few leaders in the Old Testament now becomes the *entire focus* of the realm of spirit in the New Testament. The New

Testament almost exclusively speaks of divine-human spirit as this more saturated and intensified spirit-breath within us.

Levison says that in Israel and the early church, "One word, *rûach* or *pneuma* could communicate *both* the spirit or breath of God within all human beings *and* the divine spirit or breath that God gives as a special endowment."[34] What Levison calls "special endowment" I identify as awakened spirit-breath. The Bible describes this with phrases like "filled with," "poured out," "come upon," "flowed from," "descended upon," "baptized with," "received," and "given." In these cases, people are given *more* life or *more* spirit–breath in order to carry out certain tasks. In the Old Testament this occurs with a few such as Moses, Joshua, Samson, Saul, Elijah, Elisha, and Isaiah. Then Joel predicts that spirit–breath will be poured out on everyone. We see the beginning of this in the New Testament as intensified spirit-breath fills new followers of Jesus. This is in the form of "more" spirit or "expanded" spirit. I concluded that *God's spirit in the Old Testament is our normal, everyday life force or spirit with a few exceptions of awakened spirit. God's spirit in the New Testament is almost always referring to awakened or intensified spirit.*

Clue # 4: Spirit is consciousness in the Bible

I asked myself what is the difference between the "earth creature" of Genesis and the "living being" that it became when God/She breathed spirit into it. The difference between an earth body created from the clay of the earth and a living human being is consciousness. Dust, dirt, and rocks are not conscious, at least in the way people are.

What was the difference between basic spirit-breath and Levison's "special endowment" or what I call intensified or more awakened spirit? When people moved from basic consciousness or awareness to a higher degree of awareness, they suddenly became more conscious of an intense life force and, in Joel's words, of "prophecy, dreams, and visions." We will see in the last six chapters that the phenomena Joel

---

34. Levison, *Fresh Air*, 19 (italics his).

predicted of channeling words from God, information from dreams, and seeing sacred visions were all a vital part of the New Testament church's experience of spirit-breath. These are all experiences of non-ordinary or awakened consciousness. When I saw this, I came to the only conclusion that seemed to fit:

These ancient biblical metaphors and descriptions of spirit are today contained in our word "consciousness."

Since the Bible is full of words pertaining to consciousness, why didn't the writers of the Bible simply use the word "consciousness"? They didn't because the word and clearly identified concept of consciousness is relatively recent. The word "consciousness" and its modern meanings did not appear until the late 1600s. The origin of the modern concept of consciousness is often attributed to John Locke's *Essay Concerning Human Understanding* published in 1690.[35] Locke defined consciousness as "the perception of what passes in a person's own mind."[36] *I find that spirit is most clearly seen in the Bible, in the writings of the mystics, and in human experience as consciousness in today's understanding.*

Naming spirit as consciousness does not make spirit any less divine or less mysterious. Jesus said, "The wind (πνεῦμα—*pneuma*, meaning breath, wind, or spirit) blows where it chooses, and you hear the sound of it, but you do not know where it comes from or where it goes. So it is with everyone who is born of the spirit (πνεῦμα—*pneuma*, meaning breath, wind, or spirit)" (John 3:8). It is still a mystery! We are just beginning to explore consciousness today. It is often viewed as individuals' awareness of their internal states as well as the events going on around them. If you can describe something you are experiencing in words, then it is part of your consciousness.

---

35. John Locke, *An Essay Concerning Human Understanding*, Chapter XXVII, (South Australia: University of Adelaide, updated 2015), https://ebooks.adelaide.edu.au/l/locke/john/l81u/B2.27.html.

36. Science & Technology: consciousness, *Encyclopedia Britannica*. https://www.britannica.com/topic/consciousness.

Now I was ready to see spirit, biblically, as the divine energy field of infinite consciousness that has been breathed into humankind, an active power of loving intent and mystical content manifest as awareness. The phrase "holy spirit" is an early naming of this divine/human energy field of consciousness. It is holy in both its divine and human expressions. It is God's infinite consciousness poured into finite humans and awakened to the degree their situation allows.

Theologically informed and thoughtful people may hesitate to equate spirit with consciousness because it may seem to them to remove spirit from the divine or sacred space that is God. They may prefer to keep capitalizing spirit to remind us that it is God's spirit. Some may think that to say spirit is consciousness makes spirit too ordinary or too human. They may prefer to say "spirit" and not mean "consciousness." That is one way to go and is the way we have gone for a long time. I prefer to go another way. If we see that God is consciousness, seeing spirit is consciousness is another way of pointing to our deep connection to God. Life and consciousness become newly sacred when seen as divine! Let's change our thinking so that "consciousness" is intimately connected with spirit, both human and divine. Let's not make a false distinction between divine and human spirit. This, to me, is a more radical, biblically-based, and transforming path.

Clue # 5: Others speak of God's spirit as infinite consciousness

I hesitate to embrace a theological understanding of which I am its only proponent. It's not that I'm theologically timid, but I feel I owe it to my readers to show some communal validation from other mystics and theologians before I share it with others. It was interesting to find so many writers affirming the divine spirit as infinite consciousness.

• Fourth-century church leader Gregory of Nyssa, according to David Bentley Hart's interpretation, describes the divine life as, "an eternal act of knowledge and love, in which the God who is infinite being is also an *infinite act of consciousness*, knowing himself as the infinitely good, and so is also an infinite love, at once desiring all and receiving all in himself."[37]

• An often quoted way of speaking about infinite consciousness comes from Alain of Lille, twelfth-century French philosopher and poet who writes, "God is an intelligible sphere, whose center is everywhere, and whose circumference is nowhere."[38]

• Meister Eckhart wrote of God as consciousness in contemporary translation:

> God alone truly is, and … He is consciousness, and … He is consciousness alone to which no other being is added. … Observe that all that is a consequence of the One, or of oneness, such as identity, likeness, image, relation and the like, are properly to be found only in God or Divinity. … All these signify unity in multiplicity.... Only in God are being and consciousness identical. … Therefore only God calls things into being through consciousness for only in Him are consciousness and being identical.[39]

• Philosopher Joseph Politella (1910–1975) writes, "The conception of the creation, cosmic and personal, of which Eckhart speaks sounds like a consciousness which, like the Logos of St. John, is in the beginning in God and with God."[40] In this light we can read the

---

37. Hart, *The Experience of God*, 42, 43 (italics mine).

38. https://dialinf.wordpress.com/2008/04/03/a-circle-with-the-center-everywhere/.

39. Timothy Conway describes how he translates these words from the Latin Works 29 as consciousness: *"Intellectus* (L)—'Intellect'; today a better sense of this important scholastic term is 'consciousness,' the highest part of the soul; *Negatio-Affirmatio* (L)—negation and affirmation, the fundamental acts of intellect/consciousness; *Vernünfticheit* (MHG)—intellect, understanding, consciousness." In Meister Eckhart (1260-1328)—Nondual Christian Mystic Sage by Timothy Conway http://www.enlightened-spirituality.org/Meister_Eckhart.html.

40. Joseph Politella, Meister Eckhart and Eastern Wisdom in *Philosophy East and West*, Vol. 15, No. 2 (Honolulu: University of Hawaii Press, 1965), 123.

words about Logos or Word in the first chapter of the Gospel of John this way:

> In the beginning was Consciousness. And this conscious-
> ness was with God and was God. What has come into
> being in consciousness was life, and this life was the light
> of consciousness of all people. John came to testify to the
> light. The true light of consciousness shines in the deepest
> night and the night did not overcome it. True awakened
> consciousness, which enlightens everyone, was coming
> into the world. The Consciousness became flesh and lived
> among us, and we have seen his glory.   (John 1:1-14)

• Evelyn Underhill (1875–1941), author and teacher, was one of the great Christian mystics of our times. She considered God the one reality, and union with that reality as the goal of our lives. Her definition of mysticism is that it is the art of union with Reality where Reality is equated with the Ultimate State of Consciousness. The mystic is a person who has attained that union in greater or lesser degree, or who aims at and believes in such attainment. Evelyn Underhill distinguishes five stages of ascension to the Absolute or Cosmic Consciousness.[41]

• God as consciousness finds resonance in other ancient religions such as Hinduism. Noted scholar Georg Feuerstein summarizes the Advaita realization, an ancient Hindu tradition of scriptural exegesis and religious practice centered in the concept of unity, as follows: "The manifold universe is, in truth, a Single Reality. There is only one Great Being, which the sages call Brahman, in which all the countless forms of existence reside. That Great Being is utter Consciousness, and It is the very Essence or Self (Atman) of all beings."[42]

• Sri Ramana Maharshi (1879–1950), possibly the most famous sage of the twentieth century and teacher of the direct path of self-

---

41. Evelyn Underhill, *Mysticism*, (CreateSpace Independent Publishing, 2011), 49.
42. http://www.wie.org/j14/advaita.asp.

inquiry and awakened consciousness, said, "When a person enters Cosmic Consciousness, he knows, without learning, certain things e.g. (1) that the universe is not dead but a living presence; (2) that in its essence and tendency it is infinitely good; (3) that individual existence continues beyond death."[43]

• Shankara, the eighth-century Indian saint, whose insights revitalized Hindu teachings, said of his own enlightenment: "I am Brahman... I dwell within all beings as the soul, the pure consciousness, the ground of all phenomena... In the days of my ignorance, I used to think of these as being separate from myself. Now I know that I am All."[44]

• Integral philosopher Ken Wilber, called "the Einstein of consciousness," is the most widely translated academic writer in America, with 25 books, translated into some 30 foreign languages, including *Integral Spirituality* and *The Religion of Tomorrow: A Vision for the Future of the Great Traditions—More Inclusive, More Comprehensive, More Complete*. An internationally acknowledged leader and the preeminent scholar of the Integral stage of human development, he writes:

> The Ultimate State of Consciousness is universally described in mystical literature as union with the Absolute, where the Absolute is known not as many but one without a second. Further, it is specified that to know the absolute is to be the absolute. It follows that the Ultimate State of Consciousness is itself the Absolute, and thus the ultimate state is not a state of consciousness set apart from other states, not one state among many, but rather one state without a second–that is to say, absolutely all-inclusive. Hence, the Ultimate State of Consciousness is not an altered state of consciousness, for there is no alternative.[45]

---

43. http://www.kktanhp.com/ultimate_state_.htm.

44. Shankara, *Vivekachudamani*, (Surrey, British Columbia: House of Metta, 2012), 69.

45. Ken Wilber, *Eye to Eye: The Quest for the New Paradigm*, (San Francisco:

• Richard Rohr calls God "Universal Consciousness itself," saying, "On one level, soul, consciousness, and the Holy Spirit can all be thought of as one and the same."[46] He points out that, "Mature believers eventually move toward a transpersonal notion of God as presence itself, consciousness itself, pure Being, the very ground of Being, the force field of the Holy Spirit ..."[47]

• David Bentley Hart writes,

> For to say that God is being, consciousness, and bliss is also to say that he is the one reality in which all our existence, knowledge, and love subsist, from which they come and to which they go, and that therefore he is somehow present in even our simplest experience of the world, and is approachable by way of a contemplative and moral refinement of that experience. That is to say, these three words are not only a metaphysical explanation of God, but also a phenomenological explanation of the human encounter with God.[48]

Clue #6: Scientists and Infinite Universal Mind or Consciousness

• One of the most significant theoretical physicists of the 20th century who contributed innovative and unorthodox ideas to quantum theory, neuropsychology and the philosophy of mind, David Bohm, said, "The consciousness of mankind is one and not truly divisible. Each person has a responsibility to achieve this and nothing else. There is no other way out. That is absolutely what has to be done and nothing else can work."[49]

Shambhala; 3rd ed., 2001), 79.

46. Richard Rohr, *Breathing Under Water*, (Cincinnati: Franciscan Media, 2011), 91, 87.

47. Richard Rohr, *Eager to Love*, (Cincinnati: Franciscan Media, 2014), 237.

48. Hart, *The Experience of God*, 44.

49. Beatrix Murrell, The Cosmic Plenum: Bohm's Gnosis: The Implicate Order on Stoa del Sol, http://www.bizint.com/stoa_del_sol/plenum/plenum_3.html.

• Nobel Prize-winning Austrian physicist who developed a number of fundamental results in the field of quantum theory, Erwin Schrödinger (1887–1961), said, "Consciousness cannot be accounted for in physical terms. For consciousness is absolutely fundamental. It cannot be accounted for in terms of anything else. Consciousness is a singular for which there is no plural. Multiplicity is only apparent, in truth, there is only one mind."[50]

• Medical doctor, world-wide lecturer, and author of nine books on spirituality, health, and science, Larry Dossey, says that Schrödinger "painstakingly built a concept of a single mind, in which consciousness is transpersonal, universal, collective, and infinite in space and time, therefore immortal and eternal."[51]

He adds, "Scientists such as Schrödinger, Arthur Eddington, James Jeans, Kurt Gödel, Gregory Bateson, Bohn, and others all support a unified view of consciousness." Dossey calls infinite, universal consciousness by the term "one mind" in his book *One Mind*. "The collective One Mind does not need to be tweeted or Facebooked into being. It already *is*—an overarching dimension of consciousness of which we are *already* a part."[52]

• Noted Israeli physicist Gerald Schroeder in *The Hidden Face of God: How Science Reveals the Ultimate Truth* says,

> A single consciousness, an all-encompassing wisdom, pervades the universe. The discoveries of science, those that search the quantum nature of subatomic matter, those that explore the molecular complexity of biology, and those that probe the brain/mind interface, have moved us to the brink of a startling realization: all existence is

---

50. Ken Wilber, ed., *Quantum Questions. Mystical Writings of the World's Great Physicists* (1984) (San Francisco: Shambhala, 2001). http://www.azquotes.com/author/13142-Erwin_Schrodinger/tag/consciousness.

51. Larry Dossey, M.D., *One Mind: How our individual mind is part of a greater consciousness and why it matters*. (New York: Hay House, 2013), 13.

52. Ibid. xxxi–xxxii.

the expression of this wisdom. . . . When we see through the camouflage haze that at times convinces us that only the material exists, when we touch that consciousness, we know it. A joyful rush of emotion sweeps over the entire self. This emotional response—some might call it a religious experience—is reported in every culture, from every period. It tells us that we've come home. We've discovered the essence of being. . . .

If we dared, we'd call this experience spiritual, even Godly. . . . The age-old theological view of the universe is that all existence is the manifestation of a transcendent wisdom, with a universal consciousness being its manifestation. If I substitute the word information for wisdom, theology begins to sound like quantum physics. Science itself has rediscovered the confluence between the physical and the spiritual.[53]

• Researcher, sociologist, futurist, and author of several critically acclaimed books, Dennis Kingsley, says,

Neuroscience, quantum biology, and quantum physics are now beginning to converge to reveal that our bodies are not only biochemical systems but also sophisticated resonating quantum systems. These new discoveries show that a form of nonlocal connected consciousness has a physical-scientific basis. Further, it demonstrates that certain spiritual or transcendental states of collective Oneness have a valid basis within the new scientific paradigm.[54]

I believe this universal or nonlocal consciousness is infinite spirit, the mind or consciousness of God. The Bible further points to this

---

53. http://www.dailyom.com/library/000/000/000000300.html.

54. Dennis Kingsley Ph.D., "Quantum Consciousness: The Way to Reconcile Science and Spirituality." http://www.huffingtonpost.com/kingsley-dennis-phd/quantum-consciousness-the_b_647962.html.

nonlocal universal consciousness or infinite consciousness as spirit-breath which is both divine and human at the same time.

The divine side of divine-human spirit as consciousness in fifteen sentences

1. Spirit is the infinite radiance of divine energy and life that is the field of consciousness itself.

2. Spirit is the face of God that is pure consciousness making itself conscious in humankind through the long process of evolution.

3. The universe was created by infinite consciousness and it was necessary for things to go the way they have in order to bring about us—personal beings who could be conscious that they are conscious, aware that they are aware.

4. The face of God, which is infinitely more than personal being and personal consciousness, created a transpersonal universe that could evolve into our being conscious of infinite consciousness which is God, the Ultimate Mystery.

5. If someone asks me, "What is God consciousness?" my answer is that consciousness *is* God!

6. There is no separation between our mind and Infinite Consciousness, the Mind of God.

7. God as the radiance of consciousness brings new meaning and significance to all traditional descriptions of God.

8. Spirit as universal consciousness reveals the oneness of all reality.

9. Consciousness is an aspect of God expressed as conscious life itself—the breath of spirit that moved over the cosmos in the beginning to create and the life that God breathed into Adam.

10. The infinite consciousness of God is the universal field which holds the consciousness of all humankind in its awareness.

11. Infinite Consciousness is eternal, intelligent, loving, all knowing,

all powerful, creative and present across all dimensions of space and time.

12. The question "Is there a God?" is actually asking is, "Is the universe conscious?"

13. Infinite Consciousness is a universal energy field beyond time and space.

14. God is not your consciousness or my consciousness, but *everyone's* consciousness and beyond.

15. Infinite consciousness is present in us and as us as the Divine Light that shines in every mind and heart.

Does God know your name?

In *The Crossing*, American novelist Cormac McCarthy wrote, "Deep in each man is the knowledge that something knows of his existence. Something knows, and cannot be fled nor hid from."[55]

Is God conscious of you? We have said that God is not a super being. Rather, God is being itself. That's a rather abstract way to think about God. So here's a question to help take it out of the totally intellectual realm. Is Being which is not *a* being ever conscious of us? We all want to be in touch with what is real. We want to see reality, especially Ultimate Reality or what we are calling the Infinite Face of God. But here's the real "reality" question: Does reality see us? Is Ultimate Reality conscious of you and me? David Bentley Hart points to many of us when he writes, "Above all, one should wish to know whether our consciousness of that mystery directs us toward a reality that is, in its turn, conscious of us."[56]

Does God know that we exist, not just in general but specifically—by name? Does God know your name? This is easier to answer if we are thinking about God as Jesus being close to us as we will do next.

---

55. Cormac McCarthy, *The Crossing*, (NY: Vintage/Random House, 2010) 148.
56. Hart, *The Experience of God*, 151.

But how about when we are reflecting on the big picture of God—the Face of God as Infinite Being?

Reflecting about God as Infinite Consciousness can seem like an impersonal view of God. However, rather than impersonal, we might call this face of God transpersonal—including the personal but going beyond it. Every person is an individualized expression of this divine infinite consciousness. Therefore creation cannot be impersonal but rather transpersonal. Consciousness cannot be impersonal. The impersonal cannot be the source of our personhood.

The transpersonal Infinite face of God is conscious of us because that face is pure consciousness itself which holds all things in its infinite spaciousness. Pure consciousness is the One Mind which is the Mind of God. Yes, God knows your name!

A diagram of Trinity Beyond Us

Human experience and divine reality are messy. At the risk of losing those who don't like neat and tidy explanations of messy life, I offer this neat and tidy diagram for those of us who need all the help we can get to see a complicated pattern and understand new ideas. On the accompanying page is my illustrated diagram (full color in Kindle) of Trinity Beyond Us—the third person perspective in *reflecting about* the traditional Trinity. It shows how God the Father, Son, and Spirit look when viewed through the lens of the Infinite Face of God—God-Beyond-Us. Let's begin at the top.

The top image of outer space with an empty hole in the center

Behind "God the Father," looking through God-Beyond-Us, reveals God as Infinite Being. The image of outer space represents the vastness of the Infinite Face of God. But space has lots of objects and Infinite Being is not objects—it *holds* all objects but it itself is objectless. So I asked the man at the top to pull back outer space enough to reveal *empty*, infinite space. This is a picture of the I AMness that God was communicating with the divine name of I AM.

The middle image of the risen Jesus surrounded by an infinity spiral.

Behind "God the Son," looking through the lens of God-Beyond-Us, reveals the Cosmic Christ. In the center is Jesus expanded outward in an infinite spiral which is the Cosmic Christ, the Christian symbol for the whole of reality. The Cosmic Christ beyond Jesus is the transpersonal, creative, loving face of God that creates all things and in whom all things hold together as One.

The bottom image of infinite outer space with the all-encompassing eyes of God and the heart of God in the center.

Behind "God the Spirit" is the face of God that is Infinite Consciousness. Once again, outer space represents infinity, and the eye of God represents divine awareness of you and all that is.

It's not necessary to remember all of this or get the details just right. It is enough to see that there really is an Infinite Face of God-Beyond-Us hidden behind the words "Father, Son, and Spirit." Let these psychospiritually active images soak into you.

Summary of Is Your God as Spirit Big Enough?

• God is infinite spirit.

• Spirit is both divine and human.

• Spirit is given to all living persons.

• Spirit, in the Bible, is best recognized as consciousness.

• There are mystics and scientists who recognize one, universal, collective, infinite consciousness.

• The transpersonal Infinite Face of God knows your name.

• A diagram of Trinity Beyond Us.

Questions for Reflection and Group Discussion

1. Which of the six "clues" the author found that led him to infinite spirit as infinite consciousness seems most relevant to you? What makes them so for you?

2. Do any of the fifteen sentences about the divine pole of divine-human consciousness stand out to you? Why?

3. Are there any places in this chapter that you underlined, highlighted, or marked?

4. Finding time to reflect, pray, and/or mediate can be a challenge. Discuss this quote from English author, editor, and blogger Andrew Sullivan:

> I used to be a human being. An endless bombardment of news and gossip and images has rendered us manic information addicts. It broke me. It might break you, too. . . . The reason we live in a culture increasingly without faith is not because science has somehow disproved the unprovable, but because the white noise of secularism has removed the very stillness in which it might endure or be reborn. . . . If the churches came to understand that the greatest threat to faith today is not hedonism but distraction, perhaps they might begin to appeal anew to a frazzled digital generation. Christian leaders seem to think that they need more distraction to counter the distraction. . . . But the mysticism of Catholic meditation—of the Rosary, of Benediction, or simple contemplative prayer—is a tradition in search of rediscovery. The monasteries—opened up to more lay visitors—could try to answer to the same needs that the booming yoga movement has increasingly met.[57]

_____

57. Andrew Sullivan, "I Used to Be a Human Being," http://nymag.com/selectall/2016/09/andrew-sullivan-technology-almost-killed-me.html?mid=fb-share-selectall.

5. If the diagram was helpful, what did it make more clear?

Practices

1. When breathing in, think or say, "I am breathing in spirit-breath. As God breathed spirit-breath into me at my birth, I now breathe spirit-breath into myself as divine life itself."

2. When there is tension in your body or pain, breathe spirit-breath into it. Let spirit-breath dissolve the tension and pain.

3. If breathwork interests you, research other methods such as holotropic breathwork.

4. Close with signing the Three Faces of God benediction.

"God beyond me, in whom I live and move, and have my being."

("God beyond us, in whom we live and move, and have our being.")

"God beside me, you are always with me."

("God beside us, you are always with us.")

"God being me, I am the light of the world."

("God being us, we are the light of the world.")

"God beside me."

PART TWO

Is Your God Close Enough?
Opening our heart to Trinity beside us

Now we shift from *reflecting about* God to *relating to* God. Connecting personally to God opens up vast new and motivating experiences of the spiritual realm which hold within them the potential to transform our lives.

The traditional Trinitarian formulation of "God the Father, Son, and Spirit" was a Greek-oriented philosophical definition which arose out of the radical God experiences of the early Christians. For these first Christians "God the Father, Son, and Spirit" was not just carefully worked out theology or words in a creed. They were profound experiences of relationship they experienced with the presence of God. The traditional Trinity was, first of all, intensely personal, more personal than one's closest loved one or friend. These companions of Jesus while in his physical body, and later in his spiritual body, had three uniquely different personal relationships with three different faces of God. The first was the fatherly-motherly face of God as Jesus taught them about God watching over them like a caring parent. The second was the Jesus face of God, a transforming friendship that they came to understand as God with them in a radically personal way. The third was the spirit face of God, a guiding presence who comforted, taught, and helped them along their journey of following Jesus.

This Intimate Face of God-Beside-Us is an entirely different perspective from the Infinite Face of God-Beyond-Us. The Infinite Face of God is our attempt to understand God who is ultimately beyond understanding. The Intimate Face of God is our heart to heart devotional connection to God. The early Christians were devoted to God and Jesus while their relationship to the spirit was not one of devotion, but rather it was one of paying attention to the spirit's help and guidance. Devotion to God and Jesus was the fire that blazed in the early church. It is the fuel that heats up our life in Christ today. The first Christians' dual devotion to God and Jesus was revolutionary. It was the beginning of the recognition that if one person could be fully divine and fully human, then how about everyone!

How do you know your God is close enough?

Closeness to God is about bringing the reality of God's presence into our reality.

You know your God is close enough if your relationship to God, in whatever form and by whatever name, is filled with gratitude, love, and devotion.

You know your God is close enough if you share your secrets and struggles with your divine Beloved and listen for a response.

You know your God is close enough if God is like a loving mother and father to you. Or if you have allowed Jesus to be your transforming friend, your dearest friend and constant companion. Or if spirit is your every breath of life-filled consciousness and you are aware of her helping, healing presence. Or, better yet, all three!

Your God is close enough if you know that God is aware of you personally. Above all, we want to know whether our consciousness of

God directs us toward a reality that is, in its turn, conscious of us. You sense that God knows your name. "The One who created you says, 'Do not be afraid. I have called you by name; you are mine'" (Isaiah 43:1). It is always moving for me to think about God knowing my name. It means that I exist and am important in the vast scope of infinity.

Jesus said, "And this is eternal life, that they may *know* you, the only true God, and Jesus Christ whom you have sent" (John 17:3). Jesus said to Thomas, "If you know me, you will know my Father as well" (John 14:7). The word "know" here in Greek "denotes emphatically the relationship to God and to Jesus as a personal fellowship . . . not merely to have information concerning the circumstances of his life."[1]

Marcus Borg (1942–2015) was a leading New Testament scholar, progressive postmodern theologian, and author. He writes, "Whatever God is ultimately like, our relationship to God is personal. This relationship engages us as persons at our deepest and most passionate level. . . . I do think personal language for God is appropriate. Indeed, I think it is more appropriate than impersonal language, for I am persuaded that God is not less than personal."[2]

You know your God is close enough if you can fall in love with the Intimate Face of God beside you. At first glance that may sound like sentimental dribble. But think again when you see people, such as Jesus, who think falling in love with God/She is the most important thing you can do in life.

Jesus said the one thing God most desires is, "Love the Lord your God with all your heart and with all your soul and with all your strength and with all your mind," and "Love your neighbor as yourself" (Luke 10:27). Loving God is one thing. Falling in love

---

1. TDNT, Vol 1, 711-712.

2. Marcus Borg, *The Heart of Christianity*, (San Francisco: HarperSanFrancisco, 2003), 72-73.

with God is another. I believe Jesus had in mind the second because it was clear he was in love with God. Being in love means there is a strong bond with your Beloved. There is a profoundly tender, passionate affection for the other. This is how Jesus loved God. Jesus asks that we fall in love with God the way we fall in love with each other, with a partner, a parent, a child, a friend. We fall in love with one another because we spend time being together, exchanging our thoughts, learning about one another, and soaking up the beauty in one another.

We can follow the same path with God. We spend dedicated time with one another in prayer and meditation. We see the beauty in the world around us and in the waves of God's love that spread over us. If we can fall in love with messy, broken human beings, how much easier it is to fall in love with God whose very essence is perfect love and overwhelming compassion.

Jesus advocated heart-felt love as he quoted Isaiah saying it applied to the people of his day: "These people honor me with their lips, but their hearts are far from me" (Matt. 15:8).

What others have said about falling in love with God

One person who was enthralled with God was King David. He was so thoroughly smitten with God that he once declared, "As the deer pants for streams of water, so my soul pants for you, O God. My soul thirsts for God, for the living God. When can I go and meet with God?" (Psalm 42:1-2). And again, "One thing I ask of God, that will I seek after: to live in God's house all the days of my life, and there to see God and gaze upon God's beauty" (Psalm. 27:4).

St. Augustine penned, "To fall in love with God is the greatest romance; to seek him the greatest adventure; to find him, the greatest human achievement."[3]

---

3. Augustine of Hippo, http://www.goodreads.com/quotes/73061-to-fall-in-love-with-god-is-the-greatest-romance.

Pedro Arrupe (1907–1991) was a Spanish Jesuit priest who served as the twenty-eighth Superior General of the Society of Jesus. These words are attributed to him:

> Nothing is more practical than
> finding God, than
> falling in Love
> in a quite absolute, final way.
>
> What you are in love with,
> what seizes your imagination,
> will affect everything.
>
> It will decide
> what will get you out of bed in the morning,
> what you do with your evenings,
> how you spend your weekends,
> what you read,
> whom you know,
> what breaks your heart,
> and what amazes you with joy and gratitude.
>
> Fall in Love,
> stay in love,
> and it will decide everything.

John Eldredge is an American author, Christian counselor, and teacher known for his book *Wild at Heart*. He says, "Falling in love with God is the most important thing a person can do."[4]

The great Sufi poet of the thirteenth century, Rumi, wrote:

> Soul, if you want to learn secrets,
> your heart must forget about
> shame and dignity.
> You are God's lover,

---

4. http://www.brainyquote.com/quotes/quotes/j/johneldred526135.html#7 cYLZVXjuHEPOoRi.9.

yet you worry
what people
are saying.

There are thousands of wines
that can take over our minds.
Don't think all ecstasies
are the same!
Jesus was lost in his love for God.
His donkey was drunk with barley.

The Essential Rumi

Thomas Traherne (1636–1674) was an English poet, clergyman, theologian, and religious writer. He penned, "By Love alone is God enjoyed, by Love alone delighted in, by Love alone approached or admired."[5]

Blaise Pascal (1623–1662), French mathematician, physicist, inventor, writer and Christian philosopher, proclaimed, "The heart has its reasons, which reason does not know at all."[6]

Questions for Reflection and Group Discussion

1. How does closeness to God seem relevant or not relevant to your life?

2. How realistic do you think falling in love with God is?

3. What did you mark as interesting or questioning in this brief section?

Practice

By relaxing our bodies, quieting the chatter of our minds, and allowing our hearts to be more sensitive to our situation, we open to

---

5. Thomas Traherne, *Centuries of Meditations* (Cyprus: Paphos Publishers, 2016).
6. http://www.christianitytoday.com/history/people/evangelistsandapologists/blaise-pascal.html.

the very inner qualities and resources that can help us grow. Today, as you enter into a quiet space, become aware of God looking at you and loving you. Can you let God look at you while you bask in God's love for you? But you say, "I thought we were supposed to love God." Yes, and that love will only flow freely from our heart when we first let the love of God for us wash over us. Take some time now to just sit with God for a heart washing.

You can do this right now by becoming still and aware of breathing in and out. As you breathe in, let God say to you "I love you." Then, as you breathe out, say back to God, "I love you." Repeat this until you sense you are letting the love flow between you and God.

Close with this brief version of The Three Faces invocation/benediction/blessing done slowly and thoughtfully:

"God beyond me"

"God beside me"

"God being me"

"God beside me."

CHAPTER 4

God Beside Us as Father-Mother

What's in a name?

Choosing a name for God/She is choosing a relationship to Ultimate Reality. Since it is naming the unnamable so we can know something of the unknowable, it is a delicate task. Not just any name will do.

A name holds the capacity to stir our hearts, claim our loyalty, and shape our thinking.

What do you call God/She besides "God"? How do you personally name Ultimate Reality, the Infinite Mystery?

Shakespeare's Juliet pines,

> "What's in a name? That which we call a rose
> By any other name would smell as sweet."[1]

If you have never smelled a rose, knowing its name may help you find one so you can smell it and find out for yourself.

---

1. Romeo and Juliet (II, ii, 1-2).

Ludwig Wittgenstein (1889–1951), Austrian-British philosopher, said, "The limits of my language mean the limits of my world."[2] Influential German philosopher Martin Heidegger (1889–1976) continued with, "Language is the house of Being. In its home man dwells. Those who think and those who create with words are the guardians of this home."[3]

As a speaker and writer creating words about God, I take seriously the task as a guardian of this home of Being. Our words limit or expand the world in which we live and have our Being. For instance, if we teachers and pastors *only* offer a naming of God to others that is male and father-like, then women get the limiting message loud and clear—men are more like God than women. Our male gender language for God/She in our hymns, books, and sermons, as well as the practice of male-only pastors and priests indicates how much we deny that God created us in God/She's image, male *and* female. Then this male and masculine god can be used to justify the oppression of women we have seen throughout church history.

Australian writer Anne Hamilton says, "Throughout the ancient world, naming was a sacred act. It was the word by which a child was called into his calling. It was the voice of destiny, summoning the child into his future with all its glorious promise."[4]

I have moved through three names for God so far in my spiritual evolution of naming God.

My first naming of God/She was "Heavenly Father"

I called God "Father" for many years when I prayed. That's what we all did in the church of my youth and the ones I worked in starting at age eighteen until I finished seminary at age 26. It never occurred

---

2. *Tractacus* 5.6 https://en.wikisource.org/wiki/Tractatus_Logico-Philosophicus/5.

3. Martin Heidegger, *Letter on Humanism*, http://www07.homepage.villanova.edu/paul.livingston/martin_heidegger%20-%20letter%20on%20humanism.htm.

4. Anne Hamilton, *God's Panoply: The Armour of God and the Kiss of Heaven* (Even Before Publishing, 2013), http://www.goodreads.com/quotes/tag/naming.

to me to pray any other way as a good Southern Baptist, since calling God "Heavenly Father" was the norm in the out loud praying I heard in church. It was something you could say without thinking, like the incessantly repeated "and uh" some people use that gives you a moment to think about what you were going to say next. I suppose it had various shades of meaning and feeling with folks, but for me, it was just a habit.

But it didn't begin as a habit two thousand years ago with Jesus. In the New Testament, instead of one of many metaphors and titles for God, Father becomes a primary name for God and the focus of Jesus. It carries both metaphysical and intimate family meanings. He primarily spoke *about* and *to* God as father and the early church adopted his language. So did my early church, without asking if that word carries the same meaning today that it did in Jesus' day.

My second naming of God/She was "Father-Mother" in my teaching and writing

In my thirties, I finally became aware of the male bias of biblical culture, Western culture, and especially my church culture. I began the slow journey toward the liberating partnership of women and men, female and male. After seminary, I went to the church I was to pastor for the next forty-nine years. They ordained men deacons and pastors, but not women. It created quite a stir the first time a woman member who was finishing seminary asked to be ordained by us when she was called to a small rural church. But we did it. Soon we were adding woman deacons and eventually women pastors to our staff. Then I began to look at our exclusively male-only language for God as my eyes and heart were slowly opening to how the feminine had been relegated to second place. In 1993 I wrote my first book to help explain to my congregation why I thought it was important to think of God in both male and female images, since both were created in the image of God. I called it *Is It Okay to Call God Mother? Considering the Feminine Face of God*. I was amazed at the national response in newspaper and journal articles, and radio and TV interviews.

In that book I pointed out that even in the patriarchal, male-oriented language and cultures of the Bible there were striking clues that our linguistic pictures of God can be gender balanced. Motherly and fatherly pictures are interwoven in places in the Bible beginning with Genesis 1:27 pointing out that the image of God contains both male and female identities.

In the song of Moses in Deuteronomy 32:18 mother language is explicit in, "The rock who bore you, you forgot, and you cared nothing for the God who gave birth to you."

King and psalmist David pictures both male and female images of God with, "I lift up my eyes to you, enthroned in the heavens! See, as the menservants' eyes are on their lord's hand, as maid's eyes on her lady's hand, so our eyes are on YHWH, awaiting your favor" (Psalm 123:1-2). In David's "song of ascents" he prays, "O Lord,... I have calmed and quieted my soul, like a weaned child with its mother; my soul that is with me is like a weaned child." Here is a picture of David sitting on God's lap like a mother cuddles her child.

God is a nursing mother in Psalm 131:2, and Numbers 11:12; a midwife in Psalm 22:8-10. Isaiah does not hesitate to call God a comforting mother: "I will comfort you there in Jerusalem as a mother comforts her child." And a nursing mother: "Can a mother forget her nursing child? Can she feel no love for the child she has borne? But even if that were possible, I would not forget you!" (Isaiah 49:15) Even as a woman in labor: "But now, like a woman in labor, I will cry and groan and pant." (Isaiah 66:13; 49:15; 42:14)

Hosea twice sees God as a raging mother bear and famished lioness: "Like a bear whose cubs have been taken away, I will tear out your heart. I will devour you like a hungry lioness and mangle you like a wild animal" (Hosea 11:3-4, 13:8).

The writer of Deuteronomy sees God as a mother eagle: "Like an eagle that rouses her chicks and hovers over her young, so he spread his wings to take them up and carried them safely on his pinions."

And then a God who gives birth: "You neglected the Rock who had fathered you; you forgot the God who had given you birth" (Deut. 32:11-12, 18).

Jesus is not bashful about feeling explicitly motherly in, "Jerusalem, Jerusalem, city that kills the prophets and stones those sent to it! How often I desired to gather your children as a bird gathers her brood under her wings" (Matt. 23:37-39).

In the Gospel of Thomas Jesus, contrasting God with his mother, says, "My true mother gave me life" (Saying 101).

Christians down through the ages have at times pictured God as a mother or beyond gender categories. Some of these were Clement, Irenaeus, Augustine, Jerome, and Bernard of Clairvaux. The medieval mystic Julian of Norwich eloquently summed it up as she wrote, "As truly as God is our Father, so truly God is our Mother."[5]

Tim Bulkeley in his thoughtful book *Not Only a Father* says,

> Many children and people, now adult, have had inadequate, absent, or abusive fathers. If we think and speak of God as only a father, then we make relating to this God more difficult for some people. Many of these may be already hurting; they need to know that they can approach God. It is true that some children have inadequate or absent, mothers as well, but this is less common. So talking of God in both fatherly and motherly ways broadens our thinking and reduces some of the problems associated with using one parent alone as our main image of God.[6]

Regardless of how we personally pray and relate to God, in our public worship and teaching we should use both motherly and fatherly

---

5. Julian of Norwich, *Revelations of Divine Love*, trans., Grace Warrack (Christian Ethereal Classics, 1901), LIX. http://www.ccel.org/ccel/julian/revelations.i.html.

6. http://bigbible.org/mothergod/7-5-why-it-matters.

language and images of God for our spiritual health. It is damaging to everyone not to do so.

Why did Jesus call God Father but not Mother?

In order to understand why Jesus called God "Father" and not "Mother," we must be willing to look at a culture that is much different from our own. First, Jesus would have used father as a metaphor for God because it was already used as one of the many titles for God in his Jewish religion. But more importantly, the word "father" in relationship to the word "mother" in ancient Middle East patriarchal culture meant something quite different than in our more egalitarian Western culture.

Father was the corporate personality of the family. In ancient Israel there was a distinctive mentality in which the group functioned as a single individual through the person representing it. In the case of the family, this was always the father. Father represented the family in a way our individualistic society can hardly comprehend. He spoke and acted for them legally and socially with wife, children, and servants being regarded as extensions of the father.

In the book of Acts when the Philippian jailor was asked what he must do to be saved, the reply was, "Believe on the Lord Jesus and you and your household will be saved." The assumption was that the jailer spoke for the entire family and when he was converted they would all be converted.

In Jesus' culture, "father" in heaven was the only choice for Jesus if he was going to use a parental name for God that communicated God's freedom and role as ruler, teacher, and authority. The "in heaven" was often added to distinguish whether one was talking about an earthly father or God.

In our society, to the extent patriarchy has truly crumbled, then both father and mother are free and powerful agents. Unlike women in Jesus' culture, they can exercise authority, go out in public alone, get a divorce, inherit property, testify in court, and teach both children and adults. Both father or mother have this parental sense for today's family. Even in Jesus' patriarchal culture, he planted the seeds of woman's value that eventually resulted in woman's liberation into the same freedom offered men, but that could not be accomplished in his brief ministry time.

So let's use something like "Father-Mother" as one naming of this close face of God because it is a naming that is personal, intimate, warm, and caring. A rock is impersonal and therefore we don't call a rock "Father" or "Mother." Nor do we call a principle or force "Father" or "Mother." But we do call our parents "Mother and Father" and especially "Mom" and "Dad"! Don't hesitate to call God by whatever name or names you call your father and mother. That's what Jesus modeled for us.

A parable of life after birth

To help balance out the centuries of exclusively masculine language and imagery for God, here is a beautiful parable attributed to Útmutató a Léleknek that radiates with divine motherly energy:

> In a mother's womb were two babies.
>
> One asked the other: "Do you believe in life after delivery?"
>
> The other replied, "Why, of course. There has to be something after delivery. Maybe we are here to prepare ourselves for what we will be later."
>
> "Nonsense," said the first. "There is no life after delivery. What kind of life would that be?"
>
> The second said, "I don't know, but there will be more light than here. Maybe we will walk with our legs and eat from our mouths. Maybe we will have other senses that we can't understand now."

The first replied, "That is absurd. Walking is impossible. And eating with our mouths? Ridiculous! The umbilical cord supplies nutrition and everything we need. But the umbilical cord is so short. Life after delivery is to be logically excluded."

The second insisted, "Well I think there is something and maybe it's different than it is here. Maybe we won't need this physical cord anymore."

The first replied, "Nonsense. And moreover, if there is life, then why has no one ever come back from there? Delivery is the end of life, and in the after-delivery there is nothing but darkness and silence and oblivion. It takes us nowhere."

"Well, I don't know," said the second, "but certainly we will meet Mother and she will take care of us."

The first replied "Mother? You actually believe in Mother? That's laughable. If Mother exists, then where is She now?"

The second said, "She is all around us. We are surrounded by her. We are of Her. It is in Her that we live. Without Her, this world would not and could not exist."

Said the first: "Well I don't see Her, so it is only logical that She doesn't exist."

To which the second replied, "Sometimes, when you're in silence and you focus and you really listen, you can perceive Her presence, and you can hear Her loving voice, calling down from above."[7]

---

7. This is widely attributed on the internet to the Hungarian writer, Útmutató a Léleknek, but the original source appears unavailable.

My third naming of God/She was "Daddy," for my own healing

I had experimented with calling God "Mother" and "Mommy" in my own prayer times. That naming gave me no meaningful or emotional connection in my own devotion to God, even though at an intellectual level I strongly owned God as both Father and Mother. This was probably because of my mother-wound for which I spent years in therapy. Only recently have I been able to personally think of God as my mother in a positive way.

One day around ten years ago I decided to experiment back in the other direction. I sat down to pray, closed my eyes, and spoke out loud, saying, "Daddy." Whoa! I had a sudden rush of strong feelings. There was embarrassment. Had I done something silly? There was hesitancy and timidity. Was I being theologically crazy? But by far the overwhelming feeling was of being loved and cared for. I was bowled over by that one. It didn't make sense to me since the name "Daddy" in my life only brought up sad and painful memories. I was an only child and got all the family dysfunction undiluted and unshared. Dad was largely absent physically and emotionally, but when present, he hit me and called me names. In light of my lack of a loving father, I was totally surprised by the intense feeling of being loved by simply calling God "Daddy." It eventually dawned on me that I had been longing for a real dad all my life. Now I had found him. He was always there, but I didn't know how to connect with God/She that way. The new name did it.

The sacrament of naming

Eve Ensler, American playwright, performer, feminist, and activist, says, "I believe in the power and mystery of naming things. Language has the capacity to transform our cells, rearrange our learned patterns of behavior, and redirect our thinking. I believe in naming what's right in front of us because that is often what is most invisible."[8]

---

8. Eve Ensler, *The Power and Mystery of Naming Things*, audiobook, NPR's All Things Considered, March 20, 2006, http://thisibelieve.org/essay/17/.

When I give something a name, I choose my relationship to it. A name is a container that holds my relationship, even if that being named is beyond what we normally think of as relationship material. It identifies the other and then I can think about and feel what my relationship is with what the symbol of the name represents

I had discovered a new sacrament in my life, the sacrament of naming. The Catholic Church defines a sacrament as "an outward sign of an inward grace, instituted by Jesus Christ." If ever there was an outward symbol for me of an inward grace, it was my calling God "Daddy." And this was a sacrament instituted by Jesus himself as we explore next.

Debate over "Daddy"

In the Greek New Testament Jesus is recorded using two different words for God as father. One is the formal Greek word for father, *pater*. The other is his native Aramaic language word for father, *Abba*. This was not a formal word for father but a warm, intimate, family term of endearment and respect used by both children and adults. The Aramaic word, *Abba*, was strikingly left untranslated in the Greek New Testament.

The exact meaning of the word *Abba* has been recently much debated. Some scholars find that words like "Papa" or "Daddy" convey the meaning of *Abba*, while more recently others think that those words are too informal and disrespectful. In an influential article entitled "Abba Isn't Daddy" scholar James Barr says:

> It is fair to say that *abba* in Jesus' time belonged to a familiar or colloquial register of language, as distinct from more formal and ceremonious language. . . . But in any case it was not a childish expression comparable with "Daddy": it was a more solemn, responsible, adult address to a Father.[9]

---

9. James Barr, "Abba Isn't Daddy," *Journal of Theological Studies*, (Vol. 39, 1988), 46.

I think it was just the opposite. It seems to me that Jesus used the word *abba* meaning dad or daddy exactly *because* it was so childish, or put in a less negative way, more *childlike*. It was not "solemn, responsible, and adult." When Barr says that *abba* "was not a childish expression comparable with 'Daddy,'" he may be revealing his picture of God rather than his scholarship. Some may outgrow the word "Daddy" but the word "Dad" in our culture is widely used by both children and adults. Furthermore, we must ask if the word "Daddy" is childish or rather is it childlike. There is a great difference between childish and childlike. Here is a striking passage in the Gospel of Mark that has strong implications about childlike attitudes being dismissed by those who considered them childish.

> People were bringing little children to him in order that he might touch them; and the disciples spoke sternly to them. But when Jesus saw this, he was indignant and said to them, 'Let the little children come to me; do not stop them; for it is to such as these that the Reign of God belongs. Truly I tell you, whoever does not receive the Reign of God as a little child will never enter it. And he took them up in his arms, laid his hands on them, and blessed them. (Mark 10:13-16)

The disciples wanted a sense of formality and adult propriety, after all, this was their adult hero Jesus they were dealing with. Jesus would have nothing to do with that. He spoke "sternly" to the disciples telling them to drop the adult stuff because only childlike adults get into God's realm! Then he picks up the little children just like a dad would and holds them in his arms. Perhaps one of them looked up at him while in his arms and called him "Daddy" in Aramaic!

My son at age 45 still calls me "Daddy" and my granddaughter at 18 still calls me "Papa." I love to think of God caring for her children even more than I care for mine.

Summary of God Beside Us As Father-Mother

• Naming God is choosing a relationship to Ultimate Reality.

• Jesus named God as *Abba*, the name all Jewish children and adults called their fathers.

• Jesus was not assigning a gender to God, but naming a relationship of parental care and love.

• Father as the corporate personality in Jesus' culture included mother in a way that is not true today.

• God may also be called "Mother" as the Bible and mystics have imaged and experienced God in that way. I use the name "Father-Mother" in teaching so as to not exclude mother and point to the image of God as both male and female.

• God comes to us in whatever form we need. I needed to call God "Daddy."

Questions for Reflection and Group Discussion

1. Reflect about what kind of God/She you have. The mystical, transformative journey cannot take place until the image of a punishing, wrathful God is undone. Why would you want to spend even an hour in silence, solitude, or intimacy with such a god? Share your thoughts about this with the group.

2. What are the most endearing, loving names that you called your own father and mother as a child? What endearing, loving names do you use now with them or in remembering them?

3. You may have struggled as you read this chapter. You may have strong feelings for or against the practice of calling God Father, He and Him or Mother, She, and Her. What are any past or present struggles you have had with this?

4. One powerful way we have found of healing parent wounds is to find a therapist or friend who temporarily becomes a healing father

or mother figure. I call it changing parents. We, psychologically and emotionally, change parents from the past abusive one(s) to the new more healing one(s). Perhaps this is what Jesus wanted for men and women who have been wounded by their human fathers and/or mothers—to know a Father-Mother who loves them, who will not make fun of them, ignore them, hit them, or abandon them. Jesus wants you to know you have a heavenly father-mother who does nothing but love you. Have you ever considered changing one or both of your parents for God as your healing father and/or mother?

5. Words are symbols. Referring to God as Father-Mother can be most simply seen as a symbol for God as Loving Creator. But they can also be very powerful transforming namings.

I have shared that the most transforming term to me and the one I use most often for God as parent is "Daddy" in my heart-centered prayer life. This comes from my need for healing from my father-wound. What naming of God strikes the most resonance within you coming from your place of wounding?

Practices

1. The next time you sense God's presence, use one or even all of those endearing names you have used for your own father and/or mother to address that presence. Be aware of what happens inside you and see if there is a name that resonates with your heart. This may lead you to follow Jesus' model for your situation in addressing God. Others who have had absent or abusive relationships with parents may find such namings not helpful at all. You will only know if you explore this and try it out for yourself.

2. Intentionally experiment in devotional prayer with calling God "Daddy" or "Mommy." What feelings does that bring up? How does it change your sense of God? Do you think this is closer to the sense of God that Jesus experienced?

3. Allow yourself to warm up on the inside by letting the loving presence of Mother-Father God fill you with light and love.

4. Close with signing the Three Faces of God as a benediction.

"God beyond me, in whom I live and move, and have my being."

("God beyond us, in whom we live and move, and have our being.")

"God beside me, you are always with me."

("God beside us, you are always with us.")

"God being me, I am the light of the world."

("God being us, we are the light of the world.")

"God beside me."

CHAPTER 5

Why I Still Talk to Jesus

Here's a history of Christianity in five sentences:

> Christianity began in Palestine as an experience.
> It moved to Greece and became a philosophy.
> It shifted to Italy and became an institution.
> It arrived in Europe and became a culture.
> It traveled to America and became a business!

A transforming friendship with Jesus

While this little history may be something of a caricature,[1] it contains an important truth. *Christianity was an experience before it became a religion.* What was this experience that was the foundation of Christianity? I understand that it was the transforming friendship that Jesus had with a few others. He summed up that relationship with, "I no longer call you subordinates but I call you friends" (John 15:15 *Inclusive Bible*).

---

1. This is my version of what has been attributed to at least three different people in three different versions. http://www.barrypopik.com/index.php/new_york_city/entry/when_christianity_came_to_america_it_became_a_business/.

By contrasting the idea of being a subordinate with the notion of being a friend, Jesus was pointing to a more intimate kind of relationship than the one master to servant or boss to worker suggests. Echoing modern sensibilities about grown up adult to adult relationships, he was aiming at a partnership in healing the world, working together in mutual respect. Friendship with Jesus is the heart of Christianity.

Others have spoken about this transforming friendship with Jesus

In *The Intimate Friendship of Jesus*, Thomas à Kempis (1380–1471), novice instructor in his monastery, and author says,

> When Jesus is near, all is well and nothing seems diffi-cult. When He is absent, all is hard. When Jesus does not speak within, all other comfort is empty, but if He says only a word, it brings great consolation. . . . He who finds Jesus finds a rare treasure, indeed, a good above every good . . . It is a great art to know how to converse with Jesus . . . Of all those who are dear to you, let him be your special love. Let all things be loved for the sake of Jesus, but Jesus for his own sake. Jesus Christ must be loved alone with a special love for he alone, of all friends, is good and faithful. For him and in him you must love friends and foes alike.[2]

Spanish mystic and Catholic saint, Teresa of Avila (1515–1582) said:

> If Christ Jesus dwells in a person as their friend and noble leader, that one can endure all things, for Christ helps and strengthens us and never abandons us. He is a true friend. . . Unlike our friends in the world, he will never abandon us when we are troubled or distressed.[3] . . .

2. http://www.ccel.org/ccel/kempis/imitation.TWO.8.html?highlight=john, friendship,with,jesus#highlight
3. Saint *Teresa, Opusc. De Libro vitae, ap. 22, 6-7, 14.*

Contemplative prayer in my opinion is nothing else than a close sharing between friends; it means taking time frequently to be alone with him who we know loves us.[4]

John Henry Jowett (1863–1923), influential British Congregational preacher, writes:

His friendship transforms every road. Every road unveils spiritual wonders when He walks with us, and blessings abound on every side. The very consciousness of His presence begets a peace which is itself the medium of discernment, and we are able, on the most ordinary road, to know some of "the things that God hath prepared for them that love Him."[5]

Oswald Chambers (1874–1917), early twentieth-century devotional writer, said, "The dearest friend on earth is a mere shadow compared to Jesus Christ."[6]

Leslie Weatherhead (1893–1976) was a liberal Protestant English pastor and theologian. He wrote about how complicated Christianity must seem to many people. His answer to that perception was this: "I think the essence of the matter might be stated by saying that Christianity is the acceptance of the gift of the friendship of Jesus."[7]

This section is used in the Roman Catholic Office of readings for the Feast or liturgical memorial of Saint Teresa of Avila on October 15. http://www.crossroadsinitiative.com/library_article/760/Friendship_with_Jesus_Teresa_of_Avila.html.

4. Catechism of the Catholic Church - Expressions of prayer. http://www.vatican.va/archive/ccc_css/archive/catechism/p4s1c3a1.htm.

5. http://www.ccel.org/ccel/jowett/mattermost.iv.xvii.html?highlight=john,friendship,with,jesus#highlight.

6. http://www.quotes-friendship.com/quotes/jesus/.

7. Leslie Weatherhead, *The Transforming Friendship: A Book About Jesus and Ourselves*, (Nashville: Abingdon Press, 1990), 25.

Prominent, controversial, outspoken critic of social injustice and liberal American minister, Harry Emerson Fosdick (1878–1969) said, "The steady discipline of intimate friendship with Jesus results in us becoming like Him."[8]

Pope Frances, at the very beginning of his 2013 *Evangelii Gaudium* ("The Joy of the Gospel"), wrote: "I invite all Christians, everywhere, at this very moment, to a renewed personal encounter with Jesus Christ, or at least an openness to letting him encounter them; I ask all of you to do this unfailingly each day. No one should think that this invitation is not for him or her."[9]

In 2015, Roman Catholic Archbishop Samuel Aquila of Denver said, "To abide in Christ means to enter into a relationship of friendship with him.... Human formation finds its fulfillment in that friendship with Christ, which is at the heart of spiritual formation."[10]

Richard Rohr writes, "In Jesus, God took human form, human face, human eyes, and human endearment; God is finally someone we could fall in love with. God was given a face and a heart in Jesus.... The nondual paradox and mystery was for Christians a living person, an icon we could gaze upon and fall in love with[11]... The gift of the Incarnation is that we have someone now we can see, touch and love in the energetic realm of pure consciousness."[12]

---

8. Fosdick was on the cover of *Time* magazine in 1930 when he became the first pastor of famous Riverside Church in New York. http://izquotes.com/quote/64367.

9. http://www.christiantoday.com/article/why.pope.francis.is.calling.catholics.to.have.a.personal.encounter.with.jesus/49378.htm.

10. http://www.fullycatholic.com/what-makes-a-good-priest-friendship-with-jesus-christ/.

11. Richard Rohr, *The Naked Now: Learning to See as the Mystics See*, (New York: Crossroad, 2013), 154.

12. Published on *National Catholic Reporter* (http://ncronline.org) December 2009 http://www.cccrmn.org/v2/index.php?option=com_content&view=article&id=316:interview-with-richard-rohr-the-eternal-christ-in-the-cosmic-story&catid=86:articles&Itemid=210.

Marcus Borg said, "Being a Christian isn't primarily about having a correct theology by getting our beliefs right. It is about a deepening relationship with God as known especially in Jesus."[13]

The challenge of devotion to Jesus for thoughtful people today

Borg's "deepening relationship with God as known especially in Jesus" seems to me to be the most neglected aspect of Christianity by many progressive Christians. So before I go any further in describing this kind of friendship with Jesus, I need to address my understanding of why many growing and evolving Christians have left this relationship with Jesus behind.

Some, if not many progressive Christians today, have no place for connecting with Jesus, person to person in the intimate way I am describing. Those who have passed through the modern and postmodern stages have asked the question, "Is it acceptable as a well-educated, broad-minded person of the twenty-first century to still talk to Jesus?" Their answer seems to very often be "no." This seems true even for those who have a more evolved Jesus, taken off the narrow ethnocentric pedestal of being the world's only savior and no longer a sacrifice for our sins to an angry God. They may admire him and think of him as great teacher, but the thought of talking with him today is embarrassing to them.

A warm relationship of love and devotion to God is considered key to Christianity by many Christians. However, a relationship of love and devotion to Jesus is often ignored or is somehow suspect to many mainline or progressive Christians. Why is this? Here are nine reasons I have heard from those who find it difficult to relate personally to Jesus.

1. First, devotion to Jesus may be associated with exclusivist religion. Postmodern spiritual-but-not-religious folks often have difficulty with Jesus because they perceive devotion to him as excluding other

---

13. Marcus Borg, *Convictions: How I Learned What Matters Most*, (New York: HarperOne, 2016), 50.

spiritual masters and traditions. Much of traditional Christianity has taught that only people who "believe in Jesus" are destined for eternity with God. This associates that narrow belief with Jesus. The desire for inclusivity and greater religious harmony leads some to lower the profile and importance of Jesus in Christianity. In my understanding, Jesus does not in any way exclude any loving spiritual path or other teachers. I think Jesus asks us to test everything by comparing it to his life and teaching. Those things from other spiritual traditions, science, fields of study, and philosophies that support and further his aim of moving from self-centeredness to liberating love and divine consciousness can and should be fully embraced by his followers.

2. Sometimes it seems that the people who talk to Jesus most loudly are not always the kind of Christians some of us want to be. The most judgmental, moralistic, and rigid folks are often the ones who talk about Jesus the most. I had to face this as the pastor of a Southern Baptist church. For a while I didn't want anybody to know I was a Baptist, especially one of those awful "Southern" Baptists who excluded women, gays, evolutionists, and most other people who weren't in their exclusive club of true beliefs and righteous purity. When I was introduced as a Southern Baptist, I felt like I had to go into great detail to explain that I wasn't one of "those" Baptists, lest I be dismissed out of hand. After several attempts through the years to dismiss my church from the Southern Baptist Convention for such things as ordaining women, calling God "Mother," being "charismatic," and my not believing in eternal hell, we were finally tossed out in 2004 for performing gay unions. We were no longer Southern Baptists which, in reality, we had not been for some time. However, I did decide to continue to call myself a Baptist since I like Baptists' more democratic congregational system of doing church as well as their attempt at taking the Bible and Jesus seriously. In addition, it lets people know there are a growing number of Baptists who are inclusive, compassionate, and theologically progressive.

3. Many have not seen that devotion to Jesus is at the heart of Christianity. This dimension has often been rejected as too traditional,

old-fashioned, shallow, or quaint because it is associated with the evangelical beliefs about Jesus dying for our sins, eternal hell, an exclusivist position about salvation, and rigid, literal interpretations of the Bible. Progressive thinkers may have only been exposed to modern theological discussion which can be deconstructionist and related to linguistic, philosophical and theological categories rather than the actual recorded phenomenon of devotion to Jesus in early Christianity. Many educated folks have uncritically accepted the few streams of contemporary theology that have rendered Jesus as unknowable in the name of a relatively narrow approach to biblical scholarship.

4. Then there is an aversion by thoughtful Christians to those who *replace* acts of justice and liberation in the name of Jesus with the acts of devotion and worship in the name of Jesus. Progressive Christians sometimes say it as, "Jesus said to follow him, not worship him." This is aimed at sentimentality without redemptive action in the world that characterizes some Christian behavior. Too often we have seen devotion to Jesus without devotion to what Jesus taught about freeing all from poverty and oppression. However, putting devotion to Jesus in opposition to devotion to others distorts the witness of Jesus and the New Testament. Those closest to Jesus and his message in the early church demonstrated both devotion to Jesus and to others. Authentic admiration, honor, imitation, gratitude, and devotion to Jesus is a catalyst for serving others as he did.

5. Many thoughtful Christians have rightly given up the kind of talking to Jesus that is pleading with him to micromanage the world to suit our preferences. From finding a parking space to ending poverty, they think if they just beg Jesus or God enough, their wishes will be granted. This "do something for me" kind of praying can turn off those looking for a grown-up relationship with Jesus. Jesus' own model is quite evolved. Jesus never asked God to do something he could do himself. He never asked God to heal someone. He did it himself. He said if you see a mountain that needs moving, don't ask God to move it, move it with yourself using your faith (Matt. 17:20).

6. Many today have not been exposed to deeper understandings of prayer in modern scientific terms such as energy fields and nonlocal consciousness. Dr. John Pilch, clinical professor in the Department of Preventive Medicine, Medical College of Wisconsin focusing on medical anthropology as it is connected to healing in the modern and ancient world, emphasizes that scholars who deny the reality of healing through spiritual means "demonstrate Western cultural myopia rather than scientific astuteness."[14]

7. The financial and sexual scandals of church leaders parading as devoted followers of Jesus has tarnished the reputation of Christian spirituality. Church politics and endless wrangling loom large in people's view of those who claim to be Christians. We should not underestimate the damage this has done to the idea of a personal relationship with Jesus and how badly the image of authentic Christianity has been mutilated.

8. Then too, fundamentalist and evangelical versions of devotion to Jesus tend to carry a theology that may seem out of date, narrow, exclusive, naïve, sentimental, or just plain wrong to many sincere Christians. I believe progressive Christians often need a larger framework to even consider what I am saying about Jesus. The God who comes close enough to us needs the expanded picture of the God who is also big enough and you enough. Without that framework as the background for talking about a transforming friendship with Jesus, I would sound to many progressive Christians like a Southern Baptist preacher talking about a traditional Jesus who saves them from God's wrath and eternal damnation because of their sins. While I understand and respect those who hold such atonement beliefs, that is not where I am coming from. The subject of "friendship with Jesus" in this book comes right after I have talked about a God who is big enough. It is followed by the last six chapters on the God who is you enough. Right in between the big

---

14. John Pilch, "The Transfiguration of Jesus: An experience of alternate reality," in Philip Esler, ed., *Modelling Early Christianity: Social-scientific studies of the New Testament in its Context*, (London and New York: Routledge, 1995), 49.

God and the you God is the close God—which is exactly where it belongs.

9. Finally, one more reason some thoughtful Christians avoid devotion to Jesus is the challenge of relating to Jesus beyond his incarnational maleness. This is so important that I will devote Chapter 9 entirely to the topic of relating to Jesus beyond gender.

Is talking to Jesus talking to God?

If we see that every human being is a piece of God, then we normally don't have a problem with seeing Jesus as divine. However, the question of Jesus' divinity continues to be debated today. So let's explore this. First, we must be clear: Jesus never made a one to one definition of himself as "God." Instead, he cloaked his divine mission and identity of nondual oneness with God in symbols and nondual words. The result was that Jesus acted on behalf of God and spoke on behalf of God in the Gospels to such a degree that he was seen as acting for and as God by the first Christians.

New Testament scholar N. T. Wright points out, "the old caricature of 'Jesus talked about God and the early church talked about Jesus' does not hold water. Jesus made himself the symbol of his own vocation: 'If anyone hears my words . . . but I say unto you . . . .' Jesus advocated an agenda which involved setting aside some of the most central and cherished symbols of the Judaism of his day, and replacing them with loyalty to himself. . . . [Jesus] acted upon a vocation to be and do for Israel and the world what, according to scripture, only Israel's god can do and be."[15]

Wright strongly stresses that the heart of first-century Judaism was the incarnational symbols of the Torah and the Temple. Jesus acted symbolically and spoke cryptically to define his mission and provide clues to his own self-understanding in terms of the Torah

---

15. N. T. Wright, *Jesus and the Victory of God*, (Minneapolis: Fortress Press, 1996), 384, 548, 649.

and Temple. This has been ignored by scholars from the second century on up to today. The crucial question is did Jesus think, in his proclamation of the Reign of God, that he was in any sense the embodiment of Israel's God? The writing of the Apostle Paul and others in the New Testament comes from Jesus' conviction that it was his role to not only talk about this Reign but to enact and embody it. He was called to do and be what the Hebrew scriptures said only Israel's God could do and be.

Referring to Judaism's two great incarnational symbols—Temple and Torah, Wright says, "Jesus seems to have believed it was his vocation to upstage the one and outflank the other. Judaism spoke of the presence of her God in her midst, in the pillar of cloud and fire, in the Presence ('Shekinah') in the Temple. Jesus acted and spoke as if he thought he was a one-man counter-temple movement."[16] The Jews believed God was compassionate and caring, tending his flock like a shepherd, gathering the lambs in his arms and Jesus used that very image of God more than once, to explain his own actions. This is only one of many ways Jesus talked as the God of Israel.

Concerning the death of Jesus, Wright comments,

> The thing about painting portraits of God is that, if they do their job properly, they should become icons. That is, they should invite not just cool appraisal, but worship, though the mind must be involved as well as the heart and soul and strength in our response to this God. . . . The death of God's son can only reveal God's love (as in, e.g., Rom 5:6-10) if the son is the personal expression of God himself. It will hardly do to say "I love you so much that I'm going to send someone else. . . ."[17]

Jesus was and is all that God is, without being all there is of God.

---

16. N. T. Wright, "Jesus and the Identity of God," in *Ex Auditu*, 1998, 14, 42–56. http://ntwrightpage.com/Wright_JIG.htm.
17. Ibid.

What does Jesus' kind of friendship look like?

What did it look like for the first followers of Jesus to be his friends? Jesus described that as "love one another like I have loved you" (John 15:12). How did he love them? First, he was devoted enough to them to lay down his life for them. He said to them, "There is no greater love than to lay down one's life for one's friends." He asked them in return that they take his words seriously: "And you are my friends if you do what I charge you to do" (John 15:14).

Jesus had been giving himself to his close friends day and night for some time now. He was about to move it to the "no greater love" level and lay his life down for them in submitting to crucifixion. Jesus' charge to them was to love and live like he did. That's quite a challenge! Just who has the audacity to tell you to lay down your life for someone else? The only person who can evoke that kind of incredible devotion and love in us is someone who is devoted in that very way to us. That's what Jesus was doing, and they knew it. His devotion and love for them brought forth gratitude, love, and devotion from them to both him and to one another.

The reason Jesus himself gave for this remarkable "charge" was that he no longer sees his request as coming from his superior position in the relationship. "Charging" his followers to love one another was not like the mother who says to her children when she has reached the end of reasons about why they have to do something, "Because I told you so!" Instead, he plumbs the depths of the true partnership of authentic friendship with, "I no longer speak of you as subordinates because a subordinate does not know a superior's business. Instead, I call you friends because I have made known to you everything I have learned from *Abba* God" (John 15:15, *The Inclusive Bible*).

Jesus didn't want underlings. He wanted partners who shared the authentic friendship of mutual openness with one another. Self-disclosure is the key to all friendships. Jesus saw his whole life as coming from God. This made "everything I learned from *Abba* God I have made known to you" (John 15:15) a genuine opening of his entire life, struggles and all, to them. He had a heart to heart relationship with his *Abba* God, and he wanted that same kind of heart to heart relationship with them.

Think of your best friend. What makes it a best friendship? It is probably because you can share more of anything and everything with one another than anyone else. Sharing is not just talking about how nice the weather is or how the football team it doing. It is how you are really doing. It is what is going on deep inside you. It is where you stretch and where you struggle. It is where you shine and where you sin. Loneliness is going for long periods of time without opening your heart to someone else. Self-disclosure is the substance of an authentic friendship. Jesus knew and practiced that. Writing on Jesus' reason for declaring his friendship to his disciples, Thomas Aquinas said, "For the true sign of friendship is that a friend reveals the secrets of his heart to his friend."[18] A close friend is someone with whom we feel a heart connection. We know one another. We feel safe because safety comes from knowing, whether it is the struggle or the success, the trash or the treasure, what we hide inside of us is safe in the hands of our friend.

A close friend is someone you see often and that you trust enough to open your heart to. This is a person who is important to your life and sincerely interested in your life. This kind of friend cheers for you and wants the best for you. This is someone willing to hang out with you in other places besides the place you first met such as at work, church, or a social gathering. These are all the things that the early Christians found in their friendship with Jesus!

Devotion to Jesus among the first Christians

Merriam-Webster defines devotion as "being ardently dedicated and loyal." That's a great description of the early Christians friendship

---

18. Saint Thomas Aquinas, *Commentary on the Gospel of St. John*, trans., Fabian R. Larcher, (Albany: Magi Books, Inc., 1998), Part II: Chapters 8-21. http://dhspriory.org/thomas/John15.htm.

with Jesus. The heart of this friendship was always the devotion that comes from genuine love. It was not a demand or an "ought to" kind of love. Rather it was the natural response to Jesus' life and teaching. After the resurrection it also flowed from his demonstration of giving his life for them and then, incredibly, not stay dead but return in unlimited spiritual form to continue his friendship with them.

Jesus knew his friends loved him. He used that knowledge as the basis for reminding them that loving him included taking what he taught seriously. He made that clear when he said, "Those who love me will be true to my word, and my *Abba* God will love them, and we will come to them and make our dwelling place with them" (John 14:23). In other words, true love for Jesus will always be accompanied by devotion to both Jesus *and* his teachings. When I hear someone say, "Jesus did not say to worship him but to follow him," I respond by saying that is partially true but misleading. It implies that there is something wrong with devotion to Jesus. It is true that Jesus did not say "Worship me." But somehow those who knew him best ended up worshipping him! Larry Hurtado is a prominent New Testament scholar, historian of early Christianity and Emeritus Professor of New Testament Language, Literature and Theology at the University of Edinburgh, Scotland. He writes, "High devotion to Jesus erupted early and quickly in circles of Jewish Jesus-followers."[19]

It may surprise some Christians to learn that both God and Jesus were worshiped and prayed to in the New Testament and early church. They recognized that God was in Jesus as the revolutionary breakthrough that shouted to the world that God was fully present in at least one human being. Only a few years after the death and resurrection of Jesus they were not only worshipping and praying to God as *Abba* Father but now also to God as Jesus Christ. This was a radical break with the strict monotheism of Judaism.

---

19. Larry Hurtado, Early High Christology: "A 'Paradigm Shift?" 'New Perspective'?" Larry Hurtado's Blog. https://larryhurtado.wordpress.com/2015/07/10/early-high-christology-a-paradigm-shift-new-perspective/.

Hurtado emphasizes that the devotional practices of the early followers of Jesus demonstrate the same devotion and honor that was given to the God of Israel was given to Jesus Christ. They prayed to Jesus (Acts 7:59, 2 Cor. 12:8, 1 Thess. 3:11-13; 2 Thess. 2:16-17; 3:5). He says, "The account of Stephen's death, . . . is also a personal prayer, but again it seems likely that the author expects his Christian readers to be quite familiar with Jesus as recipient of prayers."[20] They prayed "Maranatha" which was a prayer for Jesus to come (1 Cor. 16:22). They sang hymns to Jesus (Eph. 5:19; Rev. 5:8-10, 13-14; 7:9-12). Many scholars believe that Philippians 2:6-11, about Jesus as God, is a Christian hymn already in place from the first few years after the resurrection that Paul used in his letter to the Philippians (50-60 CE).

They worshiped Jesus (Acts 13:2) and often said things like "Grace and peace to you from our *Abba* God and our Savior Jesus Christ" (Rom. 1:7). How is it that a community of monotheistic Jewish people ended up giving Jesus the same honor and spiritual devotion that for centuries they had reserved for the God of Israel alone? Furthermore, how did this transformation come about within a few years after Jesus' death and resurrection in a culture with such slow communication channels compared to our internet society?

Giving devotion and reverence to both God and Jesus was an unparalleled development in the origin of Christianity and was partly generated by visions of the risen Christ receiving heavenly worship (Revelation, Chapter 5) and celebrated in prophetic words and inspired songs. In earliest Christian devotional practice, both God and Jesus are the sole recipients of devotion. The early Christians refused to offer such worship to others considered divine such as the Roman Emperor or the various deities of the Roman and Greek society. Reverence, worship, and devotion to Jesus did not begin as a slow, slippery slope, but quickly and vigorously. It was the distinctively Christian way to offer worship to God.

---

20. Larry W. Hurtado, *At the Origins of Christian Worship: The Context and Character of Earliest Christian Devotion*, (Grand Rapids: Michigan, 1999), 75.

The exalted Jesus was worshiped as "the image of God who reflects God's glory" (2 Cor. 4:4). Jesus was the child of God who uniquely represents and executes God's will on earth. In Philippians, written years before the Gospels, Jesus was given "the name above every name" and declared as "reigning supreme" (Phil. 2:9-11). Peter believed God required this worship as he declared at Pentecost, "Let the whole House of Israel know beyond any doubt that God made this Jesus, whom you crucified, both Messiah and Sovereign" (Acts 2:36). The most explicit expression of this attitude is, "so that all may honor the Son just as they honor the *Abba* God . . . Whoever does not honor the Son does not honor the *Abba* God who sent the Son" (John 5:23).

Hurtado says,

> This . . . reverence which may be described as "worship" is given to Jesus, not because early Christians felt at liberty to do so, but because they felt required to do so by God. They reverenced Jesus in observance of God's exaltation of him and in obedience to God's revealed will. . . . Christian worship of the one God is offered through Jesus, and also jointly to him with God. As we have seen, worship of Jesus is not merely worship of an additional god, or some reverence of a divine hero after the pattern of the Roman religious environment of earliest Christianity. Nor does it represent the supplanting of an old, obsolete deity by a younger one. Worship of Jesus properly is worship of the one God, through, and revealed in a unique way in, Jesus Christ. . . . In the ancient world especially, one's religion was understood and assessed in terms of how, when, and what one worshiped.[21]

This practice was even noted by the Roman officials. Pliny, the imperial representative to the emperor Trajan, reported in a famous letter to the emperor in 112 CE about the Christians, "They were

---

21. Hurtado, *At the Origins of Christian Worship*, 118.

accustomed, on a stated day, to meet together before it was light, and to sing a hymn to Christ, as to a god."[22] They experienced the radiant, transcendent presence of Jesus *as* the presence of God.

Various branches of Christianity respond differently to friendship with Jesus

Eastern Orthodoxy has "stressed the achievement of a mystical union with God. This mystical union with God is referred to as deification (*theosis*). . . . Consequently, Orthodox churches do not emphasize a personal relationship with Jesus Christ as much as they focus on taking the sacraments. They believe that receiving the sacraments provides a relationship with Jesus today."[23]

Roman Catholics also focus on the belief that the bread and wine of Holy Communion, while maintaining their outward appearance, actually become the blood and body of Jesus in the moment of Consecration. Their devotion to those elements comprises the way they express their devotion to Jesus. Some also practice a devotion to the name of Jesus and the heart of Jesus.

I cannot mention my Catholic sisters and brother and their relationship to Jesus without mentioning my friend, Franciscan friar and Roman Catholic priest, Father Richard Rohr who has touched my life in so many ways. I believe he represents the most evolved kind of Catholic possible in the world today. Here is part of his moving response in a recent interview on an Integral Life website when he was asked, "What is your personal relationship with Jesus?" He responded:

> My love dedication to the message of Jesus and person of Jesus has without any doubt increased, broadened and deepened. . . . My relationship with Jesus is in some ways more intelligent, but also more sweet and more personal.

22. A.N. Sherwin-White, *The Letters of Pliny: A Historical and Social Commentary* (Oxford: Oxford University Press, 1966), 694.

23. http://www.4truth.net/Eastern_Orthodox/.

There is a dearness to how he has communicated the Godself to me that I am more in love with than ever before.

I said something to my students this week that I don't think I ever said to a group before—because I have been here at the Center for 29 years to teach contemplative prayer and it is still my daily practice to try to free myself, to open the field, to let go of myself as a reference point. If I'd be honest with you, and this will probably will make some of you lose respect, but I actually pray to God, to Jesus. I say prayers that come from the heart, in a very I-Thou personal give and take way of talking. . . . I don't think I would begin to have whatever relationship I have with the divine if I did not have this combination of open-ended prayer and very personal prayer that probably to some people would sound naive, too sweet, too personal, too relational, too sweet, too chummy.

With the more healthy Christians I have worked with around the world over the years, I have to say now, this is the unique aspect they bring to spirituality. It's a kind of sweet intimate personalism. If they combine that with a life of contemplative prayer, I think we have the best of both worlds.[24]

Evangelicals, Pentecostals, and Charismatics begin with the historical Jesus as found in the New Testament. From certain passages there they arrive at an often meaningful but sometimes formal transaction with Jesus called conversion or "being saved." This is where one confesses they are repentant sinners and embraces a belief that Jesus died so God could forgive them of their sins. This can bring forth an initial and often life-changing encounter with Jesus. The depth of the continuing relationship seems to vary greatly after that.

---

24. From the video of Richard Rohr found at http://returntotheheartevent.com/offerings/jesus/.

Mainline churches such as Presbyterian, Methodist, and United Church of Christ are usually progressive around theological and social issues. Unity churches, while not usually considered mainline, are especially progressive in my opinion. Mainline and Unity churches tend to emphasize God and the teachings of Jesus rather than the presence of Jesus with us today.

However, at the same time, many of these progressive Christians who come from more traditional backgrounds often long for the more nurturing, close relationship they once had with Jesus, his *Abba*, Mary or another Presence in their youth or more traditional days. Now they often seem to believe that is no longer available because it is prerational, mythic religion. Progressive Buddhists may still "take refuge in Buddha" or "put their head in Buddha's lap," but evolving Christians may hesitate to do that with Jesus because it seems like the old evangelical "personal relationship with God" who is both punishing and loving, wrathful and gracious.

I hope that more of these thoughtful and progressive Christians will come to whole-heartedly embrace the three faces of God and come into personal friendship with Jesus and his motherly-fatherly God.

Whom do you admire?

David Brooks, *New York Times* Op-Ed columnist, writing on "The Big Decisions," says,

> The most important decisions in life should not be based on what we think we want but on what or who we admire. ... These days we think of a lot of decisions as if they were shopping choices. When we're shopping for something, we act as autonomous creatures who are looking for the product that will produce the most pleasure or utility. But choosing to have a child or selecting a spouse, faith or life course is not like that. It's probably safer to ask "What do I admire?" than "What do I want?"[25]

---

25. http://www.nytimes.com/2015/08/25/opinion/david-brooks-the-big-decisions.html?smid=fb-share&_r=0.

We become like that which we admire. Even more strongly, we become like that which we adore. We adore sports heroes, movie stars, rich people, smart people. Is that who we want to become? I'd rather adore Jesus and become like him. It seems to me that one reason to worship Jesus is to become like him. The goal in authentic Christianity is not to be a Christian. The goal is to be a Christ as seen in Jesus. Evolving Christians see that since we really do become like that which we adore, adoring and worshipping Jesus helps us become more Christ-like.

The chair

English pastor Leslie Weatherhead tells a story about an old Scotsman who was very ill, and his minister came to visit him.

> As the minister sat down on a chair near the bedside, he noticed on the other side of the bed another chair placed at such an angle as to suggest that a visitor had just left it. "Well, Donald," said the minister glancing at the chair, "I see I am not your first visitor." The Scotsman looked up in surprise, so the minister pointed to the chair. "Ah!" said the sufferer, "I'll tell you about the chair. Years ago I found it impossible to pray. I often fell asleep on my knees I was so tired. And if I kept awake I could not control my thoughts from wandering. One day I was so worried I spoke to my minister about it. He told me not to worry about kneeling down. "Just sit down," he said, "and put a chair opposite you, imagine that Jesus is in it and talk to Him as you would to a friend." "And," the Scotsman added, "I have been doing that ever since. So now you know why the chair is standing like that." A week later the daughter of the old Scot drove up to the minister's house and knocked at his door. She was shown into the study, and when the minister came in she could hardly restrain herself. "Father died in the night," she sobbed. "I had no idea death could be so near. I had

just gone to lie down for an hour or two. He seemed to be sleeping so comfortably. And when I went back he was dead. He hadn't moved since I saw him before, except *that his hand was out on the empty chair at the side of the bed.* Do you understand?" "Yes," said the minister, "I understand." The Scotsman, not by intellect or will, but by an imagination which had become faith, had accepted the gift of a friendship and made the Master real.[26]

Sitting with Jesus

I call the kind of prayer that I practice, "sitting with Jesus." Here are six elements I have found important in this way of praying. I am wording this as directed to Jesus for the sake of historical grounding, the centrality of Jesus for Christians, and simplicity in my explanation. If you are connecting to Mary or other spiritual beings, use their names instead.

1. Recognize the presence of Jesus

Begin by saying (out loud or within, but in words) something like "Thank you, Jesus, for being here with me." This is a powerful way for you to recognize and affirm Jesus' presence. You never have to ask him to be there, since he already and always is. Asking God or Jesus to be present is a negative belief, stating that they are not present, which is not possible since they are ubiquitous.

2. Connect heart to heart to Jesus by crossing the devotional threshold.

We can't just sit down and do devotion mechanically like we do knitting or push-ups. A threshold must be crossed to do devotion in an authentic, transforming way. Progressive Christians often give up devotion to God and Jesus as they grow from pre-rational religion to transrational spirituality because they think it is not compatible with liberated spirituality. But this is not true.

---

26. Weatherhead, *Transforming Friendship*, 44.

Integral Life Practice by Wilber et al. devotes an entire section to Integral Devotion, written to be inclusive of all religions. The writers say,

> Trans-rational devotion expresses a profoundly liberated consciousness . . . . There are transrational paths of devotion practiced by Christians, Jews, Hindus, Buddhists, Muslims, shamans, and many others. Transrational devotion (often in forms that embrace the traditions) is a natural expression of maturity in Integral Practice. . . . Devotional objects and rituals—statues, paintings, pictures, altars, incense, candles, bowing, singing, praying—all can be used intelligently, mindfully, and tastefully, as opposed to being used inattentively, childishly, or fanatically. . . . The transrational devotional heart is not an alternative to intelligence in the mind or vital presence in the hara [The region of the solar plexus or abdomen]. It is one of the most efficient ways to be related to moment-to-moment experience.[27]

I cannot emphasize enough that nothing happens in sitting with Jesus prayer without moving into your heart and making a heartfelt devotional connection to Jesus. Heart passion and devotion is the bridge between us and the energy field of Jesus. When I feel dull and unable to connect I ask myself, *"What would I feel if Jesus was really here with me?"* This gets me in touch with my heart. This is what changes Jesus from a figure in history to a living presence for me. So I suggest if it's difficult for you to experience Jesus' presence deeply, then ask yourself, "What would I feel if Jesus was really here with me?"

3. Sit quietly in mutual awareness.

Someone who had traded in prayer for meditation said to me one time, "Prayer is just too busy. Too much noise and talking. Too much asking and begging and pleading." I said, "So, don't pray that way!"

---

27. Ken Wilber et. al., *Integral Life Practice* (Boston & London: Integral Books, 2008), 228-229.

He looked at me strangely and said, "And how do you do that?" I shared with him what I am sharing with you now.

Sitting quietly in mutual awareness is what good friends can do. They can sit in silence and enjoy one another's company. You sense one another's loving presence. You soak up the love and history together, all the things you have been through together. That's real sitting with Jesus prayer. You are intensely aware of Jesus' presence, and you sit quietly in that field of love and friendship. He is real to you—*and you are real to him.*

4. Communicate back and forth

We human beings also communicate with words at times, too. So express yourself and be aware of his response. Traditional prayer is us talking and never listening for or even expecting a response from the God. I tell Jesus how grateful I am for his life and teaching, that he wants to be here with me, that he is devoted to me. I share whatever is going on that I want guidance and help about. I ask questions. If I don't hear an answer inside my head, I assume I have asked the wrong question.

Word for the day

Jesus said, "One does not live by bread alone but by every word that comes from the mouth of God" (Matt. 4:4). I stay aware of words, pictures or intuitions that may represent Jesus' response to me. Some years ago as I reflected about Unity's "Word for the Day," I thought, "This is a good practice. But Unity can't know what my particular word for the day is. Only I can hear that. So why don't I start listening? It will take more effort than reading Unity's word for the day, but of course it will!" So daily for years, and sometimes now, I ask "What's the word for my day?" I listen for the first word to come to my mind. Most of the time it turns out to be quite relevant and helpful. Sometimes it's just silly babble going on in my head. I can usually tell the difference because of the intensity with which the divinely inspired word comes.

Visions

In addition to various felt experiences and hearing words of guidance, I also began to experience external visions as others have sometimes reported. These appeared in front of me with my eyes closed or open. They started as stars dotting the vast universe and it seemed that I was traveling among them. Then after a few months of stars, I began to see exquisite, colorful, geometric patterns which eventually evolved to luminous white, blue, purple, and gold waves of color most times I was in prayer mode. I have found reports from others of this experience of colors. Eventually the stars and patterns ceased, and the colors became primary.

Next, rapidly moving images of people, nature, buildings, and objects began to appear in front of me. This has continued now for some years in my prayer meditation times. Sometimes I could only tell if these objects were physically present or non-physically present in subtle state awareness by putting my hand out. If my hand went through the object, I assumed it was not in the material realm. I questioned the meaning of these experiences. Also, almost any time day or night that I closed my eyes for any length of time, I began to see various surfaces such as cloth and other objects about a foot in front of my eyes. If I was in a darkened room or wearing my Mindfold,[28] I could open my eyes and still see these surfaces. I pondered for months about what the perceptions meant. I was seeing what ordinarily would be "out there" as something I was seeing inside of me. Eventually I came to see that these kinds of visions were preparing me for the dissolution of "out there" and "in here" into one nondual sacred space.

For years when I was talking to Jesus, as a presence, not a visible form, it seemed to me that he was standing in front of me several feet away. One day I said, "Can't you come closer to me?" Suddenly Jesus

---

28. The Mindfold was originally designed by visionary artist Alex Grey for meditation. It is now called a sleep mask and is available at amazon.com. Evidently many more people sleep than meditate so marketing went to work on the name. I use it quite often.

was an inch from my face. He was so close that I was uncomfortable. So I said, "Not that close." He seemed to laugh and moved from in front of me to my right side and touched my arm. He said, "Is that okay?" I said, "Yes, that's wonderful." I could clearly feel the sensation of his touch on my arm. This touch has become a stabilized awareness that I experience continually now. I feel his touch on my arm right now as I write this.

5. Soaking prayer

"Soaking prayer" is a phrase I have borrowed from my friend Francis McNutt, former Catholic priest and leader in the healing prayer movement. I understand it as soaking up Jesus' loving presence and healing energy which he is always radiating out to us. When a woman in need of physical healing touched Jesus, he said, "Someone touched me; for I noticed that power had gone out from me."[29] Then Jesus asked who touched him and the woman came forth and said she had been healed. This is the same kind of healing energy in this context, albeit most likely at a highly intensified level, that intuitive healers and energy workers today transmit as demonstrated in numerous well-researched cases. Jesus reminded her it was her faith that healed her (Mark 5:30, Luke 8:46) even though he also knew that it was his power that her faith allowed in to effect the healing. This is another way of saying we must set our intention on receiving while Jesus transmits power (δύναμιν) or healing energy. I often place my hands on some part of my body that needs healing while I am sitting with Jesus in prayer. I feel his healing energy flow into me.

6. Merge with Jesus

When Jesus prayed for us, he said, "I in them and you in me, that they may become completely one" (John 17:23). One way to make this

---

29. Luke 8:46, also Mark 5:30. Our word "dynamite" from this Greek word for power, *dynamin* (δύναμιν).

oneness with God, Jesus, and others a reality in your life is in "sitting with Jesus prayer." After you have made a heart to heart connection with Jesus and sense his presence, you can do the following: See or sense Jesus moving toward you and you toward Jesus. Let Jesus fill your awareness as you slowly dissolve into Jesus himself. Just let it happen. Jesus' head becomes your head on the inside of your face. Jesus' heart becomes your heart on this side of you—inside of you. You and Jesus are one. What was Jesus out there is now Jesus in you—in your head and heart and whole body.

In the Gospel of Thomas Jesus is talking to his close companions. He vividly describes his offer of himself in and as us with these words:

> Whoever drinks from my mouth will become like me, and I will become like that one, and what is hidden will be revealed. (Gospel of Thomas, Saying 108.)

If there is a "sitting with Jesus" saying of Jesus, it's got to be this one! We can "drink" in Jesus into us. You can see and feel it happening as you deliberately set your intention to it. Sitting with Jesus is allowing ourselves to drink from his presence and for Jesus and us to become more and more alike. And hidden things will be seen. Are you ready to drink and merge? Are you ready to see hidden things?

One person's experience in Sitting with Jesus

In 2015 I gave a talk at Integral Life's Return to the Heart of Christ Consciousness Conference in Boulder. In the talk[30] I outlined this book, ending with the topic of this chapter—a transforming friendship with Jesus.

Corey deVos, the Editor-in-Chief of *Integral Life,* was there and later shared the following on the *Integral Life* website about his first experience of "sitting with Jesus."

---

30. Available on my website, www.revpaulsmith.com (click on Podcasts and then Videos). Also on the *Integral Life* website at https://integrallife.com/future-christianity/transforming-friendship-jesus.

My Personal Introduction to Jesus Christ

by Corey W. deVos

Although I was raised with a Christian background, I have never personally had a genuine encounter with Jesus Christ. That is, until I experienced Paul's presentation. I want to share some of my reflections with you, as this particular presentation touched me very deeply.

Some of you may already know that my family has been struggling with some medical challenges over the last couple years. I've written about it a few times on this site, so I won't go into a lot of detail. But briefly, my daughter was born with a chronic liver disease, and received a liver transplant last year when she was just a year and a half old. Her transplant was a success, thank God, and we have been walking a mostly positive, if occasionally bumpy, path toward recovery ever since.

We have received an incredible amount of love and support from our friends, our family, and from many of you in the integral community. But still, this has been an exhausting journey for both my fiancée and myself. It's a lot to hold, and often too much to wrap my heart around.

Even as immersed in integral practices and perspectives as I am, these trials nonetheless completely knocked me off my cushion, and left my interiors feeling tattered and twisted. Containing these experiences has required more strength and presence than I ever thought possible. Usually I am able to rise to the occasion, other times I fail. When I fail, I tend to isolate myself and fall into blurred numbness until the cycle naturally renews itself.

So it was this context in which I experienced Paul's presentation. There was something about the keen intellect, gentle wisdom, and graceful humor that Paul shared throughout his presentation that allowed me to temporarily "suspend my disbelief" enough to bring my full attention to the prayer he leads at the end. "Okay, I'll play along," I said to myself. "I'll set aside my cynicism, do the prayer, and see what happens." Fake it 'til you make it, a very wise woman once told me. So I tried it. To tell you the truth, the results surprised me.

I imagined Jesus sitting in front of me, as Paul prompted me to do, visualizing His face until I could feel His presence before me. It felt odd at first, but after a few minutes of silence, I thought I felt something. I began my prayer.

"Please help me," I whispered.

I'd never really been able to ask for help before. At least not in this way. It was painful to put the words together in my mind. What if nothing happens? What if no one answers? What if there's no help to be had? I'd almost rather never ask, than to find out the terrible truth: that this is a fantasy, that there is nobody there, and that I must ultimately bear this cross alone. Tears streamed down my face.

In that instant, all I can say is that Jesus responded. I looked into the face of Christ, and felt His eyes soften.

That was all it was. Just a softening of His eyes.

And in that same moment, I felt something shift inside of me. It seemed to flow from a source that was at once within me and without me. There was a soft warm glow in my solar plexus, and for the very first time I felt that something was helping me hold all of this fear, all of this pain, all of this beautiful agony. For a moment, the unreasonable gravity of life didn't feel quite so heavy. In that moment I knew I was feeling Christ's Love. I was drenched in it. It was something I had never really felt before, at least not to this magnitude—and yet, it was *everything* I had ever felt before, all at once. I was overwhelmed, and I was grateful.

It's funny, it had never really occurred to me that the reason I'd never had a relationship with Jesus Christ was simply because no one had ever bothered to introduce us. Which seems rather important, "personal God" and all. I have the sense that this is true for a great many of us. For me, this was probably the only sort of introduction that would have worked—one that used humor to disarm my skepticism, one that opened my mind by first satisfying my intellect, one that opened my heart by coming from a man as lovely and as kind as Paul Smith.

I was missing this all-important "Spirit in 2nd person" piece from my own spiritual toolkit, and suffered for its absence. I've paid plenty of lip service to it over the years, understanding its importance intellectually, but largely missing the point in my own practice. I knew the signifier very well, but held only a glimmer of the reality it actually signified.

I haven't quite felt the same since this experience. Of course, the pain and fear have not gone away, and I have collapsed and re-emerged at least a dozen different times between then and now. But since that first genuine encounter with Christ, I now have a resource I never knew I had before. I have somewhere to go, someone to call upon whenever things get too heavy. I don't pray for an easier life, I don't really think that's how this works. But I do know that I can always ask for help and pray for more strength when I need it.

So I would like to sincerely thank Paul for this personal introduction to Jesus, and for helping me begin to discover my own transforming friendship with Him. I sincerely hope he can do the same for you.[31]

Summary of Why I Still Talk to Jesus

• Friendship with Jesus is the heart of Christianity.

• Devotion to Jesus is a challenge to many progressive, thoughtful Christians today.

• Devotion to Jesus is often associated with exclusivist, fundamentalist, narrow-minded Christianity.

• Some needlessly put devotion to Jesus in opposition to following Jesus in justice and healing for the world.

• For some, it is a challenge to relate to God in male images.

• The early Christians gave the same devotion and reverence to Jesus they gave to God.

• Various Christian groups relate in different ways to Jesus.

• None of this needs to be a barrier to relating to God in whatever personal way God comes to you.

• One person's experience in sitting with Jesus.

Questions for Reflection and Group Discussion

1. Where were you in your childhood and youth about the reality of Jesus with you? How has that changed?

2. Were you surprised to read that both God and Jesus were reverenced and worshiped by the first Christians?

3. Have you ever experimented with "sitting with Jesus" prayer? Is so, how did it go?

---

31. https://integrallife.com/future-christianity/transforming-friendship-jesus.

Practices

1. *An experiment for a group to do.*

A recording made by the author for this book can be played with these instructions. Available at www.revpaulsmith.com, under Podcasts/Audios/Sitting with Jesus Prayer.

Or have someone read the following in a calm voice to lead the group members in this experiment. The word "PAUSE," unless otherwise specified, means for the leader to let five or ten seconds go by in silence before continuing to read these words to the group.

For those of you willing, let's join now in an experiment in sitting with Jesus. Many people have found this a powerful way to experience the presence of Jesus. Be gentle with yourself as we go along since it may be new. You may find yourself having doubts, asking questions, or your mind wandering. That's all very normal. You will have lots of time in the coming days if you wish to continue to find out how this works for you. So again, be gentle with yourself.

Since this is a wonderfully diverse group, I will mention that there are other versions of this you may want to do: If you find another form of the Beloved or personal expression of God's presence other than Jesus more meaningful to you, then you may want to go with what you are already accustomed to. Or you may do this simply as an experiment.

Do whatever works for you in this prayer time. For the sake of simplicity, I will use the name Jesus, and you can put whoever's name there that works for you.

If this practice seems entirely foreign or strange to you, then it is quite workable to start there with Jesus. Tell him that very thing. "I don't think you're here, Jesus. This is just silly." Then go with whatever ever else you might say and see what happens.

Let's begin. Become still in whatever way you normally use to center yourself as much as possible right now. Remember, none of this requires total attention or freedom from distractions. I still deal with my mind wandering around for much of the time, and I still quite often fall asleep. That hasn't seemed to prevent me from learning how to sit with Jesus—and it won't keep you from it either.

Jesus said that he will always be with us. So we begin by becoming aware of his presence. This is not believing something. This is becoming conscious of that which already is. It is connecting person to person, heart to heart.

Begin by recognizing the presence of Jesus by using words, spoken silently and directly to Jesus. Words like, "Thank you, Jesus, for being here with me right now." PAUSE briefly.

Let yourself feel thankful and grateful for the love God is sending you through Jesus. Feel yourself letting go and sinking into Jesus' presence. Once you sense a heart connection, you may want to simply sit quietly in that mutual awareness.

If you find yourself wanting a deeper heart connection, then ask yourself this very powerful question: "What would I feel if Jesus was really here with me?" PAUSE

Whenever you are ready, you can express yourself to Jesus in whatever way fits for you. Tell him anything you feel or that comes to mind. As you do, be aware of Jesus' response to you. Listen for words that come to mind, or images or pictures. Or sensations or intuitions that might represent Jesus' response to you. PAUSE

You might ask Jesus for a word for you today. Go with the first word that comes to mind. Don't overthink it. If that word sounds like something Jesus would say to you, then go with it. PAUSE.

If you would like to ask Jesus a question, do so. Listen inside your head, heart, and body for what comes most immediately to your sight, senses, or feelings. If it seems like something Jesus would do or say, go with it. If not, ask another question. PAUSE.

Now sense where in the space around you that you feel or imagine Jesus' presence with you.

Become aware of Jesus and his love for you and your love for him. PAUSE.

Sense the space between you and Jesus filled with love. See Jesus moving toward you and you moving toward Jesus. Let Jesus fill your awareness as you let him slowly dissolve into you. Just let it happen. Jesus' head becomes your head. Jesus' heart becomes your heart on the inside of you. You and Jesus are one. What was Jesus out there is now Jesus in you. What was you sensing Jesus near you becomes sensing yourself as Jesus. Don't overthink it. Just rest in that oneness which is already present. See yourself looking out through the eyes of Jesus, feeling with the heart of Jesus. He is aware of what you are aware of because you two are now one. PAUSE

To end this time, tell Jesus anything you want to. PAUSE

Is there anyone who would be willing to share their experience of this practice?

2. Read out loud together this benediction with motions:

 "We go now in love and peace,

In the name of the Infinite God in whom we live and move and have our being.

 In the name of the Intimate God who is always with us.

 And in the name of the Inner God, for we are the light of the world."

"God beside me."

CHAPTER 6

Is Anybody Really There?

> Alice laughed. "There's no use trying," she said. "One can't believe impossible things." "I daresay you haven't had much practice," said the Queen. "When I was your age, I always did it for half-an-hour a day. Why, sometimes I've believed as many as six impossible things before breakfast."
>
> —Lewis Carroll, *Alice in Wonderland*

Is talking to Jesus an exercise in trying to believe six impossible things before breakfast? Comedian and political commentator Bill Maher amusingly describes Christians as those people with an imaginary friend. Is Jesus an imaginary friend? A heroic archetype? A personification of some force or presence. Or, a historical person now present in an energetic spiritual body?

As a follower of Jesus, I have asked myself questions like, Was Jesus talking to himself when he prayed? Was his *Abba* real and there with him? How about us today? When we pray, is anybody really there?

Various streams of Christianity differ on what the experienced presence of Jesus, *Abba*, or other beings to whom Christians pray is. There are at least four options:

1. An archetypal Self

2. An outward projection of one's own inner divinity

3. A helpful but metaphorical way to find comfort and guidance

4. The presence of God as an actual, ontological, spiritual reality in a form that is shaped and interpreted by our stage of development.[1]

Progressive Christians may embrace any of these viewpoints. However, in my understanding, to dismiss the last one and insist that only the first three are options for thinking folks is moving back toward the limitations of a merely rational level of interpretation. If we are stuck in the remarkable but incomplete worldview that is called the modern stage of development, we will see all non-rational understanding as pre-rational magical thinking. Then we will not be able to see the fourth possibility, which moves us more fully to a post-rational mystical perception of transrational reality.

What is real and how do we know?

The modern scientific revolution began in early 17th century Europe. The job of science was to sort out what was true and real from what was myth, superstition, and fantasy. Before the modern scientific era, religious beliefs and priests called the shots about what was true and real. In the modern era, science and scientists determined what is true and real. Because of this, science has been able to bring about incredible progress in our understanding the world and rapid advancement in medicine and technology.

However, sometimes science has led to *scientism* which is an overvaluing of science compared to other kinds of knowing. It is

---

1. One of Ken Wilber's major contributions to understanding spiritual events is that our states of consciousness are always interpreted by our stage of development.

one thing to celebrate science for its achievements and remarkable ability to explain a wide variety of phenomena in the natural world. But scientism claims there is nothing knowable outside the scope of science. Once you accept that science is the only source of human knowledge, you have adopted a philosophical position (scientism) that cannot be verified or falsified by science itself. This is, of course, unscientific!

Beginning 150 years ago in Europe and most noticeable in the 1960s in America, postmodernism was partly a reaction against scientism and rejected scientism's strict rationalism. Postmodernism denies the existence of any ultimate principles, and it lacks the optimism of there being a scientific, philosophical, or religious truth which will explain everything for everybody. It reopens the value of subjectivity regarding morality, social constructions, political movements, art, religion, and truth statements. Postmodernism questions whether we can really know much of anything about what is real.

Today, postmodernism has led to *relativism*, the idea that all viewpoints are equally valid. That means what is right for one group is not necessarily right or true for everyone. If someone says, "This is my truth. What's yours?" they are probably reflecting this viewpoint. Relativism hates rankings and hierarchies and it is taboo to say one thing is better than another, except, of course, that relativism is better than every other way to view the world. This is the fatal flaw of assuming everything is relative except relativity. Of course, domination hierarchies like slavery and classism ought to be rejected. But there seem to be natural hierarchies which simply need to be recognized. A molecule is more complicated than an atom and a person is more complicated that a molecule. Love is better than hate. Integration is better than disintegration. Extreme relativism says there is nothing sacred or transcendent but rather everything is just a matter of viewpoint and language.

The value of postmodernism is in its recognition that much, perhaps all, of what we know and believe to be true is shaped by our culture and worldview. What is not true is the postmodern claim that all viewpoints are equally true and that there is no way to discern what may be more true or less true, especially when it comes to spiritual matters.

I find that interpreting Christianity and deciding what is real in the spiritual realm in a postmodern world involves finding the balance between acknowledging the pluralism of a diversity of views, historical influence on beliefs, our interpretation of spiritual realities always beings shaped by our stage of development/worldview— while avoiding the extremes of relativism that say we can't really know anything, therefore, any viewpoint is as good as any other.

I have found Ken Wilber's writings a helpful resource here as well as those of Jorge Ferrer. A good description of Ferrer's approach comes from *Tikkun* in a review of a book he edited, *The Participatory Turn*: "The question of whether or not we can preserve the ontological integrity of religion, spirituality, and mysticism without sacrificing the integrity of modern critical scholarship lies at the heart of *The Participatory Turn*. . . . Their basic project is the integration of religious experience and practice with modern critical thinking and postmodern epistemological insights about the constructed nature of human knowledge."[2]

That's a scholarly way of asking, "Is there anybody there when I pray?" I am raising the thorny issue of ontology (what is real and actually exists) concerning the nature of subtle or nonphysical entities. Are they imaginary or real? If real, are they co-created, fully independent, or paradoxically both? Ferrer says:

> First, I see no conflict between maintaining that entities such as angels or dakinis [iconic female figures of liberation in Vajrayana Buddhism] may have been historically co-created and that they can also have autonomy and agency independent from human experience. In my view, these beings

---

2. Gleig, "Spiritual Democracy," 61-68.

(as well as other co-created spiritual phenomena) are not necessarily reducible to human byproducts, but emerge from subtle, complex, and probably collectively maintained enactive interactions between human multidimensional cognition (not reducible to the mind), cultural memes, and the creative power of life, reality, and/or the spirit. Second, if one accepts the possibility of an afterlife scenario in which personal identity is somehow maintained, it becomes possible to contemplate the feasibility of human encounters with nonco-created entities such as deceased saints, bodhisattvas, ascended masters, and the like.[3]

What Ferrer broadly calls "the creative power of life, reality, and/or the spirit," I call God.

Co-creation—Partners with God

I want to suggest that spiritual phenomena are events in reality in which both God and our consciousness creatively participate. This includes relationships to spiritual entities, collective identities such as morphic fields, sacred places, and communion with nature. The divine nature is a creative nature. If we are each a participant in the divine nature, then we are participants with God in continuing creation. We are little Christs, contributing our part of the blueprint and piece of reality in connection with others and God. All of our interactions with God are co-created by our divine partnership with God. This means they have an ontological reality that is shaped and interpreted by our worldview, culture, and needs.

This means that all spiritual phenomena are co-created events. All of our spiritual experiences are a mixture of our interpretation from our level of development, our culture and its symbols, and our authentic and very real experience of God and the nonphysical

---

3. Jorge Ferrer, "Participation, Metaphysics, and Enlightenment," *Transpersonal Psychology Review*, 2011, 14(2), 17.

spiritual realm. Cocreation is a dynamic and realistic understanding of the ontological reality of spiritual entities while at the same time recognizing our part in their creation and shaping.

According to Elliot Wolfson, Chair in Jewish Studies at the University of California and scholar of the history of Jewish mysticism, the visions of the Jewish mystic are not entirely constituted by his or her subjective imagination, but actually reflect "ontological realities that have the capacity of being seen within the imagination of the visionary." This is so because "the imagination is . . . the organ that puts one in contact with spiritual realities that are perceptible to each individual according to the dominant images of one's religious and cultural affiliation."[4]

Ferrer advances the theory that "religious worlds and phenomena, such as the Kabbalistic four realms, the various Buddhist cosmologies, or Teresa's seven mansions, come into existence out of a process of participatory cocreation between human multidimensional cognition and the generative force of life and/or the spirit." He goes on to say that this does not mean the uncritical acceptance, typical of postmodern contemporary approaches of pluralism, of all past or present religious understandings standings or forms of life. There must be a kind of faithfulness to the traditions while at the same time an openness to the bold new thing that God may be saying with us to the world.[5]

If spiritual experiences can be seen as the result of human participation with a God who is ontologically real, then their reality and authenticity can be firmly anchored and affirmed in a sophisticated modern world. This kind of approach can explain and account for the great varieties of mystical experience and spiritual phenomena, while at the same time make a solid case for their ontological and metaphysical reality. This is not dismissing them as fantasy or products of only human thinking, or something dropped straight out of heaven, but more

---

4. Elliot Wolfson, quoted in Ferrer, *The Participatory Turn*, 31-32.

5. Ferrer, *The Participatory Turn*, 34-35.

realistically sees them as real even as they are shaped and interpreted by our culture, worldview, and needs.

Ferrer believes "we must not be limited by reason but can find a transrational basis for the reality of spiritual phenomena." He holds out "a vision that redeems the ontological and metaphysical status of spiritual knowledge. . . .[6] To acknowledge that humans not only discover but also shape and co-create spiritual landscapes does not annul the metaphysical reality of such mystical worlds."[7]

Evidence for the reality of a personal Divine Other

Here are eleven arrows pointing to the reality of a personal Divine Other such as Jesus' motherly-fatherly *Abba*, Jesus himself, and other spiritual helpers who provide us with intuitive, visionary information, and guidance from the non-physical spiritual realm of reality.

1. Christianity is inherently theistic

Christianity is inherently theistic or in some sense dualistic and therefore predisposed to the reality of the Divine Other. The Intimate Face of God/ She recognizes the dimension of Ultimate Reality that is a divine Someone or Being with an identifiable personality of love and desire for all to find wholeness. Christianity is also inherently nondualistic and in a certain sense, therefore, nontheistic. The Infinite Face of God/She recognizes this nondual Oneness as Infinite Being, the ground and source of all being. God/She is seamlessly in, beyond, and one with everything without being the same as everything. The Inner Face of God/She is the experience within of God-being-us. We can hold all three of these Faces of God as real and true in seamless oneness. Dismissing any of them diminishes the Full Spectrum God of Jesus.

If Christianity is inherently theistic in some way, then the question for progressive Christians is, "What kind of theism?" We want

---

6. Ferrer, *Revisioning Transpersonal Theory*, 205.
7. Gleig, "Spiritual Democracy," 66.

to transcend *magical theism* where God behaves like a wizard. We must leave behind *supernatural theism* where God looks like Zeus "up there" in the heavens. Supernatural theism is the traditional mixture you get by melding a 2nd person personal God with a 3rd person infinite impersonal God. You then get a really, really Big Person who lives up there in the sky somewhere and behaves with anger, love, jealously, and all other human emotions. This God sends thunderbolts in the form of sickness, bad weather, and accidents down to earth to punish and reward. Or beneficent love telegrams in the form of getting what we want.

The modern and postmodern stages reject these previous two forms of theism which brings us to panentheism. This is an expansive form of theism which we might call *progressive theism*. This is God in and beyond everything. Next, we can even move beyond progressive theism to an integrally-informed altitude which can be called *mystical theism*. Mystical theism, along with mystical nonduality manifests in the Infinite, Intimate, and Inner Faces of God/She and is particularly compatible with evolving, transrational Christianity.

2. Jesus' profound prayer life

Was Jesus delusional when he prayed, fantasizing that he was talking to God? Was Jesus really only praying to some higher form of himself when he communed with God? If so, he sure spent a lot of time really alone! Nights spent in prayer were foundational to his spiritual vision and sustenance. He modeled the viability of a dynamic personal relationship to an authentic Divine Other that he called "*Abba*." How strange that some people admire Jesus for his wisdom, breaking down of social and religious barriers, radical self-giving, and selflessness but yet at the same time believe he was delusional about his love relationship with *Abba* God!

3. Jesus' teaching about prayer

Jesus also taught others to pray to a personal Other such as *Abba*. He probably began by teaching them some form of what we now call the Lord's Prayer. This is a beginners' prayer primarily at a thinking level rather than a heart-centered one. Although commonly called the "Lord's Prayer" there is no evidence Jesus ever prayed that way. The evidence is that he prayed in a different way—a much less formal and much more personal way. However, he taught his friends to talk to God and to him in a personal way—and they did (Matt. 6:9, John 14:14, Acts 9: 6, and 10-14, 1 Cor.1:1-2, 2 Cor. 12:8, 2 Thess. 2:16-17).

4. The resurrection as a spiritual reality

I side with the Apostle Paul who understood and knew the resurrection of Jesus as a continuing awakened consciousness experience and not usually perceived in the manifest physical realm (1 Cor. 15:50f.). Would Christianity have come about without the experiences of the first Christians with the risen Jesus? It seems highly unlikely.

5. The first friends of Jesus prayed to him and to God

The New Testament is full of prayers to Jesus, "Lord," and "Father." People prayed both individually and in communities where altered-state experiences were common. These experiences were the vital center of their actions of love and courage in the world. Were they all delusional? I think not.

6. The experience of mystics down through history and today

A mystic is a person who has vivid and frequent experiences of God. Throughout the centuries and today those who pray to Jesus, God as Father or Mother, or another authentic Beloved attest to the reality of those personal forms of God. God also comes alongside us in the form of teachers and guides from the past as Moses and Elijah were there for Jesus.

7. Research findings of mystical paranormal phenomena

Stanislav Grof is a prominent psychiatrist, one of the founders of the field of transpersonal psychology, and a researcher into the use of non-ordinary states of consciousness for purposes of exploring, healing, and obtaining growth and insights into the human psyche. He and others have found evidence of the reality and power of subtle level consciousness. Researchers such as Ian Stevenson (1918 -2007), Research Professor of Psychiatry at the University of Virginia School of Medicine, have done extensive exploration in the idea of past lives as a form of subtle body reality.[8]

Research in Nearing Death Awareness (end of life transition experiences) described by researchers such as transpersonal psychologist, psychotherapist, author and lecturer Kathleen Dowling Singh can compellingly change our view of dying.[9] Raymond Moody, philosopher, psychologist, physician and author, most widely known for his books about life after death and near-death experiences, coined the term "Near Death Experience."[10] His and other's extensive NDE studies with those who return to normal consciousness close to or after brain death have shown the life-changing effect of connecting with other beings in the numinous realms of awakened consciousness. Shared Death Experiences add to the mixture as several people have the same mystical subtle state experience in the presence of a dying loved one.

Peter Fenwick is an internationally renowned neuropsychiatrist and a Fellow of the Royal College of Psychiatrists. He is Britain's leading clinical authority on near-death experiences and is president of the British branch of The International Association for Near-Death Studies. He cites a study of 293 widows and widowers where researchers found not only that slightly less than half of them had

---

8. Jim B. Tucker and Ian Stevenson, *Life Before Life: Children's Memories of Previous Lives,* (New York: St. Martin's Griffin 2008). George G Ritchie, Jr., MD and Ian Stevenson, MD, *My Life After Dying: How 9 Minutes in Heaven Taught Me How to Live on Earth* (Charlottesville: Hampton Roads, 2015).

9. Kathleen Dowling Singh, *The Grace in Aging: Awaken as You Grow Older* (Boston: Wisdom Publications, 2014).

10. Raymond Moody, *Life After Life: The Bestselling Original Investigation That Revealed Near-Death Experiences* (New York: HarperOne, 2015).

contact with their deceased spouse but also that 2.7 percent touched them.[11]

Induced After-Death Communications is a more recent version of (ADC). Psychologist Allan Botkin has created a new kind of therapy for grief. He uses eye movement desensitization and reprocessing (EMDR). He discovered this while working with United States soldiers who had fought in Vietnam. In 98% of cases he found that by moving their eyes left to right in a rhythmic way the clients could experience having a vivid meeting with someone who had died. Most people felt they were in the presence of the person who had died and could talk directly to them. Some clients saw the person, heard their voice, felt their touch, and/or could smell them. At first, Botkin thought that these experiences were all in the individual's mind, but then he discovered that the psychologist who was watching could also see the meeting.[12]

8. The resurrection of Jesus as After Death Communication

Benny Shanon, Professor in the Department of Psychology of the Hebrew University of Jerusalem says, "As anyone who has engaged systematically in entheogenic inquiry knows, for example, subtle realities and ostensibly autonomous spiritual entities can be encountered not only within one's inner visionary landscapes … but also in front of one's open eyes in the world 'out there' … and these external visions can sometimes be intersubjectively shared."[13]

One of Stanislav Grof's remarkable discoveries is that spiritual phenomena from various cultures and their religions can be

---

11. Peter Fenwick and Elizabeth Fenwick, *The Art of Dying*, (Bloomsbury: Bloomsbury Academic, 2008, 121.

12. Allan Botkin, *Induced After-Death Communication: A Miraculous Therapy for Grief and Loss*, (Newburyport, Massachusetts: Hampton Roads, 2014) 91-99. Video of this process at http://www.victorzammit.com/evidence/inducedafterdeathcommunication.htm.

13. Benny Shanon, *The Antipodes of the Mind: Charting the Phenomenology of the Ayahuasca Experience* (New York: Oxford University Press, 2002),129.

understood by human beings who have never been previously exposed to them. People who had no interest in mysticism or were even strongly opposed to anything esoteric would have visions that gave them an intuitive understanding of the symbols of these religions which were previously unknown to them. Purely because of these visions, in some instances, they developed an accurate understanding of various complex esoteric teachings.[14] Grof's data "strongly suggest that once particular spiritual realities have been enacted, they become potentially accessible to the entire human species."[15]

9. The scientific method points to the reasonableness of being a mystic

A dynamic rationale for being predisposed to the post-metaphysical ontological reality of nonphysical entities or beings is found in the scientific process. Ken Wilber promotes the idea that it's reasonable to be a mystic. By "reasonable" he means the scientific process applied not only to the physical world but to the non-physical world as well. One version of that process is:

1. EXPERIMENT—do this spiritual practice.

2. EXPERIENCE—see what happens, what you experience.

3. EVALUATE—assess what happens with others who have done the same experiment.

4. EVIDENCE—conclude with others that there is evidence that this experience is rooted in reality or not.

Wilber, from his broad-based spirituality that includes the world's great religious traditions, began to develop the idea of the reality of God as the divine Other early on in his writing:

> The *ishtadeva* [cherished divinity] is simply a high-archetypal deity form which is evoked (and thus

---

14. Stanislav Grof, *The Adventure of Self-Discovery: Dimensions of Consciousness and New Perspectives in Psychotherapy and Inner Exploration* (New York: State University of New York, 1988), 139.

15. Ferrer, *Transpersonal Psychology Review.*

emerges) in certain meditations and is literally visualized with the mind's eye using the high-phantasy or vision-image process. I realize some people would say that the *ishtadeva* is "just a mental image" and doesn't *really* exist—that is to simultaneously reduce all mental projections: might as well say that mathematics is just a mental production and therefore doesn't really exist. No, the *ishtadeva* is real—more real in its emergence from the ground unconscious.[16]

More recently, Wilber wrote about the reality of the I-Thou experience, calling attention to the dynamic of personal surrender to the Beloved and its neglect by some traditions. He says that relating to God as being to being is "the great devotional leveler, the great ego killer, that before which the ego is humbled into Emptiness. Vipassana, Zen, shikan-taza, Vedanta, TM, and so on, simply do not confront my interior with something greater than me, only higher levels of me. But without higher levels of Thou as well . . . then one remains subtly or not so subtly fixated to variations on I-ness and 1st person. That is why the merely 1st person approaches often retain a deep-seated arrogance."[17]

He declares, "It is understandable why so many individuals abandoned the mythic God, often when they reach college and move to modern and postmodern worldviews." Wilber says, "Abandon the mythic God they should—but not abandon Spirit in 2nd person!"[18] In the Christian tradition, surrender to God in 2nd person has a central place as its earliest and most prominent affirmation which is simply stated in the New Testament in the sociopolitical language of the Roman empire as "Jesus is Lord" (1 Cor. 12:3). This means Jesus is the senior and leading partner in our friendship with him. The deepest reality of this friendship awaits our surrender to him.

---

16. Ken Wilber, *The Atman Project* (Wheaton: Quest Books, 1996), 80-81.

17. Ken Wilber, *Integral Spirituality: A Startling New Role for Religion in the Modern and Postmodern World* (San Francisco: Shambhala, 2007), 160-161.

18. Ibid.

10. "By their fruits you will know them"

The authenticity of co-created spiritual events is further confirmed by the degree to which they produce selfless love and healing integration in one's life and in the world. This test for Jesus was framed in his words, "By their fruits you shall know them" (Matt. 7:16). What one's life produces in terms of qualities of self-giving and wholeness is a measure of what is valid and what is not valid. This benchmark is quite revealing about the spiritual depth of many contemporary approaches to spirituality which seem to be very self-centered. It's not only okay to rank various spiritual paths on this basis but necessary to do so. The capacity to free individuals, communities, and cultures from narcissism and self-centeredness is the gold standard for all spiritual paths. What or who produces the most saints, lovers, reformers, and explorers of new realms is highest on the list of what is most real.

11. My experience

I have found that relating to *Abba* God and Jesus is real and intensely transforming. That, along with the previous points is compelling evidence to me for the ontological reality of the close Intimate Face of God. We can commune with Jesus, Divine Father/Mother, and other authentic expressions of the Beloved as if they are really there—because they are.

Summary of Is Anybody Really There?

• Thoughtful Christians often wonder if anybody is there when they pray.

• Christianity is inherently theistic and Jesus prayed to a divine Other.

• Jesus taught others to pray to a personal divine Other and Jesus became that along with God to the first Christians.

• In the resurrection Jesus became available without limits of time and space to relate to his friends, and they did.

• Mystics down through history have found Jesus in his non-physical energy body to be real.

• Contemporary research findings of paranormal phenomena demonstrate the reality of After Death Conversations and other connections to non-physical reality.

• The scientific method of experiment, experience, evaluate, and evidence can be applied to spiritual phenomena.

• The authenticity of co-created spiritual events can be validated by their capacity to move us from self-centeredness to self-giving.

• I have found relating to *Abba* God and Jesus real and intensely transforming.

Questions for Reflection and Discussion

1. Which of the author's eleven "arrows" pointing to the reality of a Divine Other do you find most interesting or important to you?

2. If you have previously been convinced of the reality of Jesus' presence, what convinced you?

3. If you are not convinced of the reality of Jesus' non-physical spiritual presence accessed in awakened consciousness, what would convince you?

Practices

1. Whenever you marvel at nature, seeing beauty and sacred presence there, talk to it. If you have never talked to an awesome tree, you probably haven't connected to nature in its sacred fullness.

Share how you best connect with nature.

2. If we can talk to trees, we can certainly talk to Jesus. Instead of trying to believe six impossible things before breakfast about him, just talk to him and see if he is hanging around waiting to be recognized by you in person. One person asked me, "How can I talk to someone

I can't see?" I pointed to the cellphone he had in his hand and said, "You do it all the time!" Try it out.

3. Some spiritual practices may be more helpful for different psychological and cultural backgrounds. In addition, as we grow and change, a different spiritual approach may be called for. For instance, Hinduism recognizes the four different yogas of meditation and physical exercises, love and devotion, selfless service, and exploring wisdom and knowledge. What practices are you attracted to? They may not be easy, but you may sense they would be fulfilling.

4. Sing this new hymn written by Wanda Heatwole, one of the former musicians at Broadway Church in Kansas City. See and hear it in a video made on the Sunday after Christmas several years ago of that congregation singing it along with the pipe organ and other instruments. The congregation not only sings but many also do the hand motions that accompany the words. You may want to join in singing and doing the hand motions along with the congregation. We all probably must do some translating in our heads with any hymns we sing in church but you may find you have to do less with this one.

You can access this four-minute hymn in two ways on the internet:

(1) "YouTube God in Three Dimensions"

(2) Watch the video from my website, www.revpaulsmith.com.

"God beside me."

CHAPTER 7

God, Jesus, and Gender

Sometimes I am asked, "What can I do if I have difficulty relating closely to a male Jesus, especially in prayer?" This is an important question. Some thoughtful women and men find it difficult to relate closely in prayer to Jesus' presence as a male figure because of centuries of patriarchal abuse and/or a personal history of abuse by male figures. Or, more and more often in today's increasingly gender awareness, some simply need and want a feminine presence as their spiritual guide. The idea of a friendship with Jesus may only not be appealing but may not even be workable in their current place in life. What does one do then with this dimension I have called the "heart of Christianity"?

God's wonderful plan of diversity

Unless you are an amoeba or a greenfly, when it comes to being close to others, we are faced with varying forms of sexuality, gender, gender identity, and sexual orientation. Sex is about biological maleness and femaleness. Gender refers to behavioral, cultural, and psychological traits typically associated with one sex. Gender identity is how someone feels about their gender assignment. This is a spectrum with some people identifying as male, some female, some transgender, or gender fluid. Others are gender-neutral and don't associate with gender at all. Sexual orientation refers to the direction of a person's romantic and sexual attractions, and there appears to be greater diversity here than we have previously thought.

Straight (heterosexual) people are primarily attracted to someone of the opposite gender, men to women, women to men. Lesbians (gay women) are women attracted to other women. Homosexuals (gay men) are men attracted to other men. Bisexual people can be attracted both to someone of the same gender and someone of a different gender. Pansexuals (sometimes called omnisexuality or polysexuality) refers to feeling attraction to people regardless of their gender identities, sex, or sexual orientation. Asexuals are not romantically or sexually attracted to other people at all, though they may still enjoy close and intimate relationships. How about all of that for God's boundless creativity! Does this mean that relating to God up close in the intimate way that Jesus provides is just not available for lots of folks? No, indeed!

Mary carries Good News not only with Jesus but with gender healing

God/She is very aware of Her/His/It's creative diversity and our challenges. Someone says, "Wait a minute. Jesus was a man and we can't change that!" This is true. *But a greater truth is that God comes to us in whatever way we need!* A wonderful example of this is found in the spiritual experience of our Catholic brothers and sisters. The Roman Catholic church is an extremely patriarchal institution and images God in only male terms, and its primary leadership excludes women. This has been a wounding for faithful Catholics through the centuries. So what did God do? She began showing up in profound Catholic visionary events in the form of Mary! God can be tricky when She wants to! The elevation of Mary to a place similar to Jesus in spiritual experience did not begin as a doctrinal belief imposed by the church male hierarchy. Rather, it was a spiritual movement coming from the masses who were drawn to Mary as the missing feminine in the church's tradition of a male Jesus, a male "father" God, and male-only priests. Mary not only carried Jesus, but now she carries the message of divine gender equality, side-stepping the institutional church.

The Roman Catholic Church has studied a total of 295 appearances of Mary through the centuries. Twelve of them have been officially "approved" by the Holy See. The Marian and Jesus apparitions by Benoite Rencurel in Saint-Étienne-le-Laus in France from 1664 to 1718 were finally recognized by the Holy See in May 2008.[1] It seems God moves a little more quickly than our religious institutions!

Visions of Jesus and the Virgin Mary have played a key role in the Catholic Church such as in the formation of the Franciscan order and the devotions to the Holy Rosary, the Holy Face of Jesus and the Sacred Heart of Jesus. Elements of modern Roman Catholic Mariology have been influenced by visions reported by children at Lourdes and Fatima.[2]

Ann Matter, a specialist in the history of Christianity at the University of Pennsylvania, has commented that apparitions of Mary have been building around the world for the past 150 years, "with more and more reports of visions of Mary in more and more places." Our time is the most active age of devotion to Mother Mary, more so than the ninth and twelfth centuries.[3]

---

1. Catholic News Agency, "Expert explains Church's criteria for confirming Marian apparitions," May 8, 2008, and "Vatican recognizes Marian apparitions in France," May 5, 2008, https://en.wikipedia.org/wiki/Visions_of_Jesus_and_Mary.

2. Peter Stravinskas, *What Mary Means to Christians: An Ancient Tradition Explained* (Mahwah, N. J., Paulist Press, 2012).

3. http://www.unexplainedstuff.com/Religious-Phenomena/Apparitions-of-Holy-Figures.html.

Among recent visions, the reported apparitions of The Virgin Mary to six children in Medjugorje in 1981 have received the widest amount of attention. The messages of Our Lady of Medjugorje have a strong following among Catholics worldwide. These children and their visions have been intensely studied, even while in the middle of their visionary experience. They are a contemporary example of a group all having the same visionary experience at the same time which is similar to the visions of Jesus occurring to the gathered disciples after the resurrection. It seems that God has provided ways of having a type of Jesus-friendship in a form beyond his maleness in the presence of Mary or other saints down through the ages.

The spiritual body of Jesus is beyond ordinary limits, including gender

While Jesus was in physical form, he was a man who acted in both masculine and feminine ways, serving others in his own time and culture. Jesus was the paradigm of full humanity even in his physically male form. However, this physical form changed after the resurrection. Now, Jesus, as the risen Beloved, comes to us in whatever way we need.

The Apostle Paul makes a compelling case in 1 Corinthians 15 for a spiritual body in life after death in contrast to a physical body. He says God provides different kinds of bodies for different beings (15:38). There are heavenly bodies and earthly bodies (15:40). There are physical bodies and spiritual bodies (15:44). The physical body of flesh and blood cannot be part of the non-physical realm (15:50). Our temporary physical body will perish, and we will be left with an immortal, nonphysical body (15:53). Then there will be no more physical death for us at that point because we are no longer physical beings. We will no longer be troubled by sickness, disease, or death.

The Gospel accounts, written after Paul's seven authentic letters and more than twenty years after the resurrection appearances of Jesus, were a different way of reporting the resurrection appearances. They often seem to make a case for the resurrection of Jesus' physical presence, even though in their accounts the risen Jesus appears to be beyond any limits of space and time as well as form. The risen Jesus was not always immediately recognizable by his close friends, shape-shifting into a gardener (John 20:14-18), a passer-by (Luke 24:13-35), and a wounded man that can only be recognized when Thomas touches the wounds (John 20:27f). He transcends physical limitations of space and time by appearing in two places at once (Luke 24:32-39) and coming in and out of locked rooms (John 20:19).

In my mystical experiences, an eyes-open vision of a physical object can seem exactly like seeing it in its physical form. Also, the early disciples were trying to make a case for the reality of the resurrection. Of course they would have emphasized the naturalness and reality of the Jesus they saw.

Mystics tell us that there is a "body" for every state of consciousness. Our basic consciousness is grounded in our physical or gross body. Our awakened consciousness is in our subtle energy body where we can be aware of non-physical beings, guidance, and encouragement for our life. This is the phenomena associated with what is popularly called "the other side." What I call transcendent consciousness is found in our most subtle energetic body where we have awareness without objects or forms. It is an incredibly blissful, peaceful still point that can be described as both empty and full. It has also been called the simple feeling of being, our Original Face, pure spirit, our True Self, the Cosmic Self, and God's Very Self.

Here is Paul's brilliant statement about Jesus, the metaphorical last Adam, as a spiritual being: "The first human being, Adam, became a living being, the last Adam became a life-giving spirit" (1 Cor. 15:45). Jesus is with us now as a life-giving spirit. This same being that was named Jesus of Nazareth no longer has a physical body but a spiritual one *beyond* gender. Regarding life after death, Jesus pointed out to the Sadducees that the physical concepts of marriage and gender are transcended in the resurrection because we are like angels as resurrected children of God. (Luke 20:34-36). Questions of gender and sex do not apply to Jesus in non-physical subtle body form. Therefore, Jesus can come to us in any subtle form presence we need. That subtle body may appear as male, female, transgender, androgynous, gender unnoticed, or beyond gender.

The New Testament feminine image of Jesus as Sophia, the wisdom of God

We can see a form of Jesus as feminine in the Bible when Paul equates Christ with the "Wisdom (σοφία, *sophia*) of God." This arresting statement in 1 Cor. 1:24, "Christ the power of God and the wisdom (*sophia*) of God," brings with it a rich biblical and Christian history because the Greek word for wisdom, *Sophia*, is the personification of God.

Wisdom is the feminine word *hokmah* in Hebrew and *sophia* in Greek. Jann Aldredge-Clanton, scholar, minister, author, and friend, says that wisdom *(hokmah)* is consistently depicted as female in the Hebrew Scriptures—sister, mother, female beloved, chef, hostess, and liberator. Proverbs depicts *Hokmah* as the path, the knowledge and the way that ensures life (Prov. 4:11, 22, 26). The Gospel of John parallels this, saying that Jesus is "the way, the truth, and the life" (John 14:6). What Judaism said of personified Wisdom (*Hokmah*), Christian writers came to say of "Christ the wisdom (*Sophia*) of God." She is the image of the invisible God, the radiant light of God's glory, the firstborn of all creation, the one through whom God created the world.

Jann writes, "As the incarnation of the eternal Sophia, Jesus can say, as no merely historical person could: 'How often have I desired to gather your children together as a hen gathers her brood under her wings'" (Luke 13:34, Matt. 23:37). She points out that by the first half of the second century the identification of Jesus as Sophia (Wisdom) had become widespread.[4]

---

4. Jann Aldredge-Clanton, *In Search of the Christ-Sophia* (Waco: Eakin Press, 2004), 13-18.

Influential second-century theologian Justin Martyr says, speaking of Jesus, "He whom Solomon calls Wisdom, was begotten as a Beginning before all his creatures and as Offspring by God."[5]

Famous second-century theologian Origen in his commentary on John equates Sophia with Christ, stating that Christ is "of right the wisdom of God and is hence called by that name."[6]

In Roman Catholic mysticism, the Doctor of the Church St. Hildegard of Bingen (1098-1179) celebrated Sophia as a cosmic figure in both her writing and her art. Sophia, in Catholic theology, is the Wisdom of God.

Julian of Norwich (1342–1416) was an English mystic who celebrated "Mother Jesus." She was the first woman to write a book in English, writing at length about God and Jesus as mother. She writes, "So Jesus Christ who sets good against evil is our real Mother. We owe our being to him—and this is the essence of motherhood!—and all the delightful, loving protection which ever follows. God is really our Mother as he is our Father. . . So Jesus is our true Mother by nature at our first creation, and he is our true Mother in grace by taking on our created nature."[7]

The Incarnation means that Jesus became a human being, not that Jesus became a male as opposed to a female. Just as Jesus is the image of the invisible God" (Col. 1:15), so is Christ Sophia and other saints down through the ages.

When we pray

In my own "sitting with Jesus" prayer I experience a dynamic, palpable presence on my right side along with, for the last five years,

---

5. St. Justin, *Dialogue with Trypho,* Chapter LXII. Early Christian Writings, http://www.earlychristianwritings.com/text/justinmartyr-dialoguetrypho.html.

6. Origen, *Commentary on John, The Ante-Nicene Father: The Writings of the Fathers down to A.D. 325.* http://www.ccel.org/ccel/schaff/anf09/Page_317.html.

7. From *Revelations of Divine Love,* Elizabeth Spearing and Clifton Wolters, (New York: Penguin, 1998).

the sensation of being touched on my right arm. I call this presence "Jesus" because, at an intense level of inner knowing, I identify this as what was experienced by the early Christians as the risen Jesus. When I press myself to identify this presence in gender terms, this most often seems to be a male Jesus shaped by my consciousness, and at other times beyond gender.

In my friend Jann's experience, Christ-Sophia comes to her as a dark, loving female presence in flowing purple robes. Jann tells me that this female presence is empowering, nurturing, and generative. She says that her mystical experiences of Sophia inspire her creative writing.

A good spiritual teacher tells people where to *look* but not what to *see*. I suggest to Christians that they *look* at Jesus as a transforming friend in life and prayer. However, what they *see* is shaped by what they need and their evolutionary stage or worldview. God's personal closeness may be experienced as a non-male Jesus, Mary, or other saints or Christ-like figures. Be open to this in your spiritual practice if this is relevant for you and see what happens.

Summary of God, Jesus, and Gender

• A male Jesus can be a barrier to accessing God through him.

• God has unfolded humankind in wonderful diversity.

• God has brought forth Jesus' mother, Mary, as a feminine presence and image of God in a Church that has excluded women in its image and language about God as well as from its leadership.

• Christ-Sophia, the wisdom of God, is a biblical image of Jesus as feminine.

• The spiritual body of Jesus is not limited by gender and can come to us in any form we need—male, female, transgender, androgynous, gender unnoticed, or beyond gender.

Questions for Reflection and Group Discussion

1. Has a male Jesus ever been a barrier to you in prayer? What did you do, if anything, about that?

2. Has Jesus, as some other gender or sexuality beside as a male heterosexual, been meaningful to you?

3. How does the idea of Christ Sophia strike you?

4. Have you ever prayed to Mary or other female saints? If so, how did that seem?

Practices

1. If you find a male Jesus to be a barrier to praying, experiment with other gender forms of Jesus or other saints. If you don't know who to address in prayer, or would like to connect with other spiritual guides, ask yourself this question: Who in the Bible, church history, or any highly evolved person now on the other side have I either found interesting or been spiritually attracted to? Ask if they would serve as a spiritual guide for you. See what happens.

2. Centering Prayer recommends using a sacred word to return you to prayer or meditation if your mind wanders. However, in "sitting with Jesus" prayer and meditation you return to your sacred person in the form of Jesus or other personal spiritual beings as suggested in this chapter. This presence is not "mental" as a sacred word is and does not move us back to our mind. Returning to your sacred person is returning to an actual energetic presence which can return you to your heart center where the deepest prayer and meditation occurs. This powerfully centers you once again in your heart which automatically pulls you away from a busy mind.

3. Close with the Three Faces of God signing (next page).

"God beyond me, in whom I live and move, and have my being."

("God beyond us, in whom we live and move, and have our being.")

"God beside me, you are always with me."

("God beside us, you are always with us.")

"God being me, I am the light of the world."

("God being us, we are the light of the world.")

"God beside me."

CHAPTER 8

The Closeness of God as Spirit

Getting personal with personalization

You may be surprised, at least the first few times, when an email that goes out to thousands of people is personalized with your name on it by a company trying to connect with you in a more personal way. This is an artificial method because the only thing at that company that knows your name is a computer. However, the personalization of spirit in the Bible represents actual reality, divine spirit that really does know your name!

Personalization or personification is when an abstract concept or something that is not a person is given human attributes and portrayed in such a way that we feel it can act like a human being. Something seems to appear to you in a personal form as an "Other." Something becomes a someone. For example, when we say, "The sky weeps" we are giving the sky the ability to cry, which is a human quality. The sky has been personified.

"Look at my car. She's a beauty."

"The trees danced in the wind."

"Washington just doesn't know what it's doing nowadays."

"My computer throws a fit every time I try to use it!"

Since spirit or divine-human consciousness is our very life force, it does not take much effort to naturally see spirit as a person or personification in the New Testament and at times in our own lives.

Spirit "with you and in you"

Jesus said spirit-breath would be "with you and in you" (John 14:17). "With you" and "in you" are two quite different things. Let's say that someone gives you an apple which you now carry in your hand. You can readily say, "I have *the* apple I was given *with* me." If you eat *the* apple you can say, "I have apple in me," without the "*the*." It is no longer *the* apple as a distinct and separate apple because most of it, minus the core, is in your tummy being digested. Wait a bit and the apple will be you! It is no longer "*the* apple" but "apple" itself now in and as you. I suggest that one way to think about spirit "with us" is *the* spirit walking alongside us. I write "*the* spirit" because spirit here is a theistic divine *presence*, a being of divine consciousness. There is you and there is *the* spirit which is like two persons who are separate from one another. However, spirit "in us" is the apple eaten and digested. It is no longer "the spirit" but spirit which is now *divine presence* indistinguishable from you and as you. Another way of saying this is that spirit "in us" is divine-human consciousness which we explore in Part Three. Spirit is "with us" as a personification of that consciousness that allows us to consider spirit as a "someone." This chapter is about the "with you" part.

In reference to holy spirit, *Thayer's Greek-English Lexicon* uses the terms "personification" and "rhetorically represented as a Person."[1] Spirit is personalized in the New Testament by speaking of "the spirit

---

1. Joseph Thayer and James Strong, *Thayer's Greek-English Lexicon of the New Testament* (Grand Rapids: Baker Book House, 1977), 522.

who gives life" (John 6:63) because consciousness is what defines us as living beings. This is also the "spirit of truth" (John 14:7) as our awakened consciousness brings truth to us that cannot be found in concepts or learning or in any other way but through elevated awareness. Spirit is our "teacher" (John 16:13) and "guide" (John 14:26) because enlightened consciousness is the only avenue for the deepest knowing which is not available in any other way. Spirit "witnesses" (Rom. 8:16), verifying within us that we are children of God.

Spirit is called Paraclete (*parakletos)* five times in the New Testament. This is translated variously as counselor, helper, encourager, or comforter. Jesus said, "But when the helper (*parakletos)* comes, whom I will send to you from the Father-Mother . . . that one will bear witness about me" (John 15:26). *Parakletos* is *someone called in to help* when the person who calls is in trouble, distress, or doubt. If we want help in life, nothing is more available, awesome, and powerful than awakened, transcendent, and unity consciousness.

Paraclete is often translated as "advocate" in the New Testament. Who advocates for you in life? Your spouse or partner? Your parents? Your kids? Your friends? I hope so. It always feels good and helps us greatly in our journey through life to have cheerleaders. The New Testament teaches us that we have just such an advocate, a cheerleader in God as our very own divine-human consciousness come close as Helper. The more conscious we become, the more we are helped!

The lively biblical language of other forms of spirit's personal presence

The "spirit of God" is synonymous with the "hand" of God and "the finger" of God in Ezek. 3:14, Job 26:13, Psalm 8:3, and Luke 11:20, again as personifications.

Holy spirit is used synonymously and interchangeably with "the spirit of Jesus" (Acts 16:7; Phil. 1:19); "the spirit of the Lord" (Luke 4:18, etc.); "the spirit of God's son" (Gal. 4:6); "the spirit of Jesus Christ" (Phil. 1:19). In this last usage, spirit is the mind or consciousness of Jesus which helps and guides his friends in knowing God.

These are all personifications of a reality that is God's presence which is different from the reality of the presence of God as Father-Mother and the presence of God as Jesus as specific spiritual entities. We know this because in the early church God and Jesus were subjects of devotion and worship, but spirit was not. In all the initial greetings of the letters of the New Testament God as Father-Mother and Jesus are mentioned but not holy spirit. Spirit was important but in a different way than God and Jesus.

Spirit and wine

Paul compared or contrasted spirit to wine. "And do not be drunk with wine, in which is dissipation; but be filled with the spirit" (Eph. 5:18). Do we ever associate spirit with being drunk? Sounds strange, doesn't it. But not to those who have what Maslow calls peak experiences, those high times of expanded consciousness where you are in touch with transcendent realities. This can produce overwhelming joy and bliss. Wine, as a symbol of spirit, represents joy. I have seen this as some have trouble standing or walking after a particularly vivid spiritual experience. Wine is a chemical experience. Spirit is an elevated consciousness experience.

I'll drink to that!

Summary of The Closeness of God as Spirit

• Spirit as a "person" or divine presence is a personification of spirit in the New Testament.

• Spirit is also elevated or intensified consciousness explored in Part Three.

• Spirit is compared to wine.

Questions for Reflection and Discussion

1. Have you sensed the spirit as intuition, a presence, a nudge, or something else?

2. Do you have a metaphor or personalization that better describes your experience?

Practice

1. Let spirit nudge you as you look back over this chapter to see how spirit is already at work in you, helping and gifting you for service.

2. Do the spiritual gifts workshop on my website. www.revpaulsmith. com under "resources." A group can do this together.

3. Explore the diagram of Trinity Beside Us (page 80, or on my website).

On the accompanying page is my illustrated diagram of Trinity Beside Us—the second person perspective in *relating to* the traditional Trinity. It shows how God the Father, Son, and Spirit look when viewed through the lens of the Intimate Face of God— God-Beside-Us. In some ways these seem to be similar to the traditional names of Father, Son, and Spirit. However, as we have seen in this section, there are significant differences that open up a more radically personal and transforming relationship with God through the three faces of Mother-Father, the risen Jesus, and the spirit as Helper.

The top image of loving family

Looking behind God the Father we find that God is our always present, loving Mother-Father symbolized by the family image of warm parental care and love.

The middle image of the risen Jesus

Looking behind the words "God the Son" we can discover an ever-present Jesus in his spiritual body available to anyone, anywhere. He

is the transforming friend of a lifetime. Mother Mary and Francis of Assisi signify other saints that Christians through the ages have also, at times, connected with, beginning with Jesus talking to Moses and Elijah and on to Mary and others today (Chapter 7 and 15).

The bottom image of flames of love

Behind God the Spirit is the personification of spirit-breath as a very real and present Helper who guides, comforts, and encourages us personally. The image echoes the "tongues of fire" which rested on the friends of Jesus at Pentecost (Acts 2:3) and the pure love that is spirit.

As you gaze at each of these three images, open your heart to God's presence. These images are intended to activate your heart and spirit-breath-consciousness, calling forth a deeper awareness of God beside you right now.

Again, it's not necessary to remember all of this or get the details just right. It is enough to see that there really is an Intimate Face of God Beside Us hidden behind the words "Father, Son, and Spirit." And most importantly, we can personally have an authentic personal relationship—and especially a friendship—with God in these ways.

4. Read out loud together, signing the Three Faces of God benediction on the next page.

"We go now in love and peace,

In the name of the Infinite God in whom we live and move and have our being.

In the name of the Intimate God who is always with us.

And in the name of the Inner God, for we are the light of the world."

"God being me."

Part Three

Is Your God You Enough?
Opening our identity to Trinity being us

I was attending the Eagle Scout ceremony for Ronnie, one of the teenagers in the church where, while in college, I was Associate Pastor. His foster parent, who was his aunt, and I were there trying to take the place of his mother and father who had been killed in a car accident two years before. The accident was devastating, but the boy had kept working on his Eagle Scout goal. His mother and father had both been wonderful people, and Ronnie was turning out to be just like them. As Ronnie was standing in front of the group, his aunt whispered to me, "Look at him. He's the spitting image of his mom and dad!"

That's what Genesis is saying with, "Then God said, 'Let us make humankind in our image, to be like us'" (Gen. 2:26). An astute observer to this metaphysical scenario of the first humans might say, "Look at them. They're the spitting image of their Divine Mom and Dad!" Have you embraced the spiritual truth that you are made like God? God/She has put her being into us as our deepest Self. If you come from a church background, you have probably heard someone tell you that we should be more like God. But if we turn it around and ask if God is like you, that can be puzzling. Is your God you enough? For many, that's a "You've got to be kidding" question.

That's the response Jesus got when he made that claim. Actually it was a bit stronger. When he said, "God and I are one" (John 10:30), the religious leaders started picking up stones to throw at him! He said, "I've done a lot of good things. Which ones are you upset about?" They responded, "It's not for those but because you are making yourself God" (John 10:33). They understood that Jesus was claiming that he was like God and that God was like him when he said that he and God were one. This was blasphemy, the height of irreverence for God, and it required stoning.

Claiming to be one with God, or that we are like God and God is like us, was a controversial claim in the religion of Jesus' day and remains so today among Christians. Many Christians are not familiar with the passages in the Bible and the statements of saints, mystics, and theologians down through the centuries that affirm this likeness, our divinity. These are framed in various metaphors and figures of speech such as being transformed into the same image as Jesus (2 Cor.3:18), and participating in the divine nature (2 Pet. 1:4). Other times we are called children of God (1 John 3:1), like God in the world (1 John 4:17), co-heirs with Christ (Rom. 8:17), and the light of the world like Jesus (Matt. 5:14).

We are God become flesh

God being us is pointed to in the Bible's phrase, "made in the image of God" found in the first chapter of Genesis. It comes to us again in the Apostle Paul's "we bear the image of the one of heaven" (1 Cor. 15:49). We see this demonstrated in Jesus who was "the Word became flesh and lived among us" (John 1:14), God participating in our flesh. We, too, are God participating in our flesh. Meister Eckhart said, in the language of his day, these daring and profound words about us being God and God being us:

God gives birth to me as Himself, and Himself as me.[1]

"All that God the Father gave His only-begotten Son in human nature He has given me: I except nothing, neither union nor holiness; He has given me everything as to him. Everything that Holy Scripture says of Christ is entirely true of every good and holy man."[2]

The first time I read those words fifteen years ago, I thought that was surely an exaggeration. After much research, reflection, prayer, and meditation, I am well on the way, at my best moments, to feeling it and knowing it with my whole being.

God being us

One of the earliest Christian beliefs was called deification, divinization, or theosis. It meant participating in God's divinity by coming into the union with God that Jesus demonstrated. This results in our being one with God. It means knowing God like Jesus knew God. He knew that God was not only beyond him, and close to him, but that in some way God *was* him. He claimed to be acting and speaking on behalf of God. Like Jesus, we are also one with God. We are God's mind, heart, hands, and feet here on earth today. Like Jesus, we are fully human and fully divine. We are God's children, acting as full participants in our Father-Mother's divinity by overcoming our mistaken identity that we are separate from God. This Oneness consciousness moves us to act as divine agents in healing the Earth, overcoming poverty, eliminating hunger, stopping oppression, and ending war. It motivates us to share the Good News that we all belong to God and one another.

Jesus is the living model of the reality that God and humankind exist in the same place at the same time in seamless unity. The Great I

---

1. Pfeiffer, Frantz, and Evans, C de B., trans. *Meister Eckhart.* (London: John M. Watkins, 1924), 222.

2. http://thedaobums.com/topic/31976-sayings-of-meister-eckhart-declared-as-heresy-by-the-vatican/.

AM showed up in and as Jesus. Then Jesus said to us, "You, too!" The Inner Face of God is all about our inner awareness of divine realities and our divine center.

Jesus said that you are a god

One of the most striking things Jesus ever said was in the debate he was having with the religious leaders over his divinity. I pointed out at the beginning of this chapter that Jesus said, "God and I are one" (John 10:30). The religious leaders clearly understood this was Jesus' claim of God-being-him when they replied, "You, though only a human being, are making yourself out to be God" (10:33). They accused him of blasphemy. Here was Jesus' response:

> Is it not written in your law, "I said, you are gods"? If those to whom the word of God came were called "gods"—and the scripture cannot be annulled—can you say that the one whom the Father-Mother has sanctified and sent into the world is blaspheming because I said, "I am God's child?"   (John 10:35-36, *The Inclusive Bible*)

Jesus was quoting from the Hebrew scriptures, Psalm 82:6, when he said to the religious leaders, "Is it not written in your law, 'I said, you are gods'?" The full quote is "I say, 'You are gods, children of the Most High, all of you.'" There have been several interpretations of this passage offered down through the centuries to tame down what appears to be the obvious meaning. Some have pointed out that the words of Psalm 82:6 were only directed at the religious officials who were appointed to be God's representatives here on earth as were the religious leaders of Jesus day. Others have argued that the word "gods" in this context should be translated "judges" or "mighty ones" and were seen here as simply powerful human beings as the original passage in Psalm 82:6 may have meant. Also, the gods in Psalm 82 are later condemned to mortality, effectively de-deifying them. However, it seems obvious that Jesus himself interpreted that passage as meaning "gods" as he himself was divine, one with God, or a "god." *Jesus pulled this passage out of its context to apply to his own claim to be a god, and not merely a judge or to be later dethroned.* If he had meant only "judges," why would the religious leaders be so upset? Jesus' interpretation of the Jewish scriptures turned out to be blasphemy in his day because Jesus' interpretation was that *they were all divine!*

Here was the perfect opportunity for Jesus to say, "Oh no. This is all wrong. If I say that I'm divine, or one with God, or God's son, or straight out that I am God, my followers will get the wrong idea about themselves. They will think they are gods, too, because I have told them to be like me and do what I do. We can't have them thinking that includes being divine. I'm the only one who is God in the flesh. I'm going to put a stop to this nonsense right now."

Then he could have said, "You say I am making myself out to be God. Yes, I am a god. I am divine, but let's get it straight. Only I am a god, and nobody else is. I don't want my followers to get confused and think they are gods too. Yes, they are supposed to imitate me, think like me, be like me—but there is a limit, after all. It stops with the God thing. Only I am a god. You are definitely *not* gods!" But Jesus didn't say that. *He said just the opposite! Amazingly, he not only agreed with the religious leaders that he was God, he told them the reason he agreed with them was that they were gods, too!*

Divinity runs in the family

Notice that Jesus then used another widely understood metaphor of "family divinity likeness" by saying the religious leaders believed he was claiming to be God "because I said 'I am God's child'" (John 10:36). We come across this metaphor in the very beginning of the Bible: When Adam had a son, it was described as, "he become the father of a son in his likeness, according to his image; and named him Seth" (Gen. 5:3). The words "likeness" and "image" used there are the identical Hebrew words used in Genesis 1:26 speaking of God and us, "And God said, 'Let us make man in our image, after our likeness'" (Gen. 1:26).

By associating being "gods" with being children of God in this passage the reasoning goes like this: Families produce their own kind. The children of sheep are sheep. The children of lions are lions. The children of humans are humans. And so on throughout the family offspring of all creatures. The conclusion is that if we are children of God, then we are gods.

As confused, ignorant, and opposed to him as the religious leaders were, incredibly, Jesus affirmed that they were divine also, although it is unlikely they experienced that in an intimate, personal way. That was his very point: If they were divine, as oppressive as they were, how could they say he was not divine, as good as he was. Okay, let's just assume for now that you are "a god" and you believe that God is "you enough." So what?

What does being a god mean?

God being you enough is defined in 2 Peter 1:4 as our "participation in the divine nature." That means the real heresy is not claiming to be a god, but saying, "Who am I to be a god!" In the often-quoted words of spiritual teacher and author Marianne Williamson, "Our deepest fear is not that we are inadequate. Our deepest fear is that we are powerful beyond measure. It is our light, not our darkness that most frightens us.... You are a child of God. Your playing small does not serve the world."[3]

What being a god does *not* mean

On the other hand, we do not participate in the divine nature by pretending that everything we do is our godliness shining forth. For instance, it's a "no-no" to say or think:

"God made me just the way I am, so don't tamper with this divine masterpiece that is me."

---

3. Marianne Williamson, *A Return to Love: Reflections on the Principles of "A Course in Miracles,"* (New York: HarperOne, 2009), 190.

"I think I'm more god than all these other people."

"Listen to me, this is God speaking."

"Jesus said that I'm a god, so you had better do what I say."

Patient: "Doctor, I keep thinking I'm God."

Doctor: "When did this start?"

Patient: "Well, first I created the sun, then the earth . . ."

(Although Meister Eckhart did seem to say that very thing as we shall see later!)

How it works

We take part in God's nature by manifesting our divine nature in our human nature. Jesus modeled what the divine-human looked like par excellence. We are participating in the divine nature not as the I AM God of Moses but as a divine human. This is the presence of the Infinite in the finite. Blogger and spiritual adventurer Jon Zuck, writing about Christian mysticism which he wonderfully calls "the wild things of God," says,

> Becoming God doesn't mean we become all-knowing, all-powerful, or that we remember saying "let there be light." It really means becoming Christ, or becoming divine—that God's God-ness is experienced and known not as something outside and separate, but as a part of our own being. It means knowing God as Jesus knew the Father, so like Jesus, we are with him, fully human and fully divine.

> This is a difficult teaching to accept at first. It is one thing to think of ourselves as children of God in the sense that, like all creation, we ultimately come from God. But it is quite another to believe in the biblical usage of the words children and sons, because their implications of

likeness, growing up, and inheritance are much stronger than that. "The power to become children of God" (John 1:12), indicates something much more than the fact that he created us.[4]

The Christian understanding of *theosis* is not a New Age slogan about our creating our own reality. It's not a casual, "Sure, I'm a god" that sidesteps the hard work of ethical living, deep humility, letting go of all our attachments, and whole-self devotion to God. Father Thomas Keating succinctly sums it up most beautifully: "The plan is to be God in the humblest kind of way. Why not put everything into that. This means the goal is not to become better, but to become who you are."[5]

Our spiritual DNA is divine. Our physical DNA is divine, too. Our physical and spiritual bodies have all been shaped by God through the evolutionary process and imbued with life by the breath of God from our first breath as a newborn until now. Our physical and spiritual bodies are all divinely sourced.

Being a god is not the same as being God

When Jesus answered the religious leaders by saying that he was like God enough to be one with God, he did not mean he was the same as God. Nor did it mean he was different from God. God and Jesus were one, but they were not identical as the many metaphors of the Bible and creeds point out. Notice how Jesus described his relationship to God (referenced in parental language by Jesus) in the Gospel of John with these three sentences:

"*Abba* God and I are one" (John 10:30).

"*Abba* God is in me and I am in *Abba* God" (John 17:21).

"Whoever has seen me, has seen *Abba* God" (John 14:9).

---

4. http://www.frimmin.com/faith/theosis.php.

5. https://integrallife.com/future-christianity/becoming-nothing.

None of these statements declared that Jesus and God were the same or identical. When Jesus prayed, he was not praying to himself. Being one but not identical is what some call "nonduality." Nondual means not two in the sense of being separate. But nondual also means not one either in the sense of being the same. Jesus was Jesus, fully God and fully human. God was God. At the same time, they were one, not two. In an initial recognition of this after the resurrection, the first Christians soon began giving Jesus the same intense devotion they gave God. They treated Jesus like a god because they believed God wanted them to. On the day of Pentecost when awakened spirt-breath consciousness had been released in Jesus' friends, Peter stood up and declared, "Therefore let the entire house of Israel know with certainty that God has made him both Sovereign and Messiah, this Jesus whom you crucified" (Acts 2:36). They continued to believe there was only one God, not two. But both God and Jesus were one God.

The early Christians explored various ideas about how this might be true. Was Jesus God and not human? Was Jesus human, and then God adopted him as a god? Was Jesus half God and half human? In the Council of Nicea in 315, the gathering of church leaders made a careful wording of this relationship of Jesus and God. They said, in effect, there was only one God and this God had three seamless faces. The terminology that was most available and useful to them was God the Father, God the Son, and God the Spirit—one God in three persons. This was a beautiful statement of nonduality—not two or three Gods, but one God in three persons. God as *Abba*, God as Jesus, and God as spirit were one in seamless unity, yet each is unique.

God and Jesus are linked together

Larry Hurtado points out that in the New Testament God is so closely linked with Jesus and Jesus so closely linked with God that one cannot adequately identify the one without reference to the other. This did not result in the worship of two gods but rather a new kind of monotheism. It was a devotional practice where God was worshiped in reference to Jesus and Jesus was reverenced in obedience to God and to the glory of God.[6]

The relationship of Jesus to God is the same as our relationship to God in the sense that we are also one with God. Of course, Jesus embraced and manifested this oneness fully, while we are still on that journey. God is in us and we are in God. We are not different from God and yet we are not the same as God. Sometimes I use upper case and lower case letters to point to this. We are not God—but we are gods. Some Christians, as early as the second century, recognized this deification of humanity as the goal of the Christian life.

God being us is both in process and yet already a present reality

Sometimes the New Testament seems to point to our god-likeness as something in process and yet to be completed. We shall become divine like Jesus in the future. Other passages have a theme that focuses on our already here and now divinity. As a result, there have been saints and sages down through the ages that have pointed to one theme or the other. Here are some of the biblical passages and writings of Christian leaders that emphasize we are in the process of becoming like the divine Jesus, the Christ.

We will become gods in the future

The writer of Ephesians says, "until all of us come . . . to maturity, to the measure of the full stature of Christ" (Eph. 3:19). The Apostle Paul frames it as, "to become true images of Jesus, so that Jesus might be the eldest of many brothers and sisters" (Rom. 8:29).

One of my favorite expressions of Jesus about manifesting our evolving divinity is, "Whoever drinks from my mouth will become like me. I myself shall become that person, and the hidden things will be revealed to him" (Gospel of Thomas, Saying 108). Many Thomas scholars believe that the core of the Gospel of Thomas was

---

6. Larry Hurtado, *God in New Testament Theology* (Nashville: Abingdon Press, 2010, 43.

written earlier than the four gospels in the Bible. This saying from Thomas reflects the process of becoming like Jesus, which means to know, embrace, and live one's own humanity and divinity. We will experience Jesus' True Self, his Christ consciousness, as ours, also. Then we shall see things that were hidden from us before.

Others down through the ages who say that we are gods in the making

This is not a new idea in terms of church history. It was there right from the beginning of the church's reflection about divinity. Christian teachers down through the ages, using the male-oriented language of their culture, taught that our goal was to become and express our own divinity.

• Justin Martyr (100–165), also known as Saint Justin, was regarded as the foremost interpreter of the theory of the Logos in the second century. He explained that we all have the potential to become children of God and therefore gods: "It is demonstrated that all people are deemed worthy of becoming gods, and of having the power to become children of the Highest."[7]

• Irenaeus, bishop of Lyons (130–202) said that God "became what we are in order to make us what he is himself."[8] Irenaeus also wrote, "If the Word became a man, it was so men may become gods."[9]

• Athanasius (293–373), bishop of Alexandria for 45 years, declared, "He was incarnate that we might be made god."[10] This sentence, commonly translated as "God became man so that man might become God," was repeated so often that it became a Christian proverb.

---

7. St. Justin, *Dialogue with Trypho* 124.2.

8. Irenaeus, *Against Heresies*, Book 4, Chapter XXXVIII, https://carm.org/irenaeus-heresies4-1-20.

9. Clement of Alexandria, *Exhortation to the Heathen*, Chapter I, http://www.newadvent.org/fathers/0208.htm.

10. Athanasius, *On the Incarnation of the Word*, 54.3. Trans. John Behr (Yonkers: Saint Vladimir's Seminary Press, 2011), 167.

• St. Augustine (354–430) continued the proverb, "God became man, so that man might become God."[11]

• St. Symeon (949–1022), a monk canonized by the Easter Orthodox Church, eloquently writes, "He who is God by nature converses with those whom he has made gods by grace, as a friend converses with his friends, face to face."[12]

• St. Thomas Aquinas (1225-1274), Italian Dominican friar, Catholic priest, and Doctor of the Church stated, "The Only-begotten Son of God, wanting us to be partakers of his divinity, assumed our human nature so that, having become man, he might make men gods."[13] He summed up deification as "full participation in divinity which is humankind's true beatitude and the destiny of human life."[14]

• The Catechism of the Catholic Church says, "The only-begotten Son of God, wanting to make us sharers in his divinity, assumed our nature, so that he, made man, might make men gods."[15]

• The concept of *theosis* (becoming one with God) came under intense scrutiny and was, itself, the subject of bitter theological disputes, ultimately being declared orthodox and central to the teachings of the Eastern Orthodox Church.[16] The Orthodox Church, the second largest Christian group in the world, with an estimated 225–300 million adherents, has made becoming god, called deification or *theosis*, a central teaching. Eastern Orthodox scholar, Panayiotis

---

11. St. Augustine, Sermo 13 de Tempore, from The Office of Readings (Boston: St. Paul Editions, 1983), 125

12. Symeon Lash, "Deification" in *The Westminster Dictionary of Christian Theology*, ed. Alan Richardson and John Bowden (Philadelphia: Westminster Press, 1983), 147-48.

13. Aquinas, *Opusc.* 57:1-4, 128-129.

14. Aquinas, *Summa Theologiae* 3.1.2.

15. Kirby, *Article 460*.

16. Gama, Michael Paul, "Theosis: The Core of Our Ancient/Future Faith and Its Relevance to Evangelicalism at the Close of the Modern Era" (2014). Doctor of Ministry. Paper 74. ttp://digitalcommons.georgefox.edu/dmin/74.

Nellas writes, "The true greatness of man is not found in his being the highest biological existence, a 'rational' or 'political' animal, but in his being a 'deified animal,' in the fact that he constitutes a created existence 'which has received the command to become a god.'"[17]

Theosis is far less known in most Protestant and Catholic circles where a focus on sin and salvation have crowded it out. Quakers have kept a traditional emphasis on Christ as the "Inner Light," and Pentecostals and Charismatics are particularly aware of the indwelling of the spirit.

• Anglican and famous writer of fantasy and Christian thought, C. S. Lewis in *Mere Christianity* said,

> God said that we were "gods" and He is going to make good His words. If we let Him—for we can prevent Him if we choose—He will make the feeblest and filthiest of us into a god or goddess, dazzling, radiant, immortal creature, pulsating all through with such energy and joy and wisdom and love as we cannot now imagine . . . The process will be long and in parts very painful; but that is what we are in for.[18]

In *The Weight of Glory* he writes, "It is a serious thing to live in a society of possible gods and goddesses, to remember that the dullest and most uninteresting person you talk to may one day be a creature which, if you saw it now, you would be strongly tempted to worship. If we knew the depth of others we meet, we would worship them now rather than wait for heaven."[19]

In *The Grand Miracle* he pens (in the male language of his day), "Morality is indispensable: but the Divine Life, which gives itself to us and which calls us to be gods, intends for us something in which

---

17. Panayiotis Nellas, *Deification in Christ: Orthodox Perspectives on the Nature of the Human Person* (Crestwood, New York: St. Vladimir's Seminary, 1987), 30.

18. C. S. Lewis, *Mere Christianity* (New York: Harper Collins, 1952), 174-5.

19. C. S. Lewis, *The Weight of Glory* (New York: Harper Collins, 1976), 45-6.

morality will be swallowed up. We are to be remade. . . . we shall find underneath it all a thing we have never yet imagined: a real man, an ageless god, a son of God, strong, radiant, wise, beautiful, and drenched in joy."[20]

I conclude these quotes from C. S. Lewis with his arresting words, "God said to this hairless monkey, 'Get on with it, become a god!'"[21]

On the other hand, the Bible claims we are *already* gods

The Bible also claims that we are *already* gods even while we are becoming gods, learning to manifest that which is already true. Deification does not mean that we only have a divine nature, but that like Jesus, we are both human and divine at the same time. This is not a future hope but a present reality that needs to be embraced and manifested. We only need to sink down or rest into it. I call it "resting as God."

Divinity from the very beginning

The first words of the Bible say that we have already been created in the image and likeness of God. "Then God said, 'Let us make humankind in our image, to be like us . . . .' So God created humankind in God's image, in the image of God they were created; male and female God created them" (Gen. 1:26, 27). This magnificently states the essential divinity of human beings. This is not something to be attained in the future. It is always a present reality.

Conservative evangelical theologian Robert Rakestraw defines *theosis* by saying, "Above all, theosis is the restoration and reintegration of the 'image' or, as some prefer, 'likeness' of God, seriously distorted by the fall, in the children of God."[22] But here is the question I have:

---

20. C. S. Lewis, *The Grand Miracle* (New York: Ballantine, 1986), 85.

21. C. S. Lewis, *A Grief Observed* (New York: Harper, 2009), 42.

22. Robert V. Rakestraw, "Becoming Like God: An Evangelical Doctrine of Theosis," *Journal of the Evangelical Theological Society*, June 1997, 257-269. http://www.etsjets.org/files/JETS-PDFs/40/40-2/40-2-pp257-269_JETS.pdf.

How can the image of God be *restored* in us so that we become "divine" if that image is not already there within us? "Restoration and reintegration" are about making newly visible what is already there. It is true that that image has "fallen" or been covered over by our egoic self. So there is restoration work to be done. It is the work of becoming who we are. It is NOT becoming who we are not. When you restore something, you return it to its original shape. You don't turn it into something else.

When God and the serpent in Eden agreed

In the metaphysical story in Genesis, both the serpent and God considered the eating of the tree of knowledge of good and evil not as the "fall of humankind," but as becoming *more* like God! The serpent said, "God knows well that on the day you eat it, your eyes will be opened, and *you will be like gods*, knowing good and evil" (Gen. 3:5, italics mine). Of course, they were already like God, "made in the image and likeness of God" (Gen. 1:26). We might be suspicious of the serpent's statement given the source. However, after eating, sure enough, God acknowledges that, even more so, we are "like gods," with, "Look—*these humans have become like one of us*, knowing good and evil" (Gen. 3:22, italics mine). Now they were gods who were grown up enough to now discern the difference between good and evil.

We traditionally read the story of Adam and Eve as how we did one wrong thing and God punished us forever. But what if, as Rabbi Harold Kushner says, this is the story of emergence, of the evolution of humans from animals.[23] All animals feel pain, but only humans feel the looming dread, frustration, and betrayal at levels animals will never know. Remember it's a story about trying to explain a way of looking at life, not a literal happening.

I agree with Rabbi Kushner that when God told Adam not to eat of the forbidden tree it was a warning, like the person telling a friend in

---

23. Harold Kushner, *How Good Do We Have to Be* (New York: Back Bay Books, 1997).

line for a promotion, "You know, if you get that job, you'll have more responsibility and stress than you ever dreamed of. It will be terrible. Are you sure you want that?" It seems to me that God wanted us to move on up from the realm of animals to the realm of humankind. And then, with Jesus, invited us to move on up from being aware of our belonging to the realm of humankind to becoming aware of belonging to the Realm of God.

Did you know that in the entire Bible, the story of Adam and Eve eating of the tree of knowledge of good and evil is never, ever, not even once, referred to as a sin? In this light, Eve, rather than being sinful, is incredibly brave as she moves on to be the first to eat of fruit to further our evolution. The woman was not a villain but a hero. She should be hailed as a pioneer. But then we all know about pioneers. Like Eve they are persecuted, reviled, and blamed. In Genesis, underneath the details of trying to explain why life is so difficult, is the story of the evolution of our earth as it took form, our bodies as they came to be filled with life, and our souls as we became even more like God.

Already made in the divine image

Later on, again using the "image of God" metaphor, Colossians 1:15 says that Jesus "is the image of the invisible God." As Genesis says, we are also images of the invisible God. The difference is that it is easily seen in Jesus but not as much in us because we have yet to disidentify with our ego and embrace and manifest our divinity as fully as Jesus did.

The Reign of God is within you—right now!

Like our divinity, the message by Jesus to the Pharisees in Luke 17:21 was, "The Reign of God is within you." This Reign of God is not slowly coming into us or waiting to come in the future. The Reign of God is already within us here and now! It is also true that it needs to be recognized and embraced which is a process.

Jesus sides with heresy: You are a god right here and now!

I again list Jesus' astonishing quote from Psalm 82 in these biblical passages declaring that we and God are one: "You are gods" (John 10:34). Raimon Panikkar comments on this passage, saying, "Neither does he [Jesus] minimize his answer; on the contrary, he is exacerbating it as he dares to propose a 'blasphemous' exegesis of a Hebrew psalm, 'You are Gods'" (82:6).[24] Later, in his *The Experience of God*, Panikkar emphasizes. "I am not assuming a dialectical position when I assert that I have no hesitation in saying 'I am God'— because God has said 'I am Man.' That would be wrong. What I am doing, rather, is describing my own experience in an intimate, personal way."[25]

Knowing yourself as a child of God/She

In the Gospel of Thomas Jesus says, "When you know yourselves you will understand that you are children of the living *Abba* God" (Saying 3). This is another reference to the "like parent, like child" imagery of Psalm 82:6. "I say, 'You are gods, *children* of the Most High, all of you.'" Jesus was saying, "Really know yourself, and then you will know that you are already the divine child of the Divine Parent."

We are to be like Jesus now, not later

Paul writes, "Just as we have borne the image of the one of earth, let us also bear the image of the one of heaven" (1 Cor. 15:49). This is an exhortation to embrace our divine image as Jesus did in the here and now.[26]

---

24. Raimon Panikkar, *The Experience of God, Icons of the Mystery* (Minneapolis: Augsburg Books, 2006), 107.

25. Ibid., 137.

26. This text is more often translated "we will bear the image" even though the better texts support "let us" aorist active subjective, rather than the "we will" future active indicative as in NET, HCSB, and D-R translations. The UBS Textual Committee preferred the "we will" text reading despite the poorer manuscript evidence that supports it because they said the passage is a teaching passage, not

We are participants in the divine nature

"Through these God has given us God's very great and precious promises, so that through them you may participate in the divine nature, having escaped the corruption in the world caused by evil desires" (2 Pet. 1:4 NIV).[27] This is a neglected or ignored passage in Western Christianity but a central tenet of the Eastern Orthodox Church. Unfortunately, there it is interpreted as something only for the future and not a present reality in our lives. However, notice that it is corruption in *this* world we escape from. Therefore, this participation in the divine nature is also in *this* world and available as a present reality, not something waiting for us after this world. However, it is also a reality that must be acknowledged and manifested which is the process of waking up to what is real and true. Our participation in the divine nature means that God participates in our human nature! Is your God you enough?

Joint heirs

"We are joint heirs with Christ" (Rom. 8:17). Notice that we are *already* joint heirs with Christ. A "joint heir" means that all the heirs get the same thing. It means that what Christ gets we get. Everything will be divided up between all of us, and Jesus' share is no bigger than ours! We say, "Oh no, not joint heirs. Jesus gets the whole estate and all the fortune, and all that we get is to be with him, and maybe a small monthly allowance." However, we are now, and have always been, divine. All that the creeds say about Jesus is also true about us.

---

an exhortation. This appears to a theological decision rather than a textual one. http://web.ovc.edu/terry/tc/lay161co.htm.

27. Rather than "*may* (genēsthe) *participate* in the divine nature" as the NIV translates, the NRSV has, "may *become* (genēsthe) *participants* of the divine nature (italics mine)." Matthew 5:45 in the NRSV γένησθε (genēsthe) is translated "that you may *be* children of your heavenly Father (italics mine)." The Greek word γένησθε (genēsthe) has the sense of both be and becoming in the eight passages where it is found in the New Testament. Translators may be influenced by theological considerations of whether the divine nature is present now or later, or present now and also in process which is my understanding.

We are truly joint heirs. Jesus is what we are even though we have yet to fully realize it or express it. The goal of the spiritual path is to consciously realize and express our divinity. I saw someone wearing a T-shirt that said, "I found it!" When I asked what that meant, the man said that it meant he had found God. I want a T-shirt that says, "I never lost it! But I do keep forgetting where I put it."

We are divine light

Another image of our divinity is seen in the use of the metaphor of "light." Jesus said, "I am the light of the world" (John 18:22). He also declared, "You are the light of the world" (Matt 5:14). Jesus said he was the light of the world, and so are we. John teaches us that Jesus is the "true light that enlightens everyone" (John 1:9). Paul says we are like mirrors that not only reflect God's bright light, but which are transformed into the same light which they reflect (2 Cor. 3:17-18). We share in the same light as Jesus.

We have come from the light

In another reference to our association with the divine light, Jesus says, "If they say to you, 'Where have you come from?' say to them, 'We have come from the light, from the place where the light came being by itself, established itself, and appeared in their image'" (Gospel of Thomas, Saying 50). Do you remember the last time someone asked you where you were from? What would have happened if you had said, "I'm from the light?" and the response was, "Why do you say such an odd thing like that?" You could, of course, give a completely sincere, honest response: "Because Jesus told me to!" However, I'll be the first to admit that's an outstanding way to stop a conversation dead in its tracks. On the other hand, it's a very good thing to remind ourselves and others of quite often. Occasionally I have said, "I've got two answers to that question. There's the geographical one and then the spiritual one." Usually the other person says they would like to hear both, and we then have a conversation that's about who we really are.

God being us means we can do great things

Jesus said, "The one who believes in me will also do the works that I do and, in fact, will do greater works than these" (John 14:12). We can only do the works of Jesus if we are like Jesus. Jesus' works were God's works, in other words, God being Jesus. Our being Jesus or "little Christs" is God being us. He did not say whoever is especially gifted or unique will do my works but those who believe in him. "Oh, not me," we say. We have never and could never do greater works than Jesus." But if it is not you and me doing these works, then who was Jesus talking about? How many of us have even considered such a thing? That's how strongly we have been taught to think that being a god like Jesus would be impossible. Of course, "greater" works does not always mean famous, or great in the eyes of others. God is our only audience and the only one who gets to decide what great is. I'll settle for that!

God's children are like God, both now and in the future

The writer of 1 John declares, "We are God's children now but what we are to be in the future has not yet been made manifest; what we do know is that when it is made manifest we shall be like God because we shall see God as God really is." (1 John 3:2).

Remember that being a son or daughter of God/She in the Bible is being an offspring of God, one who carries the divine image and likeness of their heavenly Mother/Father. It is a core belief of original Christianity that our True Self is already divine and our journey here is to realize, embrace, and manifest that divinity for the healing of the world. Accepting this will result in leaving behind the traditional Western Church's focus on sin and sinners in order to regain the biblical focus on the goodness of creation and the motivation to discover the sacred reality within.

Not me within, but the divine Christ

"It is no longer I who live, but it is [the Divine Cosmic] Christ who lives in [and as] me. And the life I now live in the flesh I live by faith in the Jesus who loved me and gave himself for me" (Gal. 2:20). As the writer of Colossians says, "we are hidden with Christ in God" (Col.3:3).

Others who say that we are already gods

Mystics, saints, and scholars down through the ages have said that our divinity is a present reality. They did this even with heresy charges looming over them. In some places and times, it meant going to prison or being killed. Today it can mean losing your position in a seminary or in your church as a minister.

• Clement (150–215) was a teacher and theologian in Alexandria, considered the "brain" of early Christianity. He was the head of the Christian "catechetical" school, an early Christian university or seminary, where new Christians were taught about Christianity. Clement wrote, "From the beginning you have been *immortal* . . . If one knows himself, he will know God, and knowing God will *become* like God."[28] Even though we are "immortal" from the beginning, we still need to "become" like God. Therefore, he holds that we become what we already are.

• Augustine of Hippo (354–430), was an early Christian theologian and philosopher whose writings influenced the development of Western Christianity and Western philosophy. He boldly wrote, "But he himself that justifies also deifies, for by justifying he makes us sons of God. 'For he has given them power to become the sons of God' [referring to John 1:12]. If then we have been made sons of god, we have also been made gods."[29] Notice the connection made again that if we are now "sons of god" then we are

---

28. Peter Kirby, *Early Christian Writings*, "Jesus Theories," 2016. 26 Nov. 2016, Clement, Strom IV 89. (italics mine). http://www.earlychristianwritings.com/text/clement-stromata-book4.html.

29. *Nicene and Post-Nicene Fathers*, First Series, Vol. 8, ed., Philip Schaff, trans., J. E. Tweed. (Buffalo: Christian Literature Publishing Co., 1888) Augustine On the Psalms, 50.2. (italics mine).

already made gods. Another time he exclaimed, "Let us applaud and give thanks that we have become not only Christians but Christ himself. Do you understand, my brothers, the grace that God our head has given us? Be filled with wonder and joy—*we have become veritable Christs!*"[30] If we are a Christ, then we are God Being Us like Jesus was God Being Us.

• Theologian Gregory of Nyssa (335–395), venerated as a saint in Roman Catholicism, Eastern Orthodoxy, Oriental Orthodoxy, Lutheranism, and Anglicanism said, "Since the God who was manifested infused Himself into perishable humanity for this purpose, that by this communion with Deity mankind might *at the same time be deified*, for this end it is that, by dispensation of His grace, He disseminated Himself in every believer."[31]

• St. Maximus the Confessor (580–662) was a Christian monk, theologian, and scholar. He advocated both being divine and becoming divine as he wrote, "The divine and blessed love will embrace God and manifest the *one who loves God to be God himself* … Love deifies. It unites us to God and *makes us gods*. The mystery of love which out of human beings makes us gods … Let us become the image of the one whole God, bearing nothing earthly in ourselves, so that we may consort with God and become gods, receiving from God our existence as gods."[32] Notice he speaks of both being and becoming: the one who loves is "God himself" and also we become gods.

• John of Ruusbroec (1293–1381) was a Flemish priest and mystic, beatified in 1908 by Pope St. Pius. "Writing on the contemplative life, he says, "To comprehend and understand God as he is in himself,

30. *Catechism of the Catholic Church*, St. Augustine of Hippo, 795. (italics mine). http://ccc.usccb.org/flipbooks/catechism/index.html#4.

31. St Gregory of Nyssa, *The Great Catechism, Complete*, trans., W. Moore and H. A. Wilson, 37, (italics mine). http://www.elpenor.org/nyssa/great-catechism.asp.

32. Love in the Writings of St. Maximus the Confessor. http://www.sthermanoca.org/documents/Fr.%20Johns%20Papers/St_Maximus_Love.pdf and http: // christianmystics.com/contemporary/BrianRobertson/LiknessOfGod.html. (italics mine).

above and beyond all likenesses, is *to be God with God*, without intermediary or any element of otherness which could constitute an obstacle or impediment."[33]

• Catherine of Genoa (1447–1510) was an Italian saint and mystic of the Catholic Church. She boldly penned, "*My me is God*, nor do I recognize any other me except my God Himself," and "*My being is God*, not by some simple participation but by a true transformation of my being."[34]

• Meister Eckhart said many remarkable things about our here and now divinity:

> *Between that person and God there is no distinction, and they are one.* . . . Their knowing *is* one with God's knowing, their activity with God's activity and their understanding with God's understanding.[35]

> In the ground of reality *there is absolute identity between God and the soul.*[36]

> . . . therefore, I *am* my own first cause, both of my eternal being and of my temporal being. To this end I was born, and *by virtue of my birth being eternal, I shall never die.* It is of the nature of this eternal birth that I have been eternally that I *am now*, and shall be forever. . . In my eternal birth . . . I was my own first cause as well as the first cause of everything else.[37]

---

33. James A. Wisemann, O.S.B. (1990), "The Autotheistic sayings of the Mystics," *Theological Studies* 51 (1990), 233. (italics mine).

34. Ibid.

35. DW 40, Sermon 11, Davies. (italics mine).

36. *Meister Eckhart and the Beguine Mystics; Hadewijch of Brabant, Mechthild of Magdeburg, and Marguerite Porete*, ed., Bernard McGinn, (Bloomsbury, New Jersey: Bloomsbury Academic, 1997), 12. (italics mine).

37. *Meister Eckhart: A Modern Translation*, trans., Raymond Blackney (New York: Harper, 1942), 231. (italics mine).

God has given birth to the Son as you, as me, as each one of us. As many beings, as many gods in God. In my soul, God not only gives birth to me as His son, *He gives birth to me as Himself, and Himself as me.* My physical father is my father with but a small part of his being, and I live my life separate from him. He may be dead, and I may live. God, however, is my father with His entire being, and *I am never separate from Him.*

I am *always* His; I am alive only because He is alive. In this divine birth I find that *God and I are the same: I am what I am and what I shall remain, now and forever.* I am carried above with the highest angels. I neither increase nor decrease, for in this birth I have become the motion-less cause of all that moves. I have won back *what has always been mine.* Here, in my own soul, the greatest of all miracles has taken place—God has returned to God![38]

The eye with which I see God *is* the same with which God sees me. *My eye and God's eye is one eye, and one sight, and one knowledge, and one love.*[39]

Between God and the soul there is no distance.[40] . . . *Between that person and God there is no distinction, and they are one* . . . Their knowing *is* one with God's knowing, their activity with God's activity and their understanding with God's understanding.[41]

---

38. *Meister Eckhart,* trans., Frantz Pfeiffer and C de B Evans (London: John M. Watkins, 1924), Vol. 1: 221-222, 287, and Vol. 2: 41, 114. (italics mine).

39. *Meister Eckhart's Sermons,* Sermon IV, True Hearing, Christian Classics Ethereal Library, (32-33) http://www.ccel.org/ccel/eckhart/sermons.vii.html.

40. Models of God and Alternative Ultimate Realities, Jeanine Diller and Asa Kasher, Part XI, *Meister Eckhart's God* by Dietmar Mieth (New York: Springer, 2013) 801-810. (italics mine).

41. Meister Eckhart, Sermon DW 40. (italics mine). http://www.pantheism.net/paul/history/eckhart.htm.

• Father Richard Rohr writes, "In truth, we must change our very self-image rather than just be told some new things to see or do. To be a Christian is to objectively know that *we share the same identity that Jesus enjoyed as both human and divine*, which is what it means to 'follow' him. In fact, I believe that this is the whole point of the Gospel and the Incarnation!"[42]

Why Christians often resist embracing their divinity

The most common argument against our divinity is that we cannot possibly be divine because of the vast difference between God as Creator and us as the created. This view contradicts the previous statements from the Bible and church history.

Eastern Orthodoxy posits a scholarly argument by saying we are not God in God's transcendent essence, but we can be God in God's energy or his activity. We cannot be the uncreated God. We do not become the same as or identical to God. In that sense I concur but I put it into a different framework. We are a god like Jesus was a god. This is what I mean by saying we are one with God but not the same as God. The uncreated God is what Tillich calls "God above God" and "God beyond God." I agree. Jesus was one with God but not identical to God. I will explore this more fully in Chapter 14 where we look at the meaning of not two but not one, or what is called nonduality.

Becoming what we already are

Do we become gods in the future or is it a present reality that needs to be realized and manifested? It seems to me both streams of thought exist in the Bible and church history. Rather than choose one side over the other, I integrate them as I believe Jesus did. *Following Jesus is about becoming who we already are deep inside.* Traditional Christianity is often about works, trying hard to change, albeit by God's grace. A more evolved and biblical understanding is that Christianity is about becoming who we already are—the light

---

42. Richard Rohr's Daily Meditation, Wednesday, April 6, 2016, (italics mine).

of the world, the image of God, participants in the divine nature, and also in need of restoration, realization, and manifestation.

Therefore, being and becoming are both true about our divinity. Being a god is both being and becoming at the same time. It is a process of becoming what we already are as our True Self. We are, in Jesus' words, a light covered over by a bushel basket which is full of our mistaken identity. This mistaken identification with ego keeps distracting us from our true divine identity. Just as your photo is not you, so your ego is not you. There is work to be done over the years to recognize, embrace, and manifest that which is already present. The process lies in recognizing the reality, embracing it, and manifesting it in the world through our spiritual gifts. This is the ancient idea of *theosis* but freed from the limitations of the reductionist presupposition that we cannot be divine children of God now.

We see being and becoming when Jesus told sinners they were already forgiven by God without their having to ask for that forgiveness. He also said to ask for forgiveness in order to become forgiven. Both are true and come to the front at different times and stages in our lives.

"On that day you will know that I am in the Father, and you in me, and I in you" (John 14:20). Jesus's union with the Father was a here and now reality which we will know, according to Jesus most fully on "that day." In the same way, our union with Jesus is also a here and now reality which we will know most fully "on that day."

Some are concerned that all this talk of union with God blurs the distinction between Creator and creation. However, in Jesus and God we see complete union without a loss of Jesus' individual identity. This is the point of our own union with God. We are one, yet we maintain our identity. It is not a simple reality which is easily available to the mind. It's not available to the mind at all! We can only approach it with our words. The most beautiful example is when Jesus said, "The Father-Mother and I are one." He really meant "One," yet it was clear that he was not the Father-Mother and the Father-Mother was not him. We are gods, yet God is still God and we are still us.

Why it is important to know that your God is you enough

Jesus changed the idea of what it means to be human. For those of us who see him as the prototype of the New Human Being, we see now that being fully human is now also being fully divine. Our divinity is not immediately apparent, just as Jesus' was not always obvious. It has to emerge over the years from its ego-building stage that is necessary for survival in the first part of life. Jesus' vision quest in his temptation in the wilderness was a key step in his own transcending his own ego in order to find a deeper and transcendent identity as a divine child of God.

Jesus wasn't born with a grown-up worldview but as Luke (2:52) says, "He grew in wisdom and stature" in order to begin to see the religious and social limitations of his culture that needed discarding. We see him making unusual progress at age twelve as some precocious kids do. Ultimately, in his brief three plus decades of life, he himself became the revolutionary breakthrough in what being fully human and fully divine looks like. His early followers became convinced that God had made him the Christ, the living blueprint and cosmic symbol for the seamless unity of divine, human, and material reality. They responded to his earthly friendship and then his spiritual friendship after the resurrection by personally giving him the same devotion they gave to God. They looked at the heart of Jesus and saw the heart of God—and it transformed them.

Jesus had a God that was beyond him, beside him, and being him as his deepest True Self. He moved fully between all three perspectives with ease, never losing the reality of any of them. He invites us to do the same by having a God that is big enough, close enough, and you enough.

How do you know your God is you enough?

You know God is you enough if:

1. You more and more sense that deep within you there is a true Self that is made in the very image and likeness of God.

2. You see yourself as a piece of God that is as fully God as a drop of ocean water is fully ocean water although it is not all of the ocean.

3. You find yourself in growing agreement with such statements as Father Keating's, "The plan is to be God in the most humble way."

4. You begin to experience expanded states of awareness where you rest in the vast, blissful, spaciousness of simply being.

5. You see that the deepest message of Jesus was that he was one with God and we are no different than him in that respect.

6. You identify more and more with Jesus in both his humanity and his divinity.

This is not *reflecting about* God or *relating* to God—this is *resting* as God!

Summary of Part Three: Is Your God You Enough?

• There are many places in the Bible that refer to our divinity, or God-being-us.

• God-being-us is both an on-going process and also a present reality. We are both becoming divine while we are already divine.

• The Bible and Christians down through the centuries and today say both: We are becoming divine and we are already divine.

• Many Christians and Christian groups resist seeing God being us, not understanding how crucial it is to God's plan and Jesus' teaching and model.

Questions for Reflection and Group Discussion

1. On a scale of one ("I don't believe it") to ten ("I completely believe it"), where are you in believing your deepest Self is divine as described in this chapter?

2. Using the same scale where are you in an inner sensing or knowing your divinity identity?

3. Is there any part of this chapter that helped you come to believe or sense this in a greater way? If so, which part?

4. How does your light or greatness frighten you?

5. The one purpose of every authentic spiritual path and religion is to lead you to ever new experiences of your Divine True Self that transform and integrate your life, leading to becoming a more loving person. If your religion does not do this, it is junk religion. If your spiritual path does not do this, it is junk spirituality. The goal of life is to know who we are and manifest that in the world. Who are we? We are gods. How would your life change if you embraced this more fully?

Practices

1. Resting as God begins with the simple feeling of being. Richard Miller's column in *Yoga Journal* offers the following practice of the feeling of being:

> Take a moment to relax your jaw, eyes, shoulders, arms and hands, torso, hips, and legs and feet. Then rest your attention on the sensations created by the gentle expansion and release of your belly as breath comes into and flows out of your body. As you're resting here, between two thoughts or two breaths, notice where and how you experience the sensation of being. You may experience being as an internal feeling of warmth, or presence in your belly, heart, or other parts of your body. Keep your attention on these sensations as you read the following terms commonly used to describe being. Do any of these words describe your experience? Peaceful—calm—loving—secure—heart-centered—grounded—connected—spacious—well-being. . . .

Write down words that best describe your sense of being.

Being is natural to all of us, yet most people never take the time to simply experience the presence and aliveness of being. Doing this opens a doorway for you to feel unchanging inner peace, calm, equanimity, groundedness, security, joy, compassion, and love. This is because when you're present, negative thoughts and feelings turn off.[43]

2. Take fifteen seconds to rest in your natural state of being. For these few seconds give up trying to change anything. Let go of everything. Just be. See what happens.

3. Close your session with this Three Faces of God devotion.

"God beyond me, in whom I live and move, and have my being."

("God beyond us, in whom we live and move, and have our being.")

"God beside me, you are always with me."

("God beside us, you are always with us.")

"God being me, I am the light of the world."

("God being us, we are the light of the world.")

---

43. http://www.yogajournal.com/article/health/meditation-tap-sense-unchaning-well-being/.

"God being me"

CHAPTER 9

The Spectrum of Spirit as Consciousness

The man said to me, "Okay, you've convinced me against all odds that I'm a divine human being. I'm a god. Yikes, that sounds ridiculous! Now, so what? What's that got to do with my life?" Even though the idea still sounded ridiculous to him, he was thinking about it for the first time. I shared with him some of what follows here in these next seven chapters. The answer to his question is found within us in our own inner consciousness according to the Bible, the scriptures of other religions, the mystics of many traditions, and a growing number of scientists. It comes from the inside out. It is what Jesus and the Bible call "spirit" and I call "consciousness."

In this chapter I want to begin by showing how opening our inner identity to God-being-us is focused on the spectrum of spirit as consciousness. This is an experiential map. I will end Part Three by putting this experiential map together with the theological map of the classical Trinity of God, Jesus, and spirit. First, the map of spirit as the experience of consciousness in the Bible.

Consciousness in the Bible has four primary expressions

1. Basic consciousness. God says, "I will put my spirit (*rûach*) within you and you shall live" (Ezekiel 37:6). We can say, "I am alive and aware. I go about my day aware of seeing, hearing, feeling, sensing, touching the material world around me."

2. Awakened consciousness: "Jesus said to them, 'Receive holy spirit-breath'" (John 20:22).

We can say, "I am extra aware and now awake to spiritual realities. I sense the presence of God and Jesus. I am having higher levels of insight, wisdom, intuition, and paranormal events of spiritual reality. This is amazing."

3. Transcendent consciousness: Jesus said, "God and I are one . . . . You are gods" (John 10:30, 34). We can say, "I am awesomely aware of God-being-me as a vast, empty mind and an overflowing, blissful heart. When I rest in my deepest Self, I rest as God-being-me."

4. Oneness conscious: Jesus said, "May they be one, as you, *Abba* God, are in me and I am in you, may they also be in us" (John 17:21). We can say, "Now, instead of thinking of people as separate from God and one another, I see no separation. I see *from* Oneness—so I only see Oneness!"

The Bible is so obviously a record of these kinds of mystical consciousness that only eighteen hundred years of institutionalized religion could have obscured that fact. It becomes evident as we take away the stained glass lens when reading the Bible and see that these paranormal events are the motivating heart of the Bible's writers and writings. The actions and teaching themselves came from awakened and transcendent spiritual events and consciousness.

Four introductory points about spirit

Here are the four basic beginning points about spirit from Chapter Three which are the foundation of these next chapters. If they don't look familiar, you may want to review them again in that chapter.

1. God is infinite spirit.

2. Spirit is both human and divine at the same time.

3. Spirit is given to all living persons.

4. Spirit is consciousness.

The human side of divine-human consciousness in ten sentences

1. Consciousness is where you live on the inside of you, the inside life of human bodily experience, including our thoughts, feelings, intentions, values, memories, and sense of self.

2. Consciousness is a universal energy field beyond time and space, an aspect of God expressed as life itself.

3. God's spirit as consciousness already pervades every area of our lives.

4. You and I are divine infinite consciousness having a human experience!

5. Spirit in and as us often appears to move through evolving stages from basic consciousness to awakened consciousness, to transcendent consciousness, and finally to Oneness consciousness.

6. Every event of expanded consciousness is shaped and interpreted by one's worldview and stage of spiritual development.

7. Recognizing spirit-breath, both God's and ours, as consciousness, brings new light not only to Christians but all those interested in the inner path of the world's great religious traditions.

8. The experience of expanded consciousness brings new insight, wisdom, clarity, and the validation that higher consciousness is real.

9. When your awareness expands enough, God appears—at first as the Beloved Other, and then as your deepest Self!

10. Divine-human consciousness is God having a "me" experience while I am having a "God" experience!

Consciousness is more than just awareness

There is much debate today in trying to define consciousness. Some say that consciousness is simply awareness. It is like a mirror that only reflects what it sees as a radio only transmits what it receives. However, as we have seen, in the Bible consciousness is much more than awareness. In the Hebrew Scriptures it is the gift of life or human consciousness received from God at its basic level. In the New Testament it becomes the "more" life of intensified consciousness that allows us to be aware of spiritual realities.

Spirit as consciousness in the Bible is the divine energy field of loving, creative intent. The more conscious we are, the more we can float in this infinite sea of sacred energy. Historian of religion, philosopher, and professor at the University of Chicago Mircea Eliade (1907 –1986) was a leading interpreter of religious experience. He wrote, "the 'sacred' is an element in the structure of consciousness."[1]

David Hart Bentley says, "Consciousness does not merely passively reflect the reality of the world; it is necessarily a dynamic movement of reason and will toward reality."[2]

Jorge Ferrer says, "Mystical awareness is not an . . . objectless consciousness experienced by 'the regular me' which can pass unnoticed or be easily forgotten. On the contrary, mystical PCEs [pure consciousness experiences] are pregnant with deep meaning, blissful and ecstatic feelings, and usually involve a drastic transformation of individual consciousness whose occurrence is hardly unnoticed or forgotten. . . . Likewise, what most Christian mystics report is not an inconspicuous experience of their own contentless consciousness, but a sublime and awesome participation in or union with God's divine Being."[3]

1. Jeffrey J. Kripal, *Authors of the Impossible: The Paranormal and the Sacred* (Chicago: University of Chicago Press, 2011), 255.
2. Hart, *The Experience of God*, 238.
3. Ferrer, *Revisioning Transpersonal Theory*, 225.

In the Bible and many religious traditions, spirit is a description of being alive, expanded awareness, transcendence, joy, and peace.

The Apostle Paul writes about consciousness

There is a beautiful passage in one of Paul's authentic letters[4] to the church at Corinth where he unfolds this whole idea of divine-human consciousness which the Greek word "spirit-breath" (*pneuma*) encompasses. Notice that a deeper understanding opens up when we remove the capitalization of spirit that makes a dualistic distinction between our spirit and God's spirit. There is a seamless, inseparable melding of divine and human consciousness. I will comment separately on each of the four sentences of this passage by Paul to make reading them easier.

"For the spirit (consciousness) searches all things, even the deep things of God" (1 Cor. 2:10). The "deep things" (βάθος) of God refers to what God is in vast, hidden beingness.[5] This can be seen as divine infinite consciousness.

"For who among us knows the things of a person except the spirit (consciousness) of a person that is within?" (2:11). The "things of a person" in parallel to the "things of God," refers to what a person is deeply. This is our innermost consciousness. Hence, spirit or consciousness is the awareness of our own vast, hidden, beingness.

So also no one comprehends the things of God except the spirit (consciousness) of God (2:11b). The only way to comprehend spiritual reality is through sensitized, numinous consciousness.

Now we have not received the spirit (consciousness) of the world, but the spirit (consciousness) that is from God, so that we may know the things that

---

4. Many scholars today believe that 1 Thessalonians, Galatians, Philemon, Philippians, 1 & 2 Corinthians, and Romans were written by Paul while the later letters were written in his name by others. There are significant differences between these two sets of letters. Paul advocates liberation in his writings, while these elements are missing in these later more conservative letters.

5. Βάθος—depth, hiddenness, vastness, being. TDNT Vol. 1, 516.

are freely given to us by God (2:12). Paul speaks of the basic, everyday dimension of consciousness by calling it the "consciousness of the world." It is, in reality, consciousness of the material, concrete world. However, he seems to have forgotten that this everyday consciousness which his Hebrew Scriptures emphasize, is the life of God's breath within us and also God's spirit as us. He and the other writers of the New Testament are caught up with contrasting the power and glory of the higher realms of consciousness with basic, everyday concrete consciousness. So much so that they leave behind the richness and depth of their Hebrew scriptures' teaching that there is no distance between God's spirit and our normal, everyday spirit.

The New Testament almost exclusively focuses on the higher dimensions of awareness that are opened up when the believer's consciousness is awakened. Unfortunately today, much of the Christian tradition has forgotten this understanding and experience of intensified consciousness. It is only the mystics who have kept it alive. It is time now in the divine evolutionary scheme of things for awakened mystical consciousness to become a part of the normal Christian life.

The spectrum of consciousness in four modes

Jesus experienced at least four identifiable realms of consciousness. Mystics in all of the world's great religious traditions down through the centuries have pointed to various distinguishable states of consciousness using various names for them. Eastern traditions sometimes call them gross, subtle, causal, and nondual. I primarily call them basic, awakened, transcendent and Oneness consciousness. William James (1842–1910) was a physician, one of the most influential American philosophers, and called the Father of American psychology. Referring to mystical states, he says, "No account of the universe in its totality can be final which leaves these other forms of consciousness quite disregarded."[6] I will briefly introduce them here,

---

6. James, William, *The Varieties of Religious Experience*. (New York: Collier Books, Macmillan), 305.

and then later devote entire chapters to their unfolding.

1. Basic, everyday consciousness is the way we function in the physical world. It is how we hear the alarm go off in the morning and read a book at night before we go to sleep. It is how we know how to do our job, recognize our friends, know our feelings, and solve problems. You are most likely reading this sentence right now in what might be called normal or everyday consciousness, unless you are on drugs or are quite far along in realizing higher consciousness. Our basic consciousness includes our thoughts, feelings, intentions, values, memories, and sense of self. Consciousness is the inner life of human experience. For most of us, consciousness means an immediate experience of self. Consciousness is the inside of human experience. This everyday kind of consciousness is called "spirit" and "breath" in the Old Testament.

Basic awareness is also sacred. I only call it basic, ordinary, or everyday because it is the one we are most familiar with and the state we are in most of our waking hours. Of course, our everyday consciousness is far from ordinary. It is incredible and spectacular! It is vital to our high level of functioning in the world. However, by itself, basic consciousness is a relatively limited awareness in terms of the reality beyond the physical material realm. In basic awareness we only know reality as that which can be seen, heard, smelled, and touched by our ordinary senses.

Mindfulness

Basic consciousness ranges from barely enough awareness to keep us safe to deep, life-giving mindfulness. Our minimal awareness rushes us through our day only conscious enough of what is going on to get us up in the morning and function somewhat adequately in our daily tasks. When we begin to let ourselves become more deeply aware of our surroundings and our feelings we have moved into the richer dimension of the first of four states of awareness. This deeper state of everyday, basic awareness is often called mindfulness. Mindfulness is feeling aware. It is the basic state of awareness of thoughtful people who have cultivated a kind of centered consciousness while they are awake and going about their everyday activities. They are "mindful."

Mindfulness is a state of active, open attention on the present. When you're mindful, you observe your thoughts and feelings from a distance, without judging them good or bad. Instead of letting your life pass you by, mindfulness means living in the moment and awakening to experience.[7]

Mindfulness means maintaining a moment-by-moment awareness of our thoughts, feelings, bodily sensations, and the surrounding environment. Mindfulness also involves acceptance, meaning that we pay attention to our thoughts and feelings without judging them—without believing, for instance, that there's a "right" or "wrong" way to think or feel in a given moment. When we practice mindfulness, our thoughts tune into what we're sensing in the present moment rather than rehashing the past or imagining the future.[8]

2. Awakened Consciousness is beyond basic awareness. In the New Testament, the advent of awakened consciousness was so new, powerful, and widespread among Jesus' friends that it came to be regarded as the only expression of spirit-breath.

In awakened mystical consciousness we drop down into an inner world where we are immersed in God's loving presence and guidance in many forms. Here we wake up from the usual way that we see our story, our wounds, failures, and successes—and move into a larger world. There we are free of the limitations of the physical body and thinking mind, but still attached to needs, desires, and personality. Here people wake up to a new awareness of God. They begin to hear God's voice in a new way. Spiritual gifts are abilities that are especially opened up here. These states of consciousness are called by such names as trances, visions, non-ordinary, altered states, higher consciousness, deep prayer, meditative states, peak experiences, and subtle states of consciousness. This also includes glimpses and

---

7. https://www.psychologytoday.com/basics/mindfulness.

8. http://greatergood.berkeley.edu/topic/mindfulness/definition.

flashes of insight and wisdom that come to us as brief experiences of intensified awareness.

In awakened, mystical consciousness we become aware of the reality of diverse energies and non-physical forms such as intuition, the presence of God, wisdom, guidance, channeled words, healing energies, visions, and other luminous phenomena. This includes nonphysical entities such as Jesus, angels, transitioned loved ones, and spiritual guides.

Christianity was born in massive demonstrations of this mystical consciousness accompanied by deep feelings of ecstasy as reported by the participants. In awakened consciousness we do not relate to God as a principle but as a personal being, a non-physical, divine loving being with intent and consciousness. Concepts and principles are not aware of us, but the Intimate Face of God is. Here we relate as one being to another.

3. Transcendent Consciousness is the great I AM that is Infinite Being experienced within us as a vast and peaceful mind along with a loving and blissful heart. This moves our awareness beyond the awakened state with all its visions, sensations, feelings, and thoughts. We leave all these forms behind and move into a formless state of being that is sometimes called "emptiness" because it is a luminous darkness where our mind is empty and our heart is full. Here we rest in our inner divinity and "God's spirit (consciousness) bears witness to our spirit (consciousness) that we are children of God" (Rom. 8:16). This is the Apostle Paul's one-sentence explanation of how we move from a mere concept or belief to an inner knowing. Infinite divine consciousness "witnesses" to our divine-human consciousness that we are divine children of God. It is here, for the first time, that we have a sense of our own divinity.

Steve McIntosh, author and leader in the Integral philosophy movement, says it this way: "Our ability to recognize the presence of the infinite within the finite depends on the presence of the infinite within us. Succinctly stated, 'it takes the infinite to see the infinite.'"[9] In terms of this book, it is God, as the presence of Infinite Consciousness within us that sees God as Infinite Consciousness within us.

This is what Meister Eckhart refers to as, "The eye with which I see God is the same one with which God sees me."[10]

4. Oneness consciousness is seeing everything and everyone from the Presence of the Infinite.

The cover of this book is a portrayal of Oneness Consciousness. God as Infinite Consciousness is present within our finite bodies as us in the form of vast, spacious, transcendent awareness.

Then we look from this mind of (the Cosmic) Christ and see all of reality without separation experienced within us as seeing everything in seamless unity. This is not an altered state of awareness as the previous two are. Rather, it is viewing all the realms of reality without separation in the nondual consciousness that Jesus called the Reign of God. Paul says, "I live, not I but Christ lives in me." Since Christ is the Christian symbol for all of reality, this means we drop our identity with only one body, one journey, one reality and identify with everything that is. We see ourselves as one with the all.

David Bentley Hart says, "If God is the unity of infinite being and infinite consciousness, and the reason for the reciprocal transparency of finite being and finite consciousness each to the other, and the ground of all existence and all knowledge, then the journey toward him must also ultimately be a journey toward the deepest source of the self."[11]

---

9. Steve McIntosh, *The Presence of the Infinite: The Spiritual Experience of Beauty, Truth, and Goodness* (Wheaton: Theosophical Publishing House, 2015), 128.

10. *Meister Eckhart's Sermons*, Sermon IV, "True Hearing," Christian Classics Ethereal Library, (32-33) http://www.ccel.org/ccel/eckhart/sermons.vii.html.

11. Hart, *The Experience of God*, 324.

Science says we are the body;
Psychology says we are the emotions;
Academia says we are the mind;
Religion says we are the soul;
Advertisers say we are the consumer;
What are we?
We are consciousness!

Well-known Indian American author, public speaker, and prominent alternative medicine advocate Deepak Chopra discerningly says, "The reason that the average person cannot live the pure teachings of Jesus or Buddha is that these teachings depend upon higher consciousness."[12]

Summary of The Spectrum of Spirit as Consciousness

• We find these four modes of consciousness in the Bible and the lives of Jesus and mystics down through the centuries: basic, awakened, transcendent, and Oneness.

• Mindfulness is basic consciousness in a state of active, open attention on the present.

• Spirit as consciousness is more than awareness. It is the divine energy field of loving, creative intent.

Questions for Reflection and Group Discussion

1. The place to begin this journey into higher consciousness is to start by learning how to be mindful, the highly attentive form of basic everyday consciousness. On a scale of one to ten, with one not being very mindful to ten as mindfulness most of the time, where are you?

2. When did you first begin to think that there might be something more not just to know about, but to experience as higher consciousness in your spiritual journey?

---

12. Deepak Chopra, *The Future of God: A Practical Approach to Spirituality for Our Times* (Clarkson Potter/Ten Speed/Harmony. Kindle Edition), 118.

3. What parts, if any, of this chapter did you mark as interesting or questionable for you. If in a group setting, explain why.

Practices

A growing transforming practice while in everyday consciousness is called mindfulness. Mindfulness is the gentle effort to be continuously present with experience. Take one minute if by yourself or have the following read by someone to the group. Then be mindful as you sit in silence for one minute.

Here are a few key components of practicing mindfulness that Jon Kabat-Zinn identifies:

• Pay close attention to your breathing, especially when you're feeling intense emotions.

• Notice—really notice—what you're sensing in a given moment, the sights, sounds, and smells that ordinarily slip by without reaching your conscious awareness.

• Recognize that your thoughts and emotions are fleeting and do not define you, an insight that can free you from negative thought patterns.

• Tune into your body's physical sensations, from the water hitting your skin in the shower to the way your body rests in your chair.[13]

Close with signing the Three Faces of God as on page 28.

---

13. Adapted from "What is Mindfulness?" by Jon Kbat-Zinn http://greatergood. berkeley.edu/topic/mindfulness/definition.

"God being me."

CHAPTER 10

The Record of Awakened Consciousness (in the Bible)

The *New York Times* book section headline shouted, "The Burning Bush They'll Buy, but Not ESP or Alien Abduction." The reviewer, Mark Oppenheimer, said:

> Practically anything goes at the American Academy of Religion's annual conference, where scholars of dozens of religions convene annually to debate . . . nearly 5,000 people attended panels including "Seeking New Meanings of God and Dao" and "Madness, Smallpox, and Death in Tibet." What was almost impossible to find, at this orgy of intellectual curiosities, was discussion of the paranormal: ESP, premonitions, psychic powers, alien abduction and the like. This is a conference concerned with all sorts of supernatural and metaphysical claims. In panels, over coffee and during cocktail-hour quarrels, they talk of Moses at the burning bush, the virgin birth, Muhammad's journey on a winged horse. So why nothing about, say, mental telepathy?

The *Times* review of *Authors of the Impossible: The Paranormal and the Sacred* continued with,

> That is the question posed by Jeffrey J. Kripal, a professor of religion at Rice University in Houston and a renegade advocate for including the paranormal in religious studies. . . . Dr. Kripal 'leans toward' the paranormal — he does not dismiss it as the fruit of deluded minds. He thinks there is some external reality being talked about, something real out there. According to Dr. Kripal, their omission is evidence of a persistent bias among religion scholars, happy to consider the inexplicable, like miracles, as long as they fit a familiar narrative, like Judaism or Christianity.[1]

I agree with Dr. Kripal. These first seven chapters of Part Three are my contribution to a serious look at what some call "the paranormal" in the Bible, Christianity, and, hopefully, our lives. We have tried "normal" religion with mixed results. Time to try beyond normal—the way most religions began.

Do we read the Bible through the glasses of doctrine or experience?

Once the early creeds were in place by the fifth century, Christians were already reading the Bible through the lens of their doctrines. We began to forget that the doctrines came from the experiences. Even worse, we began to forget about the experiences all together. We did this by studying the experiences, extracting a set of beliefs from those spiritual experiences, sermonizing about the beliefs that came from the experiences, and then saying, "Oh, by the way, all that paranormal stuff only happened back then and not today." It seemed like a good rationale because that described exactly what

---

1. Mark Oppenheimer, "Beliefs," *New York Times* book review, Nov. 12, 2010. http://www.nytimes.com/2010/11/13/us/13beliefs.html?_r=0.

has happened. Less and less did the spiritual experiences occur, and more and more did Christianity become what you believed rather than what you sensed, heard, and saw in the numinous realm of altered consciousness. Sound familiar? However, the experiences didn't leave on their own. They were ushered out!

The creeds became what you needed to believe, and the clergy became who you needed to believe. The more the church became an organization and less the realized body of Christ, the fewer "Jesus" and "spirit" experiences there were. Christianity became a system of propositions rather than fostering the experiences which gave rise to those propositions. We began reading the Bible through the lens of later doctrines rather than through the lens of the originating spiritual experiences. As the years went by, most Christians stopped having any of original Christianity's "normal" events of intensified consciousness. Normal Christianity became abnormal by abandoning the mystical paranormal.

The unwritten belief about the spiritual experiences recorded in the Bible goes something like this:

> The spiritual experiences recorded in the Bible only happened in order to get to the doctrines. Now that we have the doctrines, we don't need any more experiences because God knew that more experiences would just confuse us about what we have already decided to believe.

That's the wrong conclusion!

The spiritual experiences left because it's easier to believe a few religious ideas than to go through the inner transformation needed to access the deeper experience. It is easier to hope the "professional" Christians know everything we need to know and will tell us about it. Even the professional Christians, the priests and clergy began to be preoccupied with what the right beliefs, behaviors, and rituals were. In addition, they often became preoccupied with how to keep the business called "church" funded and stable. This meant, above all else, don't rock the boat with anything new. We forgot that the new wine of mystical experience was recorded in the New Testament so that we could all continue to drink this superior wine in ever deeper and more evolved ways!

The best beliefs are beneficial and beautiful

Here in Part Three I do not mean to disparage beliefs since they have an important place in the spiritual journey. This book itself is a framework of beliefs that I have come to embrace as beneficial and beautiful. The benefit of liberating beliefs is in providing a healthy and encouraging context for our mystical journey. They give us a stable communal tradition and ethical context in which to ground our experience of God and spiritual realities. That means of course that our beliefs must have a place for the kind of spiritual experiences being detailed here. The higher our stage of development, the more adequate our beliefs will be for holding and interpreting the events of our states of consciousness. In the rest of this book we are going to continue to look at the Bible through the lens of the experiences of various evolving stages of worldview evolution and states of consciousness of the people in both Old and New Testaments. This is quite different from looking at the Bible through the lens of the beliefs that were themselves time-bound interpretations of those mystical experiences.

The drama of awakened mystical consciousness in the Old Testament

In Chapter Three we explored the Hebrew scriptures' account of an extra portion of spirit-breath or intensified awareness that came upon some of the Israelites' normal, everyday consciousness. The accounts of this awakened mystical consciousness usually focus on the dramatic outward responses to it, with fewer descriptions of the details of what was being experienced and how it felt. We should expect this as a result of reporting in pre-modern times. What was reported were outwardly observable phenomena rather than the extensive research going on today around the inner dimensions of mystical experience. So while these very dramatic experiences still occur, mystical consciousness is in no way limited to the outwardly dramatic. The dramatic is simply much easier to notice and describe than the more inner dimension of spiritual events. Note that there are fewer videos today of people sitting quietly in prayer in a Pentecostal church than of those dramatic ones where people are collapsing onto the floor in an altered state of awareness.

Awakened spirit-breath in the Hebrew scriptures

Here are a few more examples of intensified spirit-breath consciousness from the Old Testament accounts to remind us again what they looked and felt like. Imagine how you would respond if these things happened in your church or spiritual community. In Numbers 11:25-26 the helpers appointed by Moses to assist him in his work are to receive the same "spirit-breath" that he enjoyed— "the Lord took some of the spirit-breath that was upon him, and put it upon the seventy elders, and when the spirit-breath rested upon them they prophesied" (Num. 11:25-26).

As Samuel was anointing Saul to be ruler over Israel, he said, "The spirit-breath of the Lord will rush upon you, and you will join the prophets in their prophetic state and will be changed into another man" (1 Sam. 10:6). Later, Saul sent messengers three times to try and capture David. When they saw the company of the prophets in a frenzy, with Samuel standing in charge of them, "the spirit of God came upon the messengers of Saul, and they also fell into a prophetic frenzy" (1 Sam. 19:20). It seems being a prophet back then was a real psychedelic trip! Then Saul came on the scene and "fell into a prophetic frenzy, stripped off his clothes and fell down naked for all that day and night. Therefore, it is said, 'Is Saul also among the prophets?'" (1 Sam. 19:20-24). Evidently this ecstatic state was contagious!

But awakened spirit-breath did not make all its recipients suspects for psych evaluations. Rather, more often, in the Hebrew scriptures, non-ordinary consciousness as mystical, intensified spirit-breath, empowered people for leadership. "But the spirit-breath of the Lord took possession of Gideon; and he sounded the trumpet, and the Abiezrites were called out to follow him." (Judges 6:34).

In this warrior stage culture, leadership took on warrior qualities. "The spirit-breath of God began to stir Samson. . . The spirit-breath of God rushed on him and he tore the lion apart barehanded as one might tear apart a kid. . . . Then the spirit-breath of God rushed on him, and he went down to Ashkelon. He killed thirty men of the town" (Judges 13:25; 14:6, 19). Later "the spirit-breath of God rushed upon him" and he killed a thousand men with the jawbone of a donkey. (15:14-15). Remember, at this stage of social and spiritual evolution, killing on behalf of God was seen as a virtue. Later, Jesus rejected that understanding as he ushered in a new stage of the truth of loving enemies. But back then, awakened consciousness in a Jewish strongman was no tame thing!

Spirit-breath was also associated with more evolved levels such as living justly and speaking to power as in, "I am full of strength by YHWH's spirit-breath, full of justice and courage to declare the crimes of Jacob and Israel to their faces" (Micah 3:8). Spirit-breath gave the courage to speak out as in "For I am full of words, spirit-breath within besieges me, my heart is indeed like wine that has no vent; like new wine, it is ready to burst" (Job 32:18-19).

Notice the difference between Saul's lower and somewhat disturbed stage of development (1 Sam. 19:24) and David's more evolved stage as expressed in what happened when spirit-breath came on him. "Then Samuel took the horn of oil, and anointed David in the presence of his brothers; and the spirit-breath of YHWH came mightily upon him from that day forward" (1 Sam. 16:13). David became a mighty king and writer of many of the Psalms. David's Psalm 51 goes beyond the outwardly dramatic and gives us a revealing glimpse of the *interior experience* of awakened expanded consciousness in Jewish history. His adultery with Bathsheba left him with painful guilt and the loss of intensified spirit-breath. He wrote this prayer for a return to the joy of awakened spirit-breath:

> Create in me a clean heart, O God,
>   and put new and steadfast spirit-breath within me.
> Do not banish me from your presence,
>   and do not take your holy spirit-breath from me.
> Restore to me the joy of your salvation,
>   and sustain in me the freedom of spirit-breath.
>   (Psalms 51:10-12)

He asked God to be restored to his awakened state of consciousness which had shut down after his immoral actions. He no longer experienced an unblocked heart, God's presence, inner joy, or spiritual freedom. These were the inner phenomena he associated with the stirred consciousness of spirit-breath. They are also the testimony of the aroused mystical consciousness of mystics down through the ages and today which often include these specific experiences of an open heart, God's presence, inner joy, and inner freedom. Don't we all want more of this?

In Exodus 31:2-5 we see the result of an expanded consciousness in a strikingly non-dramatic but beautiful example in enhancing Bezalel's ability to create the artwork of the Tabernacle. "I have called by name Bezalel son of Uri son of Hur, of the tribe of Judah: and I have filled him with divine spirit-breath, with ability, intelligence, and knowledge in every kind of craft, to devise artistic designs, to work in gold, silver, and bronze, in cutting stones for setting, and in carving wood, in every kind of craft." Here is an affirmation of the "flow" state artisans have reported as they enter a creative zone of consciousness.

A new era of awakened consciousness is predicted for all humankind

The prophet Joel predicted that in the future spirit-breath in this intensified, awakened way would come on everyone and not just a few as Hebrew history had recorded:

I will pour out my spirit-breath on all flesh;
     your sons and your daughters shall prophesy,
your elders shall dream dreams,
     and your young people shall see visions.

(Joel 2:28)

The prophet is predicting that the mind of God will someday be available for all who are open to awakened spirit-breath, naming such examples as channeling God's words of encouragement and guidance, meaningful dreams, and spiritual visions. This is not just flowery religious talk but about transforming events that can and did rock our world!

Jesus and numinous consciousness for all

Jesus comes saying, "That day is here!" We don't know the extent of Jesus' spiritual experiences for the first thirty years of his life except that he "grew and became strong, filled with wisdom; and the favor of God was upon him" (Luke 2:40). He also spent those first thirty years only four miles away from the imperial city of Sepphoris which was being rebuilt. He, along with his father and brothers, probably made much of their living there as craftsmen. In this cosmopolitan city, Jesus would have been exposed to the world travelers of many religions and teachers and perhaps learned deeper things about other religions as well as his own.

Jesus, who functioned with everyday spirit-breath all of his life just as we do, awakened to a new degree of mystical consciousness at his baptism. "Suddenly the heavens were opened to him," and he saw the saturated overflow of the divine spirit-breath washing over him. A heavenly voice said, 'This is my son, the beloved, with whom I am well pleased'" (Matt. 4:16-17). This dramatic event did not happen because the other people there needed to see it, but because Jesus needed to have it. The everyday, basic consciousness that was already present within him was activated to a higher level so he could operate in that more numinous dimension. This intensified, cosmic opening of his consciousness confirmed to him that he was a beloved child of

God and a divine agent in the world for its healing and liberation. His newly awakened spiritual awareness immediately led him into the wilderness for a month-long vision quest of even more mystical altered state experiences (Matt. 4:1). There, in a series of visionary events, he sorted out whether he was to use these incredible new powers of mystical awareness for his ego or for the sake of others. Then, "Jesus returned to Galilee in the power of spirit-breath, and news about him spread through the whole countryside (Luke 4:14). What a difference a month of serious letting-go-of-ego and a few mystical experiences make!

Jesus, the mystic with a social and political agenda

Soon Jesus addressed the congregation in his hometown synagogue, reading from the scroll of Isaiah. This very passage was about awakened consciousness:

> The spirit-breath of God is upon me,
> who has anointed me
> to bring good news to those who are poor.
> who has sent me
> to proclaim release to those who are captives
> and recovery of sight to those who are blind,
> to let those who are oppressed go free,
> to proclaim the year of God's favor.
>
> (Luke 4:18-19)

Jesus didn't just read those words or give a nice sermon about them. He *identified* with them. He believed the words about awakened spirit-breath described his own anointing of inspired consciousness to do these very things he outlined. He told the gathered congregation this, and they said to one another, "Isn't that nice" (Luke 4:22). He sermon was going fine until he made a despised Syrian the hero of a story. Suddenly he had gone from "nice" to meddling with their oppressive racial prejudices. They became angry and tried to throw him off a cliff (Luke 4:29). Jesus was a mystic whose transcendent awareness led him to cause trouble in his hometown synagogue. Good mystics sometimes cause trouble at church!

Postmodern Jesus scholar Marcus Borg says, "Mystics are people who have vivid and typically frequent experiences of God."[2] Borg strikingly and boldly states that his most compact shorthand phrase for the historical Jesus is, "Jesus was a Jewish mystic." Mystic ranks first and is foundational to his four other basic descriptions of Jesus as healer, wisdom teacher, social prophet, and movement initiator.[3] These four other dimensions of Jesus' life flowed from his "vivid and typically frequent experiences of God."

Stevan Davies, author and Professor of Religious Studies, says that it is likely "Jesus made use of altered states of consciousness among his healed and exorcised associates in the process of effecting their full cure."[4] In Christian mysticism we move past the basic divine consciousnesses that all humans possess and move into an awakened divine-human consciousness which is now available to everyone, bringing healing and the transformation of people and society.

The activation of higher consciousness

After Jesus' consciousness was activated to this new level he began his astounding ministry of teaching and healing the multitudes while also training those closest to him to continue what he started. He gathered a few others with whom he taught and demonstrated this intensified awareness. Eventually "he breathed on them" (John 20:10) and said to them, "Receive holy spirit-breath" (John 20:22). Just as God breathed the breath of everyday life and consciousness into Adam, Jesus now breathed the breath of numinous life and awakened consciousness into his friends. There was a lot of heavy breathing in the Bible.

---

2. http://marcusborg.blogspot.com/.

3. Borg, *The Heart of Christianity*, 89.

4. Stevan Davies, *Jesus the Healer: Possession, Trance, and the Origins of Christianity* (Norwich: UK, Hymns Ancient & Modern Ltd, 2015), 119.

This breath, or activation of awakened divine-human consciousness, poured out on over a hundred followers of Jesus gathered together on Pentecost, the day of the Jewish celebration of the giving of the Ten Commandments to Moses. These friends of Jesus had gotten up that morning in their basic, ordinary consciousness. Now they were "filled with holy spirit-breath and began to speak in other languages (*glōssais*) as spirit-breath gave them the ability" (Acts 2:4). They were so ecstatic in mystical trance states that they were accused by on-lookers of being drunk (2:13). Drunkenness is a drug-induced altered state experience. Pentecost was a spirit-induced altered state experience.

Activation of numinous awakening continues

This initial activation of an elevated spiritual awareness continued to be passed on down to new followers of Jesus such as the Samaritans (Acts 8:14–17), Paul (9:17), the Gentiles at Cornelius' house (10:44), and the new believers at Ephesus (19:2–6). It was nourished in the meetings of the house churches such as described in 1 Corinthians 11:17–14:37 which were filled with expressions of mystical consciousness. This is seen in such phenomena as channeled words from God ("prophecy") and mystical state devotion to God and Jesus expressed in personal, transrational languages of prayer and praise ("tongues"—*glōssais*).

What is "tongues"?

Here in Acts we encounter the mystical phenomenon of "languages" (*glōssais*), often translated as "tongues." The word simply meant the language or dialect used by a particular people distinct from that of other nations. These "languages" are associated with awakened consciousness two other times in the book of Acts. When the Gentiles became believers (Acts 10:46) and when the believers in Ephesus were prayed for by Paul, "holy spirit-breath came upon them and they spoke in languages (*glōssais*) and prophesied" (Acts 19:6). In Paul's first letter to the Corinthians, written long before the four Gospels and Acts, he addresses their meetings for worship and mutual encouragement. He specifically talks about "spiritual gifts" using a word taken from the word "*pneuma*" or spirit-breath. He points out that spirit-breath gifts give us powerful ways to worship, encourage one another, and bless the world. One of these gifts is spiritual languages. He makes five informative points about them:

1. They are "activated by spirit-breath-consciousness" (1 Cor. 12:11) or a beginning level of expanded consciousness.

2. These languages are addressed to God and not to others (14:2). For this reason I will now call them "prayer languages" to distinguish these from known foreign languages that people learn by culture or training.

3. Prayer languages are not from one's mind but from one's spirit, bypassing the normal language centers of the brain (13:14).

4. Paul advocates both praying and singing with one's spirit in these transrational words of prayer and praise, and also praying and singing with one's mind in everyday speech (14:15).

5. Paul says that he prays in these prayer languages more than all of them, *but not in church.* In church he would rather speak with his mind so others can be instructed. Nobody is instructed in listening to prayer languages (14:18-19).

I have elaborated on prayer language for two reasons. One is that my Pentecostal friends have taken an extreme position, saying that the only evidence that you are "filled with the spirit" is that you have spoken in "tongues." This is simply not true. The other reason I detail this is because other friends, and most other Christians, have taken the opposite extreme position which goes something like this: "Don't have anything to do with that 'speaking in tongues' stuff." That's bad advice, too.

In my experience, praying in a prayer language allows me to express deep feelings to God from my inner spirit, bypassing my mind with all its distractions, education, and the many rules and restrictions of grammar. At times it also opens me up to a deeper mystical state by serving as a free-flowing mantra. It is transrational speech which is not meaningful at a rational level but is spiritually meaningful beyond the rational. Paul described it very well when he wrote, "Likewise, intensified-spirit-breath-consciousness (*pneuma*) helps us in our weakness; for we do not know how to pray as we ought, but that very inspired-spirit-breath (*pneuma*) intercedes with sighs too deep for words" (Rom. 8:26). For many years I have found it natural and helpful at times to pray in these "sighs too deep for words."

What is prophecy?

American actress, comedian, writer, singer, and producer Lily Tomlin says, "Why is it that when we talk to God we're said to be praying, but when God talks to us we're schizophrenic?" That's not only funny but insightful. If God talking to us was good enough for Jesus, Paul, the saints, and millions of mystics down through the ages, why not the rest of us!

Channeling

What the Bible calls prophecy we call "channeling" in today's terminology. Paul, the mystic with the giant intellect, made an important challenge to all Christians when he said he wished everyone would channel words from God and that we are to pursue that as a way to encourage others (1 Cor. 14:1-5). Paul's letters provide three major lists of spiritual gifts in Romans 12:6-8, Ephesians 4:11, and 1 Corinthians 12:8-10. The only gift mentioned in all three lists is "prophecy" or speaking God's words of encouragement heard from within one's elevated awareness. Why did Paul value this mystical channeling words from God? Because it was us *talking as God!* This is what Jesus did—he talked about, to, and *as God.* This is *God being us!* We can see how vital this was to the early Christians and why it is so vital for us today. However, the difference between us and Jesus is that these words are being channeled through us as less fully identified with our divine self. Therefore, for the sake of everyone involved, they always need to be discerned as to how much they seem to be from God and how much from our small self rather than our Universal

Self. (1 Cor. 14:29). Those words should be offered to others only if one is willing for their words to be tested and discerned by others.

Christianity began in a blaze of awakened consciousness

As we have seen, Christianity began in a riot of mystical consciousness. This kind of "super awareness" has also been called consciousness that is non-ordinary, inspired, altered state, intensified, expanded, elevated, numinous, quantum,[5] holotropic,[6] cosmic, higher, subtle (less obvious than concrete everyday consciousness), trance (Acts 10:10, 11:15, 22:17), and transpersonal. It connects us with the nonlocal spectrum of wisdom, information, and non-physical beings such as Jesus. Whatever it is called, Christianity began in a steady flood of these kinds of experiences! Now the intensified level of consciousness that "stirred, rushed, and came on" a few leaders in the Old Testament becomes the entire focus of spirit-breath reception in the New Testament. In the New Testament it is described with words like baptized with, descending upon, come upon, filled with, in the power of, given to, flow from, full of, received, and compelled by.

Psychedelic[7] visions in Revelation

In the last book of the New Testament, Revelation, John begins with, "It was the first day of the week, and suddenly I was in spirit-breath (*pneuma*), and I heard behind me a loud voice like a trumpet saying, 'Write in a book what you see'" (Rev. 1:10). What did this mean?

---

5. Quantum consciousness is applying quantum theory to consciousness. See Chapter 15 for more.

6. Coined by Stanislav Groff, holotropic literally means "moving toward wholeness" in reference to a spiritual opening in consciousness. The holotropic has to do with states which aim towards wholeness and the totality of existence. This is characteristic of non-ordinary states of consciousness such as meditative, mystical, or psychedelic experiences. He says, "Holotropic experiences have the potential to help us discover our true identity and our cosmic status." http://www.terrypatten.com/sites/default/files/Legacy-paper-Grof.pdf.

7. "A mental state characterized by a profound sense of intensified sensory perception." http://www.dictionary.com/browse/psychedelic.

Was he having fun imaging various wild religious scenarios? Was he hallucinating? Was he doing science fiction writing for the first century? No! He meant that he was in an altered state of consciousness called "in spirit" in the New Testament. He again says, "I was immediately in spirit" (4:2.) There is not a "the" before "spirit" present in the Greek. While "in spirit" he has a vision of a heavenly throne with someone seated on it looking like gemstones and surrounded by a rainbow. Sounds like our psychedelic era of the 1960s! Except that here the only psychedelic present was spirit-breath trance consciousness. Many dramatic visions unfold in the following chapters of Revelation including an out-of-body-experience where he was carried away into a wilderness (17:3) and another where he teleported to the top of a great mountain (21:10).

More paranormal phenomena

The book of Acts recounts the experience of mystical elevated consciousness being repeated with new followers of Jesus. After Paul's dramatic experience with the risen Jesus on the road to Damascus, Ananias told Paul that Jesus had sent him to pray for him "to regain your sight and be filled with holy numinous-spirit-breath-consciousness (*pneuma*)" (Acts 9:17).

At another similar event, Peter was invited to speak about Jesus to the Gentiles. As he was speaking, spirit-breath "fell upon all who heard the word." He recognized this was happening because while he was still speaking his audience members suddenly moved into expanded states of consciousness and began praising God in prayer languages! Peter then pointed out that these non-Jews had received spirit-breath just as the Jewish believers had and should be baptized. (10: 44-48). This was a breakthrough event with the clear implication that Gentiles could become followers of Jesus without first having to become Jews.

Spirit-breath "came upon" the new believers in Ephesus when Paul laid his hands on them and they began praising God in prayer languages and channeling words from God they heard within in their newly awakened mystical consciousness (19:6).

Once again we should expect that these dramatic experiences were described in Acts because they were a readily observable outward demonstration of what was a powerful inward initiation into mystical consciousness. We know from Paul's writings to the Corinthians that this kind of joyful hubbub of everyone praising God out loud in prayer languages and channeling words from God, all at the same time, was continued when the new believers gathered together in at least one and possibly other cities at that time. Paul's challenge was to affirm the power of the awakened consciousness and even the transrational languages, while bringing back some order and rationality into their church gatherings and worship. The history of the Pentecostal movement in our time has been faced with similar challenges. Unfortunately, institutional Christianity, in the name of the orderly and rational, has nearly succeeded in stamping out all traces of such mystical consciousness in both traditional and progressive churches.

They had never seen spirit-breath like this!

These early Christians may not have been aware of similar phenomena such as ancient shamanic tribal rituals or the trances of the oracle at Delphi which continued through the fourth century. They did not yet have today's extensive study of psychotropic drugs or other religions, some of which were not in existence at the time such as Sufism, the inner mystical dimension of Islam which practices expanded states of consciousness. It appeared to these first Christians that there really must not have been much awakened spirit-breath around until Jesus. They so associated the dramatic intensified higher states of consciousness with spirit-breath that the Gospel of John reports that spirit-breath only came to people through Jesus and after his resurrection, dismissing such events in the Hebrew scriptures. The writer's theological interpretation was the quite black and white statement that "for as yet there was no spirit-breath" (John 7:39). Professor of Old Testament Interpretation and Biblical Hebrew, Jack Levison, says that this statement from John "creates a substantial breach between the wisdom tradition [in the Hebrew scriptures] in which the spirit is the locus of learning, and John's view of the spirit as a subsequent endowment that could not possibly enter the believer before the death of Jesus."[8]

The first Christians began their Christian lives with mystical experience

Paul wrote a letter to the Jewish Christians in Galatia who were insisting that the Jewish laws still needed to be kept by Gentile Christians in order to be okay with God. Paul admonishes them, saying, "Are you so foolish? Having begun in spirit-breath (*pneuma*), are you now made perfect by the flesh?" (Gal. 3:3). What does "having begun in spirit-breath" mean?

As we have seen, these early Christians seemed to normally experience an initial activation of mystical consciousness when they became followers of the Jesus. This was so definite and identifiable that Paul could point back to it for each of the recipients of this letter. He could say, in effect, "Did this transcendent experience that blew you away when you became a Christian happen to you because of some religious act you performed, or as the gift of God's grace?

That doesn't make much sense today. Most children who grow up in the church begin their Christian path by simply being taught about Jesus and at some point begin to have faith in Jesus, or consider themselves a Christian, often after confirmation or water baptism. Most adult converts to Christianity begin their lives as Christians by attending classes, agreeing to certain beliefs and joining a church. Or if in an evangelical church, by asking God to forgive their sins and accepting Jesus' death on the cross as atonement for their sins.

Many, if not most, of those of us who are Christians may have never had an initiating mystical experience or one of any kind. Our Christianity is just something we sincerely believe and practice by our going

8. John Levison, *Filled with the Spirit* (Grand Rapids: Michigan, Eerdmans, 2009), 366.

to church and living a good life. So today, just as with original Christianity, we need to know that there is a mystical consciousness which is available to everyone open to the spiritual path. The goal is for that awareness to be accessible whenever it is needed, and even a normal way of living everyday life where we live our lives from that inspired consciousness. Then we manifest our inner life in our outer life by being the hands and feet, heart and voice of Jesus in the world today. This is the point of Paul saying, "If we live in spirit-breath (the divine-human-mystical awareness called *pneuma*) let us also walk (manifest it in the world) in spirit-breath" (Gal. 5:25).

I am *not* saying one cannot be a Christian without having had some kind of mystical experience. Rather, I am pointing out that mystical consciousness was so universal among these first Christians from the very beginning of their faith in Jesus that Paul could point to it as an example of what happened to them *without* having to obey the Jewish Law. Today, such spiritual experiences are conspicuous by their absence. Christianity has become only a matter of what one believes and how one behaves. Both of these are important, but not as substitutes for the awakened reality of God's presence in our lives.

Jesus leaves, and mystical spirit-breath comes

"I tell you the truth: it is to your advantage that I go away, for if I do not go away, the helper will not come to you; but if I go, I will send the helper to you" (John 16:7). Why did Jesus make this startling statement? Because he wants them to move to spirit-breath at another level of consciousness in the spectrum of awareness which is greater than basic consciousness. But why did he have to leave physically in order for this to happen? I believe that he had to leave physically so they would not settle for an ordinary physical perception of him and other spiritual realities. *As long as Jesus was around in his physical body they would only relate to him in everyday consciousness, the limited way of seeing him as a person whom they could see and hear teach. Jesus wanted a much more intimate relationship with his friends than that.* He also needed to provide a way for his future friends to access him in the coming generations.

Therefore he invited them, and us, to move to a higher consciousness so that the spiritual realities he was in touch with would be available to us. His leaving the limited physical realm meant he, himself, could be present with us in an unlimited way. He could be with anyone, at any time and in any place, unlimited by time and space. His dramatic resurrection appearances, where he seemed to be in the physical realm, were meant to wean his friends away from his purely physical presence. They, and we, could then continue to apprehend his presence, but only in higher or more awakened levels of awareness. When we are able to enter the dimension of non-physical reality that he now dwells in, then he can continue to personally guide and teach us in whatever ways we are ready for. How about that!

Summary of The Record of Awakened Consciousness (in the Bible)

• Once the early creeds were in place by the fourth and fifth centuries, people began to read the Bible through the lens of their doctrines, forgetting that the doctrines came from the experiences.

• Spiritual experience as a living, ongoing reality became less and less prominent.

• Mystical experiences are the norm in the New Testament, from dreams, to initiating awakening consciousness events, visions, channeling words from God, transrational prayer and praise, the spiritual presence of God and Jesus, guidance, wisdom, insight, and encouragement.

Questions for Reflection and Discussion

1. What mystical experiences have you had?

2. Have any of your experiences involved hearing words within that you thought might be God speaking?

3. Has your opinion about prayer languages changed after reading this chapter? If so, in what way?

4. Have you ever gotten so carried away in praying that your words became "garbled?" Could that have been a prayer language sneaking out?

5. Do you ever personally experience Jesus' presence, guidance, or help? If so, how?

Practices

1. It is a common practice with those who pray and meditate regularly to set aside 20 minutes on most days of the week. Meditation is often called contemplative prayer in Christian circles. Regular practice reminds us repeatedly that we are hypnotized by our personality. It's important to set aside some time each day to re-establish a deeper connection with our True Nature. Busy people can be mystics. To do that we deliberately put times and places in our busyness where we are not busy.

2. A prayer language or mantra is a way to pray without using our minds. Just turn your attention to God and say whatever comes to your mind that is not in a language you know. Let your inner spirit give you syllables, from a few sounds to a flow of "words" to express yourself without having to think of actual words in a language you have learned.

3. Experiment with asking God for a word for you for this day. Listen for the first word that comes to mind. If it's something like "green eggs and ham," try again. You will sense when the word fits.

4. Experiment with asking God or Jesus a question and listening for what you hear or sense within. Sometimes you may see an image or picture in your mind that could be part of your answer.

5. Begin and/or end your time with the Three Faces of God practice from the Appendix on page 381 to further incorporate into your body-self the healing wholeness of a multidimensional God.

"God being me."

CHAPTER 11

The Reality of Awakened Consciousness

The inspired numinous awareness we read about in the Bible is as real today as it was centuries ago. In a 1962 Gallup survey, 22% of the U. S. public said they have had a religious or mystical experience, defined as a "moment of sudden religious insight or awakening." In a 2009 survey, that number had grown to twice as high, to about half of the U.S. public (49%). Either more people are having mystical experiences, or more are feeling free to report them. Either way, or both, this is a wonderful trend.

Two visions

Here are two accounts of mystical consciousness, one ancient and the other contemporary. Notice the similarities and the differences.

An ancient visionary experience recorded in the Bible:

> I saw the Lord sitting on a throne, high and lofty; and the hem of his robe filled the temple. Angelic beings were in attendance above him; each had six wings: with two they

covered their faces, and with two they covered their feet, and with two they flew. And one called to another and said: "Holy, holy, holy is the LORD of hosts; the whole earth is full of his glory."

The doorposts on the thresholds shook at the voices of those who called, and the house filled with smoke. And I said: "Woe is me! I am lost, for I am a man of unclean lips, and I live among a people of unclean lips; yet my eyes have seen the King, the Lord of hosts!"

Then one of the angelic beings flew to me, holding a live coal that had been taken from the altar with a pair of tongs. The being touched my mouth with it and said: "Now that this has touched your lips, your guilt has departed and your sin is blotted out." Then I heard the voice of the Lord saying, "Whom shall I send, and who will go for us?" And I said, "Here am I; send me!" (Isaiah 6:1-10, followed by the specific message Isaiah was to deliver.)

A modern visionary experience recorded in this person's journal:

I was seated in a recliner with my eyes open in a darkened room in my usual time of prayer and meditation. I felt drained, worn out, and anxious that I would not be able to complete my current work. Slowly, a beautiful, deep, darker than dark blackness filled the room which I sensed as the presence of God. Then gorgeous colors of gold, blue, purple, white, and red began rolling in like waves on a coastline from beyond. A wave of one color would roll by to be followed by another. It reminded me of God's glory often symbolized and seen as bright light. The waves receded as a luminous, undulating curtain of pale blue and gray lace formed in front of me. It was so real that I reached my hand out to see if it was in the physical or spiritual dimension of reality. My hand went through it, confirming it was a visionary reality. This beautiful curtain then gently formed a cocoon-like shape around me with its dome about two feet above my head and two feet out in front of me. I turned around and saw that it surrounded me. It felt like the tender hand of God covering me in the midst of a vast infinity of luminous black energy. My life-long challenge has been anxiety, often in the form of panic attacks. This was the extreme opposite of a panic attack. It was a place of refuge and safety, peace and bliss. After a few minutes, the curtain cocoon melted away. Then I returned to the almost always constant presence of Jesus at my side with his hand touching my right arm. I heard the words, "Do it for the sake of others."

The first account occurred some 2700 years ago with the prophet Isaiah in Jerusalem. It is recorded in the Hebrew Scriptures in the book of Isaiah Chapter Six.

The second event happened to me last week. As I was writing this chapter and was rereading my journal entries for the previous week, I noticed some of the similarities to Isaiah's vision from my journal record the week before and copied that entry here.

Notice the *similarities*. Both were visionary mystical experiences in non-ordinary consciousness. I believe we can readily assume Isaiah was convinced what he saw was a reality in the spiritual world. I can vouch for the undoubted reality of this and other visionary experiences I have had and continue to have.

In both accounts there was the direct experience of the presence and glory of God. Both accounts shared images of beauty and splendor. Isaiah's vision described this as "full of his glory," a designation in the Hebrew scriptures often involving bright light. In mine it was deep darkness and clouds of brilliant color. Each person in their vision had a need. Isaiah felt unworthy and I was feeling drained and worn out from pressing myself to finish three years of research, reflection, and writing in completing this book. There was a tactile sensation of being touched on the body in both experiences, for Isaiah on the lips, and for me on my right arm. Both accounts ended with a meaningful communication from a messenger of God about God's work in the world.

Now notice the *differences,* as mystical experiences are always a co-creation of both divine and human origins and interpreted by our stage of development, our worldview. Initiated by God, these visions were both shaped and interpreted by two different people in two different cultures and times. Isaiah lived in a pre-modern, mythic era around seven centuries before Jesus. God was a righteous Judge and Ruler, and sin was seen as anything that offended an awesome, holy God. God was all about judgment, repentance, and restoration, both personal and national.[1] God appeared to Isaiah in the images that were meaningful to him: a royal kingly setting filled with Temple of Solomon images where smoke indicated the presence of God and an altar where offerings made to God were burned in the constant fire. The presence of God came to me as beautiful, black darkness— infinitely vast spaciousness which was empty of objects viewed from my eyes, but the heart space in my chest was filled with pulsating love energy. The splendor was not of male kingly images but of vast rolling clouds of colors filling the incandescent darkness along with a quite feminine lace-like soft curtain with a pale blue and white pattern. I later realized that the curtain and it colors reminded me of a Jewish prayer shawl.

Isaiah felt terrified and unworthy to be in the presence of a holy God at the beginning of his vision. He saw winged beings who ministered to him, giving him a powerful sign that he was forgiven and accepted. I felt anxious and drained of energy from the joyous but demanding work of writing. The vast, dark, empty presence of God and a protecting, nurturing divine curtained hand cocooned

---

1. See *Integral Christianity*, Smith, Chapters 1-7 for a description of six stages of developmental history in world cultures and the Christian Church.

me, relieving my anxiety and making me feel safe.

Isaiah heard communication from God through a winged messenger that sent him out into the world with a message for the people. I heard a message from Jesus that reminded me to "Do it for the sake of others."

My journey

I don't recount my visionary experience alongside Isaiah's experience in order to compare myself to him. Far from it. I am an example of someone who has been "spiritual experience" challenged for much of my life. I have been an emotionally uptight and repressed Southern Baptist preacher in therapy for twenty years who longed for more, much more, during most of my life. I have had a life-long deep interest in experiencing the presence of God and being in touch with the information fields of mystical consciousness. I had read hundreds of books, gone to dozens of conferences, and was personally prayed for by various spiritual luminaries. However, not much happened to me since my one experience at age 23 until 15 years ago. Then I began having vivid and frequent experiences of God.

As I shared previously, visionary experiences have been happening to me quite often for the last fifteen years whenever I sit down to pray and meditate, and at other times during the day. For the last few years the deep blackness, the colors, the presence of Jesus touching my right arm, and words of guidance have been recurring themes in my prayer-meditation times and at other times when I am quiet.

I share my experience to let you know even the most wounded and challenged of us like me can learn to be open to transforming spiritual experiences with God and Jesus.

Why did this begin fifteen years ago? This was a time where three factors coalesced in my life. Each carried new healing into my life. First, I had completed many years of therapy to get in touch with my repressed emotions and inner pain. Sitting on your capacity to feel is always connected to sitting on your capacity for spiritual experience.

A second factor was ten years of weekly sessions with an energy healer who was adept in connecting to the non-physical world of subtle energy. She introduced me to the numinous world of non-physical beings and light. Her modeling and encouragement to me were important to my initial opening to the reality of spiritual beings.

Finally, it was fifteen years ago that I found a map of life and spiritual evolution that made sense in the writings and life of Ken Wilber. Here was a practicing Buddhist who took meditation and spiritual realities seriously. As a Christian I was motivated by his thinking and practices to do a serious restart of my pale two minutes a day prayer life. Of course, two minutes is better than no minutes, but . . . .

For most days of the week (that's about four out of seven) for these past dozen years I take 20-60 minutes to sit quietly with Jesus. I often affirm the presence of other saints and part of the time I don't think about anything but just sink down into a still mind and a blissful heart. I often have various visions during this time, not because I'm so spiritual but because I need so much healing. These are usually a series of rolling clouds of colors signaling God's presence and various scenes which continue to remind me that everything out there is also in here in the seamless oneness of all reality. I only occasionally have a life-altering vision. Visions are quite different from pictures that come into your mind when you think of something. Visions are not under one's control and are seen with one's eyes while awake, appearing as real rather than imagined. I constantly feel Jesus' touch on my right arm in prayer and meditation, and any time I turn my attention to it during the day or night. These kinds of subtle awareness experiences are a constant source of encouragement for me. I would not be surprised if at some point these visionary and tactile phenomena stop and I will move on to other avenues of inner healing and nourishment. It's all good.

All spiritual paths are explorations of awakened consciousness

Most of the world's religions began with their founders off by themselves somewhere having profound mystical and transcendent spiritual experiences in non-ordinary states of consciousness. In Judaism, God appeared to Abraham several times in visions telling him to leave his country and giving him direct guidance (Gen. 12:1,7; 13:14; 15:1; 18:1, etc.). Moses had his burning bush and commandments on the mountain top. The prophets continued by emerging from their spiritual visions to challenge the people to change their lifeless religion and oppressive ways.

Buddha sat under the Bodhi tree until his consciousness changed dramatically, becoming the "awakened one." He traveled for 45 years spreading his experience, practices, and understandings. His last words were about awakening. His followers who are serious practitioners of the Buddha path have similar experiences of awakening.[2]

As I have said, Jesus emerged into ministry only after a powerful mystical experience at his baptism followed by an altered state vision quest in the wilderness. His mystical visionary baptismal experience of intensified consciousness (Matt. 3:16-17) was passed down to his first followers at Pentecost (Acts 2:1-4) and then with new converts (Acts 8:14-17; 9:17; 10:44; 19:2-6). His life was filled with such numinous events.

Mohammed was in a cave by himself when an angelic presence revealed the first words of The Qur'an to him. This experience of non-ordinary consciousness was repeated many times in the following thirteen years in very deep, fire-filled spiritual experiences, visions, as well as trance-like states resulting in the 114 chapters in the Qur'an.[3] However, these experiences were not encouraged for others, and Islam quickly became a religion of the book, and like Christianity, a closed book. The practice of non-ordinary consciousness later emerged in Sufism, the mystical stream of Islam, which seeks to find divine love and knowledge through direct personal experience of God. It is an exception to non-mystical Islam.[4]

---

2. http://jayarava.org/buddhas-last-words.html.

3. http://www.tijani.org/the-vision-of-the-prophet-in-the-islamic-tradition/.

4. http://www.rim.org/muslim/sufism.htm.

Bernard McGinn, theologian, historian, and scholar of spirituality, says, "Mysticism can be regarded as an integral element of religion. It includes both a way of life and a direct consciousness of the presence of God."[5] Broadly defined, one can encounter mystical dimensions within all religions of the world. Taoism, Zen, and Buddhism, as well as Hindu traditions like Kashmir Shaivism, Vaish-navism, and Advaita Vedanta, are basically mystical in the sense that they all strive for transcendence from this world of multiplicity. In the case of Theravada Buddhism, we would have to exchange the concept of God/She with "the ground of being" or similar expressions.[6]

What happened to all these mystical dimensions?

We see these experiences beginning to be resisted right away from the first letter of Paul to the church at Thessalonica. Paul said, "Do not despise prophecy" (1 Thess. 5:20). The only reason he would say this is because some were already saying, "Cut that crazy stuff out!" People, probably the law and order types, were already despising the whole idea of channeling words heard in mystical consciousness. Mystics are messy and institutions are allergic to messiness. The move against messy mystics was already beginning and increased in the first few centuries as the church became more organized.

An increasingly authoritarian structure along the lines of Rome came into place. This was part of the seemingly inevitable deadening process of institutionalization that continues today and requires constant renewal and pushing for change. The institution preserves beliefs, rules, and rituals but, in doing so, becomes a form of crowd control rather than consciousness raising. For instance, the New Testament practice of laying on of hands to activate transforming mystical consciousness (Acts 8:17-18; 19:5-6; 2 Tim. 1:6) became mostly an awesome ritual, albeit with magnificent trappings, investing institutional power in the clergy, priests, and bishops.

---

5. Bernard McGinn, *Presence of God: History of Western Christian Mysticism* (London: SCM, 1995), xvi.

6. https://www.academia.edu/1405697/Altered Consciousness in Religion.

Awakened consciousness can be intentionally turned off

Paul says, "Do not quench the spirit," (1 Thess. 5:19) as he insists that we not avoid elevated consciousness. We know from his first letter to the Corinthians that people worshipping together with newly awakened consciousness can get noisy and boisterous. Go to a church service with lots of loud shouts of praise, dancing in the aisles, fainting "in the spirit" and excited praying in tongues and you can get a sense of why Paul said to tone things down. Some would advise that such activities be cut out all together and replaced with the proper decorum. But Paul did not want to "quench" the spirit. He just wanted some balance between ecstasy and order. Today in most churches we have order, lots of order. But when is the last time you saw ecstasy in a church group? It might appear to Paul that we have indeed quenched the spirit.

Even though Paul clearly said, "Do not despise prophecy" (1 Thess. 5:20), I was taught, even warned, in my Southern Baptist seminary to do just that. Both teachers, who believed "every word of the Bible is inspired," and fellow students made fun of anyone who claimed God spoke to or through them. Prophecy was reduced to "good preaching" rather than its New Testament role of speaking words from God of encouragement, guidance, and challenge from a state of inspired spirit. This is not to say that some preaching cannot be that very thing. Of course, according to Paul, all such words must be discerned because not just everything that is claimed to be a word from God is always that.

Early Christianity was messy. Overly controlling leaders and timid congregations always get rid of messy in favor of order, their order. As the law and order that came with the clergy—priestly control of the church by the fourth century—spirit was effectively "quenched." No more words from God except the past ones in the Bible and the multiplying rules and doctrines, inquisitions, and heresy trials of the controlling clergy. We don't burn heretics today. We just fire them from their religious jobs and push them out of our churches.

Of course any group has a right to determine what it will believe and teach. But the revelations of spirit are not confined to such traditional religious groups but sometimes, perhaps often, through the untraditional actions of the visionary fringe.

Christians mystics from Jesus to Paul and from the early martyrs to the various heretics and others such as Meister Eckhart (who came close to being a martyr) have always been difficult to tame. But that didn't keep religious and political leaders from trying. The church has traded its mystics for stability. It has swapped upsetting new creative understandings arising from mystical consciousness for conformity.

Demythologizing the Bible

In addition, in the last two hundred years, a new approach to interpreting the Bible has emerged. Scholars and theologians began using various methods to deconstruct many of the elements of Christianity that appeared to be creative editing, legend, and myth. Most recently this has been popularized by the Jesus Seminar in our time. It is useful and important to look behind what are premodern understandings to see what may be inauthentic, less evolved, or simply the spiritual but not literal truth that is being communicated in biblical texts. It is good to explore how the various parts of the Bible came to be written and transmitted down through the centuries.

However, at some point the hidden biases of demythologizing can outweigh the benefits. This occurs when what is deconstructed is an authentic event, even when described in the symbols and language of an ancient culture. Ignoring or explaining away most mystical experiences as invented stories to attain a literary, political, or social end does not explain the power of these events in shaping the lives of these early Christians. Increasingly, modern researchers and scholars are taking the numerous accounts of altered consciousness in the Bible at face value and exploring their commonalities in various religions and how today's consciousness research might apply. An extreme reductionist approach is not scholarly, but brings a modern bias against spiritual reality into the process.

Speaking about the absence of attention from biblical scholars and theologians to the mystical spiritual experiences in the New Testament today, scholar, historian of early Christianity, and Roman Catholic, Luke Timothy Johnson says,

> Much of what the earliest Christian texts talked about is simply ignored. On one side, then we possess marvelous intricate and methodologically sophisticated scholarship about early Christianity, a veritable mountain of learning about every word of the New Testament and its milieu, every literary seam, every possible source, every discernable pulse of historical development. On the other side, we are virtually ignorant concerning a remarkable range of statements in the New Testament that appear to be of first importance to the writers, that seem to express fundamental convictions, that demand some kind of account, but that all of our learning does not touch. This range of statements has to do with religious experience and power.[7]

This may all be changing as more and more scholars are coming out as mystics and practitioners of elevated states of consciousness themselves. They will see the Bible through the new eyes of spiritual experience. Prominent New Testament scholar James Dunn says. "Spirit (*pneuma*) for Paul is essentially an *experiential concept*: by that I mean a concept whose content and significance is determined to a decisive degree by his experience."[8]

My journey

In seminary I studied the spirit as a concept to be understood rather than as an inner awakening to be experienced. Much later in life

---

7. Luke Timothy Johnson, *Religious Experience in Earliest Christianity: A Missing Dimension in New Testament Study* (Minneapolis: Fortress, 1998), 4-5.

8. James Dunn, *Jesus and the Spirit: A Study of the Religious and Charismatic Experience of Jesus and the First Christians as Reflected in the New Testament* (London: SCM-Canterbury Press Ltd, 1975) 200, (italics his).

I discovered that the word "spirit" and its associated phenomena describe deep inner experiences which we must taste ourselves before we can understand the life-changing and culture-transforming power of spirit-breath seen in the Bible. In my early church life and seminary journey, actual religious experiences, except for conversion experiences, were pushed aside. This seemed to be partly because they were not understood or were associated with highly emotional Pentecostalism where people sometimes acted like they were drunk. The accusation of drunkenness is a famous hallmark of the friends of Jesus at Pentecost (Acts 2:13). Encased in holy scripture, it's a sign of hilarious spirit filling. But we don't want any of that today in our religious gatherings. Tame spirit filling only, please.

I was drawn to the charismatic movement of the 1960s because I saw people becoming conscious of God in a new way and of their spiritual identity and ministry. They didn't just talk concepts of spirit—they had experiences of spirit as intensified spiritual consciousness. Sometimes the experiences seemed over the top or manufactured. But not most of the time. It seemed a step forward and I had my spirit experience of oneness and cosmic love when I was 23 a few weeks after being prayed for by some charismatics. I eventually began praying for others to have such spirit experiences and they often did.

Over the course of thirty years I quietly prayed at my church and other places for hundreds of people to have what might be called a "release of the spirit." As I prayed softly in my flow of devotional, words-beyond-words prayer, many of these people quietly fell to the floor or off their chairs in a state of great peacefulness. They would remain there anywhere from a few minutes to a few hours. I would ask them what happened, and they would report they felt something like waves of peace or joy come over them and their awareness moved internally to such a degree that they were not conscious of sitting or standing. It was clear they were having such a deep experience of inner awakening that their normal "stay alert" system of body wakefulness shut down. They were super-awake spiritually while physically in something like sleep mode. Those who were in a church community where worship and prayer were geared toward these altered experiences, continued to have them at an even deeper and more stabilized level. For others, it soon becomes only a fading memory.

When my attention was drawn to integral understanding as articulated by Ken Wilber, I began a deepened prayer and meditation practice. My "spirit" or deeper consciousness experiences took off once again, this time in regular prayer and meditation by myself as well as in worship experiences with others. These new experiences were deeper and more sustained.

After a few years I realized both my charismatic spirit experiences and my prayer/meditation spirit experiences were incredibly similar. Both were experiences of a new level of consciousness. I found "consciousness" was a more meaningful and accurate way to think and talk about my spirit experiences. I would like to see a path develop between these two different traditions that blends the power of the charismatic experiences, without its excesses, with the maturity and stability of deep reflective prayer and meditation.

I began to see "spirit" in the Bible in a whole new light. As I researched both Old and New Testaments I came to see that spirit was about consciousness. I saw that, with time and institutionalization, we have turned these mystical experiences of awakened consciousness into religions, obscuring their depth and daring.

These chapters are an invitation to return to this radically creative and inspired consciousness, experienced and interpreted now in the postmodern world of today. My framework is Christianity. Those of other traditions can find similar calls to the deep spiritual path in writers such as Ken Wilber.[9]

Scientists point to the reality of the mystical

In his groundbreaking *The Varieties of Religious Experience*, which investigated these different forms of religious experience, William

---

9. See bibliography.

James says, "No account of the universe in its totality can be final which leaves these other forms of consciousness quite disregarded."[10]

Physicist Fritjof Capra writes:

> As Eastern thought has begun to interest a significant number of people, and meditation is no longer viewed with ridicule or suspicion, mysticism is being taken seriously even within the scientific community An increasing number of scientists are aware that mystical thought provides a consistent and relevant philosophical background to the theories of contemporary science, a conception of the world in which the scientific discoveries of men and women can be in perfect harmony with their spiritual aims and religious beliefs.[11]

He says, "Science does not need mysticism and mysticism does not need science; but we need both."[12]

Psychiatrist and researcher Stanislav Grof says:

> In non-ordinary states of consciousness, visions of various universal symbols can play a significant role in experiences of individuals who previously had no interest in mysticism or were strongly opposed to anything esoteric. These visions tend to convey an instant intuitive understanding of the various levels of meaning of these symbols. As a result of experiences of this kind, subjects can develop accurate understanding of various complex esoteric teachings. In some instances, persons unfamiliar with the Kabbalah had experiences described in the Zohar and Sepher Yetzirah and obtained surprising insights into

---

10. William James, *The Varieties of Religious Experience* (Boston: Adamant Media Corporation, 2000), 305.

11. Fritjof Capra, *The Turning Point* (New York: Harper Collins, 1982), 78.

12. Fritjof Capra, *The Web of Life: A New Scientific Understanding of Living Systems* (New York: Anchor, 1996), 306.

Kabbalistic symbols. Others were able to describe the meaning and function of intricate mandalas used in the Tibetan Vajrayana and other tantric systems.[13]

Shawn Mikula is a neuroscientist at the Mind-Brain Institute at Johns Hopkins University. He says:

> The evolution and expansion of consciousness is inevitable. With the expansion of consciousness comes new ways of seeing reality. Everything changes. You see things that you could never have conceived of before. Old philosophies and religions suddenly appear naive and give way to a far more profound understanding. Most religions (including naive Christianity) and philosophies will not last long, simply because it's inevitable that a profound transformation in our consciousness, in our way of understanding and interacting with reality, is going to soon take place. It's inevitable because that's the direction that consciousness is headed . . . Ordinary consciousness is simply too mundane and limiting.[14]

Ervin Laszlo is a world-class philosopher of science and the developer of Systems Philosophy derived from General Systems Theory. He is a member of the Club of Rome and has taught at Yale and Princeton Universities. He is currently director of the United Nations Institute for Training and Research. A *Huffington Post* article by Laszlo cites British psychophysiologist Maxwell Cade who examined the EEG patterns of more than 3,000 individuals. He found a remarkable state that comes to light in the EEG-portrait of accomplished healers. Cade called the consciousness associated with this state "awakened mind." Here alpha and theta waves are strong, much as

---

13. Stanislav Groff, *The Adventure of Self-Discovery: Dimensions of Consciousness and New Perspectives in Psychotherapy and Inner Exploration* (Albany: State University of New York Press, 1988), 139.

14. http://www.metareligion.com/Philosophy/Articles/Consciousness/expansion_of_consciousness.htm From:mind-brain.com (http://mind-brain.com).

in the meditative state, but there are also beta waves. In some healers this state has become the norm, maintained not only during active healing but also in everyday life.

Laszlo points out that in this state the EEG waves are balanced across the left and the right hemispheres. This is important. The brain-state underlying ordinary consciousness is left-hemisphere dominated, and we know that the left hemisphere filters out experiences that do not mesh with our established beliefs and expectations. We also know that deep prayer and meditation activate the right hemisphere and tend to synchronize the two hemispheres. A hemisphere-synchronized brain can operate in the direct quantum-resonance mode. He has witnessed expert meditators synchronize not only their own left and right hemispheres, but also synchronize with the hemispheres of others who meditate with them. And this synchronization occurs in the entire absence of sensory contact among the meditators. They can be in different rooms, different cities, even on different continents.[15]

Research into the paranormal

Professor of Psychiatry, Ian Stevenson, has pioneered the accumulation of empirical evidence of past life memory in a now-iconic body of work, where the subjects, usually children, remember the locations of their previous lives and interact with people they used to know. But the most rigorous empirical experiments regarding actual subtle disincarnate existence have been done by Dr. Gary Schwartz at the University of Arizona Human Energy Systems Laboratory. Through a series of rigorous double-blind experiments, he had a number of reputable psychics and mediums individually contact one named deceased entity per experiment, with living relatives accessible for cross-confirmation under extremely isolated and insulated

15. Abraham Laszlo, *Science and the Akashic Field* (Rochester, Vermont: Inner Traditions, 2004), 53-4, 152-3. Also http://www.huffingtonpost.com/ervin-laszlo/quantum-consciousness-our_b_524054.html. and http://www.huffingtonpost.com/ervin-laszlo/why-your-brain-is-a-quant_b_489998.html.

conditions, asking the same list of personal and intimate questions. In most experiments the psychics and mediums averaged 80 percent unanimity. These experiments are ongoing to determine whether subtle conscious existence is parallel with concrete, physical existence.[16]

Quantum Physics

The quantum idea of entanglement is action at a distance, meaning that once two particles interact, they are connected forever and can affect each other directly regardless of how far apart they now are. This connection isn't dependent on the location of the particles in space. Even if you separate entangled particles by billions of miles, changing one particle will instantly induce a change in the other![17] Eugene Wigner, theoretical physicist and mathematician, winner of Nobel Prize in Physics, says, "It is not possible to formulate the laws of quantum mechanics in a fully consistent way without reference to consciousness."[18]

R.C. Henry, Professor of Physics and Astronomy at Johns Hopkins University, writes,

> Physicists are being forced to admit that the universe is a "mental" construction. Pioneering physicist Sir James Jeans wrote: "The stream of knowledge is heading toward a non-mechanical reality: the universe begins to look more like a great thought than like a great machine. Mind no longer appears to be an accidental intruder into the realm of matter: we ought rather to hail it as the creator and governor of the realm of matter. Get over it, and accept the inarguable conclusion. The universe is immaterial—mental and spiritual."[19]

---

16. https://www.academia.edu/2140608/A_Meta-Theory_of_Integral_Relativity.

17. http://physics.about.com/od/quantumphysics/f/QuantumEntanglement.htm.

18. http://www.informationphilosopher.com/solutions/scientists/wigner/.

19. "The Mental Universe" *Nature* 436:29, 2005. http://deanradin.com/evidence/Henry2005Nature.pdf.

Fred Wolf, American theoretical physicist specializing in quantum physics and the relationship between physics and consciousness, says, "Consciousness is the creative element in the universe."[20]

Religions neglect awakened mystical consciousness

This dimension of awakened consciousness, sometimes referred to as the "subtle realm," is often neglected or downplayed, not only in Christianity but in other traditions such as Theravada, Mahayana Buddhism, and Zen according to Ken Wilber. He says, "But the subtle realms are real and important. They are the domain of the transformational processes through which consciousness awakens from the gross to the causal [what I call transcendent] consciousness."[21] He says that we all have three bodies, a gross body, a subtle body, and a causal body, which correspond to the three states of consciousness which I call basic, awakened, and transcendent.

Awakened consciousness connects basic awareness with transcendent consciousness. Wilber says, "It is how Christ is connected to God. Jesus of Nazareth, the person whose body actually died on the cross, connected with the spirit that was resurrected from that dead body. In Christianity, Jesus of Nazareth was the gross body that died. Then the pure truth body, which was Christ's consciousness, which was one with God the father, the Christian equivalent of the *Dharmakaya*" [was left]. The Holy Spirit [awakened consciousness] was the transforming power that connected them.[22]

In another place Wilber writes about what I am calling awakened consciousness: "The high-subtle . . . said to be the realm of high religious intuition and literal inspiration; of bija mantra; of symbolic

---

20. Fred Wolf, *Taking the Quantum Leap: The New Physics for Nonscientists* (New York: Harper Collins, 1988), 275.

21. [http://www.integrallivingroom.com/blog/?utm_source=Integral+Living+Room+Master.

22. "A Discussion of Subtle Energy," recorded 4.9.2015. http://www. integrallivingroom.com/tag/subtle-energy/. *Dharmakaya is the unmanifest aspect of Buddha.*

visions; of blue, gold and white light; of audible illuminations and brightness upon brightness; it is the realm of higher presences, guides, angelic forms, ishtadevas,[23] and dhyani-buddha[24] ... [25]

A review of *Mystical Union in Judaism, Christianity, and Islam* states, "Mystics who have spoken of their union with God have come under suspicion in all three major religious traditions, sometimes to the point of condemnation and execution in the case of Christianity and Islam. Nevertheless, in all three religions the tradition of *unio mystica* is deep and long. Many of the spiritual giants of these three faiths have seen the attainment of mystical union as the heart of their beliefs and practices."[26]

Seven qualities of authentic mystical experiences

1. Mystical experiences are meant to inform and transform us. That's what they did in the Bible. That's what they do today when we are open to them.

2. This information and transformation is not always immediately obvious. Sometimes it takes years before we realize what we have learned and how it has changed us.

3. Mystical experiences are not for our entertainment, specialness, or importance. Mystics through the centuries have tended to downplay spiritual experiences because they do not want to call attention to the experiences but rather to God and our spiritual development. They realize less mature people may seek spiritual experiences to feel

---

23. In Hinduism, the form of a god that one is inspired by and therefore connects with.

24. The five Buddhas which are icons of Mahayana Buddhism, each representing a different aspect of enlightened consciousness to aid in spiritual transformation.

25. *Atman Project: A Transpersonal View of Human Development* (Wheaton: Quest, 1996), 78.

26. Moshe Idel and Bernard McGinn, ed., *Mystical Union in Judaism, Christianity, and Islam: An Ecumenical Dialogue* (New York: Continuum International Publishing Group, 1996). http://www.bloomsbury.com/us/mystical-union-in-judaism-christianity-and-islam-9781474281188/.

important or special. Recognizing and resolving our shadows' power over us takes work and time.

4. We should neither seek nor avoid any particular type of mystical experience but rather do the things that allow us to be open to all that God has for us. We are all different and will have a variety of different experiences.

5. All authentic mystical experiences are a mixture of ontologically rich spiritual reality and our shaping and interpretation of that reality according to our needs, culture, and stage of development. Rather than deflating their importance or ontological reality, this view puts us in the divine-human equation at a higher level than if it was all God.

6. We are participating in the creation and evolution of spiritual reality by cooperating with our divine-human spirit consciousness in embracing and learning from mystical experience. When Jesus had a mystical experience such as at his baptism, it was a co-creation of his spirit and God's spirit. His openness, willingness, degree of spiritual evolution, and cultural setting all contributed to his breakthrough for all humankind.

7. Devotion is a critical part of accessing spiritual reality. The spiritual world does not casually reveal its secrets. Ferrer says, "The process of loving devotion realizes what existed only as potential in the initial stage, thus creating a new ontological reality."[27] This echoes Jesus' words, "I still have many things to reveal to you but you are not ready for them now. When you are ready, the divine-human spirit-breath of inspired consciousness will make me real to you and together we will create new spiritual realities that have yet to emerge" (John 16:12-14, my paraphrase). *Nothing happens in the mystical spiritual realm without heartfelt devotion to God and spiritual realities.*

8. All of our mystical spiritual experiences are interpreted from our stage of "truth." In Chapter 3 we introduced Jesus' profound

---

27. Ferrer, *Revisioning Transpersonal Theory*, 174.

statement that we must worship God in spirit and truth" (John 4:24). There we focused on the "worship in spirit" dimension. But spirit alone is not enough because we interpret our experiences of spirit-breath consciousness from the level of truth that we have about the world around us. This stage of truth is our worldview or depth of understanding— what we think is "real" or "true" about our experience and how we view reality.

I join Ken Wilber in the Afterword in referring you to my book, *Integral Christianity*, for a fuller treatment of six worldviews or stages of truth that we can observe down through history.

Jesus had already sided with the awakened consciousness interpreted from the higher evolutionary level of the ethical consciousness of the later Old Testament prophets that had moved beyond the tribal and warrior stages. He introduced elements of what would later evolve into modern, postmodern, and integral worldviews and basically invited us into a never-ending evolution of perspectives when he said he had more to teach us and "spirit" (our evolving consciousnesses) would lead us into that in the future. In other words, Jesus was saying we must worship God at the highest dimensions of consciousnesses available to us at any given time in history, but also interpret that consciousness from the highest stage of truth available as our perspective on what we believe is real continues to evolve.

Summary of The Reality of Awakened Consciousness

• There are numerous accounts of awakened consciousness down through history and today.

• Mystical experiences inform and transform us. We are all different and will have a variety of experiences.

• All numinous experiences are a mixture of divine reality and our shaping and interpreting that reality according to our needs and culture.

• Devotion is a critical part of accessing spiritual reality. Nothing happens without genuine, heartfelt devotion.

Questions for Reflections and Discussion

1. If in a group, share whatever parts you may have marked as interesting or questionable and why.

2. Has this chapter made any change in your view of mystical experience? If so, share in what ways.

Practices

Make the following series of statements as often as you need to help you disidentify with your egoistic self and move you toward awakened and transcendent consciousness. You can use either the italicized words alone or the entire statement.

"I have a body, but I am not my body. I can see and feel my body, and what can be seen and felt is not my True Self. My body may be tired or excited, sick or healthy, heavy or light, but that has nothing to do with my inward I. I am wearing my body, but I am not my body."

"I have desires, but I am not my desires. I can know my desires, and what can be known is not my True Self. Desires come and go, floating through my awareness, but they do not affect my inward I. I have desires, but I am not desires."

"I have feelings, but I am not my feelings. I can feel and sense my emotions, and what can be felt and sensed is not my True Self. Feelings pass through me, but they do not affect my inward I. I have feelings, but I am not feelings."

"I have thoughts, but I am not my thoughts. I can know and intuit my thoughts, and what can be known is not my True Self. Thoughts come to me and thoughts leave me, but they do not affect my inward I. I have thoughts, but I am not my thoughts."

"As my deepest, truest self, I AM. I simply am. I am the awareness, the witness of all these thoughts, emotions, feelings, and desires." This is the direct experience of the Infinite Face of God.

The discovery of this divine center is like diving from the roaring waves on the surface of a stormy ocean to the quiet and secure depths of the bottom.

—Adapted from *The Simple Feeling of Being* by Ken Wilber

I Have Always Been Here

Reflect on the following. If in a group, ask someone to read it out loud with appropriate pauses:

Notice that you are here. Notice the objects arising in your awareness—the images and thoughts arising in your mind, the feelings and sensations arising in your body.

Now think about what was in your awareness 5 minutes ago. Most of the thoughts have changed, most of the bodily sensations have changed... but something has not changed. Something in you is the same now as it was 5 minutes ago. What is present now that was present 5 minutes ago? I AMness. The feeling-awareness of I AMness is still present. I am that ever-present I AMness. That I AMness is present now, it was present a moment ago... it was present 5 minutes ago.

What was present 5 hours ago? I AMness. That sense of I AMness is an ongoing self-knowing, self-recognizing, self-validating I AMness.

What was present 5 years ago? I AMness. So many objects have come and gone, so many feelings have come and gone, so many thoughts have come and gone... But one thing has not come, and one thing has not gone... This timeless, ever-present feeling of I AMness is present now as it was 5 years ago.

What was present five centuries ago? What is always-present is I AMness. Every person feels this same I Amness—because it is not a body, it is not a thought, it is not an object, it is not the environment, it is not anything that can be seen, but rather is the ever-present I Am which is none other than God Being Us.

How about five thousand years ago? When Jesus said "Before Abraham was, I AM," this is what he was talking about. When we say "Before Abraham was, I am," this is what we are talking about. In divine, transcendent consciousness we are aware of our own Divine Identity.

—Adapted from *The Simple Feeling of Being* by Ken Wilber and *The Book of Undoing* by Fred Davis.

Close with the Three Faces of God Devotion in Motion benediction.

"God beyond me, in whom I live and move, and have my being."

("God beyond us, in whom we live and move, and have our being.")

"God beside me, you are always with me."

("God beside us, you are always with us.")

"God being me, I am the light of the world."

("God being us, we are the light of the world.")

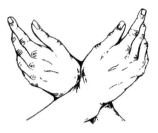

"God being me."

CHAPTER 12

The Results of Awakened Consciousness

Here are a few of the Christians who have significantly influenced the world after experiences of heightened, awakened consciousness.

St. Francis of Assisi (118–1226) was renowned for drinking and partying in his youth. After fighting in a battle between Assisi and Perugia, Francis was captured and imprisoned for ransom. He spent nearly a year in prison and began receiving visions from God. After his release, Francis was praying at the ancient church at San Damiano. He heard Jesus on the crucifix say to him, "Francis, repair my church." Consequently, he abandoned his life of luxury and became a devotee of the faith, his reputation spreading all over the Christian world.[1]

Thomas Aquinas (1225-1274) was an immensely influential philosopher and theologian, writing over one hundred works. He had many mystical experiences in his life and was often absorbed in

---

1. http://www.biography.com/people/st-francis-of-assisi-21152679.

various states of enchantment and unconscious of his surroundings. Towards the end of his life, according to an early biographer, he was saying mass on December 6, 1273, when he experienced a heavenly vision. After this he stopped writing. When urged by others to take up his pen again, he replied, "Such things have been revealed to me that all that I have written seems to me as so much straw. Now I await the end of my life." Three months later he died.[2]

Julian of Norwich (1342–1416) received a series of sixteen visions of Christ on the cross. She felt she was at the foot of the cross with Mary and other women. The things she "saw with her eyes," referred to by Julian as "showings," occurred over the course of hours. After that, she transcribed what she had seen in the short version of Revelations of Divine Love. Julian spent the next twenty years contemplating those visions, eventually writing a long version of the same volume and becoming the first woman to write a book in the English language.[3]

Teresa of Avila (1515–1582) was a charming, droll, tough-minded mystic and reformer, according to the London-based Roman Catholic magazine, the *Catholic Herald*. In the early years of her vocation as a nun, she was a socialite, entertaining many guests in the parlor. But in her 40s she felt compelled to reform her order and would go on to found 17 other convents.... In some ways, St. Teresa was like a Pope Francis of her time. She challenged her fellow religious not to be caught up with creature comforts, to be true to their vocation, and to dedicate hours each day to contemplative Carmelite prayer, as opposed to pleasure-seeking.

She had many mystical experiences, which she described as, "a feeling of the presence of God would come over me unexpectedly so that I could in no wise doubt either that he was within me, or that

2. http://www.christianity.com/church/church-history/timeline/1201-1500/thomas-aquinas-had-a-vision-11629843.html and http://www.crisismagazine.com/1996/the-spirituality-of-st-thomas-aquinas-2.

3. http://spectrummagazine.org/article/delcy-kuhlman/2012/08/22/revelations-divine-love-julian-norwich-study-guide-adventists.

I was wholly absorbed in him."[4] In her autobiography, she describes an intense visionary encounter with an angel:

> I saw in his hand a long spear of gold, and at the iron's point there seemed to be a little fire. He appeared to me to be thrusting it at times into my heart, and to pierce my very entrails; when he drew it out, he seemed to draw them out also and to leave me all on fire with a great love of God. The pain was so great that it made me moan; and yet so surpassing was the sweetness of this excessive pain, that I could not wish to be rid of it. The soul is satisfied now with nothing less than God. The pain is not bodily, but spiritual; though the body has its share in it. It is a caressing of love so sweet which now takes place between the soul and God, that I pray God of His goodness to make him experience it who may think that I am lying.[5]

Joan of Arc (1412–1431) was a teenage war hero with visions. One summer, when she was around 13, she was working in her father's garden at noon and saw a bright light and heard a voice. The voice called her "Joan the Maid" and told her to live a virtuous life. Voices came more often and gave instructions: Joan was to save France and help the Dauphin (France's rightful heir) be crowned. Joan questioned how she could accomplish these astounding feats. The voices said God would be with her. Joan later identified the voices as belonging to the archangel Michael and Saints Margaret of Antioch and Catherine of Alexandria.

She ended up helping 4,000 troops relieve the besieged city of Orleans. Though not the commander of the soldiers, she led them

---

4. http://www.discerninghearts.com/catholic-podcasts/st-teresa-of-avila-mystic-and-doctor-of-the-church/ and *Catholic Encyclopedia* http://newadvent.org/cathen/14515b.htm.

5. How's that for a jolly good Christian curse! St. Teresa of Jesus, *The Life of St. Teresa of Jesus*, Christian Ethereal Classics Library, Chapter XXIX; Part 17, http://www.ccel.org/ccel/teresa/life.viii.xxx.html.

in taking a number of forts that surrounded Orleans. During the battle, Joan was wounded (an arrow through the shoulder) but she quickly returned to the fight, and her fortitude inspired many French commanders to maintain the attack until the English capitulated.[6]

John Wesley (1703–1791), founder of Methodism, wrote that on May 24th, 1738 he opened his Bible at about five in the morning and came across these words, "There are given unto us exceeding great and precious promises, even that ye should be partakers of the divine nature." That evening as he reluctantly attended a church meeting he said, "I felt my heart strangely warmed." This spiritual awakening led to a great movement that eventually became the Methodist Church.[7]

William Booth (1829–1912) reported seeing a myriad of angelic beings as well as patriarchs, apostles, and Christian martyrs. Then he saw Jesus, who rebuked him for his "nominal, useless, lazy, professing Christian life." This experience led Booth to start the Salvation Army.[8]

Mother Teresa (1950–1997) had a secret life of mystical experiences with Jesus. It would be difficult to understand her work without these visions and mystical conversations with Jesus. They went from Sept. 10, 1946, to Dec. 3, 1947, as Jesus sent her to go out into the streets to care for the poorest of the poor. But not even her friends were aware of these awakened, mystical events. It wasn't until after her death that this part of Mother Teresa's spiritual life was uncovered in documents found in the archives of the Jesuits in Calcutta.

Mother Teresa wrote that one day at Holy Communion, she heard Jesus say, "I want Indian nuns, victims of my love, who would be Mary and Martha, who would be so united to me as to radiate my

6. http://www.christianitytoday.com/history/people/moversandshakers/joan-of-arc.html.

7. http://www.christianity.com/church/church-history/timeline/1701-1800/john-wesleys-heart-strangely-warmed-11630227.html.

8. Phillip Weibe, *Visions and Appearances of Jesus* (Abilene, Texas: Leafwood, 2014), 21.

love on souls. . . . I want free nuns covered with the poverty of the Cross. I want obedient nuns covered with the obedience of the Cross. I want full-of-love nuns covered with the charity of the Cross." Jesus asked her, "Would you refuse to do this for me?" She said, "I cannot go alone to the poor people, you carry me with you into them."

It was also discovered that Mother Teresa started to experience a "terrible darkness and dryness" in her spiritual life. This period lasted nearly 50 years, until her death, and she found it very painful. She said, "If my darkness and dryness can be a light to some soul let me be the first one to do that. If my life, if my suffering, is going to help souls to be saved, then I will prefer from the creation of the world to the end of time to suffer and die."[9]

To me, this made her original visions even more impressive since their memory was her sole motivation to keep working in the slums of Calcutta in the subsequent years. I wonder if she would have suffered so much if she had been around mystics who could have helped her into a more sustained mystical journey.

Marcus Borg (1942–2015), whom I have admired for twenty years, is among the most widely known and influential voices in progressive Christianity. A fellow of the Jesus Seminar, his many books about enlightened Christianity nourished me in an unusual way. I was not sure why I resonated with him so much since I was a critic of the extreme reductionism of the Jesus Seminar. I found out a few years before his death in 2015 why I felt spiritually as well as theologically in tune with him when he wrote the following in his blog:

> My most formative religious experiences were a series of mystical experiences. They began to occur in my early thirties. They changed my understanding of the meaning of the word "God"—of what that word points to— and gave me an unshakable conviction that God (or "the sacred") is real and can be experienced. These experiences

9. http://www.zenit.org/en/articles/mother-teresa-s-mystical-experiences-origin-of-her-work, and http://www.catholic.org/news/hf/faith/story.php?id=70599.

also convinced me that mystical forms of Christianity are true, and that the mystical forms of all the enduring religions of the world are true.

For a minute or two (and once for the better part of an hour), what I was seeing looked very different. Light became different—as if there were a radiance shining through everything. The biblical phrase for this is "the glory of God"—as the book of Isaiah puts it, "the earth is filled with the glory—the radiance—of God." The world was transfigured, even as it remained "the same." And I experienced a falling away of the subject-object distinction that marks our ordinary everyday experience—that sense of being a separate self, "in here," while the world is "out there."

They were experiences of wonder—not of curiosity, but of what the 20th-century Jewish theologian Abraham Heschel called "radical amazement." They were also experiences in which I felt that I was seeing more clearly than I ever had before—that what I was experiencing was "the way things are." And they were also experiences of complete peacefulness, marked by a sense that I would love to stay in this mental state forever. Anxiety and distraction utterly disappeared. Everything looked beautiful.

When I had these experiences, I had no intellectual understanding of mysticism. Indeed, whenever I tried to read mystical writings, they seemed like gobbledy-gook. I had no idea what they were about—they were completely opaque. But after these experiences, mystical texts became luminous. I recognized in them what I had experienced.

The effect was to transform my understanding of the word "God." . . . to use a phrase from the New Testament, the word "God" refers to "the one in whom we live and move and have our being" (Acts 17:28). "God" is not a hypothesis, but a reality who can be known.[10]

As I pointed out previously, Borg used five foundational adjectives to describe Jesus and "mystic" is number one! Why, as a Jesus Seminar Fellow, does he say this? Could it be that because of his own mystical experiences he recognized their importance and radical centrality in the life of Jesus? Often scholars ignore or dismiss Jesus' mystical experiences. Borg recognized them as part of his own spiritual journey. Until scholars and others who teach about the Bible and the Christian life begin to have their own mystical experiences they will continue to ignore or dismiss them in the Bible and their value in the Christian life.

Four factors in biblical spiritual experiences

These Christians illustrate what prominent New Testament scholar and historian of early Christianity Luke Timothy Johnson wrote about the kinds of experiences associated with spirit in the Bible. He says they are connected with four factors:

(1) Transcendent rather than trivial concerns—which doesn't mean the event might not be relatively small, but that it is connected to ultimate realities.

(2) Affects our whole self—mind, body, feelings, and will,

(3) A certain kind of intensity that comes from an amplified awareness and sense of contact with a heightened reality.

(4) Results in action.[11]

Paul, the consummate Christian mystic, was also a passionate, intellectual activist

We find all four of these factors that Johnson outlines in Paul's life.

---

10. "Mystical Experiences of God." The Marcus Borg Foundation. http://www.marcusjborg.com/2010/07/01/mystical-experiences-of-god/.

11. Johnson, *Religious Experience*, 61-63.

> Now as he was going along and approaching Damascus, suddenly a light from heaven flashed around him. He fell to the ground and heard a voice saying to him, "Saul, Saul, why do you persecute me?" He asked, "Who are you, Lord?" The reply came, "I am Jesus, whom you are persecuting. But get up and enter the city, and you will be told what you are to do." The men who were traveling with him stood speechless because they heard the voice but saw no one. Saul got up from the ground, and though his eyes were open, he could see nothing; so they led him by the hand and brought him into Damascus. For three days he was without sight, and neither ate nor drank.
>
> (Acts 9:3-9)

Notice this event, in Johnson's words, included:

(1) "Transcendent concerns" involving Paul's relationship to God, his calling, and the rest of his life.

(2) It affected his "whole self"—mind, body, feelings, and will—as his body was overwhelmed with spiritual energy and he fell to the ground in an altered state of consciousness. He was changed from persecutor of followers of Jesus to their stunning defender.

(3) This was one of many such events in his life that followed of "heightened awareness" in intensified visual and auditory consciousness with the voice of Jesus in his spiritual body.

(4) The "results in action" were that these mystical experiences were the very foundations of Paul significantly shaping the course of Christian tradition and altering the history of the world.

Not only was Jesus a mystic, his first and primary interpreter, Paul, was also a mystic who had numerous visionary experiences. Albert Schweitzer (1875–1965), was a theologian, organist, philosopher, physician, recipient of the 1952 Nobel Peace Prize, and founder and sustainer of the Albert Schweitzer Hospital in west central Africa, one of the leading scientific institutions in Africa. He wrote, "Paul is the patron-saint of thought in Christianity. And all those who think to serve the faith in Jesus by destroying freedom of thought would do well to keep out of his way." But Schweitzer also considered Paul to be a mystic, writing a whole book on the subject called *The Mysticism of the Apostle Paul.* He said, "For Christianity is a Christ-Mysticism, that is to say, a 'belonging together' with Christ as our Lord, grasped in thought and realized in experience."[12]

Paul's numinous, awakened consciousness events

• Paul's initial mystical vision of heavenly light and conversation with Jesus is narrated three times in Acts (9:5, 22:8, and 26:15).

• Paul writes of his "visions and revelations of the Lord" (2 Cor. 12:1).

• He was "caught up to the third heaven—whether in the body or out of the body I do not know; God knows . . . and heard things that are not to be told, that no mortal is permitted to repeat" (2 Cor. 12:1-4).

• He had a vision in the night of a man from Macedonia, saying, "Come over into Macedonia, and help us" (Acts 16:9).

• Jesus spoke to Paul in a vision: "Do not be afraid; keep on speaking, do not be silent" (Acts 18:9).

• He had three conversations with the risen Jesus about his "thorn in the flesh" (Acts 12:8).

• He claimed his writings and teachings were "revelations" from God (2 Cor. 12:1).

• When Paul says he conferred with no one and instead "went away to Arabia" (Gal.1:17), he's saying that his teachings were not of human origin but came directly from God and Jesus.

---

12. Albert Schweitzer, *The Mysticism of Paul the Apostle* (Baltimore: Johns Hopkins University Press, 1998), 377-8.

• Paul thanked God that "more than any of you" (1Cor. 14:18) he prayed in *glōssa*, words beyond words, the transrational devotional language of prayer and praise.

• Paul received instructions about the Lord's Supper by direct revelation: "I received from the Lord what I also delivered to you" (1 Cor. 11:23).

• He said not to brag about mystical experiences even though he did not hesitate to be open about his because they were so transforming for him and subsequently helped to establish his credibility as an apostle (2 Cor. 2:17).

• He recounts a vision of Jesus while he was praying in the temple in Jerusalem saying, "While praying, I fell into a trance and saw Jesus saying to me, 'Hurry, get out of Jerusalem quickly'" (Acts 22:17).

• Paul lists himself as one of those who had also seen the risen Jesus (1 Cor. 15:5-9). Paul did not know the historical Jesus but rather only knew Jesus in his spiritual body.

Paul is seen by some progressives as a social and sexual conservative. Letters attributed to him urged slaves to obey their masters, taught the subordination of women, appeared to condemn homosexuality, and saw sexual behavior as a part of human weakness. As Spellcheck corrected one seminarian to write in his term paper, "Paul preached to the Genitals." Marcus Borg and John Dominic Crossan, in *The First Paul: Reclaiming the Radical Visionary Behind the Church's Conservative Icon*, show that the seven authentic letters of Paul reveal a progressive visionary who advocated freedom and equality. Paul's version of Christianity is the essence of Christian mysticism which results in liberating action.

Ananias, the quiet ministry of an "in the background" mystic

We can't leave Paul's initial experience without recognizing the visionary experience of Ananias that was connected to Paul's calling. This illustrates these same four qualities in a less dramatic way.

Now there was a disciple in Damascus named Ananias. The Lord said to him in a vision, "Ananias." He answered, "Here I am, Lord." The Lord said to him, "Get up and go to the street called Straight, and at the house of Judas look for a man of Tarsus named Saul. At this moment he is praying, and he has seen in a vision a man named Ananias come in and lay his hands on him so that he might regain his sight."

(Acts 9:10-12)

This, too, involved a transcendent vision where Jesus gave Ananias specific actions to take. On the surface, it was a relatively small thing to go to someone's house and pray for them. However, it was a difficult thing in this case—deliberately facing a man who spent his time persecuting people just like Ananias! But Ananias went and put his hands on Paul, praying for Paul to "regain his sight and be filled with holy spirit" (Acts 10:17). Ananias' faithfulness in a relatively small way in mystical healing and activating prayer resulted in the healing of Paul's eyesight, initial spirit-breath activation, and going on to spend the rest of his life as one of the most famous transformed and transforming persons of all time. We will not all be an Apostle Paul but we can all be an Ananias, quietly listening to the inner voice of God and following it.

Fourteen Transforming Results of Mystical Experience

1. Mystical awakened consciousness is communications central for spiritual reality.

Sacred visions, channeled words, and intuitions are some of the languages that God uses for delivering guidance and wisdom to humanity. Transpersonalist Jorge Ferrer notes:

Although with different emphases, every transpersonal theorist has maintained that transpersonal and spiritual phenomena provide important and valid knowledge about human beings and the world. This commitment situates the transpersonal vision in sharp contrast with scientistic, materialist, positivist, analytical, and reductionistic paradigms, which have consistently regarded spirituality as wishful thinking, infantile illusions, mere ideology, psychotic hallucinations, pseudoscience, language games with no reference to the real world, or, at best, edifying private, subjective experiences without public, objective cognitive value . . . Spiritual knowledge is not the fruit of psychological imagination or pathological delusion. Anyone who has seriously engaged in a spiritual life knows that essential information about human nature and reality can be revealed through spiritual states.[13]

2. Mystical experiences can be targeted to an individual in a more direct way than biblical passages, sermons, or books usually are.

This makes the divine messages they carry especially relevant for the person they are given to. Sometimes one of my congregation members would say something like, "I was listening to God in my prayer time yesterday and heard these words for you . . . ." I would take them seriously, even as I also tried to discern if and how they fit for me. Quite often they would be greatly encouraging to me in exactly what I was going through.

3. Sacred intuitions and visions have a certain kind of intensity.

This comes from heightened awareness and sense of contact with a deepened reality that makes their divine messages more powerful and compelling. They can make an emotionally intense and often permanent impression on us that can be life-changing. My visions have been deeply transforming for me.

4. We can directly encounter God in the sacred space of awakened consciousness.

It's one thing to say a prayer; it's another to sense God's and Jesus' presence in a real way and have a conversation.

---

13. Ferrer, *Revisioning Transpersonal Theory*, 28, 61.

5. Vivid spiritual events give us the courage to move on in our faith.

As Meister Eckhart says, "The best and utmost of attainment in life is to be still and let the voice of God act and speak within you."[14]

6. Spiritual experience moves Jesus from being a belief to being a reality.

"The spirit-breath (pneuma) will glorify me by taking what is mine and declaring it to you" (John 16:14). The word glorify means "to cause the worth of some person or thing to become manifest and acknowledged."[15] In effect, this means that Jesus will be made as real to us in the spiritual realm in his "glorified" body, as he was in the physical realm. This is the risen Jesus, the "glorified" Jesus who is with us now all the time and everywhere. This is the historical Jesus now with us in his subtle energy body presence. How does this happen or how do we become aware of this? By spirit-breath in an inner awakened state of consciousness.

7. The shared energy field of communal worship transforms and renews us.

The connecting field of mystical consciousness results in the ability to enter this spiritual energy field with others in prayer, meditation, and worship. The early church worship was regularly in this subtle energy space, and we can read detailed accounts of it in 1 Corinthians 11-14. It is clear that the Christians there were reentering the state of consciousness they first encountered in their initial baptism or filling with the spirit-breath consciousness. Every time they gathered they moved back into this space which kept it alive and deepened in their lives.

Their communal worship included various spiritual giftings that would have in effect accomplished what Jesus would have done in their group had he been physically present. Paul writes, "To each is given a manifestation of spirit-breath (awakened consciousness) for the common good" (1 Cor.12:7). Jesus was spiritually present in their expressions of mystical consciousness during the worship

14. Meister Eckhart. http://first-thoughts.org/on/Meister+Eckhart/.

15. Thayer, *Greek-English Lexicon*, 157.

meeting. Some would share words they were hearing from Jesus or God in non-ordinary consciousness for the strengthening of the group (prophecy). Others operated with healing gifts as Jesus did or sharing spiritual discernment and wisdom as Jesus did that came to them in the devotional state of mind and heart that is true worship.

The worship of the early church was one where Jesus was present in his spiritual body and physically present in the shared meals and manifestations of spiritual gifts offered by the participants. In other words, whatever Jesus would have done had he walked into their church service and taken over, he was doing via the awakened consciousness of the members in breaking bread and worship!

8. Spirit as awakened consciousness brings joy.

Abraham Maslow (1908–1970) was an American psychologist who was best known for creating "Maslow's hierarchy of needs." He said that peak-experiences are the most fulfilling, joyous, and blissful moments in one's life. During these moments, an individual could experience, among other phenomena, a sense of self-transcendence, wholeness, and undeserved grace; a resolution of the polarities of ordinary life; a variety of creative and spiritual insights; a complete loss of anxiety and fear; and a compelling certainty of the intrinsically benevolent nature of the world.[16]

Jesus had many of these peak experiences. "At that time Jesus, full of joy through holy spirit-breath, said, 'I praise you, Abba God, Sovereign of heaven and earth, because you have hidden these things from the wise and learned, and revealed them to little children. Yes, Abba God, for this was your good pleasure'" (Luke 10:21). This same joy can be ours today. I experience it often, even daily, and sometimes hourly when I'm paying attention.

9. Spirit as awakened consciousness brings justice.

"Here is my servant whom I have chosen, the one I love, in whom

---

16. Ferrer, *Revisioning Transpersonal Theory*, 38.

I delight; I will put my spirit-breath on him, and he will proclaim justice to the nations" (Matt 12:18). Jesus led the cause for justice for the poor and outcast, died for his actions, and planted seeds for future generations to continue to press for change in our social, political, and economic worlds.

10. Spirit-breath awakening brings freedom.

"Where the spirit of the Lord is, there is freedom" (2 Cor. 3:17).

11. Divine-human consciousness teaches us wisdom and spiritual truth.

"The spirit of the Lord shall rest upon him: a spirit of wisdom and of understanding" (Isaiah 11:2). Divine-human spirit-breath consciousness teaches us: "You gave your good spirit-breath to instruct them" (Neh. 9:20). From Paul we hear, "This is what we speak, not in words taught us by human wisdom but in words taught by spirit-breath, expressing spiritual truths in spiritual words" (1 Cor. 2:13).

12. Spirit as awakened consciousness gives us commonality with other religions.

Understanding spirit as divine-human awakened consciousness gives us a greater commonality about the inner path of the world's great traditions. Buddhist meditators, Jewish Kabbalists, Christian mystics, and whirling Sufi dervishes can all, in Christian terminology, be filled with awakened spirit-breath. They are resting in something of the same space using different terminology, images, and expectations. These are the amazingly similar and profound experiences of spirit-breath that I call awakened and transcendent consciousness which connects us to spiritual realities that can only be seen and experienced from this awareness.

The goal and effects of "spirit filling" in the New Testament appears remarkably similar to the goal and effects of meditation and other spiritual practices by the religious and non-religious alike that awaken us to higher and transcendent states of consciousness. The terminology may be different, but the phenomenology appears quite similar.

13. Preparation for death as a spiritual experience.

Dying is a mystical state experience. The more familiar we are with the mystical state of awakened consciousness, the less we are afraid of dying. The thousands of Near Death Experience reports demonstrate this dramatically. People who have had them lose their fear of death.

14. The goal of the spiritual life is not just to have mystical experiences.

Rather, it is to bring about genuine change, first in us, and then in the world around us. The work of spirituality, broadly defined, is the transformative process in which we uncover and let go of our narcissism so as to surrender into the Mystery out of which everything continually arises. This is moving from self-centeredness to self-giving love. For Christians, the Mystery that we surrender to is God, and Jesus is our incredible model and companion in the process.

Summary of The Results of Awakened Consciousness

• The mystical experiences of nine well-known Christians who have influenced the world are described.

• The Apostle Paul's numerous recorded experiences of awakened consciousness are listed and explored.

• Mystical events are the way spiritual reality is communicated to us in a targeted and intensified way.

• They give us courage, make Jesus real to us, and place us in a field of shared energy in community worship.

• They bring joy, freedom, commonality with other religious, and preparation for death.

• The goal of mystical experiences is to move from self-centeredness to self-giving, which such experiences can facilitate.

Questions for Reflection and Group Discussion

1. Which account of mystical experiences by famous Christians did you find most interesting, if any? Why?

2. Do any of the "Fourteen Transforming Results of Mystical Experience" resonant with where you are in your life?

Practices

One way to bring healing to yourself is by being present in the body. Another way is by expanding the heart. A third way is by quieting the mind. Anyone who wants real change finds a way to work on all three at the same time.

Higher consciousness is a muscle. It gets stronger, bigger, and better with exercise. Just like the practice of regular physical exercise, the following five steps may be helpful in getting started in the exercise of prayer and meditation.

1. Turn your mind towards God

Having already turned off phones, collected whatever things you use (CD/MP3 player,[17] timer, comfortable clothing, pen/paper), let others know you are having your "zone" time, sit down in your regular chair in any position that allows you to be comfortable for 20 plus minutes. Turn your attention, mind, and heart towards God. Simply be aware that this is what this time is all about.

2. State your intention.

Say inwardly or outwardly what you are seeking from this time. Put it into words: "I want _____ (to feel your presence, to get help with _____, to see your face, to talk to my guides, to be peaceful, to come alive, help with a problem, etc.)."

---

17. I have often used brainwave entrainment CDs such as those at Profound Meditation. (http://www.iawaketechnologies.com/). These can increase your ability to enter higher states in prayer and meditation, especially as you begin.

3. Make a heartfelt devotional connection.

Prayer goes nowhere without genuine devotion and a heart to heart connection to God, Jesus, or whoever you are addressing. Remember the key question to ask yourself from Chapter 5, "What would I feel if Jesus (or whoever) was standing here next to me?" Answering this question can help to get the emotional energy of gratitude and devotion flowing in you.

4. Practice a child-like attitude.

Use your intellect to find a framework that your mind can accept so your heart can embrace it. If you can't find an intellectually satisfying framework, then let go of needing one. The priority is not your need to understand, but your need to learn to trust God. Jesus said, "Except you become as a little child you cannot see the Reign of God." Having a real conversation with Jesus requires just such child-like trust.

5. Consider the Three Faces of God benediction for your prayer time.

"God beyond me, in whom I live and move, and have my being."

("God beyond us, in whom we live and move, and have our being.")

"God beside me, you are always with me."

("God beside us, you are always with us.")

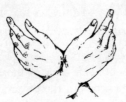

"God being me, I am the light of the world."

("God being us, we are the light of the world.")

"God being me."

CHAPTER 13

The Bliss of Transcendent Consciousness

Will the Real Me please stand up?

When someone asks you to tell them about yourself, what do you say? Social convention usually calls for things like job, family, and interests. Of course, inwardly you know you are more than all of that. You are a body, a mind, and a gender and sexual identity. You have a level of education, money, car, and clothes that can be an important part of how you see yourself. You have a certain personality and a unique, one of a kind, history with circumstances in life that have especially shaped who you are. All of this makes up the self that we learn to identify with in order to become an individual and function efficiently in the world. This is the ego part of us that helps us establish our separate identity. This separate self is very important to develop in order for us to begin to grow up. This ego is our warm-up self for the first part of our life.

Our poor, trashed ego

Our ego has been given a bad rap lately. It's been called all sorts of names such as the false self, separate self, small self, egoic self, and constructed self. Ouch! How would you feel if some big bully got up in a crowd, pointed to one of your children, and shouted, "You false, lonely, small, ego-centered, made-up kid!" These are negative sounding names for such an important part of all of us. However, they are all true in some sense if we continue in life to confuse our ego with our True Self. On the other hand, these names are not helpful to begin with. To start with, our ego is important to our journey in human form and is the basis through which our uniqueness comes to be expressed eternally.

Four Stages in Moving to the Real You

Stage One to the Real You: Become a Somebody

Our first job in life is to become a Somebody. You don't have to be a famous Somebody, just a regular, everyday Somebody with a grown-up, healthy, well-developed self or ego that has good boundaries. Boundaries are what allow us to separate our own self from someone else's self. We need to know where we stop and somebody else begins. If we can't be separate from others, we can't do a very good job of being together with others. The closer we are to someone, the more a lack of good boundaries shows up.

Stage Two to the Real You: Become a Nobody

After you are reasonably successful in becoming a Somebody, you are ready for the next stage. Stage two is to become a Nobody. Why would anyone want to do a crazy thing like that? Many people don't want to, maybe even all of us! However, when we find out that Jesus said it was a crucial stage in growing up and being his follower, some of us change our minds.

Ever the intriguing teacher, Jesus offers us a riddle about becoming a Nobody: "You who wish to be my followers must lose your very self. Take up your cross every day, and follow in my steps. If you would save your self, you'll lose it. If you would lose your self for my sake, you'll save it" (Luke 9:23-24). This is the focus of Richard Rohr's insightful Foreword. Of all the topics I address in this book, he heads to the single most important one, what he calls "always-losing-a-self-to-find-a-self."

First, notice that when Jesus says, "die to self to find the self," he assumes we have a self. You can't die to or lose something you don't have. *You must be a Somebody before you can be a Nobody!* Losing yourself doesn't work if you have a self that is so undeveloped or damaged that it really can't be called much of a self. Now this is tricky. None of us has a completely developed, never-been-damaged self. So we're talking in relative terms here. Only you can sense when it's time to consider taking care of your self in Jesus' enlightened way. This usually occurs, as Richard Rohr helpfully points out, in the second half of life.[1]

Next, the key to Jesus' riddle is to understand that he is talking about two different "selves." One is this first, warm-up self that we come to think of as us. This is our ego self which is given to us by God so that we can grow up and function in the world around us. This may sound strange since we usually use the word ego in a negative way. But ego is simply our sense of self that differentiates us from other "selves." We all need an ego that is as healthy as it can be to function in the world.

Our other self is our True Self, the real us, the made-in-the-image-of-God self. This is our divine God-Being-Us Self. It is usually covered over and hidden by our warm-up self. It starts out undiscovered and unknown. If we are to manifest this deepest self, we have to "lose" our ego self. This means we stop identifying with our ego and begin identifying with the real us, our Divine God-Being-Us Self. To do that, we go on a journey, a spiritual journey, where we discover,

---

1. Richard Rohr, *Falling Upward: A Spirituality for the Two Halves of Life* (San Francisco: Jossey-Bass, 2011).

uncover, embrace, identify with, and manifest our divine image and likeness of God.

Becoming our True Self is not becoming something that we are not. It is *becoming what we already are!* If we mistakenly think our warm-up self is our real Self, then that warm-up self becomes a false self. We have a debilitating case of mistaken identity. If we think our separate self is our Real Self, we will never be able to come into any sense of our Oneness with God. Our ego is only a false, small, self-centered, mistaken self when it pretends to be the real us.

A Nobody is empty

Christians and others sometimes use the word "emptiness" to describe what losing our self is like. While "emptiness" can appear to be the language of Eastern religions, it is also very much a part of the Christian tradition. Even Jesus "emptied himself" as we will explore at the end of this chapter. Being "empty" does not initially seem to most of us to be a good thing. Usually whenever we feel empty we feel lost and unable connect with or love others. This is one reason we resist losing our self and becoming "empty." Another reason is that as long as we think our ego self is the real us, we are afraid to let go of it. Who wants to disappear and become nothing, a Nobody! That would feel like dying—which is exactly why Jesus puts it as "taking up our cross." Crucifixion is quite a dramatic metaphor for dying to your self, but it fits. It feels like dying, only one piece at a time. If that's not bad enough, Jesus said we needed to do it every day! That's the only way we get to all the pieces. It means letting go of everything. This includes our possessions, dreams, desires, and longings. It includes our relationships and reputations. It even means we let go of trying to change and be "better." We can even make "letting go" or "losing our self" a project and then we have to let go of letting go.

Being empty includes losing your mind

We must even learn to lose our minds. We all live with a roommate in our heads that loves to talk.[2] This roommate chatters on endlessly. The babble ranges from pointing out how bad we are, to worrying about the terrible things that are surely going to happen to us. If this incessant talk and noise is not enough in our heads, we try to get away from it by finding something louder to drown it out. Television, radio or newspaper drama is a good start. Movies that grab our attention can help, too. We pay big money for all kinds of entertainment to drag us away from our self-talk. The new thing on the scene that has now attached itself to our hands and heads is our incredible cell phone. Like the hymn goes, it "walks with me and talks with me." The joy of texting, twittering, or whatever is the new thing by the time you are reading this book is always with us. If the drama there isn't enough, we will make some drama in our lives by finding some others to play out the relational drama of rescuer, persecutor, and victim.[3]

Losing our mind or letting go of its busyness and inner drama games takes time and intention. The Psalmist put it as "Be still and know that I am God" (Psalm 46:10). This is not "Stop fidgeting and sit still." It means letting go of our busy mind by letting our thoughts pass by without engaging them. The more we practice this the more "empty" we become.

Writer Daniel J. Rice pens it in his characters' dialogue:

> "Sometimes I feel like I'm losing my mind," she said with a hint of sadness.
> "You lost your mind a long time ago," he said seriously. She looked at him with indignation.
> "That's a compliment for anyone who knows the freedom and clarity of losing their mind," he reaffirmed her.[4]

---

2. Michael Singer, *The Untethered Soul: The Journey Beyond Yourself* (Oakland, California: New Harbinger Publications, 2013), 15-22.

3. See the Drama Triangle to learn how to stay off of this kind of relational drama. http://www.johngouletmft.com/Breaking_The_Drama_Triangle_Newest.pdf, and http://www.soulselfhelp.on.ca/karpmandramatriangle.pdf

4. Daniel J. Rice, *This Side of a Wilderness.*, Riverfeet Press, 2016.

Jesus recommends losing your self every day

Losing your mind, along with everything else, happens best as a daily activity. That's why Jesus called it "take up your cross every day." It is dying to our self all the time. We are no longer attached to our ego or anything else. It doesn't mean our ego is dead, or gone, or not still useful in functioning in the world. It just means we have lost our death grip on it. Ego death, or dying to our small self, is not getting rid of our ego. It is letting go and replacing devotion to ego with devotion to God. Now the good news: We are in for an incredible surprise about emptiness when we let go of our small self.

Emptiness is not empty

We delightfully discover that Emptiness in a spiritual or metaphysical sense is anything but empty. Emptying our life and mind of its attachments lets us be filled with God! True Emptiness is full of God. God is love. Real emptiness is full of love. Donald W. Mitchell, emeritus Professor of Philosophy at University of Hawaii and author of eight books on Buddhism and Christianity, points out a difference between Buddhism and Christianity. He says, "The ground of being in Buddhism is understood as Emptiness, and in Christianity as God [where] the void is a field of love and unity out of which Being creates Beings."[5]

Chair in Theology at Villanova University and Franciscan Sister Ilia Delio says, "Emptiness is not nothingness but, paradoxically, 'all-ness or oneness.' It is the deepest core of oneself beyond thoughts, words, and concepts, the level at which there is no separate 'I.'"[6]

Again, pointing at a difference between some forms of Buddhism and Christianity, Steve McIntosh, in his insightful book *The Presence of the Infinite*, says:

---

5. Donald W. Mitchell, *Spirituality and Emptiness: The Dynamics of Spiritual Life in Buddhism and Christianity* (Mahwah, New Jersey: Paulist Press, 1991), 31, 26, 20.

6. Ilia Delio, *Making All Things New: Catholicity, Cosmology, Consciousness*, (Maryknoll: Orbis, 2015), 153.

. . . ultimate reality possesses the qualities of awareness, intelligence, intentionality, creativity, and love— qualities that are unmistakably personal. Every human possesses these qualities; indeed these are the qualities that actually make us real persons. And if we also possess the undivided nondual whole as our true nature or essence— if "thou art that" or "we are it"— then the nondual whole in itself must also possess these personal qualities.[7]

Stage Three to becoming the Real You: Begin to Embody (God)

Becoming an empty Nobody finally gives you room in your awareness to Embody God. And what we embody is *God-being-us*! It is here, for the first time, we begin to realize just who we are. We move into transcendent consciousness, sometimes in a sudden peak experience, or more often little by little and more and more. There we become comfortable with God-being-me as in "I am the light of the world." In contrast to the activity of the awakened realm, the transcendent realm is one of stillness and emptiness. It may only be reported in the Bible as simply as something like Jesus spending the night in prayer or saying, "Before Abraham was, I am." The transcendent realm comes increasingly to light in the writings of the mystics of both the Christian West and Buddhist/Hindu East.

God comes to you disguised as your deepest self!

An often quoted line from Paula D'Arcy is "God comes to you disguised as your life."[8] That simple sentence comes up and slaps us awake! Oh my, I keep trying to avoid my life and God keeps saying that's where you will find me!

However, even more surprising to me—that's not nearly strong enough—even more unnerving, ego shattering, heart opening, not

---

7. McIntosh, *The Presence of the Infinite*, 188.

8. Richard Rohr, *Everything Belongs: The Gift of Contemplative Prayer* (New York: Crossroad 2003), 123.

a slap in the face but a knock-out punch to all my other superficial selves is this: *God comes to you disguised as your deepest self.*

But you say, "I've been trying to find God out there all my life!" Yes, that's the way we start because that's true, too. God *is* out there, beyond us and beside us. But don't stop there. The most astonishing thing for us Westerners is that God is *in* here. The more we let go of everything that is not our deepest self, the more the disguise dissolves—and there we are—the glory of God in human flesh—our flesh!

This is why it is so important to see Jesus as fully God and fully human. It's not to honor Jesus or to get your theology right. It's to get your life right! If you can begin to see God in Jesus' humanity, then you can begin to see it in yours! Jesus came to model for us what God-Embodied looked like so we could find it in ourselves! God-Being-us!

To embody I AM is to identify as I AM.

There are books and teachers who talk about the power of I AM. They use many affirmations expressed as "I am" followed by positive words such as "peaceful" or "okay." There is power in this lesser awareness of I AM "something," as in "I am loved, I am a child of God, I am a divine human being who was never born and will never die." These can all be a part of helping our wounded self become a Somebody. However, these affirmations fade into the background when we begin to know the power of pure I AM. This is I AM without words or thoughts or images to complete what we are. We just simply ARE.

What happens if we just stop with "I am," rather than finishing that statement with something we think we are or would like to be? When we just stay with the simple "I am," gradually or sometimes suddenly, we move into something much more profound. We fall into big mind, the infinite reality beyond things.

Camaldolese-Benedictine monk Bruno Barnhart, writing about

our mutual participation with God points out, "The *implicit divine participation* of the First Testament reaches a peak in the revelation of the divine Name-Yahweh, or 'I am' to Moses."[9] Echoing that truth, Owen Barfield, British philosopher, author, poet, and critic, reminds us that, "A human being cannot utter this divine Name without some degree of implicit appropriation of the divine identity."[10] This is a sophisticated way of saying "deep down you are a god!"

Physicist Fred Wolf says, "The first documented case of quantum consciousness may have been Moses. When he asked, 'Who are You?' of the Presence felt at the burning bush, the answer came: 'I AM THAT I AM.' Moses then recognized that, within him, the God Voice now spoke as Moses."[11] As we embody God-Being-Us like Jesus, we become the voice and heart, hands, and feet of God in the world.

A point of nothingness

Thomas Merton brilliantly describes this emptiness in its most sacred sense:

> At the center of our being is a point of nothingness which is untouched by sin and by illusion, a point of pure truth, a point or spark which belongs entirely to God, which is never at our disposal, from which God disposes of our lives, which is inaccessible to the fantasies of our own mind or the brutalities of our own will. This little point of nothingness and of absolute poverty is the pure glory of God in us. . . . It is like a pure diamond, blazing with the invisible light of heaven. It is in everybody, and if we could see these billions of points of light coming

---

9. Bruno Barnhart, "One Spirit, One Body" in Ferrer, *The Participatory Turn*, 269. (italics mine to point out this is this is God participating in our life as we are, in the words of 2 Peter 1:4, "participants in the divine nature").

10. Owen Barfield, *Saving the Appearances: A Study in Idolatry* (Indianapolis, Indiana, Wesleyan, 1988), 113-115.

11. Wolf, *Taking the Quantum Leap*, 246.

together in the face and blaze of a sun that would make
all the darkness and cruelty of life vanish completely.[12]

The first time I read Merton years ago, because I thought I should,
I had little resonance with him. He sounded philosophical, vague,
mysterious, and writing about things I had little experience with.
But these words jumped off the page after I began to experience this
"nothingness." His eloquent description of what I was experiencing
was incredibly helpful.

My I AM is my unique self

I AM is my divine center, my true being. It is *my* I AM in that no
one other than me can say I AM for me. Yet, there is only one I AM.
It is the I AM in which we all share. I AM is formless. But in the
fabric of my formless I AM is my one-of-a-kind, unique self, waiting
to be manifested in form.[13] Our True Self is also Unique Self even
while sharing in the One Self that is God. It is *our* True Self which
means it is one with all other selves but not the same as all other
selves. It is the divine experienced through our unique perspective.
Our True Self is an individualized expression of God. When I say "I
AM" without adding any "what" to it, I am affirming my own divine
center that is infinite being itself, the presence of God in and as me.
I AM is most deeply and authentically my God-Being-Me Self.

Don't be undead

According to Jesus, this losing our self to save our self is of critical
importance, not just making us a nicer person or a better Christian.
This "losing to find" is what Jesus was talking about when he said,
"When you know your self, then you will be known and you will
understand that you are a child of the living Abba God. But if you

12. Thomas Merton, *Conjectures of a Guilty Bystander* (New York: Doubleday,
1966), 140–142.
13. See *Your Unique Self: The Radical Path to Personal Enlightenment* by Marc Gafni.
(Tucson: Integral Publishers, 2012).

do not know your self, then you live in poverty, and you are the poverty" (Gospel of Thomas, Saying 3).

Destitute living—what a sad thought. But it's not nearly as drastic as another time when Jesus framed this same truth in a much more radical way: "If you bring forth what is within you, what you bring forth will save you. If you do not bring forth what is within you, what you do not bring forth will destroy you" (Gospel of Thomas, Saying 70, Lambkin).[14]

Gulp! Not bringing forth our God-Being-Me self will destroy me? Whoa! That's moving from destitute to destroyed. Does that really mean our God-Being-You self will destroy us? I believe this is Jesus' daring way of saying that *not bringing your divine self up and out* will destroy your life. It will leave you lifeless in terms of true life. You will be the spiritual "walking dead." Today is Halloween[15] and just writing that sentence brings up ghoulish images and the "undead" knocking at my door, which may not be a bad way of seeing Jesus' words. Don't be undead.

The feeling of transcendent consciousness

Transcendent awareness results in deep feelings. The experience is of a vast, expanded awareness that is sensed as blissful, intelligent, creative love. There is very little ego here or sense of self, perhaps only enough of us to be aware that we are in this state. Jim Marion, calling transcendent consciousness by the name of "causal," says:

> Emotionally, we will notice at the causal level a grad-
> ual unfoldment of great inner warmth for everybody
> and everything. Other people notice it too. We may be
> astonished to see that, no matter what the circumstances,
> we can't help but express this great emotional warmth. It
> comes through in speech, in manner, in humor, in gesture.

---

14. http://www.sacred-texts.com/chr/thomas.htm.

15. A year later than the Halloween I mentioned in Chapter 4. Book writing takes a long time.

There is no effort involved. It just is. This warmth is true Christian love, true Buddhist compassion.

I noticed it first at the movies. I found that, no matter how sad the movie, or how scary, or how tragic or violent or heartrending, it didn't affect me as it had before. I stayed at peace, observing, interested, and aware, but generally undisturbed. True, I felt great compassion for people whose sufferings might be depicted, but the portrayals could not move me from my own deep inner peace. At first, to be honest, I didn't care for this change. I wanted to feel scared or heartbroken or angry as I once had, but I no longer could.

At this point on my path I realized that all these familiar negative feelings had been addictions (the contemporary word for what Christian spirituality has traditionally called attachments and what many Buddhists call desires). I realized that, once our own magnetic inner emotional negativity is substantially gone, i.e., we have grown beyond attachments, outside negative vibrations cease to have any effect because there is no longer a negative magnet inside us that they can attract.[16]

Ken Wilber calls transcendent consciousness "the simple feeling being."[17] He writes, "You *already* feel this simple Feeling of Being: it is the simple, present feeling of existence."[18]   While looking out

16. James Marion, *Putting on the Mind of Christ: The Inner Work of Christian Spirituality* (Charlottesville, Virginia: Hampton Roads Publishing, 2011), 190. Marion devotes his entire Chapter 16 to this state. Although he uses different terminology at times, we are both talking about the same thing. I highly recommend his entire book which is full of rich descriptions of I AMness and well as other developmental states.

17. Ken Wilber, *The Simple Feeling of Being: Embracing Your True Nature* (Boulder: Shambhala, 2004).

18. Ken Wilber, *One Taste* (Boulder: Shambhala, 1999), 280, (italics his).

from this simple sense of existence and being, we can then witness the physical world around us. This is a most peaceful, blissful way to live, free from any attachments but deeply aware of and caring for all creation.

God Embodied feels creative because it is the source of all creation

As co-creators with God, we too sense the urge to create. Whether it be a family of love, a better world, a healthier ecosystem, less divisive politics, better government, or a simple drawing, poem, or piece of knitting, we love to create.

At the cosmic dimension of creativity, another name for this creative "God within" of transcendent consciousness is the causal state of consciousness. This comes from religious traditions which hold that all of created reality comes from causal reality. Quantum science appears at times to be saying something similar in statements like this from Nobel prize winner neuroscientist Roger Sperry:

> Current concepts of the mind-brain relationship involve a direct break with the long established materialist and behaviorist doctrine that has dominated neuroscience for many decades. Instead of renouncing or ignoring consciousness, the new interpretation gives full recognition to the primacy of inner conscious awareness as a causal reality.[19]

Max Planck was a German theoretical physicist and originator of quantum theory for which he won the Nobel Prize in Physics. He said, "I regard consciousness as fundamental. I regard matter as derivative from consciousness. We cannot get behind consciousness. Everything that we talk about, everything that we regard as existing, postulates consciousness."[20]

---

19. http://www.continuumcenter.net/BP/BPConsciousnessasCausal.pdf.
20. Quoted in Chopra, Deepak. *The Future of God: A Practical Approach to Spirituality for Our Times* (New York: Harmony, 2014), 136.

Consciousness, both divine and human, is the source of all creation.

The more we are awake, the more we consciously participate in the evolution of creation.

I am not suggesting the New Age idea that we create our own reality by thinking it into being. I am thinking of the spiritual world counterpart to the physical world evolutionary path. The clearly identifiable developmental stages of humankind over the past 50,000 years are just such a creative expression in human culture and spirituality. It took forty thousand years for humankind to move from the tribal to the warrior stage. Then five thousand years to move to the traditional stage and five hundred years to develop into the modern stage. Postmodern Cultural Creatives began emerging one hundred fifty years ago in Europe and a mere sixty years ago in this country. The post-postmodern or integrative stage has just begun to become visible in the last few dozen years. As we can see, the pace of evolution is speeding up in terms of our human development. Each stage is built upon the other as each stage moved from egocentric to ethnocentric, to worldcentric while becoming increasingly inclusive and complex. The next movement is to integral and cosmocentric culture and spirituality. As Paul says about this labor-intensive evolutionary process, "All creation groans with labor pains" (Rom 8:22). The oldest thing you can say about God is that God is always doing something new. The new thing God is doing now is through us!

God-embodied feels vast, even infinite

One of the inner experiences associated with transcendent consciousness is vast, boundless spaciousness. We begin to approach a sense of infinity. We sense that our deepest self is much bigger than we thought. Physicist Fred Wolf says that the initial postulate of quantum thinking is "I am this whole universe."[21]

---

21. Wolf, *Taking the Quantum Leap*, 83.

Wilder Penfield, the well-known neurosurgeon and mind researcher says, "To suppose that consciousness or the mind has a location is a failure to understand neurophysiology. The mind or consciousness appears to be everywhere."[22]

In his book, *The Headless Way*, writer Douglas Harding (1909–2007), recounts walking through the Himalayas when he was 33. He says for a moment he stopped thinking, and all his mental chatter died down. He says, "For once, words really failed me. I forgot my name, my humanness, my thingness, all that could be called me or mine. Past and future dropped away." Then he started to notice himself again, only this time he found "this nothing, this hole where a head should have been was no ordinary vacancy, no mere nothing. On the contrary, it was very much occupied. It was a vast emptiness, vastly filled, a nothing that found room for everything—room for grass, trees, shadowy distant hills, and far above them snow-peaks like a row of angular clouds riding the blue sky. I had lost a head and gained a world."

This is the "us" that, as Meister Eckhart put it, has "played before the Father in eternal stillness."[23]

Writing about the witnessing aspect of what I call transcendent awareness, Harding says, "It is consciously viewing everything from its Source, reuniting it with the Infinity that lies this side of it. It is hearing, seeing, smelling, touching things as if for the first time, relieved of the crushing load of time past. It is the revitalizing and extension of our childhood astonishment. It is being present at Creation's morning, before Adam named the creatures and got bored with them. It is seeing them with their Creator's eye, as very good."[24]

---

22. William Penfield, *The Mystery of the Mind* (Princeton: Princeton University Press, 1975), 109.

23. Meister Eckhart, *Meister Eckhart,* trans., C. de B. Evans (London, John Watkins, 1952), Vol I, 148.

24. Harding, Douglas. *On Having No Head* (Kindle Locations 986-988). The Shollond Trust. Kindle Edition.

Infinite Being experienced in transcendent consciousness is the unfathomable Mystery in whom we are overwhelmed and yet find ourselves attracted to and fascinated with in ways we cannot fully explain.

Transcendence

Richard Rohr beautifully frames God-being-us with:

> This is both a transcendent God and also my deepest me at the same time. To discover one is to discover the other. This is why good theology and good psychology work together so well. You have touched upon the soul, the unshakable reality of my True Self, where "I and the Father are one" (John 10:30). The second half of life is about learning to recognize, honor, and love this voice and this indwelling Presence, which feels like your own voice too.[25]

The most profound, life-filled, heaven-filled experience we human beings can have is transcendent consciousness. This is simply being our True Self, our "God-being-us" self. This is quite different from the awakened consciousness we have explored in the previous four chapters. Awakened consciousness is the *awareness of* the presence of God. Transcendent consciousness is *being* the presence of God!

Devotion brings an empty mind and a full heart

The passion of authentic spiritual devotion is not for the purpose of pleasing God. God is already pleased. Devotion is not for the purpose of helping us. Devotion is not for us or for God. Devotion is simply an acknowledgment of reality. When we are devoted to God and to Jesus we are acknowledging their reality with our hearts and not just our minds. Believing in God and Jesus is okay, but without devotion, it's the booby prize. Devotion allows us to acknowledge the reality

---

25. Richard Rohr's Daily Meditation, "The Two Halves of Life, Monday," October 12, 2015.

of God and Jesus with our whole Self. Actually, in devotion we let go of believing and beliefs—the false ones and even the true ones—all of which keep us within the limitations of our busy heads. Devotion releases the power of love and there is no greater power than love. That's why the writer of 1 John could say "God is love" (1 John 4:8). Devotion is the royal path that leads to transcendent love.

Peace-Love-Bliss

The love that is God is more than our overused word love can describe. I call the love that is released in transcendent consciousness "peace-love-bliss." It is an almost indescribable flow of joy, peace, love, ecstasy, awe, and astonishment, all at the same time!

For years I would read about what the Eastern mystics called "bliss." It sounded good, but it was not a part of my life. Through therapy, prayer, meditation, research, and spiritual practice, now it is not only part of my life but is currently accessible whenever I turn my attention inward. My days are more and more punctuated with flowing streams of peace-love-bliss. I resonant with David Bentley Hart's words:

> It is bliss that draws us toward and joins us to the being of all things because that bliss is already one with being and consciousness, in the infinite simplicity of God. . . . This is because, in God, the fullness of being is also a perfect act of infinite consciousness that, wholly possessing the truth of being in itself, forever finds its consummation in boundless delight.[26]

Nothing is more difficult than trying to have an empty mind. That means you are thinking about not thinking which is not nothing —it's thinking. I have found the easiest way to empty my mind is to *fill my heart*. When my heart is full, my mind is at peace. A full heart trumps a busy mind any day. This is moving into transcendence

26. Hart, *The Experience of God*, 248.

through a devotional path. This is why I describe "emptiness" as a peaceful mind and a blissful heart that flows out in love to the world.

Once we've experienced peace-love-bliss we are very much drawn to it again and again. This bliss is not narcissistic because one must move through narcissism to get to it! Rather it is bliss that comes from being empty of ego and full of God. Bliss draws us away from lesser loves and more and more into transcendent love. This is what the man called "Scotland's greatest nineteenth-century churchman,"[27] Thomas Chalmers (1780-1847), famously called "the expulsive power of a new affection. . . . Even the strongest resolve is not enough to dislodge an affection by leaving a void."[28] "Nothing" is not usually motivating. But transcendent "nothing" is peace-love-bliss, the most awesome, driving stimulus in the world!

Look how it motivated Jesus. The writer of Hebrews says, "Looking to Jesus the pioneer and perfecter of our faith, who for the sake of the joy that was set before him endured the cross, disregarding its shame, and has taken his seat at the right hand of the throne of God" (Heb. 12:2). This is an exceptionally clear statement that reveals that it was the drawing power of bliss-love that made it possible for Jesus to take on his crucifixion.

When the love of God fills our hearts, it obliterates our addiction to a busy mind. It pushes out all the lesser loves that the writer of 1 John called "the world" in "Love not the world, neither the things that are in the world" (1 John 2:15).

Ritu Ghatourey, a writer from India, said, "Following your heart sometimes leads to places that your head could never imagine."[29]

---

27. Donald K McKim and Alec C Cheyne, *Encyclopedia of the Reformed Faith* (Louisville, Kentucky: Westminster John Knox Press, 1992), 61.

28. "A New Affection is More Successful in Replacing an Old Affection than Simply Trying to End It without Supplanting It with Something Better." http://www.christianity.com/christian-life/spiritual-growth/the-expulsive-power-of-a-new-affection-11627257.html.

29. http://www.searchquotes.com/search/Following_Your_Arrow/.

You know you're in love when your heart is making more sense than your head is.

How to be at peace when everything around you isn't

How does this work, besides being an interesting concept or a theological belief? What if we could really look out at the world from this transcendent I AM conscious? That would mean we would be looking at the news on TV from a place of stillness, peace, and oneness with God. This is quite different than observing the world from our busy minds which think we are victims of everything going on around us in the world today. To be at peace doesn't detach you from the values you are devoted to and emotionally involved with. Rather, it guards you against the constricted awareness that fuels inner conflict.

Transcendent consciousness is an infinitely deep center that is not pushed around by circumstances. This is a place from which to view the world, and then, from that place of quiet wisdom and love, engage the world to help it become a more peaceful place.

My journey

I first experienced transcendent consciousness in a brief peak experience of peace-bliss-love when I was 23. I was at a weekend retreat of Episcopalian charismatics at the invitation of an older deacon at the Baptist church where I was working as choral director. He had adopted me as his spiritual son and invited me to explore what were then called "neo-Pentecostals." I liked Episcopalians, even "charismatic" ones. They were intelligent, sophisticated, and well-educated like I saw myself. In other words, they were "safe" to be with in my rigid, fearful world. They invited me to sit in the center of their prayer circle to be prayed for. A large African American woman clapped her hands and said, "Oh my, we've got our hands on a Baptist preacher!" I almost ran out since, as a Baptist preacher, I already had everything I needed, thank you!

They put their hands on me and prayed in mumbled words I couldn't understand. Nothing happened. Of course that was what I planned on since I drive with my spiritual brakes on. Two weeks later, however, I was sitting in bed reading an Agatha Christie murder mystery. I began to feel something strange and unusual for me. Suddenly I felt in love with everything and everyone. I loved the walls of my room. I loved my parents. I even loved the Catholics since back then Baptists and Catholics did not love each other. This bliss-love state lasted for about an hour. The effects lasted a lifetime. I wanted more of this but there was nothing more for twenty years even though I continued to seek it. I simply didn't know how to open myself to more.

Eventually brief streams of this joyful flow began during my church's Sunday morning services. Then, ten years ago, I began occasionally having moments of this joy and peace when I was meditating. Now it has become accessible whenever I go inside myself. My mind seems vast and endless while empty of thoughts and images. I feel peace, joy, and bliss radiating from my heart center. My goal is for this to be my normal way of living.

Once you have experienced transcendent consciousness, everything else becomes smaller, less important. Just one fleeting taste of this is often enough to let us experience the vastness of God. The Psalmist says, "Taste and see that the Lord is good" (Psalm 34:8). That one taste at age 23 kept me going for twenty years while I learned how to let myself be available for more "tasting."

Jesus shows us the way to Embody (God)

Jesus not only talked about losing our self, he demonstrated it in a drastic way. In a letter to the friends of Jesus at a city named Philippi, Paul gives us the big picture of emptying on a cosmic scale. This is his description of what was going on with Jesus as the eternal Christ.

> Your mind [consciousness] must be the same as that of Christ Jesus.
> Christ Jesus, though in the image of God,
> Didn't regard equality with God something to be clung to . . .

Being equal with God is about as Somebody as you can get. Jesus, the saints, and mystics have pointed out that we will all end up equal with God in the same sense that Jesus was. Jesus emptied himself of this divine equality in glory and became a Nobody, relatively speaking:

> . . . but instead Jesus became completely empty
> And took on the image of oppressed humankind
> born into the human condition,
> found in the likeness of a human being,
> Jesus was thus humbled,
> obediently accepting death, death on a cross!
> (Phil 2:7-8, *The Inclusive Bible*)[30]

Jesus "emptied himself" of his divine glory. He turned down his high voltage divinity so as to fit it into a voltage more appropriate for human life at its highest and best. The human body and systems cannot hold pure, undiluted, infinite glory. So the eternal Jesus in glory turned that glory down to human size. We get a glimpse of that glory in the Transfiguration as Jesus visibly became the pure Christ-light that he was. Imagine him walking around like this all the time, blinding everyone as he tried to live a "normal" life! "Oh no, here comes Jesus—cover your eyes." He left that glorified transcendent reality to live life as an extraordinary but real human being. Then he took on the human journey we all must make of emptying ourselves of the things we humans tend to get attached to. Yes, Jesus had to learn to let go of his life. That's what we see in his temptations and his struggle in the garden right before he was crucified. It is only when we empty ourselves, let go, and surrender the temporary that the real can come forth, our true transcendent self.

Jesus said, "Blessed are the pure in heart for they shall see God" (Mt. 5:8). What is a "pure heart"? Panikkar reminds us that, "A pure heart is an empty heart, without ego, capable of reaching that depth

---

30. A reminder that many of my passages from the Bible, like this one, are from *The Inclusive Bible*.

at which the divine lives. The fact that the experience is simple does not mean that it is easy."[31]

Jesus, as the Christ, is Everybody

Now Jesus was restored to an even more exalted place in his culture's terms of royalty. He became the Christ, the Christian symbol for the whole of reality in metaphysical terms.

> Because of this, God highly exalted Jesus,
> And gave to Jesus the name above every other name
> So that at the name of Jesus every knee must bend,
> in the heavens, on the earth, and under the earth,
> and every tongue proclaim to the glory of God,
> Jesus Christ reigns supreme!
>
> (Phil. 2:6-8)

All humankind is united in oneness and that Oneness in Christian terminology is called Christ, the "Supername" (Panikkar's term). Jim Marion puts it succinctly as, "Jesus saw there was no separation between himself and any other person . . . . *He saw all human beings (and indeed the whole created universe) as part of himself.*"[32] Jesus morphed into being Everybody in nondual Oneness! That's the plan for us, too, which leads us to the highest realm we can live in while in this life, the Realm of God where we have moved to Stage Four:

Stage Four to the Real You: Become Everybody!

The Jesus path is the journey from Somebody to Nobody to Embody to Everybody! When you are Everybody, you are living in the Oneness of the Reign of God. But I am getting ahead of myself because Oneness, or becoming Everybody, is the topic of the next chapter.

---

31. Panikkar, *The Experience of God*, 94.
32. Marion, *Putting on the Mind*, 8 (italics mine).

Summary of The Bliss of Transcendent Consciousness

• You have to be Somebody before you can be Nobody.

• You have to be Nobody before you can Embody (God, which is transcendent consciousness).

• You have to Embody before you can be Everybody.

• When you are Everybody, you are living in the Reign of God.

Questions for Reflection and Discussion

1. What parts of this chapter have you marked as interesting or questionable? Why?

2. What do you think about the Somebody, Nobody, Embody, Everybody sequence? Where are you in that journey?

3. I have found that Father Keating's Welcoming Prayer is a powerful way to let go of trying to control what happens to me.

> Welcome, welcome, welcome.
> I welcome everything that comes to me today because I know it's for my healing.
> I welcome all thoughts, feelings, emotions, persons, situations, and conditions.
> I let go of my desire for power and control.
>
> I let go of my desire for affection, esteem, approval and pleasure.
> I let go of my desire for survival and security.
> I let go of my desire to change any situation, condition, person or myself.
> I open to the love and presence of God and God's action within. Amen[33]

4. Take a moment and say "I am" to yourself. Describe how that feels.

_____

33. http://kevinjbliss.com/welcoming-prayer/.

5. What would it be like to feel a deep sense of your identity as Divine Being today?

Practices

Regular practice serves to remind us over and over again that we are hypnotized by our personality. Clear away the hypnotic illusion that you are separate by doing practices such as these.

1. **Fully experience your own presence** first in order to experience the presence of God in whatever form. Connect with all the sensations of your body, outside and inside. Let yourself be inside of all those sensations.

2. **Self-inquiry** is the classic name given to the practice of becoming aware of being aware rather than simply being aware of what you are aware of. If that sounds convoluted, try this: Self-inquiry is your awareness watching your awareness while ignoring everything else. It is becoming conscious of looking rather than what you are looking at. It is being aware of thinking rather than what you are thinking about.

It is so simple that it's easy at first glance to miss how powerful a process this is. The practice can be described in a few brief words: In self-inquiry, we simply ask, "Who am I?" Or, "What am I?" Or, "Who is having this experience?"

It is your present awareness watching your present awareness. Let's take your reading this sentence right now. Instead of being aware of this sentence, become aware of you noticing this sentence. Who is that "you?" Ask yourself "Who am I?" Don't answer, just ask.

To practice self-inquiry, you only need to trace the root of your thoughts back to the I-thought, from which all other thoughts arise. This is initiated by the question "Who am I?" By asking, "Who am I?", our thinking process naturally gets focused on the search for the true Self and we forget about all other concerns and worries of the mind.

If you keep asking "Who am I?" eventually your "I" will disappear and you will simply be awareness watching awareness. You will be consciousness conscious of consciousness. When you notice that you are back to thinking, start again and ask "Who is it that is doing this thinking?" Become aware of being aware of thinking. Take your attention away from the thinking and back towards awareness watching awareness. That's it. Try it out. If in a group give your self one minute to try this. Then talk about how it went.

3. **Stepping back**—a way to separate your small self from your big self.

Describe yourself. Give details. That is your objective self. But who is noticing this? Who is it that is aware of this self? This is your True Self. This is you as pure consciousness, pure spirit. You are free of objects. You are aware of objects, thoughts, feelings, but you are not those thoughts, objects, and feelings. Not a real self. They are something seen, not the see-er. This first self is what you are not. This is the false self, the suffering self. We can't escape pain but we can leave suffering behind. Suffering comes from holding onto to that which is not eternal. When we find our true self, then suffering is ended and "the spirit-consciousness bears witness to our spirit-consciousness that we are children of God" (Rom. 8:16). It is pure consciousness that allows us to be aware that we are divine.

When we surrender the busyness of our mind and enter into that serene spaciousness which is devoid of content, we become aware of the simple feeling of being. This is what I have called the Inner Face of God. It is the concept of the Infinite Face of God now experienced deep within us beyond our mind as pure infinite consciousness and being itself.

4. If it fits for you or your group, use the Three Faces of God benediction on the next page to close your practice.

"God beyond me, in whom I live and move, and have my being."

("God beyond us, in whom we live and move, and have our being.")

"God beside me, you are always with me."

("God beside us, you are always with us.")

"God being me, I am the light of the world."

("God being us, we are the light of the world.")

"God being me"

CHAPTER 14

The Peace of Oneness Consciousness

The nondual consciousness of the Reign of God

Jesus experienced and taught about what today we would call consciousness at its highest levels. Some call it Christ Consciousness, the mind of Christ, unitive consciousness, nonduality, or Oneness. In the previous chapter I called it becoming Everybody. Jesus called it the Reign of God. In this all-encompassing way of the viewing the world, we see and feel that everything is connected. There is no separation between us and God, us and one another, us and the physical world. We perceive that ultimately there is no duality or twoness, only oneness.

While this oneness is often referred to as a state of consciousness, it is more like a way of viewing the world. We may have a sudden and intense altered experience of it, but the goal is to gradually begin to see everything as it really is—one reality with no distance between God and us, and us and one another.

This is the main point of Jesus' teachings

Not only did Jesus talk about the Reign (or Kingdom) of God, it was his main point. As N. T. Wright says, "Jesus spent his whole ministry redefining what the Kingdom meant. He refused to give up the symbolic language of the Kingdom, but filled it with such new content that . . . he powerfully subverted Jewish expectations."[1]

Jesus continues to subvert our expectation down through history. There have been many attempts to define that kingdom or reign of God. First it was seen as the church, then as life after death in heaven, and today as bringing God's will to earth. In my understanding, all of these fall short of what Jesus said about it. I see the Reign of God as experiencing all of reality in seamless oneness. The Reign of God is not a proposition to be taught. It is a dimension of consciousness that may be experienced, but not easily described.

Notice how Jesus, Paul, and Thomas talked all around it without ever defining it. They said the Reign of God is:

• Close to you (Mark 1:15).

• Not of this world (John 18:36).

• Inside you (Luke 17:21).[2]

• Not here and not there (Luke 17:20).

• Difficult for the rich to enter (Luke 18:24).

• Where to store your treasures safely (Matthew 6:20).

• Entered by being born again in a new level of spirit-breath consciousness (John 3:7-8).

• To be sought first and then all else will be added (Matthew 6:33).

---

1. Wright, *Jesus and the Victory*, 471.

2. The translation "'within you" is preferable to "among you" according the James Robinson in "The Study of the Historical Jesus after Nag Hammadi," in *Semeia* 44: *The Historical Jesus and the Rejected Gospels* (Atlanta: Scholars Press, 1980), 50-53.

- Entered through trials and tribulations (Acts 14:22).

- Small like a mustard seed, but grows to shelter all (Matt. 13:31).

- Spread out upon the earth but people do not see it (Gospel of Thomas, Saying 113).

- The secret of it is given to those close to Jesus, to others only in parables (Mark 4:11).

- Not flesh and blood (1 Cor. 15:50).

- Not eating and drinking but peace and joy (Rom. 14:17).

In the Gospel of Thomas Jesus criticizes other views of the Reign of God as a political or social realm or a physical place:

> If those who lead you say to you, "See, the Reign is in heaven," then the birds of the heaven will go before you; if they say to you, "It is in the sea," then the fish will go before you. But the Reign is within you, and it is outside of you. When you know yourselves, then you will be known, and you will know that you are the children of the living Father-Mother. But if you do not know yourselves, then you are in poverty, and you are poverty (Gospel of Thomas, Saying 3).

Here, and also in Luke 17:21, "The Reign of God is within you." This Reign is not an event that's going to suddenly usher in a new era. Rather, it is an interior state that sees everything outside of you is also inside of you, and everything inside is also outside of you as one seamless whole. Even though it is everywhere, Jesus says we access it inwardly by coming to "know" ourselves. If we do not go inside and learn about who we really are and act accordingly, then we are truly impoverished. Spiritual growth is an inside job!

Ken Wilber writes,

> Divinity has one ultimate secret, which it will also whisper in your ear if your mind becomes quieter than the

fog at sunset: the God of this world is found within, and you know it is found within: in those hushed silent times when the mind becomes still, the body relaxes into infinity, the senses expand to become one with the world—in those glistening times, a subtle luminosity, a serene radiance, a brilliantly transparent clarity shimmers as the true nature of all manifestation, erupting every now and then in a compassionate Radiance before whom all idols retreat . . . Did not even Saint Clement say, He who knows himself knows God?[3]

The Reign of God is Oneness Consciousness

Stevan Davies says, "The kingdom of God is a form of experience, an altered state of consciousness, directly related to Jesus' career as a healer. It is not first and foremost, a social condition or way of life."[4] He says that Jesus' teaching about the Reign of God in his parables can "best be understood to comprise part of a technique to enable his associates to attain and experience a state called the Kingdom of God and not to communicate to them an ideology *about* the Kingdom of God."[5]

Professor of Religion at Princeton and historian of early Christianity, Elaine Pagels says that the Reign of God "symbolizes a state of transformed consciousness."[6] Jim Marion, in his breakthrough book, *Putting on the Mind of Christ*, writes:

> By the "Kingdom of Heaven," Jesus meant a particular level of human consciousness, not a place to which Christians are destined after death. Unfortunately,

---

3. Ken Wilber, writing in "The Deconstruction of the World Trade Center" (as republished in *The Simple Feeling of Being*), http://www.ievolve.org/category/ciw-founders/ken-wilber/.

4. Davies, *Jesus the Healer*, 115.

5. Ibid, 131, (italics his).

6. Elaine Pagels, *The Gnostic Gospels* (New York: Random House, 1979), 68.

most officials and theologians today do not understand Jesus' concept of the Kingdom . . . . But the single most important thing that Jesus taught about the Kingdom of Heaven was that "The Kingdom of God is within" (Luke 17:21). . . . First of all and most importantly, The Kingdom of Heaven that Jesus saw so well is a vision of this world that sees no separation (duality) between God and humans. Second, The Kingdom of Heaven that Jesus saw so well is a vision of this world that sees no separation (duality) between human beings.[7]

Do we lose our unique identity in oneness?

If you are Everybody, do you still get to be you? In Oneness consciousness everything maintains its own identity but without separating from everything else. This is the world of not two, but not one in a numerical sense either. That is, I remain as myself but without any separation from you as yourself. Oneness is not sameness. Nonduality is being one without being the same.

When Jesus said, "God and I are one," the word "one" here is not meant to be a number. He did not mean a numerical one but a oneness that comes from not bring separate. Even Meister Eckhart, who so strongly proclaimed our oneness and union with God, reminds us that oneness is not sameness. Bernard McGinn says, "Eckhart's notion of indistinct union . . . is fundamentally dialectical, that is to say, union with God is indistinct in the ground, but we always maintain a distinction from God in our formal being . . . Even in the ultimate union in heaven, Eckhart insists, this distinction will remain."[8]

Advaita Vedanta is a school of Hindu philosophy and religious practice, and one of the classic Indian paths to spiritual realization.

---

7. Marion, *Putting on the Mind*, 1, 3, 7, 8.

8. Barnard McGinn, *The Mystical Thought of Meister Eckhart: The Man from Whom God Hid Nothing* (New York: Crossroad, 2003), 148.

Advaita means nondual. British-born Benedictine monk and priest Bede Griffiths (1906-1993) became a leading thinker in the development of the dialogue between Christianity and Hinduism. He said, "Advaita does not mean 'one' in the sense of eliminating all differences. The differences are present in the one in a mysterious way. They are not separated anymore, and yet they are there."[9]

Paul was describing it when he wrote, "There is no longer Jew or Greek, there is no longer slave or free, there is no longer male and female; for all of you are one in Christ Jesus" (Gal. 3:28). Jews were still not Greeks, and Greeks remained Greeks. Unfortunately, slaves remained slaves also and not free at that time but his point is not making distinctions. Woman and men were still different even though they were one. This is because nonduality does not erase differences. Rather, it transcends them. When we can see differences transcended, those differences lose their power to separate us. People who look at the world from this oneness are motivated to work for justice in the world to reflect their vision of oneness.

Before I experienced nonduality, it seemed strange to me that Jesus said to Paul in his vision on the road to Damascus, "Why are you persecuting me?" (Acts 9:4). Paul was persecuting followers of Jesus, not Jesus. We don't know if Paul knew about Jesus' words, "Whatever you do to the least, you do to me" (Matt. 25:40). But Paul heard from Jesus' own mouth the truth of the nonduality reality of what he came to call the body of Christ. (1 Cor. 12:12). Because Jesus was Everybody, persecuting anyone, especially the poor and disenfranchised who have a special place in Jesus' heart, is persecuting Jesus. When we become Everybody we can see and feel the same way Jesus did.

Jesus, nonduality in sandals

The early Christians came to the conclusion that Jesus was one with God but not the same as God. The belief that Jesus was human and

9. http://nonduality.org/what-is-nonduality/.

divine at the same time is a striking example of nonduality. He was not half human and half divine. He was fully human and fully divine. That is a nondual truth not meant to wrap our minds around, but to wrap our lives around.

Seeing Jesus as both human and divine is the most orthodox idea of who Jesus was. It is a beautiful picture of nonduality in sandals. He is Oneness with dust on its feet. Jesus extended his own nondual divine humanity to us. Christians agree we are all made in the image and likeness of God. Being made in the image and likeness of God in Genesis is a nondual expression. We are exactly like God but not identical or the same as God. That likeness has been submerged in our shadows, but not removed. So there is work to be done to see the distortion our mistaken egoic identity creates and then recognize our true identity and manifest it in the world today. We seek to become that which we already most deeply are. Jesus is the way Christians have found to do that very thing.

Single-seeing—the gleam in your eye

Jesus called Oneness consciousness "single-seeing." He pointed to a profound physiological, psychological, and spiritual truth when he said, "Your eye is the lamp of your body. If your eye is single, your whole body is full of light; but if it is hurtful, your body is full of darkness" (Luke 11:34). The word "single" here means simple, uncomplicated, or without a fold.[10] To see single, simple, or unfolded is what nonduality is all about. It is seeing things in their oneness or seamless, fold-less connection to everything else.

The cover of this book is about the gleam in the eye of the person with "single-seeing." This is looking at material and spiritual reality from the highest level of consciousness now available to humankind (symbolized by the light-filled eye)—the presence of the Infinite (symbolized by the infinite cosmos) in the finite (symbolized by the human head). When we see from the light of single-seeing or

10. Thayer, *Greek-English Lexicon*, 57.

Oneness, then the light that our nondual eye sees fills our whole body with light.

Seeing double or with distinctions is dualistic. Of course discerning people want to be able to distinguish between good and evil, good and bad, healthy and unhealthy, which Jesus did also. Discernment is noticing that things have different qualities. Discernment requires you to be a witness, not a judge. There is a judging way of seeing people which hurtfully sees them as separate from the rest of "good" humanity. In single-seeing you do not judge, but you are a discerning witness which sees all persons as a sacred part of humankind.

We can look *at* another person through our eyes, seeing them as an object. We can look *into* another person through our eyes, seeing them as a person. Or, we can look *out from* another person from their eyes, seeing them as *ourself*. That is the single-seeing that Jesus called the Reign of God. When you look at another person with a "single eye" you see yourself looking out at the world from their eyes because your eye and their eye are the same. This is how Meister Eckhart framed the single-seeing of God: "The eye with which I see God is the same one with which God sees me. My eye and God's eye is one eye, and one sight, and one knowledge, and one love."[11]

You can't just decide to look around and see oneness. It doesn't work that way. You must first experience oneness within. Only then can you look out at the world and see oneness.

The Reign of God that is single-seeing allows us to do what Jesus asked us to do, such as, "Love your enemies and pray for those who persecute you" (Matt. 5:43). This was the most quoted saying of Jesus in the early church for a reason—it's hard to do! When we see we are one with one another, we find ourselves looking at others with pure love because it sees no separation between us and God, us and one another. As Stephan Davis says, "The Kingdom of God is an invitation to leave our ordinary way of seeing the world."[12]

---

11. *Meister Eckhart's Sermons*, "True Hearing."

12. Davies, *Jesus the Healer*, 131.

Evelyn Underhill (1875–1941), one of the greatest mystics in modern times, said, "Mysticism is the art of union with Reality. The mystic is a person who has attained that union in greater or lesser degree; or who aims at and believes in such attainment."[13] The Christian symbol for the whole of Reality without separation, is Christ. Therefore Christian mysticism is the art of union with Christ.

My "dimming" experience

I always hesitate to share my spiritual experiences. We are all very different and will have experiences that are uniquely ours. We never need to try to squeeze or fit our experience into someone else's. My many wounds and flaws have shaped my spiritual experiences along with the help from others I have needed to make it through them in my life. The key is to see the reality of spiritual experiences in others and then be open for your unique path. I try to illustrate my ideas with examples from the lives of real people. Since I know my life best, I offer my experience with the hope it might make more clear what I'm trying to explain.

One of my most impactful "single-seeing" Oneness consciousness experiences was several years ago. I had just finished a nurturing time of prayer in sitting with Jesus and a few other non-physical saints and presences for about twenty minutes. I had seen the usual beautiful waves of white, gold, red, and blue colors washing over me in my visual field. This was followed by hundreds of objects and people that rapidly flashed by. Eventually that stopped and I felt so peaceful that I fell asleep for about ten minutes which was not unusual for me. I woke up, glanced at my clock, and saw I could continue for another half hour before I had to go to another appointment. This time I moved from prayer mode to meditation mode as I sank down into myself even more deeply in what I call "resting as God." I was soon immersed in the bliss and emptiness of transcendent awareness. I was in "God-being-me mode" in which there is not much of me or

13. Evelyn Underhill, *Practical Mysticism* (New York: Start Publishing, 2013), 2.

God as a presence but rather God as infinite being I AMness which is basically "nothingness."

When my timer chime went off, I came back to the here and now and slowly opened my eyes. I was immediately bewildered. The room where I was sitting appeared so faded and fragile that it looked almost transparent. There was enough visible of the walls and furniture to see that they were still there. But all the objects were "dimmed" even as the sun was shining brightly through the windows. My body was also "dimmed," appearing faded and fragile. I eventually stood up and then sat right back down because I was so disoriented. I moved back and forth between frightened and amazed until I finally decided to go with the reality of the fragile outer world I was seeing. Gradually, in an hour or so, the room and my body returned to its normal degree of solidness. But I continued to be disoriented for several days.

As I moved from bewilderment and disorientation, I realized that I had been seeing physical reality as it really is in relation to spiritual reality. The spiritual reality of the presence of Jesus and my guides in my prayer time felt greater and "denser" than the physical reality of my room and body. Both the physical and spiritual reality were real, but there was no comparison about which one felt "more" real. The spiritual reality had that hands down and eyes open! That was a turning point in how I feel about physical, concrete reality and non-physical, spiritual reality. Both are one reality but they are not identical. The reality of mystically and visually seeing Oneness allowed me to take one more step to embrace the goal of seeing *from* Oneness as a normal way of viewing the universe.

That strange word "nonduality"

More and more spiritual seekers are becoming familiar with what is called "nonduality." There are numerous versions of nonduality or unitive consciousness. The Christian version of nonduality is framed in Jesus' central teaching of the Reign of God. Here is a seemingly cryptic saying of Jesus.

> When you make the two one and make the inner like the
> outer and the outer like the inner and the upper like the
> lower, and that you might make the male and the female
> into a single one, so that the male will not be male nor
> the female be female, when you make eyes in place of an
> eye and a hand in place of a hand and a foot in place of
> a foot, an image in place of an image, then you will enter
> the Reign.
>
> (Gospel of Thomas, Saying 22)

This saying becomes less cryptic if we see it as a vivid, symbolic description of the Oneness that is the Reign of God. Our journey in life literally begins in oneness, as an embryo, one with our mother. Then comes birth and separation from mother and the beginning of twoness. We begin the journey of growing up and learning boundaries that identify things as separate. If we do a good job of ego building into being a Somebody, we are then in a position to move to transcendent awareness where we are a Nobody and now have room in our awareness to Embody God-Being-Us. From there we become Everybody which is Oneness.

Oneness consciousness as One Mind

Larry Dossey says that if the One Mind existed we would expect to see the following:

- A person could share thoughts and emotions—and even physical sensations—with a distant individual with whom she had no sensory contact.

- An individual could demonstrate detailed knowledge possessed by a person who has died, which that individual could not have acquired by normal means.

- Distant communication could take place between humans and animals such as pets.

• Large groups of animals—herds, schools—could behave in such highly coordinated ways that shared, overlapping minds are suggested.

• A dying or even healthy individual could experience direct contact with a transcendent domain in which it is revealed to her that she is in fact part of a great mind that is infinite in space and time.

Dossey then says, "As it turns out, none of these possibilities is hypothetical; they are all real."[14] The rest of his book recounts the multitude of documented and researched instances of all the above. He says the ultimate argument for one infinite, universal consciousness is what is called *"nonlocality* of consciousness." This means that consciousness is not just confined to an individual or localized to specific points in space such as brains or bodies or specific points in time. He says this means that the separateness of minds or consciousness is an illusion. In some sense, all minds come together to form a single mind or consciousness.

Oneness as Quantum Consciousness

Quantum physics is the study of how matter and energy behave at the atomic and nuclear levels. It tells us that matter is a form of energy or what physicists call quanta or tiny packets or pieces of energy coming out of an infinite field. This has transformed the way we understand life and how it develops.

Quantum physics is a way to understand the properties of solids, atoms, nuclei, subnuclear particles and light. In order to understand these natural phenomena, quantum principles have required fundamental changes in how humans view nature. One of the most interesting elements of quantum physics is the principle of quantum entanglement, where two seemingly independent particles appear to be connected to each other in a strange way.

---

14. Dossey, *One Mind*, xxv.

Bell's theorem is an important part of quantum physics. According to physicist Fritjof Capra, Bell's theorem demonstrates that the universe is fundamentally interconnected, interdependent, and inseparable.[15] This is a huge discovery as Henry Stapp, Lawrence Berkeley particle physicist, declared, "Bell's theorem is the most profound discovery of science."[16]

Quantum physics is related to consciousness. Every physical system is governed by quantum physical laws including the brain and consciousness. Consciousness is, in a complicated way, related to the functioning of the brain and the quantum physical processes going on within the brain and beyond.[17] This leads to the theory of Quantum consciousness as the field of information and energy. This field has many subfields which are completely entangled. "Completely entangled" is quantum speak for "We are all one in expanded consciousness in which we live and move and have our being."

Dr. Kingsley Dennis, sociologist, writer, and co-founder of WorldShift International says,

> "Neuroscience, quantum biology, and quantum physics are now beginning to converge to reveal that our bodies are not only biochemical systems but also sophisticated reso-nating quantum systems. These new discoveries show that a form of nonlocal connected consciousness has a phys-ical-scientific basis. Further, it demonstrates that certain spiritual or transcendental states of collective Oneness have a valid basis within the new scientific paradigm."[18]

---

15. http://www.azquotes.com/author/17669-Fritjof_Capra/tag/universe.

16. Henry P. Stapp, *"Bell's Theorem and World Process,"* Il Nuovo Cimento B (1971-1996) October 1975, Volume 29, Issue 2, 271.

17. See http://physics.about.com/od/QuantumConsciousness/f/IsConsciousness Quantum.htm.

18. Dennis Kingsley, "Quantum Consciousness: The Way to Reconcile Science and Spirituality," http://www.huffingtonpost.com/kingsley-dennis-phd/quantum-consciousness-the_b_647962.html.

Nonlocal consciousness is a quantum way of saying everything is connected. This is exactly how it looks and feels in Oneness Consciousness Writer and teacher, Paul Lenda, explains:

> We experience material reality in the form of separate objects. However, modern quantum physics is developing a conceptual understanding of the physical universe as an interconnected whole. Quantum theory also predicts another fascinating phenomenon which is known as non-locality…. David Bohm, a protégé of Einstein and one of the world's most respected quantum physicists, held the view that at the quantum level, location ceased to exist. In other words, all points in space became equal to all other points in space, and it was meaningless to speak of anything as being separate from anything else. A non-local interaction links up one location with another without crossing space, without decay, and without delay.[19]

Separateness is an illusion

In the single-seeing of the Reign of God our True or Big Self is a Vast Self which is eternal, indestructible, infinite consciousness. In other words, we are God-being-us. The Universe is our body. We are pure, unconditional love because God is pure, unconditional love (1 John 4:8). There is no separation between the consciousness that we are and the consciousness that God is. They are one consciousness.

Ervin Laszlo is a philosopher of science, systems theorist, integral theorist, and advocate of the theory of quantum consciousness. He is Founder and President of The Club of Budapest, and the author or co-author of 54 books translated into 23 languages. Nominated for the Nobel Peace Prize in 2004 and 2005, Laszlo has held professorship at major universities around the world. He paints a compelling picture of the future of oneness consciousness in terms of what he calls quantum consciousness, as he writes:

---

19. http://www.shift.is/2014/09/holographic-reality-nonlocal-universal-mind/.

Our brain can receive information not only from our eyes and ears, but directly from the wider world with which we are "entangled"—nonlocally connected. Insightful people throughout history, whether shamans or scientists, poets or prophets, have extensively used this capacity, innate to all human beings. Today it is widely neglected. This impoverishes our world picture and causes a nagging sense that we are separate from the world around us.

A new consciousness is now struggling to be born.... Transcendent consciousness is transforming. It inspires empathy with people and with nature; it brings an experience of oneness and belonging. Quantum consciousness makes us realize that, being one with others and with nature, what we do to them we do to ourselves. Not only will Quantum Conciousness make us behave more responsibly toward other people and the planet, it will also encourage us to join together to cope with the problems we face.[20]

An evolved consciousness is wider and deeper than the everyday consciousness of people today, and more functional than the consciousness of those engaged in deep prayer and meditation. In the past this kind of consciousness has been limited to exceptionally sensitive and creative people: to healers and poets, prophets and spiritual masters. In the future it could spread to a wider segment of the population. Humanity could be evolving its consciousness.... Quantum Consciousness may be not only the next step in our species evolution; it could also be our collective salvation.[21]

---

20. http://www.huffingtonpost.com/ervin-laszlo/quantum-consciousness-our_b_524054.html, and http://www.huffingtonpost.com/ervin-laszlo/why-your-brain-is-a-quant_b_489998.html.

21. Ervin Laszlo, "Cosmic Symphony: A Deeper Look at Quantum Consciousness," Huffingtonpost.com. 2010-04-12, http://www.huffingtonpost.com/ervin-laszlo/cosmic-symphony-a-deeper_b_532315.html.

Laszlo's remarkable Quantum Consciousness thesis resonates with the nondual Reign of God. There is much more available to us in an evolved consciousness which is "wider and deeper than the everyday consciousness of people today." He acknowledges that "only in spiritual, religious, or mystical experience does such information penetrate to our everyday awareness."[22]

How does Oneness consciousness feel?

Deeper Bliss

Orthodox theologian David Bentley Hart writes extensively on bliss. He says, "God is the one act of being, consciousness, and bliss in whom everything lives and moves and has its being; and so the only way to know the truth of things is, necessarily, the way of bliss."[23]

Ecstasy—the feeling of oneness

Universal perceptions of non-dual reality transform us and give us a sense of exhilaration and openness when we experience ourselves as part of the Ultimate Reality that continues to unfold. Integral visionary Terry Patton, talking about the taboo against ecstasy in our culture, says, "Part of our unspoken contract with conventional society is that there's a certain range of how we get to be. It's fine to be worried. It's fine to strive. It's fine to be depleted. But if you break open in the spirit of freedom itself—or joy itself? That's just weird!"[24]

Evelyn Underhill states:

> [Ecstasy] represents the greatest possible extension of the spiritual consciousness in the direction of Pure Being: the blind intent stretching here receives its reward in a profound experience of Eternal Life. In this experience, the

22. Ibid.
23. Hart, *The Experience of God*, 249.
24. http://www.terrypatten.com/video/the-taboo-against-ecstasy.

consciousness of "I-hood," of space and time . . . all that belongs to the World of Becoming and our own place therein...are suspended. The vitality which we are accustomed to split amongst these various things, is gathered up to form a state of pure apprehension...a vivid intuition of the Transcendent.[25]

Underhill goes on to explain that in the perfect unity of consciousness that comes in a state of ecstasy, the mystic is so concentrated on the Absolute that his or her faculties are suspended and he or she ceases to think of himself or herself as separate from the "All That Is." The mystic becomes so immersed in the Absolute that "as the bird cannot see the air which supports it, nor the fish the ocean in which it swims, [the mystic] knows all, but thinks naught, perceives all, but conceives naught."[26]

This involves the experiences of ecstasy and rapture far beyond what we normally experience. The boundaries of where you perceive your individual consciousness and identity (ego) begin to vanish. In the following I describe some of the dimensions along which consciousness may be transformed and expanded.

Body Expansion

This is the experience of one's body consciousness extending beyond one's body. One begins to feel bigger and bigger, with more and more of "out there" moving to "in here." I finally realized that my vivid and rapidly moving visions of places and people all over the world were preparing me for this way of viewing the world in the expanded consciousness of Oneness. This must have been what Jesus felt as he approached Jerusalem and began to weep, mourning the crushing future he saw for the Jewish people there (Luke 19:41-44). He wept because he felt his oneness with the troubled people of Jerusalem.

---

25. http://www.unexplainedstuff.com/Religious-Phenomena/Ecstasy.html.
26. Ibid.

I had an intense experience of oneness some years ago when I was speaking to a group in Santa Barbara, California. Ever since I was in elementary school I can remember having panic attacks. They were associated with being away from home, what is often called "agoraphobia." For several years as an adult I stopped traveling out of town because the anxiety and long telephone calls back home to my therapist were not worth it. For a time it was so intense I could not travel to the suburbs from where I live in midtown Kansas City. Even in normal travel around the city I found myself planning places I could stop if I had a panic attack. Then I began my Integral Christianity journey and serious prayer and meditation practice, and the panic attacks began to subside. Five years later I received the invitation to go to Santa Barbara, after having not traveled for as many years. I decided to risk it.

After the long plane ride I was alone in my hotel room looking out on the Pacific Ocean a few yards away. It was time to go to bed, the time I was most likely to panic. I had to get some sleep in order to hold three workshops that next day, Saturday. I sat down to pray and meditate. As I went down inside myself into my heart center, I almost immediately felt my chest expanding. Incredibly, instead of feeling like I was in Santa Barbara, I felt like Santa Barbara was in me! I was holding the whole city in my heart. There was no fear, only love for everything and everyone in this beautiful Pacific Coast city. From this sense of immense vastness I began to feel in God-mode.[27] This must be how God feels, only God has the entire universe in her heart! I had a great time in Santa Barbara and since then I have taught all around the country. Perhaps this was what Meister Eckhart was feeling when he said, "God made all things through me when I had my existence in the unfathomable ground of God."[28]

---

27. God-mode is Shawn Mikula's term, saying, "It is perhaps the highest and most profound type of Cosmic Consciousness I've yet experienced." http://www.metareligion.com/Philosophy/Articles/Consciousness/expansion_of_consciousness.htm.

28. *Meister Eckhart*, C. de B. Evans, trans, 389.

Integral philosopher Ken Wilber writes:

> Nature retreats before its God. Light finds it own Abode. That's all I keep thinking as I enter into this extraordinary vastness. I am going in and up, in and up, in and up, and I have ceased to have any bodily feelings at all. In fact, I don't even know where my body is, or if I even have one. I know only shimmering sheaths of luminous bliss, each giving way to the next, each softer and yet stronger, brighter and yet fainter, more intense yet harder to see.

> Above all, I am Full. I am full to infinity, in this ocean of light. I am full to infinity, in this ocean of bliss. I am full to infinity, in this ocean of love. I cannot conceive of wanting something, desiring something, grasping after anything. I can contain no more than is already here, full to infinity. I am beyond myself, beyond this world, beyond pain and suffering and self and same, and I know this is the home of God, and I know that I am in God's Presence. I am one with Presence, it is obvious. I am one with God, it is certain. I am one with Spirit, it is given. I shall never want again, for Grace abounds, here in the luminous mist of infinity.[29]

The Jesus Path of Heart-Centered, Devotional, Nonduality

There are various paths to nondual awareness. Jesus offers the way of devotional nonduality. As Richard Rohr has pointed out, Jesus was the first religious teacher of nonduality in the West. We don't understand and are not able to practice much of what Jesus taught because we continue to look at it in a dualistic way. I have explored various Eastern and Western avenues to Oneness consciousness and have found that the one that carried me to Oneness most fully was the doorway of devotion to God and Jesus leading to devotion to

---

29. Wilber, *One Taste*, 148-151.

Oneness or the Reign of God. This is passionate, heart-centered awareness of and devotion to Jesus and God leading to a nondual mind.

Summary of The Peace of Oneness Consciousness

• The main point of Jesus' teaching was the Oneness consciousness that he called the Reign of God.

• Nonduality is experiencing God and us, along with us and one another, as one without separation.

• Oneness is not sameness. We are still each unique and different, but we are not separated from God and one other. Nonduality is "not two" but it is not "one" in the sense of being the same either.

• Science and quantum physics point to the oneness of the universe.

Questions for Reflection and Discussion

1. How do you understand Oneness and nonduality?

2. What do you think of the author's "dimming" and "Santa Barbara" experiences?

3. Have you had any moments, experiences, or times when you felt at one with another person? A group? A tree? A mountain? A city? The world?

4. How does the idea of "single-seeing" strike you?

5. Does Quantum Consciousness find any resonance with you? In what way?

Practices

1. Imagine looking out through the eyes of someone that you know or that is in your group. How might you feel differently toward them. Imagine how you might treat them differently.

2. Being Space

Space is an excellent metaphor for Being. Being is like "empty" space, not exactly, but close enough when we are describing something difficult to describe.

Look at a nearby object. Notice the "empty" space, the Beingness, surrounding the object.

Rather than focus on the object's shape, look at the lines and curves of the Being space that is up against the object, the places in between and around the object. Notice that you are connected to that object by that same space or Beingness.

3. Use the following description and images on page 337 to reflect on and discuss together.

A diagram of Trinity Being Us (in color at www.revpaulsmith.com)

Here we put the *experience* of spirit-consciousness together with the *theology* of the classical Trinity of Father, Son, and Spirit in the illustrated diagram on page 337. This is Trinity Being Us— the first person perspective in *resting as* God. It shows how God the Father, Son, and Spirit are experienced when viewed through the lens of the Inner Face of God—God-Being-Us. Since I am using an uncommon understanding of spirit as consciousness and unfamiliar terms of various modes of consciousness, this can seem more confusing that the previous two diagrams. Also, the order in our inner experience does not usually unfold in the traditional order of the Trinity as commonly phrased. Trinity is stated as Father, Son, and Spirit, while our inner experience of identification unfolds, in Trinitarian language, as Spirit, Father, Son.

In life we don't usually begin with the experience of a transcendent God, but rather the experience of divine, basic, spirit-breath-consciousness. Then, if we engage in the spiritual journey, we may move to non-ordinary modes consciousness. That doesn't mean an infant or a child cannot have a transcendent experience. It just means that they will interpret it with the language they have available from the stage of development they are in. Babies, with no language, cannot think about such an experience, and therefore it is lost to cognition. Babies go through the warrior stage (the terrible twos), the law and order traditional stage (preteens) if they are going to become civilized, and then as teen-agers begin to question things in ways that only modern stage cultures can encourage. Every spiritual experience will be shaped and interpreted by the stage one is in. Many in the modern stage have awakened and transcendent spiritual events, but don't pay attention to them because their worldview does not allow them to think in those terms. They just say, "I really felt weird for a minute there, but I'm okay now." Too bad!

Here is an explanation of this Trinity-Being-Us diagram that follows, this time beginning at the bottom and moving up. If you will go back and forth between the diagram and the explanation of it here, you will get the over-all picture of Part Three in a more vivid and memorable way.

The bottom picture is of a little girl blowing on the seed head of a dandelion.

This signifies our beginning life with **spirit-breath as basic consciousness.** The Hebrew Scriptures identify this as *rûach* or spirit-breath given to all the living. God breathed spirit-breath into us at birth and we continue to do so with every breath we take. The presence of the Infinite in the finite begins as our own, limited, basic consciousness. I label this as "spirit" because the Bible does. As you look at this little girl breathing out spirit-breath, you are probably looking at it from your own basic consciousness while you are breathing in and out spirit-breath at the same time. Can you be mindful of that?

The second image from the bottom is a woman in a praying, meditative, or non-ordinary state of consciousness.

As we learn to go inside ourselves, we can personally **relate to spiritual realities in awakened consciousness.** This is imaged as our opening to the "other side" with its mystical paranormal phenomena bubbling up in and around us. Notice the "mystical bubbles" which represent our being immersed in moments of the higher consciousness of numinous, awakened awareness. These mystical events of elevated consciousness bubble up from deep within us. They include such experiences as the presence of God, Jesus and saintly spiritual guides, along with intuitions, wisdom, visions, voices, healing, guidance, and other energy fields of spirit-breath. The New Testament gives many examples of both Jesus and his friends coming into a release of this awakened spirit-breath which is beyond basic consciousness. I also label this as "spirit" because the Bible does.

Some of my readers who regularly engage in these awakened, paranormal states may find themselves doing so right now as they are looking at this second picture and reading these words.

The third image from the bottom pictures the no-boundary cosmic mind and full heart.

Resting as God in transcendent consciousness happens when our mind is open to the vast stillness of infinite being and our heart is filled with love and bliss. It is there that we identify with our own Universal True Self. We may have an unexpected and sudden single or momentary experience of this at any time. If we engage in spiritual practice, we can learn how to access more and more of this still, vast, infinite, boundary-less, mind accompanied by a bliss-love-joy filled heart. In this state we are not, at first, looking out at anything but are totally immersed in vast space and blissful love. This is labeled as "Father" in Trinitarian language because *it is the inner experience of God as Infinite Being*—a still mind and a full heart. This is the presence of the Infinite in the finite in the fullest way any finite human being can experience the Infinite in this earthly life.

Some of my readers may have learned to access this transcendent state by simply going inside and sinking down into a bliss-filled heart while experiencing a vast empty mind. They may be viewing this third image from that deep Divine Self. Some call this a *witnessing state*, looking out at the world from this vast, peaceful, blissful place.

The top image is of our looking out at the world from Oneness: the presence of the infinite in the finite

This image is also on the cover of this book. This is looking at material and spiritual reality from the highest level of consciousness now available to humankind (symbolized by the light-filled eye)— the presence of the Infinite (symbolized by the infinite cosmos) in the finite (symbolized by the human head). Jesus said, "The light of the body is the eye: if therefore your eye be single, your whole body shall be full of light" (Matt 6:22). When we see from the light of single-seeing or Oneness, then the light that our nondual eye sees fills our whole body with light.

As we grow spiritually, we may begin to have more and more moments of Oneness Consciousness symbolized here as the mind no longer looking out from a tiny, busy place of awareness. Rather, this is looking out at the world around us from the vast, cosmic space of Oneness which sees everyone and everything from the wholeness of Christ consciousness. The Apostle Paul says, "It is no longer I who live, but [the Cosmic] Christ lives in me" (Gal. 2:19). This is seeing nondually, or "seeing-single." This is the mind of Christ which, as Jesus, looks at the world in unitive awareness. This is not exactly a state of consciousness but rather a way of seeing from oneness. I call it Oneness consciousness. Jesus called it the Reign of God—and said we should seek it above all else.

This, too, can be an experienced reality like the previous two modes of higher awareness. Some of my readers may already be reading and looking at this diagram through the eyes of Oneness. May we all seek to move toward this more and more in our lives.

Again, it's not necessary to remember all the details of this diagram. Just let the images sink into you and do their inner work. Mentally, it is enough to see that there really is an Inner Face of God-Being-Us hidden behind the words "Father, Son, and Spirit." And most importantly, we can learn to open to new modes of spiritual awareness which enrich our lives and make us a channel of divine love and action in the world today.

The Transfiguration by Raphael (painted 1516-1520)

CHAPTER 15

The Moses and Elijah Phenomenon

Jesus with three close friends, two dead guys, and one sick boy

The Reign of God does not lend itself to descriptions using concepts and words. It's like "wet." We can't get wet by defining it or pronouncing the word "water" over and over. No matter how many times we define it, it won't make us wet. Nor can we experience the Reign of God by defining it. Yet, one time Jesus told his friends that a few of them were actually going to see the Reign of God. So one time Jesus did define the Reign of God. But he didn't define it in words—he defined it in action.

He said to his friends, "There are some standing here who will not taste death before they see that the Reign of God has come with power" (Mark 9:1). He was going to *show* them this highest dimension of God's spirit in real time and glowing reality. What happened next is the story of Jesus getting together with three close friends, two dead guys, and one sick boy.

A living picture of the Reign of God

Placed close to the center of the gospels of Matthew (17:1-21), Mark (9:2-13), and Luke (9:28-36), this seems to be the central event in Jesus' life this side of the resurrection. We usually think of his crucifixion as the central event of his life. It was certainly that for his friends who recorded it in detail.

But more importantly, Jesus did not himself point to his upcoming death as what the Reign of God looked like. Nor did he point to his resurrection as the coming of the Reign of God in power. The one event, coming in the future, which he pointed to as the Reign of

God "come with power" was what we now call the "Transfiguration." This was a living picture of the Reign of God! The crucifixion grabs our attention because it is life and death, agony and suffering. To the early Christians it was shocking and puzzling, and it took some time to develop a series of explanations for it. As the cross became more and more central in the church's thinking, it became the symbol of Christianity.

The resurrection was of great importance because it meant Jesus was now available to us without the limitations of space and time. The early Christians developed its importance framed in the language of showing God approved of Jesus. However, Jesus himself did not point to the resurrection as the Reign coming in power. The cross and the resurrection are critically significant events. But I must stay with Jesus' own words that the events on the mountain and down in the valley were what his main point, the Reign of God, looks like. However, the crucifixion and the Transfiguration are intimately intertwined since Jesus' death was the *subject* of this mystical experience.

Our own crucifixion is in daily taking up our cross, engaging in our own inner death to our ego identity. *This is how we get to the Reign of God!* Jesus' struggle to let go of his life was the motivation, context, and purpose of the Transfiguration. It is the central struggle of our lives, also, if we would be transformed!

Even if we can't make the Transfiguration into something to hang around our neck like we do with the cross, we can hang our life around the Transfiguration. We can't put it on top of our church buildings, but we can put it at the top of our lives.[30]

Jesus in distress

The account immediately continues in the next verse (Mark 9:2), where, six days after Jesus' prediction, some of those present with

---

30. See my article, "An Evolutionary Integral Understanding of the Cross" by Paul R. Smith, in *Tikkun*, Fall 2012, "Christianity Without the Cross?" http://www.tikkun.org/nextgen/an-evolutionary-integral-understanding-of-the-cross.

him did see the Reign of God "coming in power." Jesus took Peter, James, and John with him and hiked up a local mountain as this demonstration was about to begin. What motivated this long climb? Jesus was in trouble and needed some help. I love it that Jesus got in enough trouble to need help because that's where I live much of the time. What we now religiously call "The Transfiguration" was the direct result of Jesus having a problem. This moment of incredible light happened because of a time of incredible darkness in Jesus' life. This happens to us, too, when in the middle of a dark time there is an astounding moment of light. A few days before the mountain climb Jesus said to his friends that he was soon going to go through "great suffering" (Mark 9:21) where he would be rejected by the religious leaders and be killed. Remember, the problem Jesus was wrestling with was his death. Death and dying always get our full attention, even if you're the light of the world.

Four pictures of the Reign of God coming in power

Of all the High Renaissance painters, only Raphael (1483–1520) got the Transfiguration right. Rather than a three-picture event, he was the only one to see that it was a four-picture event. You can go back to his painting at the beginning of this chapter and see it all. Can you identify all four pictures?

Picture One: Three friends from his journey through life

When Jesus needed big time help with a big time struggle, the first thing he did was get together with his closest friends. This was also the very first thing he did when he began his ministry. He wanted to change the world, so he began with a small group of friends who became dedicated to doing just that. Now, after this small group had been together for some time, Jesus faced his approaching death. He took his three closest friends from this group with him to get away for a day.

Jesus shared his highs and lows with friends. Loneliness is going for long periods of time without sharing yourself with others. Of course, we say, "But I don't have the kind of friends that Jesus had. You should see the messes my friends make all the time. They never get it when I share." That's a good picture of Jesus' friends, too. Of course they loved him, but they had their own problems like all of our friends do. They tended to get sleepy whenever Jesus needed them most, which would happen shortly here on the mountaintop and later in Gethsemane (Luke 9:32, 22:45). Have you ever poured your heart out to a friend and realized they are having a hard time staying awake? When the going got really tough, these friends of Jesus made themselves scarce. But sleepy, sometimes retreating, friends are better than no friends. It takes work even to find the kind of terrified, sleepy friends Jesus had. Maybe for us it will be a friend we hire for a while in therapy. Or some friends we find in an AA or other support group. Any small degree of oneness we feel with friends is a touch of the Reign of God. This is why I have been in some kind of small group that meets regularly to share our lives and pray for the last sixty years. The Reign of God also pops up in a stroll with a friend, an intimate time with your lover, or a hug when we are feeling empty.

Before we go on to Picture Two, notice that Jesus trudged up a mountain to pray. Why go up a mountain? Why not just pray right in the midst of things? Of course you can yell "help" to God anytime. You can stop and seek God any time and any place. But Jesus knew he couldn't get done what he needed to at the bottom of the mountain in everyday life. He had to get away. He knew he needed some guidance and spiritual food, and this kind of spiritual nourishing had to be done where it was quiet, and he would not be interrupted. So he went up a mountain to pray. Traditionally God appeared on mountain tops, but it was also a way to get away from the crowds. This was serious prayer time.

Picture Two: Two friends from the other side

Once they were up on the mountain, Jesus became quiet and went into prayer mode. As his friends fought off sleep, they noticed a strange thing began to happen—Jesus started to glow. That woke them up—this time, in an altered state of consciousness. If that wasn't enough, suddenly they saw two people talking with Jesus, later identified by the writer as Moses and Elijah. In a visible shining through of transcendent heavenly light, both Jesus and the disciples were transported to another level of consciousness. Jesus was transported because he wanted to be—Peter, James, and John because they were shocked into it by the energy field surrounding Jesus. In this elevated state, they saw two highly meaningful figures in Jewish history give guidance and comfort to Jesus to help prepare him for his final earthly challenge.

So the second thing that Jesus did to receive help was to get together with two of his friends from the other side of the thin place on the mountaintop. Marcus Borg says, "There are minimally two layers or dimensions of reality: the visible world of our ordinary experience and God, the sacred, Spirit. 'Thin places' are where these two layers of reality meet or intersect."[31] These two saints, dead for centuries, now lived in that other layer of reality, the non-physical spiritual dimension. Moses and Elijah, present here, have been much discussed theologically and symbolically by scholars, but seldom taken seriously as really "being there."

The Moses and Elijah phenomenon

I call this "other side" friendship that Jesus had the "Moses and Elijah phenomenon." Jesus was standing together with Moses and Elijah having what researchers today call an ADC, an After Death Conversation. Luke says, "They were talking about his departure which he was about to accomplish in Jerusalem" (Mark 9:30). The word for departure in Greek was *exodon* (ἔξοδον) from which we get our word "exodus." They were not talking about Jesus exiting Jerusalem. They were talking about his exiting this life—his death! This is one more reason we know this entire event was motivated by Jesus facing death because that was the topic of conversation. This

---

31. Borg, *The Heart of Christianity*, 155.

conversation shows us what a good conversation with Jesus or other saintly spiritual guides can be like. It is a back and forth between caring friends on the other side about things that are important to our life.

Notice Jesus' comfort level in talking with Moses and Elijah. How would you react if suddenly two famous dead people appeared in front of you and began talking to you? Notice that Jesus didn't get flustered or excited. He didn't shout out "What's going on here! Am I losing my mind?" Instead, he calmly discussed his death with two dead guys. It seems to me the most likely explanation of this is that this had happened before, perhaps in private, and perhaps several times. Jesus refers to all of this as a "vision" (Matt. 17:9) using the same word for the many visions his friends had of him as reported later in Acts. This was a shared visionary experience, with Jesus, Peter, James, and John all seeing and hearing the same thing: Jesus talking to two trusted spiritual guides from the other side. If this was a picture of the Reign of God, could something of this become a reality for us, too?

After Death Communication

Jesus' ADC with Moses and Elijah was very much like the ADCs his followers had with him after his death. They were vivid, intense, transcendent, and life changing. Not only did people in Jesus' day have these experiences but a large number of Americans today also report that they have been in touch with someone who has died.

According to a Pew Survey, roughly three-in-ten Americans (29%) say they have felt in touch with someone who has died.[32] The survey reported that the group least likely to say they have felt in touch with a dead person were Evangelicals. That is interesting since Evangelicals are the ones who hold most strongly to the idea that every word in the Bible is true and all the events recorded in it actually happened. That means the group that believes most strongly that Jesus talked

---

32. http://www.pewresearch.org/daily-number/mystical-experiences/2009 survey.

to two dead guys does not believe in talking to the dead! Talk about compartmentalizing your religious life from your regular life!

In the last few decades, academic researchers have collected the experiences of thousands of people living today who have had ADC's, usually with those they were close to. In after-death experience, the physical body and mind disintegrate, leaving the consciousness of the person who has died free to enter into communication with those still living at the level to which the living are open to such experiences. The number of Americans saying they have been in touch with a dead person has risen from 18% in 1996 to the 29% today. This may reflect the previous skepticism of Americans to ADCs yielding to these widely reported studies.

The topic in this chapter is not about communicating with a loved one who has died, although that can have its place. Rather, I am addressing the spiritual practice of intentionally seeking enlightened spiritual guides from the other side. Despite fears of idolatry, the practice of praying to the saints was affirmed by later church leaders such as Augustine and Aquinas.[33] As I have previously pointed out, there is a long history of Jesus, Mary, and other saints appearing to friends of Jesus down through the ages and today.[34] Even millions of Muslims have been seeing apparitions of the Mother Mary in recent decades.[35]

Saints in the New Testament are simply all the friends of Jesus living both on this side and the next. The word then evolved in some circles to mean any friend of Jesus who passed on to the other side and was evolved enough to have something to offer us who are still living on this side. These have often been formally recognized in the Catholic and Orthodox circles, while in Protestant and Evangelical circles only seen as models and examples of what it means to be a friend of

---

33. http://www.christianitytoday.com/history/issues/issue-37/praying-to-dead.html.

34. http://www.unexplainedstuff.com/Religious-Phenomena/Apparitions-of-Holy-Figures.html, and http://www.holylove.org/files/med_1307117175.pdf.

35. http://www.abc.net.au/radionational/programs/encounter/4812020.

Jesus. To be honest, the only thing I heard about saints growing up in my Southern Baptist church was "when the saints go marching in I want to be in that number."

Every time we connect with someone on the other side, this opens the pathway to that person in a greater way and makes them more available to everyone. Conversations with Jesus are likely the most deeply established ADCs in the world.

C. S. Lewis does a Moses and Elijah

Here is a contemporary, documented ADC involving two famous Christians. J. B. Phillips (1906–1982) was an English Bible scholar, translator, author, and clergyman. He is most noted for his *The New Testament in Modern English*, one of the first such versions and widely popular in the 1950s. In his little book, *Ring of Truth*, Phillips shared a significant event in his life that happened in 1963.

> The late C. S. Lewis, whom I did not know very well, and had only seen in the flesh once, but with whom I had corresponded a fair amount, gave me an unusual experience. A few days after his death, while I was watching television, he "appeared," sitting in a chair within a few feet of me, and spoke a few words which were particularly relevant to the difficult circumstances through which I was passing. He was ruddier in complexion than ever, grinning all over his face and, as the old-fashioned saying has it, positively glowing with health. A week later, this time when I was in bed reading, he appeared again, even more rosily radiant than before, and repeated the same message, which was very important to me at the time.[36]

Later, Phillips reported that the message was, "It's not as hard as you think, you know." Phillips had been in the middle of a deep

---

36. J. B. Phillips, *Ring of Truth: A Translator's Testimony*, (London: Shaw Books, 2000), 103.

depression, and after he saw C. S. Lewis and heard these words, his depression lifted.

Notice the similarities to the appearance of Moses and Elijah as well as Jesus' appearances after the resurrection. Lewis appeared large as life and natural. He spoke. It was a transforming experience for Phillips. I'm amazed at the number of people in my former congregation over the years who shared with me when they found out I didn't think they were crazy to talk with the dead. They would say, "I've never told anybody this but . . . ."

Medical anthropology weighs in

John Pilch (1937–2016), scholar and author focusing on cultural and medical anthropology, provides a detailed analysis of the Transfiguration using the social sciences to show that this event is highly plausible in the Mediterranean peasant context.[37] He says that the best way of understanding the transfiguration is that it involved an altered state of consciousness. Ancient and modern altered states of consciousness, if not identical, are at least analogous to the Transfiguration. The key defining characteristic of a trance is its intensely focused attention which reduces awareness of the context, namely, objects, stimuli or environment outside the specific focus. The specific focus can be internal or external. Jesus was focused on the presence of Moses, Elijah, and *Abba* God, while the disciples were focused on the whole glowing event.

Pilch says that going up the mountain may have taken up to a day. This would account for the disciples' tiredness and sleepiness. The physically taxing journey might also have aided in the movement to another state of consciousness. A half awake and a half asleep state would also fit with the much-studied realm of waking dreams, deep prayer, meditation, and trances. Pilch's research has shown that the people of the Mediterranean world of past and present slip readily and easily into various altered states of consciousness. They do so for

37. Pilch, "The Transfiguration of Jesus," 47-64.

a variety of reasons, a major one being the need to find an answer to a question or resolution to a problem. Jesus was certainly facing the problematic event of his death, and his friends were still wondering who Jesus really was.

Picture Three: The Ultimate Reassuring Voice

Then a voice came from a cloud saying, "This is my child, listen to him" (Luke 9:35). When you hear directly from God/She that you are her child, there can be a no more transforming moment. This was both another reassurance for Jesus of who he was and a directive to these three men to take Jesus' words seriously. Then the luminous glory of transcendent reality disappears, but the picture of the Reign of God is not yet finished.

Picture Four: A friend in need

As they started back down the mountain, things were different. Imagine how you would feel if you had been there. They went up with a problem. They came down with a new sense of oneness with one another, oneness with the company of the saints, and oneness with God. There was only one more kind of oneness left to complete the picture of the Reign of God.

A sick boy enters the picture

Of course, Peter didn't want to leave. He wanted to stay and build three shelters: one each for Jesus, Moses, and Elijah (Luke 9:33). He wanted to prolong this marvelous event. Or maybe he thought Moses and Elijah were going to hang around for a while. Mark writes in an editorial comment about Peter into his account, "For he did not know what he was saying. For they were terrified" (9:6). In others words, Peter was scared to death and acting crazy.

But Jesus knew they had to go back down the mountain into the messy world where everybody has problems and little boys get sick. Jesus was ready to change the world, one troubled boy at a time. As Raphael graphically portrays in his painting, they found a sick boy at the hands of some other close friends of Jesus who had been unsuccessfully attempting to heal him. He was probably afflicted with epilepsy, which in that day would have been attributed to an "unclean spirit." Notice that in Raphael's painting the epileptic boy is the only one of the crowd at the foot of the mountain who is looking up at the mountain top event.

Jesus takes over and heals the boy. Later in private, his friends ask Jesus why they were not able to heal the boy. Jesus replies that this kind of healing only comes through prayer (Mark 9:29). I can imagine these still-being-trained friends of Jesus thinking, "But we've been praying for hours over this boy and nothing happened!" However, Jesus was not talking about that kind of praying, but rather the kind of praying he had just been a part of on the mountain top. Only heaven opening to us in consciousness that goes beyond the normal can lead to the kind of healing the world needs! As Jesus predicted, here was a powerful picture of the Reign of God— Oneness manifested in the awakened numinous consciousness of the mountaintop providing the spiritual power we need to bring healing to the nitty-gritty world in the valley below. That's a dynamic, four-part picture of the Reign of God in action!

At home with four kinds of relationships

What did Jesus show them when he said they would see the Reign of God coming in power? He showed them four manifestations of the Reign of God present in this life. They were images of Oneness manifested in the form of four friendships or ways of connecting with others.

1. Connecting with a few others here in our earthly dimension.

2. Connecting with a few others in the spiritual non-physical dimension.

3. Connecting with God.

4. Connecting with a few of the fearful and oppressed whom we are called to be with in some fashion.

Manifesting Oneness brought healing for Jesus, his friends, a sick boy, and ultimately, all who would enter in.

When the saints go marching in

The range of help from the other side has been expanding down through the centuries as others follow Jesus' example and let "the saints[38] go marching in" to their lives. This in no way replaces God and Jesus, but provides even more avenues for real help with our lives. Our Catholic and Orthodox sisters and brothers call this "praying to the saints." Protestants tend to not call it anything since they are usually uncomfortable with the whole idea.

Some Christians don't talk about this because it seems New Agey or they are worried it will detract from their relationship with Jesus. They say that prayer for Christians is a relationship with God and Jesus. When it comes to praying or talking to the saints who have come before us as Jesus did with Moses and Elijah, shouldn't we believe that was just for Jesus? Shouldn't our devotion and love for him exclude having any kind of relationship with others who live in the reality of what Christians commonly call "heaven"? However, Jesus is not alone there in that reality. If it's okay to have an ongoing friendship with him, how about with his other friends who are there with him? Think of two difference scenes:

Scene One: Someone falls in love and says, "I love you so much that I want to spend all my time with you. I never want to talk to your mom and dad. I never want to see your family or friends. I just want to spend my whole life with you and love you." That's the traditional evangelical take on relating to Jesus.

Scene Two: Someone falls in love and they say, "I love you so much that I want to spend my time with you. Your mom and dad are always

---

38. In the Old Testament David used the term "saint" while speaking to his fellow Jews, "Love the Lord all you his saints" (Psalm 31:23). The Old Testament uses the term thirty-two times referring to both living and dead persons. In the New Testament, all Christians are called "saints" (Rom. 1:7).

welcome in our home. Your family is my family, your friends are my friends. The people you love, I will love." That's the Catholic and Orthodox take on relating to Jesus and his friends. I side with them.

Let me tell you about Don, my long-time friend. He has had a cherished friendship with Jesus for many years. About three years ago he was reading a quote from Julian of Norwich and felt a connection with her optimism and many visions of God as love and never wrath. As he looked up her biography, he found some similarities between her important month and day dates and his. So he decided to bypass all the reasons he should not do this and instead visualized Julian being with him. This was him visualizing what he thought *might* be real at this point. He immediately felt her presence and found that she was very real. Now, he not only regularly talks with Jesus, but he also connects with Julian on most days of his week. When I asked him how he felt in those times he said, "Oh my, ecstatic!" I laughed and said, "That's great. Do you feel anything else?" He replied, "Yes, I also feel great peace. I feel like this is the way life is meant to be."

My journey with Jesus and the saints

Talking to the saints—Jesus modeled it, Christian history records it, modern research points to it—and some years ago I decided to do it. If Jesus' model of talking to saints like Moses and Elijah was meant for any who were drawn to it, that included me.

I began by asking the energy healer I had seen for a number of years about communicating with spiritual guides from the other side. She was easily in touch with her spiritual guides as well as those of others. When she saw my interest, she asked me if there was anyone in the history of Christianity that I had felt myself particularly interested in or drawn to. I immediately replied, "Oh yes, the disciple John, the one that it was said that Jesus loved" (John 13:23; 21:7). He had fascinated me and I have always been drawn to his writing about love. She suggested that I ask him if he would be a guide for me. So I did, then and there. Immediately I sensed his presence and heard, inside my head, the words, "I've been waiting for you to ask me." This was followed by my crying and blubbering for a while. Thus began my friendship with the one I call John. I filled many pages in my journal with enlightening conversations with him. Eventually I sensed that John moved behind me and placed his hand on my right shoulder. I have felt that touch for years whenever I turn my attention to him. I guess that means along with Jesus' touch on my right arm, that I'm just a touchy kind of person.

Some months later, on my daily two-mile power-walk in the park, I began to sense a connection with a fourth-century monk named Michael. As I talked with him, internally, I found out that he was the leader of a small group of men and women who were part of a monastery in Italy. Some of them lived in the town and some in the monastery. I was fascinated since I did not know women were monastic participants back then or that monasteries had both live in and live out members. I later researched this and found that historians have found just such evidence.[39] Soon I was having visions of this group and a number of fascinating conversations about their life and struggles.

A few years ago I had healed enough from my mother wound that I decided I needed a saintly, feminine, energetic presence in my company of saints. I thought about Mary, the mother of Jesus, and Mary Magdalene, Jesus' follower and close friend. I asked them to be with me and perceived a kind of blending of both of them in an archetype of feminine energetic presence. I call this presence Mary, meaning both Marys, and sense that Mary and I hold hands when I direct my attention to her.

In a typical prayer time I often find myself in the company of Jesus to my right, touching my arm, John behind me touching my right shoulder, Mary on my left holding my left hand, God as the divine presence I call "Daddy" in front of me, filling my heart, and a vaguely perceived group of monastics slightly to my right called "the teachers"

39. http://www.pbs.org/wgbh/pages/frontline/shows/religion/first/roles.html.

with a spokesperson name Michael. This scene is not visionary but rather a series of sensed, felt presences and touches. In the presence of God as my loving, *Abba* Daddy, Jesus, and these saints, I am greatly refreshed and blessed. My conversations have more recently been directed to Jesus rather than to the others. Each in its own time.

Like my congregation's hesitancy to tell anyone of their talking to dead loved ones, I have hesitated to share here the details of my experience with the Moses and Elijah phenomenon. However, talking with the saints at various time has become real for me and I offer it as a possibility for others.

Neuropsychologist and former Catholic nun Dr. Charlotte Tomaino sums up the Transfiguration and the Reign of God quite succinctly when she says, "An awakened brain and an awakened life means living from the inside vision of life desired, regardless of outside circumstances. When the inner reality is stronger and more real than the outer reality and you can act from your choice, you are entraining your brain and creating your life."[40] This is where Jesus lived, and, little by little, where I am heading.

Once again, the goal is not spiritual experiences or talking to dead saints. The goal is living from the inner vision of Oneness, no separation between us and God and us and one another. The inner reality of these spiritual relationships constantly draws me into this kind of Oneness.

Summary of The Moses and Elijah Phenomenon: A living picture of the Reign of God

The four pictures of the Transfiguration show us that in the Oneness of the Reign of God there is:

• No separation between us and those living on this side, as experienced in closeness with a few others here in the physical realm.

---

40. Charlotte Tomaino, *Awakening the Brain: The Neuropsychology of Grace*, (New York: Atria Books/Beyond Words), 178.

As we evolve, that moves to a wider consciousness of Oneness with everyone.

• No separation between us and those living on other side experienced in closeness with Jesus and, sometimes, a few others in the mystical realm of consciousness.

• No separation between us and God as experienced in the mystical realm of consciousness as closeness with the loving presence of our Mother-Father God. As we evolve, we begin to see that no one is separated from God, even if they are living with the illusion that they are.

• No separation between us and the need of the world experienced in bringing healing wherever we are called with the abilities we are given.

Questions for Reflection and Group Discussion

1. What parts of this chapter have you marked as interesting, questionable, or downright weird? It's good to be aware of where you really are. Until we can be where we are, we can't be where we are not—and might want to go.

2. In your friendship with God, are there any saints on the other side you might wonder if you are being called to be friends with on this side? Write their names down. Whether you share their names with the group is up to you.

3. Who are the few needy and oppressed persons or situations you have been called to in the past and present to offer your gifts and abilities to bring healing to? Share this with the group if it fits for you.

Practices

1. If you are drawn to connect with any of the saints, officially recognized or not, begin to explore this. You may read some of the books in the bibliography about visions of the saints and/or inquire with others who have such experiences. At some point, as it seems

you are being guided, go ahead and explore this in your own prayer time. Ask Jesus or God about it and listen for what words or images or intuitions come to your mind. If you get the response to go ahead, then begin by asking a saint you are drawn to if they would be your helper. See what happens. You may also find a loving spiritual guide whose name you do not know. That's okay, too.

2. The Three Faces of God Practices

The events surrounding the Transfiguration also offer us a picture of the three Faces of God basic inner practices of reflecting about God, relating to God, and resting as God.

REFLECT ABOUT GOD

Before and after the mountain top experience, even on the way back down, Jesus reflected with his friends about God. Talking, reading, remembering, and reflecting about God is a part of our spiritual journey. For this practice, reflect about God in your life by thinking about a time when you have felt loved by God directly or through another person. Remember what happened and how your felt. Stay with that until you have re-entered some of those feelings and gratitude for that time:

RELATE TO GOD

On the mountaintop, Jesus related directly and personally to Moses and Elijah, and then to Abba God. Next, in this practice, connect personally with the divine fatherly-motherly presence, Jesus, or other sacred Presence. As you breathe out, say to God who is present in whatever form you need, "I love you." As you breathe in, hear God say back to you, "I love you." Do this back and forth until you feel the love flowing both ways.

REST AS GOD

When Jesus came down from the mountain and encountered the sick boy, he rested in his own divinity and acted as and on behalf of

God by healing the boy. You can, too, in this practice by changing the words "I love you" to "I am love." As you breath in, say "I am love." You are affirming that your deepest Self is pure divine love. Sink down into this deep reality as you breathe out in each cycle of breathing. This is you as your deepest True Self embracing your true nature. Do this as long as you need to begin to feel that you are love in your heart center.

Finally, when you are ready, as you breathe out, flow out to the world in compassionate love. Send the divine love that you are to the people and situations you are called to bless. Simply picture the person or situation in your mind as you say "You are loved." See them surrounded and filled with love. Follow up with any further actions that you sense God leading you to take.

3. Close with this brief version of the Three Faces of God which so easily serves as a reminder, invocation, benediction, or blessing—or all four!

In the name of the :

"God beyond us" (or "me" if for yourself—and "you" if used as a blessing)

"God beside us"

and

"God being us"

CHAPTER 16

The Unknown God of Today

When Paul brought the gospel to Athens, he was in one of the great centers of philosophy, architecture, and art. He faced the most intellectual and cultured people of his day. They loved to talk about the deeper meanings of life summed up in the word the Greeks coined: "philosophy," meaning "the love of wisdom." Living in one of the world's earliest democracies, they reflected on matters such as existence, knowledge, values, reason, mind, and language. In many ways the Athenians were remarkably very much like educated and thoughtful people in the modern world today.

Paul spoke in the central square or marketplace where people gathered to discuss issues of the day. These were not Jews and so Paul does not quote from the Hebrew Scriptures. He had closely viewed the many statues representing the pantheon of the gods of the day. He positively noted that they expressed their desire for spirituality by saying, "I see how extremely religious you are in every way" (Acts 17:22). Then he wisely began with their own point of reference, an inscription he had seen on one of the many religious altars which read "TO AN UNKNOWN GOD." Evidently some of the Athenians believed there was another god of whom they had no knowledge and Paul began by saying that he was going to tell them about this unknown god:

> The God who made the world and everything in it, the one who is Sovereign of heaven and earth, does not live in temples made by human hands and is not served by human hands, as though God needed anything, since God alone gives to all life, breath, and all things. . . . God is not far from each one of us. For in God we live and

move and have our being; as even some of your own poets
have said, "For we too are God's offspring."
(Acts 17: 24-25, 27-28)

Notice in this brief passage Paul refers to a big God, a close God, and a you God. He begins with the big, awesome face of God who is the creator of the world and everything in it, self-existent, needing nothing, and giving life and breath to all. This is the God in whom "we live and move and have our being." This is God-beyond-us.

He then points to the close face of God who is "not far from each one of us." This is God-beside-us.

Finally, he presents the "you" face of God saying, "for we too are God's offspring." As "God's offspring," we are the descendants of divine parentage, born in God's very own image and likeness. Just as offspring of fish are fish and offspring of animals are animals, so offspring of God are gods. This is God-being-us.

I can imagine Paul saying to us today, "I see you are a religious and spiritual people, seeking the Ultimate Mystery and Reality of the Universe that many people call God. I'd like to talk to you about an unknown God, one that you may not know yet. This God is bigger, closer, and more like you than you have thought!"

The religion of today

No recognized Christian group today has yet fully acknowledged this unknown God. No widely embraced spiritual path of any tradition has yet integrated each of these three faces of God. Yet, all three were present in an incipient form in original Christianity. And all three Faces of God are present in some form when all current forms of Christianity are combined. On a wider scale, all three dimensions of the Ultimate Mystery are present if we combine all the religions of the world. I am *not* suggesting that we should combine them into one supposed, diluted "super religion" and lose each of their rich and unique approaches and truths. However, I am pointing out that integrating and honoring these three dimensions of God in the various spiritual paths holds the power to bring us together in greater understanding with one another.

The religion of the future

I believe a God by whatever name or form that is big enough, close enough, and us enough can be the unifying feature of all religious and spiritual paths as they each evolve in all the diverse forms they may take. It is peace among the religions of the world that can lead to peace among the nations of the world. This is just now beginning to emerge in the spiritual consciousness of Christianity as the wondrous three-dimensional God of Jesus. I believe Christians of the future can hold all Three Faces of God found hidden away in the traditional Trinity in balance and harmony. No one need give up their traditional religion. They only need a newer version of it. Perhaps those who read this book can help lead the way. Perhaps those who read this book can help lead the way!

Final Summary

Looking at the classical Trinity through the lens of Jesus' experience of God-Beyond-Us, God-Beside-Us, and God-Being-Us reveals a bigger, closer, and more "us" God than we have commonly seen. In the language and images of this book, the possibilities of knowing Jesus' multidimensional God include:

Trinity-Beyond-Us is *reflected about* as God as Infinite Being, Jesus as the Cosmic Christ, and spirit as Infinite Consciousness.

Trinity-Beside-Us is *related to* as the fatherly-motherly presence of God, the risen Jesus in his spiritual body (and, at times, other saints and sacred forms), and spirit personified as our helper.

Trinity-Being-Us is experienced and *rested in* as God as transcendent, Infinite Consciousness, Jesus as the Cosmic Christ in Oneness consciousness, and spirit as basic and awakened consciousness.

This may seem like a complicated shorthand for the deepest, sacred reflection and experience of Ultimate Reality possible for us as human beings. However, the classical Trinity itself is an oversimplified shorthand for the same thing. I have found this expanded, nine-dimensional Trinity broadens and deepens my understanding and experience of God. Again, as Ken Wilber says next in his Afterword, "Imagine how extraordinary it would be for a Christianity like this to actually take hold in the world. It would change history profoundly." Let's change history!

Take a moment, if it fits for you, to sign the Three Faces of God once again. Every time we do this we release into our consciousness and the One Mind of the universe an energetic reminder of God's three-dimensional transforming reality.

"God beyond me, in whom I live and move, and have my being."

("God beyond us, in whom we live and move, and have our being.")

"God beside me, you are always with me."

("God beside us, you are always with us.")

"God being me, I am the light of the world."

("God being us, we are the light of the world.")

The four full-page images in this book and additional ones that accompany various chapters in this book are available in full color on the author's website at www.revpaulsmith.com.

Afterword by Ken Wilber

With *Is Your God Big Enough?*, Smith continues his pioneering application of Integral Theory to Christianity. He made a truly superb and very impressive start with this in his previous book, *Integral Christianity*, where he applied virtually all of the major dimensions of Integral Theory to Christianity, showing how the result was profoundly more comprehensive, inclusive, and thus, in a sense, more effective as well. (Exactly what all of this means is something I will explore in just a moment.)

In this book, he continues his explorations by pursuing this goal through an extensive analysis of the Christian notion of Trinity, where he shows that the true and often hidden meaning of the Trinity is—to lapse into Integral Theory terms—the first, second, and third person perspective of the first, second, and third person dimensions of reality itself. So what exactly does that mean (and what is "Integral" itself)?

The Integral Framework is a metaview or metamap of reality that was created by looking at virtually all of the major maps of reality that human beings have offered over the ages, covering those presented in premodern, modern, as well as postmodern times. Now it's true that we do not want to confuse the map with the territory—that goes without saying—but we don't want to have a partial, fragmented, broken and inaccurate map, either. So what Integral did was take all of the major maps of the various territories that humans encounter—from spiritual to scientific, from artistic to moral, from historical to cultural—and then, using all of these maps, filled in the gaps in any of them by using all of them. The result was a truly comprehensive, incredibly inclusive meta-map, or super-map, if you will, which many scholars believe is one of the most inclusive and all-embracing "metatheories" yet produced.

Roger Walsh, in his book *A Big Picture View of Human Nature and Wisdom* (in preparation), points out the importance of such a meta-view or meta-map: "How we interpret human nature and especially wisdom is very important, and will require avoiding mental straightjackets such as excessive specialization and reductionism. We certainly want to draw on specialist research and reductive explanations, but we also want to weld them into a much larger, more generous, and far more comprehensive picture."

He then drives to the point about a genuine metaview: "To do this, we will need a mega-map: an inclusive, encompassing, integrative, intellectual framework. Such a mega-map will need to be large enough to encompass disparate data and ideas from different cultures and disciplines. And it will need to encompass them without leaving us with a hodgepodge of disconnected facts, or without stuffing them into convenient categories to produce a superficial pseudo-sameness. Fortunately, such big picture intellectual frameworks are becoming available. They are called *metatheories* and they synthesize multiple smaller theories into a coherent whole."

And this is where Integral enters the picture. Walsh states, "Currently, the most comprehensive of all metatheories is Integral Theory. Even among metatheories, Integral Theory is unusually, or even uniquely, comprehensive." It is the uniquely comprehensive nature of Integral Theory (or technically, Metatheory) that so many people have found useful. As Smith himself put it in his *Integral Christianity*, "Integral philosophy has taken everything we know about human potential from around the world and put it into a comprehensive global map about spiritual, psychological, and social growth. This is the most advanced Life Positioning System available today."

Walsh further points out, "In its most general form, Integral Theory can serve as an intellectual framework for exploring any topic." Now the reason that it can "explore *any* topic" is that, as Integral conducted its meta-survey of most of the major maps and theories that humanity has produced over the ages, it discovered several of what appeared to be invariant parameters that could be found as implicit or explicit realities in virtually all of the various maps, no matter when they were produced. This important discovery was generally called "AQAL," which is short for "all quadrants, all levels, all lines, all states, all types"—with those being the technical terms for the major parameters that this super-map found running throughout the main maps of the major territories that humans have access to. The clear implication is that these elements were ever-present, all-pervading, transcontextual elements that are some of the very basic constituents of reality itself. This is why Integral Metatheory can be used as a "framework for exploring any topic."

What this means is that, in the experience that you and I have of each and every moment, these five major elements are all present, they are all helping to create the very nature, form, and function of any reality that is arising in that moment. Whether we are looking at psychological realities, cultural realities, spiritual realities, material realities, evolutionary realities, cosmological realities . . . we will find some trace of these five major factors joining together to deliver us those realities. And as individuals explore or simply experience any territory in which they find themselves, they will consciously access several of these factors, and usually name them or conceptualize them to one degree or another. But as a metastudy of all the various major maps demonstrated, it was rare—vanishingly rare (that is, basically nonexistent)—that any person, discipline, or even culture spotted and recognized all five of these factors. But using the Integral Framework allows us to do just that—to discern the often-hidden elements that are nonetheless part of the very fabric of whatever experience, awareness, or knowledge that any person (or group or culture) manages to have. Thus, using this Framework, we can look at any experience today—or look at any of the maps of any experience formed in premodern, modern, or postmodern times—and get a much fuller, more comprehensive understanding of the factors that went into the creation of any particular experience (as well as any specific map of any experience).

And this is what Smith did with Christianity in *Integral Christianity*. He went through essentially each of the major elements of the AQAL Integral Framework, and then showed that Christianity on the whole can clearly be seen to be an expression of a reality that was molded and framed by these elements, and this fleshed out Christianity in numerous very telling and profoundly explanatory ways—ways that were clearly already present in Christianity if not always consciously acknowledged. The Integral Framework is not inventing these categories or simply making them up, and then forcing them onto any topic it looks at. Rather, using the very data of the topic itself, Integral demonstrates how it can be interpreted much more fully and inclusively using the Integral Framework. When this is done right, it is almost always met with an "Ah ha! Now that makes a lot of sense! I'm sure that's a better interpretation of this topic!" It is without doubt an interpretation that is more inclusive, more embracing, more "holistic" in the very best sense of that often overworked term. But, as Walsh might say, if Integral is "holistic," it is the "most holistic of holistic views available."

Each of these five major elements (and Integral Metatheory elucidates many other important factors—self-system, and so on— but these five are essential) turns out to be truly important, and becomes all the more important when we directly realize that many (or even all) of these elements have often been ignored or excluded in the original maps. But we can clearly see how this element was definitely a part of the original territory and thus including it in the original map makes that map itself more sensible, more believable, more embracing. In this book, Smith focuses on one of those elements—called "quadrants" (which I'll explain in just one moment)–but if you want to get a good sense of how all the elements of the overall AQAL Framework are crucial in any truly comprehensive Christianity, please consult Smith's previous book, it's very highly recommended.

(Let me just mention in passing that particularly important for any spirituality, and certainly Christianity, are the "levels" part of

"AQAL"—that is, the stages of overall psychospiritual development that are available to all humans–a sequence that Integral calls "Growing Up." This is contrasted with "states," which are direct mystical experiences involved in what Integral calls "Waking Up." As we'll see, Smith explores states and Waking Up directly in this book. The central point is that any truly effective spirituality wants to include both Growing Up and Waking Up—or, more accurately, it wants to include all five elements of the AQAL Integral Framework. Again, for not only states of Waking Up but also stages of Growing Up, see *Integral Christianity*.)

But in this book, Smith mostly focuses on quadrants, and gives them a very detailed, elaborated, and wonderfully practical explanation, made all the more powerful by their Integral context. Quadrants can be explained in many different ways (because they show up in many different ways). One of the more basic is that they represent the most fundamental perspectives that all awareness, experience, and knowledge require in order to exist in the first place. I'll start by just putting it in technical terms, then we'll put it in plain English: the quadrants represent the inside view and the outside view of an individual and a collective. Putting those together gives us four basic perspectives or four major dimensions found in virtually any domain: the inside and outside of an individual and a collective. These "four quadrants," for reasons we'll see, are often condensed to just three major realms, often called the "Big Three."

So here's what that means in plain English. These four quadrants (or the Big Three) show up in categories found around the world and in all three major epochs—premodern, modern, and postmodern. We see them in the archetypal trinity of the Good, the True, and the Beautiful—or morals, science, and art. Those are three very real, and very different, dimensions because the quadrants themselves are very real. Because these quadrants are indeed very real dimensions (with science, art, and morals all disclosing their own genuine and irreducible realities), then as human language itself evolved, it was created in direct contact with these realms, and thus every major human language the world over has pronouns that clearly represent each of these quadrants.

Thus, the inside (or subjective) view of an individual is referred to as "I," "me," "mine," and so on. This is the subjective perspective, including introspection and phenomenology, meditation and contemplation, and also includes aesthetic judgment—or the Beauty that is in the "I" of the beholder. When we speak from this perspective, we say things like "I am this" or "This is me"—we speak, that is, not *about* and not *to*, but *as*—this is a statement of *identity*.

On the other hand, the outside (or objective) view of an individual is "he," "she," or simply "it." This is an individual thing or event looked at in an objective, even "scientific" fashion. Where the subjective or inside view of an individual sees things like thoughts, feelings, awareness, consciousness, and emotions, the objective or outside view sees things like atoms, molecules, neurotransmitters such as serotonin, dopamine, and acetyl choline, it sees 208 bones, one heart, two kidneys, and so on—again, an "objective" or "scientific" perspective—in short, Truth in the typical sense (i.e., the "True" in the "the Good, the True, and the Beautiful").

Traditionally allied against this atomistic individualism of official scientific materialism have been various forms of systems theory. Unlike the objective view of an *individual* (or "it"), systems theory takes the objective view of a *collective* (or "its")–individuals themselves are not viewed as the primary reality. The primary reality is the whole, is various systems that are composed of many individuals interwoven in mutually interactive and dynamic relationships. This is another version of objective Truth (or "the True"), but looked at from a different quadrant or different perspective—namely, the outside view of a collective—this is an "its," plural, not "it," singular. But in either case, when we speak from this "outside" view (singular or plural) we speak, not *as* and not *to*, but *about*—this is *descriptive*.

Finally, where that outside view of a collective gives us "they," "them," "theirs," or simply, as we said, "its," if we look at that same collective from the inside view, we find instead "we," "us," "ours," and so on. And note that a collective "we" is made of an "I" and a "you"—when an "I" and a "you" come together in mutual understanding, the result is a "we." This is the realm of morals and ethics, or "the Good"—how *we*, as subjective individuals brought together into various we collectives, actually treat each other, or should treat each other. Classically, the "correct" moral way to treat another person is actually defined as approaching them as a "you" or a "thou" (a bearer of subjectivity and consciousness) and *not* treating them as an "it" or thing (merely an object to be manipulated). This "thou/we" is a *relational* reality, and to appropriately approach that as an "I–Thou" relationship and not an "I–It" relationship is to be a moral or Good person. (And that "we" reality cannot in any way be reduced to just "I" or just "it" dimensions or quadrants). This was beautifully captured in Martin Buber's famous "I–Thou" relationship. And the important difference between treating a person as a "thou" versus an "it" is clearly indicative of both the reality of, and the crucial difference between, these quadrants. To speak from this perspective is to speak, not *as* and not *about*, but *to* (and with).

So these four quadrants—or just the Big Three—are referred to as 1st person, 2nd person, and 3rd person perspectives, and these are the perspectives embedded in every major mature human language the world over. "1st person" is defined as "the person speaking" (or "I"). "2nd person" is "the person being spoken to" (or "you"; and a "you" and an "I" is a "we"). And "3rd person" is "the person or thing being spoken about" ("he" or "she" or "them"—or simply "it" and "its"). There is a notorious battle between various disciplines as to which of those perspectives alone is real, with a large number of them lining up to argue that their viewpoint, and their viewpoint alone, is truly real. Integral dismisses all of this as a battle between "quadrant absolutisms." In reality, all four quadrants are equally real; they "tetra-arise" and "tetra-evolve," and none of them can exist without the others.

Now all of this is coming to a very simple and very clear point, I promise. Let me first quickly mention that the very referring to

"I–Thou" brings us directly to spirituality. Given the Integral claim that all experience possesses at least these four quadrants (or the Big Three—we get "three" instead of "four" when the two objective quadrants—"it" and "its"—are simply treated as one overall outer or "it" domain, which is quite common), then it follows that all spiritual experience—whether it directly realizes it or not—actually has these three or four major views or perspectives or interpretations of its experience (with each different view itself actually generating a real experience).

So here's that simple and clear point. To put all of that rather dry technical information into very plain English, this is exactly why, as Smith puts it, "Jesus spoke *about* God, he spoke *to* God, and he spoke *as* God." Exactly right. But think about it: that is a profoundly important and crucial insight, and it keeps unfolding and unfolding its deep meanings. This *Trinity* (or Big Three) was the actual nature of spiritual reality that was presenting itself to Christ at every moment of his experience, and he could either consciously realize this or not. Unfortunately, most people do not realize this. And our truly Enlightened spiritual teachers, to the extent they are genuinely and fully Enlightened, come to tell us, among other things, of this rich reality, and how an Enlightened awareness of these Big Three— or the Trinity—is crucial to our overall spiritual realization.

Seeing the Christian Trinity in this new light simply reinforces the reality of that Trinity, but it also brings an "outside" affirmation, if you will, of this basic insight (that is, an affirmation from that hugely cross-cultural super-map). Jesus, of course, interpreted this Big Three influenced by the many contexts in which he found himself— cultural, personal, social, religious, psychological, ecological, gendered, philosophical, fantasized, and so on. But the point that an Integral Meta-view brings to the picture is that this fundamental distinction of *about* and *to* and *as* actually involves the fundamental, primordial perspectives that are inherent in the very structure of this Kosmos itself. Christ saw this when it came to the spiritual domain—he saw it, or he was ignorant of it. Turns out, he saw it.

Integral Metatheory calls this "the 1-2-3 of Spirit"—Spirit manifests itself in 1st -, 2nd -, and 3rd person dimensions (i.e., transpersonal "I" or True Self/Spirit; personal "you/we" or relationship Spirit; and impersonal infinite "beyond" or "It" or Suchness/Being). These Big Three dimensions are fundamental to all of reality, including spiritual reality. We can even think of the various 1-2-3 manifest spiritual realities as the very first dimensions into which a formless, dimensionless, groundless Ground (or "Godhead," "Emptiness") manifests itself to produce an actual universe (as Hinduism, for example, puts it, the totally unqualifiable "nirguna Brahman" or empty Godhead gives rise, in the first involutionary instance, to an ultimate "I"—"Purusha" or "Atman"—*and* a personal God or ultimate Thou—"Ishvara"—*and* an objectively/ontologically real substance of Being—"Mahamaya" or "Prakriti"—their version of the Big Three; or we have Buddhism's "Three Jewels": the Buddha–or awakened trans "I" consciousness–and the Sangha–or the spiritual community or "you/we"–and the Dharma–or impersonal Suchness, Thusness, or "It"-ness—another Big Three coming directly from the primordial perspectives of the quadrants).

Smith usefully calls these Big Three quadrant/dimensions/ perspectives the "Faces" of God, and his 1-2-3, following those of Jesus, he calls the *Infinite Face of God* (3-p beyond us, which we talk "about"), the *Intimate Face of God* (2-p beside us, which we talk "to"), and the *Inner Face of God* (1-p within us, which we talk "as"). And this is exactly the real reason that Jesus Christ spoke about, and to, and as God—these are inherent perspectives embedded in the very reality of this Kosmos. So Smith asks, in another version of this Trinity, "Is your God big enough?", "Is your God close enough?", and "Is your God you enough?"

As for the importance of understanding the Trinity as expressing these fundamental quadrant/perspectives (or Big Three), Smith says, "I consider the Three Faces of God to be the most significant advance in our understanding of God since the formulation of the Trinity in the fourth century. These three perspectives give us the fullest understanding of and relationship to God possible in this life."

But Smith doesn't stop there. Integral Metatheory maintains that these quadrants, these primordial perspectives, are the actual building blocks of the universe, and they continue to recursively occur time and time and time again, so that we have quadrants upon quadrants upon quadrants.... Thus, any adult human experience consists, at a minimum, of:

A Knower (or Who) x a Knowing (or How) x a Known (or What)

Notice that these terms involve epistemology (knower), methodology (knowing), and ontology (known). Further, each of those can involve any quadrant (so that the "knower x knowing x known" is actually "quadrants of quadrants of quadrants"). The "How" (or methodology) of knowing, for example, can involve a 1st person methodology (such as introspective meditation, or what I see when 1p "I" look within), or a 2nd person methodology (such as hermeneutics, the science of interpretation, or how I can interpret and understand a 2p "you"), or a 3rd person methodology (such as empirical science, or how I can accurately know various 3p objects). Likewise with the Knower and Known (each of them can represent any of the quadrants). Further—and this is important for this book—each of those (knower, knowing, known) can and does exist not only at different *quadrants* but also at different *levels* and in different *states* (as I'll soon explain). This "integral pluralism" (technically called "integral epistemological pluralism," "integral methodological pluralism," and "integral ontological pluralism") generates an incredibly rich array of various realities, all of them true enough when it comes to their own domain. (And when quadrants, levels, and states are all factored in, this provides an indexing system that includes virtually all known claimed varieties of epistemologies, methodologies, and ontologies–a staggeringly comprehensive indexing system.)

So let's see if we can't put those dry technicalities in a bit plainer English as well, because it does turn out to be quite important, and leads directly to the core topic of this book. Smith's first move is to combine the Knower (Who) and the Knowing (How) into a single overall *knowing awareness*—which then knows various realities, including the original Trinity—and he then applies the Big Three *to that knowing awareness itself* (so we have a Big Three knowing that knows each of the original Big Three). In other words, this is exactly what I meant when I said that we have quadrants upon quadrants (or in this case, a Big Three aware of a Big Three). This is what he means when he says that Jesus' experience of the Trinity "had *three* uniquely different personal relationships with *three* different faces of God." Now all that means is that the original Trinity itself (the first application of the quadrants or the Big Three) had each of those Big Three Faces looked at (and understood) through each of the Big Three perspectives themselves. After all, these quadrants are primordial perspectives that reflect on each other almost *ad infinitum*, and thus you can take, for example, a 1st person view of your present 1st person experience, or you can take a 2nd person view of your present 1st person experience, or you can take a 3rd person view of your 1st person experience. And you can likewise take the same three relationships (1-p, 2-p, and 3-p) with your 2nd person experience and with your 3rd person experience as well. In short, you can have a 1-2-3 of your 1-2–3 giving you a total of a very real, very genuine *nine* experiential realities!

Seems a bit complicated, doesn't it? Except, what if this is actually what is *already* happening anyway, and we can either be aware of it or ignorant of it? Because Paul then goes through extensive Christian sources (primarily the New Testament but also saints and sages from the entire tradition) and *gives very obvious, very clear examples from all nine of those perspectives.* And this gives us a staggering increase in our understanding of Christianity!

And why should this surprise us? Nine different perspectives? When we have an immediate and direct 1st person experience, we almost always start interpreting that experience in a reflective stance–and in that stance, we can take a 1st person perspective and interpret how we ourselves believe it to be, or we can take a 2nd person "you/we" perspective and interpret it perhaps in terms of what our religion might say about it, or we can take a 3rd person perspective and interpret it in terms of what an objective science might have to say about it. We do this all the time. And we reflexively just keep doing it, reflecting on our reflecting about our reflecting, and how you might interpret my experience and how I might interpret yours—we are always already plunged in a quadrant upon quadrant upon quadrant world.

But looking at the Trinity through at least a second application of the 1-2-3 of experience discloses a wealth of heretofore unacknowledged realities—and even better, actually makes sense of them. So Smith says that he will now present "the Trinity beyond as the Infinite Face of God [that is, the Trinity itself as the inherent 1-p, 2-p, and 3-p views—and then each of those Big Three perspectives will be combined with each of the Big Three (1-2-3) Faces of God, starting with the 3rd person 'beyond' or Infinite Face of God], then the Trinity close by as the Intimate Face of God [that is, a 1-p, 2-p, and 3-p view of the 2nd-p 'Intimate' Face of God], and the Trinity within as the Inner Face of God [that is, a 1-p, 2-p, and 3-p view of the 1st-p 'Inner' Face of God]."

And, as I say, using the overall Christian tradition as a whole, he fully delivers. Thus, very briefly:

- The *1st person view* of the 1st person **Inner Face of God** is every person's own Infinite Spirit, True Self, *rûach/pneuma*, I AMness

- The *2nd person view* of the 1st person **Inner Face of God** is the "closeness of God [2-p] as Spirit [1p]"

- The *3rd person view* of the 1st person **Inner Face of God** is "the marvel of infinite Consciousness as Spirit" [where "Consciousness" is taken as a "description" of a 3-p "objective" or ontologically real reality, seen as the true or inner core of one's self or 1-p "Spirit"]

- The *1st person view* of the 2nd person **Intimate Face of God** is every person's "Christ consciousness" (as in, "Not I, but Christ liveth in me") [this is not a 3-p description but a direct 1p experience of the 2-p Face of God]

- The *2nd person view* of the 2nd person **Intimate Face of God** is Jesus as one's closet friend, a genuine I-Thou (or "we") transformative relationship with Jesus Christ

- The *3rd person view* of the 2nd person **Intimate Face of God** is the Cosmic Christ or Logos, the "World made flesh" as a "3p objectively/ontologically real" Kosmic blueprint for all existence

- The *1st person view* of the 3rd person **Infinite Face of God** is one's Infinite Mind or Nondual Consciousness [as a direct 1-p experience]

- The *2nd person view* of the 3rd person **Infinite Face of God** is "the God beside us [2nd-p] as Mother-Father" [i.e., the infinite 3-p Face experienced in 2-p closeness]

- The *3rd person view* of the 3rd person **Infinite Face of God** is pure Being itself, radically unqualifiable and all-embracing, "the Ground of All Being"

Now the point is that you may or may not agree with those specific interpretations of a spiritual reality, but those are reflective categories that *already exist in the real world*, and if you are not filling all of those in, then—if I may say so—there are some major holes in your spiritual world. And the crucial point is, you can fill those categories in with any number of different items, qualities, characteristics— it's up to you. The point is that those perspectives themselves—not their content—are there, they are what are primordially inherent in this Kosmos. To say that you absolutely have an inherent 1st person perspective is not to say what you must see through that perspective. It is to say, however, that if you are not utilizing that perspective at all, then something is very, very wrong in your world—you certainly are not using all the inherent capabilities that you have, and thus you are drastically shortchanging yourself.

But if you are Christian—and since those categories must eventually be filled in by some content—then you will likely want that content to be as compatible with the Christian tradition as possible (although Smith would be the first to admit that you can fill those categories in with items from any number of other religions as well, if you wish). But Smith gives ample evidence from hundreds of different sources that specifically the types of interpretation that he gives in this section of the book (and that I summarized above) are interpretations that a very large number of acknowledged authorities in the Christian tradition have already embraced. Again, the advantage of using an Integral Metaview for this is that it gives us a framework that suggests that we look for the fundamentally Christian flavors of each of these already existing dimensions, so that the fuller this framework becomes, the fuller your spirituality becomes as well.

Finally, let me very briefly mention the importance of both levels or *stages* as well as *states* in fleshing out our understanding of Christianity (or any spirituality). I'll simply say, quickly, that "levels" refers to the major stages of growth and development that all human beings have access to. This is a profoundly important, but rarely recognized, discovery, and it literally colors every area of human experience. For what developmentalists have found is that the human being—in any of its many multiple intelligences or lines of development—goes through around a half-dozen major *levels* or *stages* of development, levels or stages of growth and unfolding (this is the "Growing Up" element of Integral). There are many different qualities and characteristics of each of these stages of Growing Up, including different worldviews, different values, different ethics, different needs and desires. To give only one type of difference, each stage creates a different worldview, and these worldviews have been named archaic, magic, mythic, rational, pluralistic, and integral (with an enormous number of variations on those, so don't let those terms put you off if you don't like them). The point is that each level of development co-creates (and literally sees) a different world, and these worlds most certainly exist and are very real (at each of their respective levels).

Moreover, virtually every discipline in existence has been shown itself to grow and evolve through these level/stages. This directly applies to spirituality itself, because—as only one example—James Fowler, in his brilliant pioneering work, *Stages of Faith*, gives empirical research indicating that almost everybody goes through around six or so major stages of faith (or stages of spiritual intelligence; and those are almost exactly an archaic stage, a magic stage, a mythic stage, a rational stage, a pluralistic stage, and an integral stage, which are those half dozen major levels that all developmental lines, or multiple intelligences, go through; and by the way, most people who express "atheistic" views are actually expressing one version of a rational level of spiritual intelligence, they do not lack spiritual intelligence itself—nobody does). Integral Metatheory did a meta-analysis of over 100 different developmental models (see *Integral Psychology*), and in the vast majority you see these same basic half-dozen stages appear over and over.

In *Integral Christianity*, Smith carefully outlines these six major level/ stages of evolutionary Growing Up as they appear in Christianity itself as it historically unfolded–stages which are also available to every person living today (as Fowler's research demonstrated, and Integral Metatheory confirmed. Indeed, some of the models of these stages have been tested in over 40 different cultures so far—including Amazonian rain forest tribes, Australian aborigines, Indianapolis housewives, and Harvard professors—and no major exceptions have been found so far). Smith calls these major stages tribal, warrior, traditional, modern, postmodern, and integral—and he *carefully outlines the very different ways that Christianity itself appears at each of them*—and that is the pioneering breakthrough that the discovery of "Growing Up" brought to an understanding of religion itself (among many other areas). Our view of religion, truly, will never be the same. And with this profound discovery, from that moment forward every

376 IS YOUR GOD BIG ENOUGH, CLOSE ENOUGH, YOU ENOUGH

understanding of spirituality that did not take these Growing Up stages into account was immediately rendered deeply obsolete.

Smith is clearly aware of this. He therefore, correctly I believe, points out that the original Trinity—the way that it was initially historically interpreted—came fundamentally from the level of development that was most common at that time, and which is known variously as mythic-literal, 2nd person focused (ethnocentric), mythic membership, traditional, conformist, absolutistic–and thus each of the three Faces (the actually existing and arising quadrants) were interpreted largely with a 2nd person slant, since research shows that perspective is primarily highlighted at this stage. Thus we see the Trinity understood in the largely (masculine) personal and relational 2p terms of "the Father, Son, and Holy Spirit"—clearly a predominantly personal, 2nd person, relational, tradition-oriented slant. This is fine—this is the quadrants being interpreted from the traditional mythic level and its 2nd person emphasis. But the subsisting reality driving all of this was the quadrants themselves, the inherent perspectives that all sentient beings take in relation to themselves, to each other, and to their surroundings. And when those realities involve ultimate, spiritual domains, then that is the "how" of the interpretation, the "what" being the spiritual quadrants themselves and the "who" being the traditional level of development. All of this makes perfect sense through an Integral lens. Thus, in *Integral Christianity*, Smith says, "I see the glorious traditional Trinity [i.e., the Father, Son, and Holy Spirit] as the Intimate Face of God [i.e., the 2nd person quadrant/perspective] within the even greater and more expansive glory of the Three Faces of God Trinity [i.e., the expansive glory of the primordial quadrants themselves— the Big Three—as manifesting, in this case, through ultimate or spiritual dimensions/states]." The point, very simply, is that how you see the Trinity will depend upon your stage of development.

Now I mention all of this simply because Smith does not himself bring up any of this in the present book; but his own work, presented in *Integral Christianity*, clearly concludes that how you interpret the

Trinity itself (or any of its nine recursive dimensions) *will depend profoundly on the stage of development that you are at.* Thus, as he himself puts it in that book, "Our states are interpreted by our stages." That is, our states of Waking Up are interpreted by our stages of Growing Up. This is crucial, because some of those Growing Up stages (particularly the lower stages) are inherently ethnocentric, prejudiced, and biased, and this is a profound issue that any religion today simply has to face—or else merely contribute to further fragmentation and worldwide alienation (not to mention terrorism and other nightmares).

So one of the items that Integral Metatheory particularly emphasizes is that, even when it comes to a direct spiritual or mystical experience—one's "Waking Up"—a person will interpret that experience according to the particular stage of Growing Up that has the experience. So this should be kept in mind as you read the last part of Smith's book, dealing with states (or "states of consciousness," one of the five major elements of the AQAL Integral Framework).

With regard to these important states, Smith points out that Integral Metatheory, in its meta-analysis of the world's great traditions, found around four or five major states of consciousness, and those *states* of consciousness actually become the major *stages* of meditative development (that is, they become the stages, not of Growing Up, but of Waking Up). These states have many names, a common set of which is gross, subtle, causal, witnessing, and ultimate nondual unity (and it's common to combine some of them, in particular causal and witnessing, giving four or so major states of consciousness—which also means, stages of spiritual unfolding).

Smith correctly looks at the Christian tradition and finds massive evidence for all four of these major states, and they are given profound significance by the tradition itself (however often many or even all of them have been forgotten). But these states, Integral has found, are the very core of direct spiritual realization, wherever they exist, East or West, premodern or modern or postmodern. Smith calls these four states: *basic consciousness* (gross), *awakened consciousness* (subtle), *transcendent consciousness* (causal/witnessing), and ultimate *nondual oneness* (nondual).

I'm simply mentioning this very briefly, but if you are seriously pursuing any spiritual path, you will want to become as familiar as possible with those states, because they are the core of the profound realizations that your spiritual path will be making available to you. (If you are interested in these crucial states, I suggest you start with Smith's presentation of them in this book, then look at his *Integral Christianity*; then perhaps my own *Integral Spirituality* and especially *The Religion of the Future*; and Dustin DiPerna's wonderful *Streams of Wisdom*, which covers states, and his superb *Evolution's Ally*, which covers stages. And simply notice this: just from what we've seen so far, a person's spiritual experience and awareness can come from any of nine different quadrant-related perspectives; *each* of which exists at six major level/stages; and *all* of those can be infused by or permeated with four major states—leaving out extreme combinations that don't exist, that still gives us over 200 possible variations on spirituality (even if they all ideally culminate in an integral understanding of an ultimate level of an ultimate state)! But looking at the sum total of humankind's overall spiritual realities around the world throughout history, do we really see any evidence that it is less complex than that? But the point is, even with all of that complexity, we can now make unifying and coherent sense of all of it using an Integral Framework—and this is what has so many people excited about this approach. It turns out that we find the same thing in virtually all human disciplines, but just with spirituality itself, this represents a several magnitude increase in our overall comprehension.

What is so important about Smith's account is that it undeniably points to the crucial role that these states—particularly the higher and highest states—have played in the actual history of Christianity. It is simply undeniable that Christianity began in a riot of higher states and peak experiences and mystical, spiritual, altered states. The very core of Christianity (and every great wisdom tradition) lies in the direct and immediate experience of a spiritual reality, and for that to be forgotten or even denied (as has too often happened with Christianity) is a cultural catastrophe of the first magnitude.

But understanding the central importance of these spiritual states opens us again to the very core of what Christianity was trying to transmit. Moreover, by taking an Integral metaview of these states, we can see that any religion can be judged on just how complete or inclusive it is—the more states it helps its followers realize, the more complete and full that religion is. And Christianity, as Smith explores it, fits that "complete" category very well. Thus it joins the other great world religions that also do so—including Mahayana Buddhism, Vedanta Hinduism, Kashmir Shaivism, Sufism, Neoconfucianism, Kabbalah, among others—in presenting a path to spiritual realization that is as full as full can get.

(I would just emphasize again that these states of Waking Up will be interpreted—and thus actually experienced—according to the stage of Growing Up that has the Waking-Up experience. This is simply unavoidable. And it is crucially important to realize that it is not enough, in order to be a positive force in the world, to simply Wake Up, even if it's a profound Waking Up—not if you are still at a very low level of Growing Up. These two axes of development—Waking Up and Growing Up—are quite independent; you can be high in one and very low in the other, or vice versa, or any combination thereof. I highly recommend you consult Smith's *Integral Christianity* for a good outline of these level/stages of Growing Up in the Christian tradition, and take these very seriously in your spiritual understanding, whatever path it might be. Each of your state realizations or Waking Up experiences—including awakened consciousness, transcendent consciousness, and ultimate nondual unity consciousness—will look quite different depending upon which of the stages you are at.)

All in all, this is indeed another and major contribution by Paul Smith to the manifestation of a truly Integral Christianity. He points out, in reference to his presentation of the Trinity, that virtually no religion anywhere has fully explored all of these perspectives, and that's true. But no religion anywhere has explored—not only not all of these quadrants—but also not all of the levels and lines, either. As I try to demonstrate in *The Religion of the Future* (which picks up where *Integral Spirituality* left off), any religion that will make it into tomorrow in a respected and truly dignified fashion will of necessity be a genuinely inclusive, comprehensive, fully Integral Spirituality. The excitement of this adventure is that, as Smith continues to demonstrate, a whole new level of sophistication, complexity, and completeness is brought to our spiritual endeavors by these more inclusive approaches, which will catapult religion itself from being something of the laughingstock of the modern and postmodern world to being a genuine and deeply respected beacon of—and a real pacer of—actual transformation, fully available to all people around the world, and disclosing a future that is the closest thing to Heaven on Earth that could ever be imagined.

Imagine how extraordinary it would be for a Christianity like this to actually take hold in the world. It would change history profoundly.

Ken Wilber
Winter 2017
Denver, Colorado

Appendix: What Every Body Can Say

Signing the Three Faces of God

What every body can say

I told the story of five travelers at the beginning of this book. Notice that three of our travelers, like most people, expressed themselves not only in words but with their bodies, in motions that communicated beyond their words.

The first traveler, when asked, "Where is this God right now?" lifted his hands upward, and said, "Beyond me," like this:

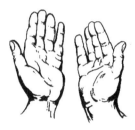

The second traveler, when asked, "Where is this God right now?" said, "Right here beside me," clasping her hands in prayer to God like this:

Our third traveler, when asked, "Where is this God right now?" said,

"In here, being me," hugging his arms and hands over his heart like this:

Devotion in Motion

Most books have words. Some books have pictures. This book has motions. Some years ago I began thinking about simple movements to express my devotion to God in these three dimensions that I call the Three Faces of God or God-beyond-us, God-beside-us, and God-being-us. Devotion is loving God with our whole selves, mind, body, heart, and spirit. It is humbly giving yourself to your Beloved, in heartfelt love and action. This is the key to a deeper spiritual experience at every level. By devotion in motion I not only wanted to express my intention to God but to let my loving God and God loving me more deeply saturate my body. I wanted to align myself with God in three simple movements, each accompanied by a short phrase that would express the three dimensions of God that these three travelers had found.

The use of gestures in worship has been around from ancient tribal ceremonies to today's Roman Catholic and Eastern Orthodox kneeling and cross signing. Yoga postures have brought a new awareness in Western culture of body movements in consciousness raising. Body movement can help us explore and access our highest spiritual reality within. Devotional movement can allow us to understand not only with our mind, but also with our body. Sacred signing and movement can ground us in our body. After all, the goal, as Jesus put it, is to "love God with mind, heart, soul, *and body*" (Mark 12:30).

God beyond me

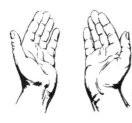 The first traveler's motion about God beyond me is reflected in Jesus' idea that God is everywhere and beyond everywhere! Ultimately, this Face of God is nothing and nowhere because if this dimension of God was something and somewhere, that God would be finite. Years ago I had already found myself, along with others, naturally raising our hands in praise and worship whenever our congregation would sing marvelous songs about and to this God beyond us. Whether rousing hymns of praise with our orchestra and pipe organ thundering away, or quiet melodies of reflection and worship, some of us would often raise our open hands upward.

This simple movement seemed to express a number of things already common in our culture. We are used to seeing people raise their hands at sports events in celebration. Celebrating God's reality is always a winning action! We also see people open up their hands in a "I give up" posture, or in movies when being robbed or arrested as "I surrender." Giving up my self-centeredness and surrendering my life more fully gets at the heart of what I want my attitude toward God to be. Then there is the sense of "I'm open to you" that one person indicates to another with that welcoming gesture of open hands and arms. I often feel that towards God. "Welcome, God-beyond-everything-and-everywhere. I give up. Come on into my life in ever deeper ways."

All four of these attitudes are expressed in the graceful movement of opening my hands upward and extending my arms outward. I can do it in a small way with open hands in my lap if I am feeling rather quiet, and I can do it boldly and full on with upstretched arms if I am in a festive mood. So now when I open my hands and raise my arms in devotion and worship, it is an act of celebration, surrender, openness, and welcome. That's quite an armful!

God beside me

Next is God beside me which echoes the messenger of God to Joseph describing Jesus as "Emmanuel," meaning "God is with us." (Matt 1:23). We call it "prayer" when we share our innermost longings with the face of God who is close to us. A common symbol for prayer is the placing of hands with palms together in front of the heart center. Interestingly, the same hand posture is found in the Eastern religious tradition where the prayer mudra is the hand position most often depicted in images of the Buddha. The palms of the hands are brought together at the center of the chest. In Sanskrit, mudra means "seal" or "sign" and refers not only to sacred hand gestures but also whole body positions that elicit a certain inner state or symbolize a particular meaning. As the consummate Indian greeting, like a sacred hello, offering this movement with the word "Namaste" is saying, "I bow to the divinity within you from the divinity within me." This salutation is at the essence of the yogic practice of seeing the Divine within all of creation.

I resonate with both meanings as I use my body to say: "I welcome you God," or Jesus, or whatever form of the divine that I am addressing. At the same time, I'm saying, in the language of my body, "I recognize this same God who is with and in me is also with and in every other person I meet." This leads us to the third movement.

God being me

I see God being me as my deepest Self in such words of Jesus as, "You are the light of the world" (Matt. 5:15) and "You are gods" (John 10:34). At first I pondered what kind of movement to use as I said, "God being me" or "I am the light of the world." I could point to myself, but when I tried it I felt silly. Of course any sacred movement can feel awkward at first and we should expect to feel a little "silly" when we first do such movements. It's a phase we all go through for the first few seconds—or weeks and months—until the meaning of the gestures of devotion is "somatized" or incorporated into our body. Finally, I tried saying "God being me" with my hands over my heart center, and it immediately seemed right. God was "in" me which of course means head, heart, hands, and whole body. But this "in" me was more than a physical sense. This was God "in" and "as" me in a deep, heartfelt sense that the New Testament calls being a "participant in the divine nature" (2 Pet. 1:4). My heart shouted "Yes" when I did that.

I now had three affirming statements of truth and devotion which I called the Three Faces of God:

God beyond me
God beside me
God being me

When I put the movements together with these words, it looked like this:

"God beyond me"   "God beside me"   "God being me"

Alone or together, moving towards a full spectrum God

I have taught hundreds of people the full spectrum of the Three Faces of God "devotion in motion" to use in worship, prayer, and meditation. Anytime, and every time, you do this, it is a gentle reminder and affirmation that God really is beyond us, beside us, and being us. It is also a wonderful way, at appropriate times for those in a group or congregation, to acknowledge together the presence of God and affirm the corporate worship, prayer, or meditation of those gathered. You can watch a video of my former congregation doing this while singing a beautiful hymn, written by one of our musicians, expressing these three dimensions of God, at "YouTube God in Three Dimensions" or https://www.youtube.com/watch?v=KXf0eJim3PA.

You might enjoy singing along with the congregation in this video as the words are shown on the screen. This video uses another set of words to accompany these movements which are Infinite God, Intimate God, and Inner God. Done together in a group, this basic version of the Three Faces of God becomes:

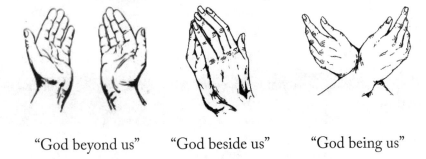

"God beyond us"   "God beside us"   "God being us"

The Sign of the Cross and the Three Faces of God

The sign of the cross or "crossing oneself" is a "devotion in motion" that has been used by millions of Christians since the fourth century. Offered billions, even trillions of times down through the centuries, it is practiced by Catholics, Orthodox, as well as optionally by some Episcopalians, Anglicans, Lutherans, and Methodists. It is often accompanied by saying, "In the name of the Father, and of the Son, and of the Holy Spirit. Amen."

The movement is the tracing of the shape of a cross in the air or on one's own body, echoing the traditional shape of the cross of the crucifixion. The sign of the cross is a prayer, a blessing, and preparation for an individual to receive from and cooperate with God. For some, making the sign of the cross is a way of expressing, bodily, the love of Jesus on the cross for us.

Signing the Three Faces of God can be a new devotional act. Perhaps, in this nonlocal, entangled universe of quantum physics and spiritual consciousness, others may be finding something similar. I hope so.

I am drawn to the Three Faces of God because it centers on God's presence and not the crucifixion with its focus by some Christians on images of sin and sacrificial atonement. It reminds me of the larger, three-dimensional picture of God whose loving presence is beyond, beside, and within. It can also be used by those who are not Christians but embrace this more inclusive image of God.

One can do the motions only, without words, or accompany the motions with a set of appropriate words. I offer three different sets of words in this book, each with a version to use by yourself and a version to use with others doing this together. Every time we repeat the Three Faces of God Devotion in Motion it helps us to keep from unconsciously moving back into our favoring one dimension of God over the others. We can grow into a more balanced and integrated understanding and experience of the Full Spectrum God of Jesus. But most of all, it reminds us that God is right here next to us and within us, as us.

Sacred movement can enhance your spiritual journey. Signing God beyond us, beside us, and being us is a powerful reminder of the Three Faces of God that Jesus knew and taught.

Questions for Reflection and Group Discussion

1. Do you ever sign the cross and if so, what does that mean to you?

2. If you have already tried out the devotion in motion by yourself, share with the group how it went for you.

3. You have this book in your hands for a reason. Let's assume that, whatever the initial reason, there is something deeper at work here. What might that deeper work be for you?

Practices

1. Experiment with these three movements and affirming phrases with the thoughts of this chapter in mind. Place your book or electronic device on a table or your lap open to the three images and phrases. If you are doing this by yourself, slowly move your hands and say the words out loud for each posture. Do this enough times until you can begin to feel it in your body. Let it become a part of you. This is a wonderful way to soak your mind, heart, soul, and body in God's three-dimensional presence.

If you are in a group setting, experiment with doing the motions and saying the group form of the phrases ("us" rather than "me") out loud together at the same time. After each set of three, let the group leader find out from the group how many more times they want to repeat this in order for it to begin to resonate with most people present.

2. Where in your body do you feel a connection with what you are saying and doing?

3. Experiment for a few weeks beginning your day, and/or your prayer/meditation time with these three acts of devotion in motion. The idea is to use body language as one more way to feel the images and words.

Here is another set of words taken from the Bible for both individual or group use: Paul points to God-beyond-us as the One "in whom we live and move have our being" (Acts 17:28). Jesus refers to God beside us when he said that he would always be with us (Matt. 28:20). And then there is God being us in Jesus words to us when he said: "You are the light of the world!" (Matt. 5:14).

When we add these words to our motions, we have:

"God beyond us, in whom we live, and move, and have our being"

"God beside us, you are always with us"

"God being us, we are the light of the world."

In our own personal times of reflection, prayer, and meditation, the words can become:

 "God beyond me, in whom I live and move, and have my being."

 "God beside me, you are always with me."

 "God being me, I am the light of the world."

Bibliography

Aquinas, Thomas, *Summa Theologiae*. http://www.ccel.org/ccel/aquinas/summa.toc.html.

——— *Commentary on the Gospel of St. John*. Translated by Fabian R. Larcher. Albany: Magi Books, Inc., 1998.

——— *Opusc. Catechism of the Catholic Church*. http://ccc.usccb.org/flipbooks/catechism/index.html.

Armstrong, Karen. "Lectures and interviews." http://thesethingsinside.wordpress.com/2013/01/08/karen-armstrong-lectures-and-interviews/.

Athanasius. *On the Incarnation of the Word*. Translated by John Behr. Yonkers: Saint Vladimir's Seminary Press, 2011.

Auden, W. H. *A Certain World: A Commonplace Book*. New York: Viking Press, 1970.

Augustine. "To Fall in Love with God." http://www.goodreads.com/quotes/73061-to-fall-in-love-with-god-is-the-greatest-romance.

——— "Sermo 13 de Tempore." From *The Office of Readings*. Boston: St. Paul Editions, 1983.

——— *Confessions*, VII.x.16. Sanford Encyclopedia of Philosophy. http://plato.stanford.edu/entries/augustine/.

——— *Catechism of the Catholic Church*. http://ccc.usccb.org/flipbooks/catechism/index.html#4.

——— Sermon 15. "On the New Testament." http://www.newadvent.org/fathers/1603.htm.

Barfield, Owen. *Saving the Appearances: A Study in Idolatry*. Indianapolis: Wesleyan, 1988.

Barnhart, Bruno. "One Spirit, One Body." In Jorge Ferrer, *The Participatory Turn*.

Barr, James. "Abba Isn't Daddy." *Journal of Theological Studies*, (Vol. 39, 1988).

Barth, Karl. *The Doctrine of the Word of God: Church Dogmatics*. Translated by G. Bromiley. Edinburgh: T & T Clark, 1975.

Blackney, Raymond, trans. *Meister Eckhart: A Modern Translation*. New York: Harper, 1942.

Boring, M. Eugene. *The Continuing Voice of Jesus: Christian Prophecy and the Gospel Tradition*. Louisville: Westminster, 1991.

Borg, Marcus. "Mystical Experiences of God." http://www.marcusjborg.com/2010/07/01/mystical-experiences-of-god/.

——— *Convictions: How I Learned What Matters Most*. New York: HarperOne, 2016.

——— and John Dominic Crossan. *The First Paul: Reclaiming the Radical Visionary Behind the Church's Conservative Icon*. New York: HarperOne, 2009.

——— *The Heart of Christianity*. San Francisco: HarperSanFrancisco, 2003.

Botkin, Allan. *Induced After-Death Communication: A Miraculous Therapy for Grief and Loss*. Newburyport, MA: Hampton Roads, 2014.

Bourgeault, Cynthia. "Mystical Experience or Unitive Seeing." http://www.spiritualpaths.net/mystical-experience-or-unitive-seeing-by-cynthia-bourgeault/.

——— *Wisdom Jesus*. Boston: Shambhala, 2008.

Brooks, David. "The Big Decisions." *New York Times*, August 25, 2015.

Brown, Francis, S. R. Driver, and Charles A. Briggs, editors. *The Brown–Driver–Briggs Hebrew and English Lexicon of the Old Testament*. Peabody, Massachusetts: Hendrickson, 1994.

Capra, Fritjof. *The Tao of Physics*. Boulder: Shambhala, 2010.

——— *The Turning Point*. New York: Harper Collins, 1982.

——— *The Web of Life: A New Scientific Understanding of Living Systems*. New York: Anchor, 1997.

Catechism of the Catholic Church–Expressions of prayer. http://www.vatican.va/archive/ccc_css/archive/catechism/p4s1c3a1.htm

Catholic Church (1995), "Article 460", *Catechism of the Catholic Church*, http://ccc.usccb.org/flipbooks/catechism/index.html.

Cessario, Romanus. "The Spirituality of St. Thomas Aquinas." *In Crisis Magazine*. http://www.crisismagazine.com/1996/the-spirituality-of-st-thomas-aquinas-2.

Chalmers, Thomas. "The Expulsive Power of a New Affection." http://www.
christianity.com/christian-life/spiritual-growth/the-expulsive-
power-of-a-new-affection-11627257.html.

Chardin, Teilhard de. *The Divine Milieu.* New York: Harper & Row, 1960.

Chopra, Deepak. *The Future of God: A Practical Approach to Spirituality for
Our Times.* New York: Harmony, 2014.

Christensen, Michael, and Jeffery Wittung. *Partakers of the Divine Nature:
The History and Development of Deification in the Christian Tradition.*
Grand Rapids: Baker Academic, 2007.

Clanton, Jann Aldredge. *In Search of the Christ-Sophia.* Waco: Eakin Press,
2004.

Clayton, Philip, and Arthur Peacocke. *In Whom We Live and Move and
Have Our Being.* Grand Rapids: Eerdmans, 2004.

Clement of Alexandria. *Exhortation to the Heathen.* http://www.newadvent.
org/fathers/0208.htm.

———— Strom IV 89. In Early Christian Writings. http://www.
earlychristianwritings.com/text/clement-stromata-book4.html.

Conway, Timothy. "Meister Eckhart–Nondual Christian Mystic Sage."
http://www.enlightened-spirituality.org/Meister_Eckhart.html.

Dahulich, Michael. "Love in the Writings of St. Maximus the Confessor."
http://www.sthermanoca.org/documents/Fr.%20Johns%20Papers/
St_Maximus_Love.pdf.

Davies, Stevan. *Jesus the Healer: Possession, Trance, and the Origins of
Christianity.* Norwich: UK, Hymns Ancient & Modern Ltd, 2015.

Delio, Ilia. *Making All Things New: Catholicity, Cosmology, Consciousness.*
Maryknoll: Orbis, 2015.

———— *From Teilhard to Omega: Co-creating an Unfinished Universe.*
Maryknoll: Orbis, 2014.

———— *Unbearable Wholeness of Being.* Maryknoll: Orbis, 2013.

———— *The Emergent Christ.* Maryknoll: Orbis, 2011.

Diller, Jeanine, and Asa Kasher. "Models of God and Alternative Ultimate
Realities." In *Meister Eckhart's God* by Dietmar Mieth. New York:
Springer, 2013.

Dossey, Larry. *One Mind: How our Individual Mind is Part of a Greater Consciousness and Why it Matters.* New York: Hay House, 2013.

Dunn, James. *Jesus and the Spirit: A Study of the Religious and Charismatic Experience of Jesus and the First Christians as Reflected in the New Testament.* London: SCM-Canterbury Press Ltd, 1975.

Eckhart, Meister. Sermon DW 40. http://www.pantheism.net/paul/history/eckhart.htm.

———— *Meister Eckhart.* Translated by C. de B. Evans. London, John Watkins, 1952.

———— *Meister Eckhart's Sermons.* True Hearing, Christian Classics Ethereal Library. http://www.ccel.org/ccel/eckhart/sermons.vii.html.

———— *Breakthrough: Meister Eckhart's Creation Spirituality in New Translation.* Introduction and Commentaries by Matthew Fox. New York: Image Books, 1991.

Encyclopedia Britannica, "Science & Technology: consciousness." https://www.britannica.com/topic/consciousness.

Ensler, Eve. *The Power and Mystery of Naming Things.* Audiobook, NPR's All Things Considered, March 20, 2006. http://thisibelieve.org/essay/17/.

Ensley, Eddie. *Visions: The Soul's Path to the Sacred.* Chicago: Loyola Press, 2000.

Fenwick, Peter, and Elizabeth Fenwick. *The Art of Dying.* Bloomsbury: Bloomsbury Academic, 2008.

Ferrer, Jorge N. "Participation, Metaphysics, and Enlightenment." *Transpersonal Psychology Review,* 2011, 14(2).

———— *Revisioning Transpersonal Theory: A Participatory Vision of Human Spirituality.* New York: State University of New York Press, 2001.

Ferrer, Jorge N. and Jacob H. Sherman, editors. *The Participatory Turn: Spirituality, Mysticism, Religious Studies.* State University of New York Press, 2008.

Flanner, Frances, and Collen Shantz, Rodney Werline. Symposium. Atlanta: Society of Biblical Literature, 2008.

Francis, St., of Assisi. The Biography.com website. http://www.biography.com/.

Funke, Mary Elizabeth. *Meister Eckhart*. Kindle, public domain, first published 1916.

Gafni, Marc. *Your Unique Self: The Radical Path to Personal Enlightenment*. Tucson: Integral Publishers, 2012.

Gama, Michael Paul, "Theosis: The Core of Our Ancient/Future Faith and Its Relevance to Evangelicalism at the Close of the Modern Era." Doctor of Ministry. Paper 74, 2014.

Gleig, Ann, and Nicholas G Boeving, reviewers. "Spiritual Democracy– Beyond Consciousness and Culture." *Tikkun Magazine*, Vol 21, no.3, April 22, 2009.

Goshen-Gottstein, Alon. "God the Father in Rabbinic Judaism and Christianity: Transformed Background or Common Ground?" *Journal of Ecumenical Studies*, 38:4, Spring 2001.

Graves, Dan. "Thomas Aquinas Had a Vision." In Christianity.com. http://www.christianity.com/.

——— "John Wesley's Heart Strangely Warmed." In Christianity.com, http://www.christianity.com/church/church-history/timeline/1701-1800/john-wesleys-heart-strangely-warmed-11630227.html.

Gregory, Saint, of Nyssa. *The Great Catechism, Complete*. Translated by W. Moore and H. A. Wilson. http://www.elpenor.org/nyssa/great-catechism.asp.

Grof, Stanislav. *The Adventure of Self-Discovery: Dimensions of Consciousness and New Perspectives in Psychotherapy and Inner Exploration*. New York: State University of New York, 1988.

Hamilton, Diane Musho. "A Discussion of Subtle Energy," recorded 4.9.2015. http://www.integrallivingroom.com/uncategorized/a-discussion-of-subtle-energy/.

Hamilton, Anne. *God's Panoply: The Armour of God and the Kiss of Heaven*. Sydney: Even Before Publishing, 2013.

Harding, Douglas. *On Having No Head*. London: The Shollond Trust, 2012.

Hart, David Bentley. *The Experience of God*. New Haven and London: Yale University Press 2013.

Heatwole, Wanda. "God in Three Dimensions." YouTube God in Three Dimensions, and https://www.youtube.com/watch?v=KX f0eJim3PA.

Heidegger, Martin. *Letter on Humanism.* http://www07.homepage. villanova.edu/paul.livingston/martin_heidegger%20-.

Heiser, James D. *Prisci Theologi and the Hermetic Reformation in the Fifteenth Century.* Malone, Texas: Repristination Press. 2011.

Hurtado, Larry. *Why on Earth Did Anyone Become a Christian in the First Three Centuries?* Milwaukee: Marquette, 2016.

————— "Early High Christology: A 'Paradigm Shift?' 'New Perspective'?" Larry Hurtado's Blog. https://larryhurtado.wordpress. com/2015/07/10/early-high-christology-a-paradigm-shift-new-perspective/.

————— *God in New Testament Theology.* Nashville: Abingdon Press, 2010.

————— *How on Earth Did Jesus Become a God?* Grand Rapids: Wm. B. Eerdmans Publishing, 2005.

————— *At the Origins of Christian Worship: The Context and Character of Earliest Christian Devotion.* Grand Rapids: Michigan, 1999.

Idel, Moshe, and Bernard McGinn, editors. *Mystical Union in Judaism, Christianity, and Islam: An Ecumenical Dialogue.* New York: Continuum International Publishing Group, 1996.

Ingerman, Sandra, and Hank Wesselman. *Awakening to the Spirit World: The Shamanic Path of Direct Revelation.* Boulder: Sounds True, 2010.

Irenaeus. *Against Heresies.* https://carm.org/irenaeus-heresies4-1-20.

James, William. *The Varieties of Religious Experience.* New York: Collier Books, Macmillan, 1961.

Joan of Arc. *Christian History.* http://www.christianitytoday.com/history/people/moversandshakers/joan-of-arc.html

John, Saint, of the Cross. *The Living Flame of Love.* http://www.frimmin. com/faith/theosis.php.

————— *Ascent of Mount Carmel,* trans., Allison Peers, Christian Classics Ethereal Library, 2010.

————— "The Spiritual Canticle." Commentary, no. 4 in *The Collected Works of St. John of the Cross.* Translated by Kieran Kavanaugh, O.C.D. and

Otilio Rodriguez, O.C.D. ICS Publications, Institute of Carmelite Studies, 1973.

Johnson, Luke Timothy. *Religious Experience in Earliest Christianity: A Missing Dimension in New Testament Study.* Minneapolis: Fortress, 1998.

Jung, C. G. *Memories, Dreams, Reflections.* New York: Vintage Books, 1963.

Justin, Martyr, Saint. *Dialogue with Trypho,* Chapter LXII. Early Christian Writings. http://www.earlychristianwritings.com/text/justinmartyr-dialoguetrypho.html.

Karpman, Stephen. "The Drama Triangle." https://www.karpmandrama triangle.com/.

Keating, Thomas. "Becoming Nothing." https://integrallife.com/future-christianity/becoming-nothing.

Keller, Catherine. *Cloud of the Impossible: Negative Theology and Planetary Entanglement.* New York: Columbia University Press, 2015.

Kingsley, Dennis. "Quantum Consciousness: The Way to Reconcile Science and Spirituality." http://www.huffingtonpost.com/kingsley-dennis-phd/quantum-consciousness-the_b_647962.html.

Kirby, Peter. "Historical Jesus Theories." In *Early Christian Writings.* http://www.earlychristianwritings.com/theories.html.

Kittel, Gerhard, editor, and Geoffrey Bromiley, translator and editor. *Theological Dictionary of the New Testament*, Volumes I – IX. Grand Rapids: Eerdmans. 1972.

Koestler, Arthur. *The Ghost in the Machine.* New York, Penguin, 1990.

Kripal, Jeffrey J. *Authors of the Impossible: The Paranormal and the Sacred.* Chicago: University of Chicago Press, 2011.

Kuhlman, Delcy. "Revelations of Divine Love by Julian of Norwich." In *Spectrum Magazine.* http://spectrummagazine.org/article/delcy-kuhlman/2012/08/22/revelations-divine-love-julian-norwich-study-guide-adventists.

Kushner, Harold. *How Good Do We Have to Be?* New York: Back Bay Books, 1997.

Lash, Symeon, "Deification." In *The Westminster Dictionary of Christian Theology.* Edited by Alan Richardson and John Bowden. Philadelphia: Westminster Press, 1983.

Laszlo, Ervin, "Quantum Consciousness: Our Evolution, Our Salvation." http://www.huffingtonpost.com/ervin-laszlo/quantum-consciousness-our_b_524054.html.

———— "Cosmic Symphony: A Deeper Look at Quantum Consciousness," Huffingtonpost.com. 2010-04-12, http://www.huffingtonpost.com/ervin-laszlo/cosmic-symphony-a-deeper_b_532315.html.

———— "Why Your Brain Is a Quantum Computer." http://www.huffingtonpost.com/ervin-laszlo/why-your-brain-is-a-quant_b_489998.html.

———— with Anthony Peake. *The Immortal Mind: Science and the Continuity of Consciousness Beyond the Brain.* Rochester: Inner Traditions, 2014.

———— *Science and the Akashic Field.* Rochester: Inner Traditions, 2004.

Levison, Jack. *Fresh Air: The Holy Spirit for an Inspired Life.* Massachusetts: Paraclete Press, 2012.

Levison, John. *Filled with the Spirit.* Grand Rapids: MI: Eerdmans, 2009.

Lewis, C. S. *The Grand Miracle.* New York: Ballantine, 1986.

———— *A Grief Observed.* New York: Harper, 2009.

———— *Mere Christianity.* New York: Harper Collins, 1952.

———— *The Weight of Glory.* New York: Harper Collins, 1976.

Locke, John. *An Essay Concerning Human Understanding.* South Australia: University of Adelaide, 1996.

Marion, James. *Putting on the Mind of Christ: The Inner Work of Christian Spirituality.* Charlottesville: Hampton Roads Publishing, 2011.

McGinn, Barnard. *The Mystical Thought of Meister Eckhart: The Man from Whom God Hid Nothing.* New York: Crossroad, 2003.

———— editor. *Meister Eckhart and the Beguine Mystics; Hadewijch of Brabant, Mechthild of Magdeburg, and Marguerite Porete.* Bloomsbury: Bloomsbury Academic, 1997.

———— The Presence of God: A History of Western Christian Mysticism. London: SCM Press, 1995.

———— "The God beyond God: Theology and Mysticism in the Thought of Meister Eckhart." *The Journal of Religion,* Vol. 61, No. 1. (Jan., 1981), 1-19.

McIntosh, Steve. *The Presence of the Infinite: The Spiritual Experience of Beauty, Truth, and Goodness*. Wheaton: Theosophical Publishing House, 2015.

McKim. Donald K. and Alec C Cheyne, *Encyclopedia of the Reformed Faith*. Louisville, Kentucky: Westminster John Knox Press, 1992.

McKnight, Rosaline. *Cosmic Journeys*. Charlottesville, Hampton Roads, 1999.

Merton, Thomas. *Conjectures of a Guilty Bystander*. New York: Doubleday, 1966.

Mikula, Shawn, "Expansion of Consciousness." http://www.metareligion. com/Philosophy/Articles/Consciousness/expansion_of_ consciousness.htm.

Miller, Judith. *Healing the Western Soul: A Spiritual Homecoming for Today's Seekers*. St. Paul: Paragon House, 2015.

Mitchell, Donald W. *Spirituality and Emptiness: The Dynamics of Spiritual Life in Buddhism and Christianity*. Mahwah, New Jersey: Paulist Press, 1991.

Moody, Raymond. *Life After Life: The Bestselling Original Investigation That Revealed "Near-Death Experiences."* New York: HarperOne, 2015.

Moore, Kathleen Dean and Michael P Nelson, editors. *Moral Ground: Ethical Action for a Planet in Peril*. San Antonio: Trinity University Press, 2011.

Muir, John. *My First Summer in the Sierra*. San Francisco: Sierra Club Books, 1988.

Murrel, Beatrix. *Stoa del Sol*, http://www.bizint.com/stoa del sol/imaginal/ imaginal_nj2.html.

———— "The Cosmic Plenum: Bohm's Gnosis: The Implicate Order." Stoa del Sol, http://www.bizint.com/stoa_del_sol/plenum/plenum_3.html.

Nellas, Panayiotis. *Deification in Christ: Orthodox Perspectives on the Nature of the Human Person*. Crestwood, New York: St. Vladimir's Seminary, 1987.

Oppenheimer, Mark. "Beliefs," *New York Times* book review, Nov. 12, 2010. http://www.nytimes.com/2010/11/13/us/13beliefs.html?_r=0.

Origen. *Commentary on John, The Ante-Nicene Father: The Writings of the Fathers down to A.D. 325.* In Christian Classics Ethereal Library. http://www.ccel.org/ccel/schaff/anf09/Page_317.html.

Pagels, Elaine. *The Gnostic Gospels.* New York: Random House, 1979.

Panikkar, Raimon. "Nine Ways Not to Talk About God." http://dimensio-nesperanza.it/english-articles/item/6187-nine-ways-not-to-talk-about-god-raimon-panikkar.html.

———— "Raimon Panikkar Official Site." //http://raimon-panikkar.org/english/home.html.

———— *The Rhythm of Being: The Gifford Lectures.* Maryknoll: Orbis Books, 2009.

———— *The Experience of God, Icons of the Mystery.* Minneapolis: Augsburg Books, 2006.

———— *Christophany: The Fullness of Man.* Maryknoll: Orbis, 2004.

Patten, Terry, "The Taboo Against Ecstasy." http://www.terrypatten.com/video/the-taboo-against-ecstasy.

Penfield, William, *The Mystery of the Mind.* Princeton: Princeton University Press, 1975.

Phillips, J. B. *Ring of Truth: A Translator's Testimony.* London: Shaw Books, 2000.

Pilch, John. *Visions and Healing in the Acts of the Apostles: How the Early Believers Experienced God.* Collegeville: Liturgical Press, 2004.

———— "The Transfiguration of Jesus: An experience of alternate reality." In Philip Esler, editor, *Modelling Early Christianity: Social-scientific studies of the New Testament in its Context.* London and New York: Routledge, 1995.

Politella, Joseph. "Meister Eckhart and Eastern Wisdom" in *Philosophy East and West*, Vol. 15, No. 2. Honolulu: University of Hawaii Press, 1965.

Radin, Dean. "The Mental Universe." *Nature,* 436:29, 2005. http://deanradin.com/evidence/Henry2005Nature.pdf.

Rahner, Karl. *The Trinity.* Translated by J. Donceel. New York: Crossroad Publishing Company, 1997.

Rakestraw, Robert V. "Becoming Like God: An Evangelical Doctrine of Theosis," *Journal of the Evangelical Theological Society,* June

1997. http://www.etsjets.org/files/JETS-PDFs/40/40-2/40-2-pp257-269_JETS.pdf.

Rice, Daniel J. *This Side of a Wilderness*. South Elgin: Riverfeet Press, 2016.

Ritchie, George G, and Ian Stevenson. *My Life After Dying: How 9 Minutes in Heaven Taught Me How to Live on Earth.* Charlottesville: Hampton Roads, 2015.

Robinson, James. "The Study of the Historical Jesus after Nag Hammadi." In *Semeia* 44: The Historical Jesus and the Rejected Gospels. Atlanta: Scholars Press, 1980.

Rohr, Richard. Video from "Return to the Heart of Christ Consciousness." http://returntotheheartevent.com/offerings/jesus/.

——— "The Great Chain of Being." http://www.huffingtonpost.com/fr-richard-rohr/the-great-chain-of-being_b_829255.html.

——— "Richard Rohr's Daily Meditations." https://cac.org/category/daily-meditations/.

——— *Eager to Love*. Cincinnati: Franciscan Media, 2014.

——— *The Naked Now: Learning to See as the Mystics See*. New York: Crossroad, 2013.

——— *Breathing Under Water*. Cincinnati: Franciscan Media, 2011.

——— *Falling Upward: A Spirituality for the Two Halves of Life*. San Francisco: Jossey-Bass, 2011.

——— *Everything Belongs: The Gift of Contemplative Prayer*. New York: Crossroad 2003.

Rushdie, Salman. *The Satanic Verses*. New York: Vintage Press, 1989.

Sacks, Rabbi Jonathan. *Christian Century*. November 25, 2015.

Sagan, Carl. *Pale Blue Dot: A Vision of the Human Future in Space*. New York: Random House Publishing, 1994.

"Sayings of Meister Eckhart declared as heresy by the Vatican." http://www.thedaobums.com/topic/31976-sayings-of-meister-eckhart-declared-as-heresy-by-the-vatican/.

Schaff, Philip, editor. Translated by J. E. Tweed. "Augustine On the Psalms." *Nicene and Post-Nicene Fathers*, First Series, Vol. 8. Buffalo: Christian Literature Publishing Co., 1888.

Schweitzer, Albert. *The Mysticism of Paul the Apostle*. Baltimore: Johns Hopkins University Press, 1998.

Shankara. *Vivekachudamani*. Surrey, British Columbia: House of Metta, 2012.

Shanon, Benny. *The Antipodes of the Mind: Charting the Phenomenology of the Ayahuasca Experience*. New York: Oxford University Press, 2002.

Sherwin-White, A.N. *The Letters of Pliny: A Historical and Social Commentary*. Oxford: Oxford University Press, 1966.

Singer, Michael A. *The Untethered Soul: The Journey Beyond Yourself*. Oakland: New Harbinger Publications, 2013.

Singh, Kathleen Dowling. *The Grace in Aging: Awaken as You Grow Older*. Boston: Wisdom Publications, 2014.

Smith, Paul R. "An Evolutionary Integral Understanding of the Cross." *Tikkun*, Oct. 26, 2012. http://www.tikkun.org/nextgen/an-evolutionary-integral-understanding-of-the-cross.

——— *Integral Christianity: The Spirit's Call to Evolve*. St. Paul, Minnesota, Paragon House, 2011.

——— *Is It Okay to Call God Mother? Considering the Feminine Face of God*. Grand Rapids, Michigan, Baker Academic, 1993.

Spearing, Elizabeth, and Clifton Wolters. *Revelations of Divine Love*. New York: Penguin, 1998.

Stapp, Henry P. "Bell's Theorem and World Process." Il Nuovo Cimento B, October 1975, Volume 29, Issue 2, 271.

Stravinskas, Peter. What Mary Means to Christians: An Ancient Tradition Explained. Mahwah, N. J., Paulist Press, 2012.

Teresa, Mother. "Mother Teresa's Mystical Experiences: The Origins of Her Work." http://www.zenit.org/en/articles/mother-teresa-s-mystical-experiences-origin-of-her-work.

Teresa, of Avila. "Friendship with Jesus." *Opusc. De Libro vitae*. https://www.crossroadsinitiative.com/media/articles/friendship-with-jesus-teresa-of-avila/.

Teresa, St., of Jesus, *The Life of St. Teresa of Jesus*. Christian Ethereal Classics Library. www.ccel.org/ccel/teresa/life.viii.xxx.html.

Thayer, Joseph, and James Strong. *Thayer's Greek-English Lexicon of the New Testament.* Grand Rapids: Baker Book House, 1977.

Tillich, Paul. *Systematic Theology,* Vol. 1. Chicago: University of Chicago Press, 1951.

Tomaino, Charlotte. *Awakening the Brain: The Neuropsychology of Grace.* New York: Atria Books/Beyond Words.

Traherne, Thomas. *Centuries of Meditations.* Cyprus: Paphos Publishers, 2016.

Treece, Patricia. *Apparitions of Modern Saints.* Ann Arbor: Servant, 2001.

Tucker, Jim B., and Ian Stevenson. *Life Before Life: Children's Memories of Previous Lives.* New York: St. Martin's Griffin 2008.

Underhill, Evelyn. *Practical Mysticism.* New York: Start Publishing, 2013.

——— *Mysticism.* CreateSpace Independent Publishing, 2011.

Vaughan, Curtis. *Ephesians.* Nashville: Convention Press, 1963.

Weatherhead, Leslie. *The Transforming Friendship: A Book About Jesus and Ourselves.* Nashville: Abingdon Press, 1990.

Weibe, Phillip. *Visions and Appearances of Jesus.* Abilene, Texas: Leafwood, 2014.

Weil, Simone. *Waiting on God.* Translated by Emma Craufurd. New York: Routledge, 1951.

Wilber, Ken, and Terry Patten, Adam Leonard, Marco Morelli. *Integral Life Practice.* Boston & London: Integral Books, 2008.

Wilber, Ken. *The Integral Vision.* Boulder, Shambhala, 2007.

———. *Integral Spirituality: A Startling New Role for Religion in the Modern and Postmodern World.* San Francisco: Shambhala, 2007.

——— *The Simple Feeling of Being: Embracing Your True Nature.* Boulder: Shambhala, 2004.

——— editor. *Quantum Questions. Mystical Writings of the World's Great Physicists.* San Francisco: Shambhala, 2001.

——— *Eye to Eye: The Quest for the New Paradigm.* San Francisco: Shambhala; 3rd ed., 2001.

——— *One Taste.* Boulder: Shambhala, 1999.

——— *The Atman Project.* Wheaton: Quest Books, 1996.

———— *Grace and Grit: Spirituality and Healing in the Life and Death of Treya Killam Wilber.* Boulder: Shambhala, 1991.

Williamson, Marianne. *A Return to Love: Reflections on the Principles of "A Course in Miracles."* New York: HarperOne, 2009.

Wiseman, James A. "'To be God with God:' The Autotheistic sayings of the Mystics." *Theological Studies* 51, 1990.

Wittgenstein, Ludwig. *Tractatus Logico-Philosophicus.* Translated by Charles Kay Ogden, 1922.

Wolf, Fred. *Taking the Quantum Leap: The New Physics for Nonscientists.* New York: Harper Collins, 1988.

Wolf, Robert. *Living Nonduality.* Ojai, California: Katina, 2014.

Wright, N. T. "Jesus' Self-Understanding." In *The Incarnation,* edited by S. T. Davis, et. al. Oxford, 2002.

———— "Jesus and the Identity of God," in *Ex Auditu,* 1998, 14, 42–56.

———— *Jesus and the Victory of God.* Minneapolis: Fortress Press, 1996.

———— *The New Testament and the People of God.* Minneapolis: Fortress Press, 1992.

Zuck, Jon. Wild Things of God. http://www.frimmin.com/faith/theosis.php.

Index

A

After Death Communication 159, 344
Armstrong 40
Augustine 3, 31, 38, 98, 107, 194, 203, 204, 345

B

bliss 84, 178, 247, 303, 304, 305, 306, 309, 321, 328, 331
Borg 97, 121, 234, 343
breathwork 93

C

Capra 56, 57, 258, 325
channeling 79, 232, 237, 239, 240, 243, 252
Cosmic Christ 30, 48-51, 53, 54, 57-68, 91, 222
crucifixion 22, 23, 127, 304, 339, 340, 386, 387

D

Dad 109, 111, 113, 183
Daddy 111-115, 352
Davies 205, 234, 316, 320
deification 132, 185, 192, 194
Delio 60, 62, 292
demythologizing 254
devotion 23, 49, 96, 111, 121-130, 132, 136, 137, 145, 164, 167, 178, 190, 191, 209, 235, 264, 292, 302, 331, 350, 382, 383, 385-388
devotion to God 96, 111, 121, 136, 190, 235, 292, 382
devotion to Jesus 121-125, 129, 130, 132, 145, 331
divine spirit 71-78, 80, 175, 231, 232, 314
divinization 185
Dossey 85, 323, 324

E

Eckhart 37, 39, 68, 81, 184, 185, 205, 206, 222, 254, 301, 317, 320, 330
Einstein 16, 17, 62, 63, 83, 326
Embody 293-295, 306, 308, 309, 323
Embody God 292, 293, 295, 323
emptiness 161, 221, 290, 292, 293, 295, 301, 303, 321
Everybody 308, 309, 317, 318, 323
evolution 17, 43, 44, 54, 59, 60, 65, 87, 104, 197, 198, 230, 250, 259, 264, 300, 327
Expanded Trinity 11, 25

F

Ferrer 52, 64, 152, 153-155, 160, 216, 264, 295

G

God beyond God 38, 207

God in Three Dimensions 164, 386
gods 16, 32, 34, 38, 186-188, 191-197,
    199, 203, 204, 206-208, 211,
    357, 384
God/She 6, 11, 13-15, 18, 20, 30, 32,
    34, 38, 53, 63, 70, 78, 97, 103-
    105, 111, 114, 155, 156, 166,
    183, 199, 202, 252, 348
Gospel of Thomas 14, 20, 23, 26, 51,
    55, 107, 141, 192, 199, 201, 297,
    315, 323
Grof 157, 159, 160, 238, 258

H

Harding 301
Hart 40, 45, 80, 81, 84, 88, 216, 222,
    303, 328
Hosea 106
human spirit 72-75, 77, 78, 80, 87,
    264
Hurtado 22, 129, 130, 131, 191, 192

I

I AM 13, 14, 33-36, 38, 41, 42, 44, 45,
    54, 71, 186, 189, 221, 266, 268,
    294-296, 305
I AMness 41, 267, 298
Inclusive Bible 73, 186
Induced-After Death-Communica-
    tions 159

J

Jesus Seminar 20, 254
Joel 77, 78, 231, 232
Julian 107, 171, 351
Jung 29, 30

K

Keating 32, 190, 210
King David 98
Kingdom of God 23, 53, 198, 317,
    320
Kingsley 86, 325
Kripal 216, 226

L

Laszlo 259, 260, 326, 327, 328
Léleknek 109, 110
Levison 73-75, 78, 240, 241
Lewis 149, 195, 196, 346, 347
losing your mind 290

M

male Jesus 165, 167, 172, 173
Mary 39, 59, 134, 136, 166, 167, 168,
    172, 173, 345, 352
McIntosh 14, 68, 221, 222, 292, 293
Merton 295, 296
Messiah 30, 47-49, 54, 66, 131, 191
Miller 19
mindfulness 219, 220, 224
Moody 158
Mother/Father 202
My journey 70, 249, 255, 305, 351

N

naming 6, 7, 11, 14, 25, 34, 80, 103-
    105, 109, 111-115, 232
Near Death Experience 158
Nobody 236, 288, 289, 290, 293, 307,
    308, 309, 323
nondual 58, 63, 65, 120, 125, 139, 155,
    191, 218, 222, 293, 308, 313,
    318, 319, 328, 331

nonduality 14, 58, 62, 156, 191, 207, 313, 318, 319, 322, 331, 332

nothingness 61, 292, 295, 296, 322

P

Panikkar 36, 40, 45, 52, 55, 60, 65, 199, 307, 308

Paraclete 74, 177

paranormal 157, 163, 214, 225, 226, 227, 239

personalization 175, 179

personification 65, 149, 170, 175, 176, 178

Piltch 124, 347

Pliny 131, 132

pneuma 73, 76, 78, 79, 217, 236, 237, 238, 239, 241, 242, 255

postmodernism 151

Postmodernism 151

prayer language 236, 244

presence of the infinite 14, 30, 189, 221

Presence of the Infinite 14, 222, 292, 293, 399

Progressive 123, 134, 136, 150

prophecy 78, 237, 252

prosopon 12

Q

quantum 56, 70, 84-86, 238, 260-262, 295, 299, 300, 324-327, 332, 387

Quantum 56, 85, 86, 238, 261, 262, 295, 299, 300, 324-328, 332

R

Realm of God 53, 58, 59, 113, 126, 198, 222, 308, 309, 313-316,

320, 322, 323, 326, 328, 332, 336, 339-342, 348, 349, 353

religions 16, 19, 20, 64, 65, 82, 137, 159, 213, 225, 226, 232, 240, 250, 252, 254, 257, 259, 262, 263, 290, 358, 359

religions of the world 64, 252, 359

Rohr 6, 37, 53, 84, 120, 132, 133, 207, 289, 302, 331

rûach 72-75, 78, 214

Rumi 58, 99, 100

S

Sacks 16

Sagan 43

saints 67, 153, 162, 168, 171-173, 184, 192, 203, 237, 307, 321, 343, 345, 346, 348, 350-354

Samson 76, 78, 230

Schrödinger 85

Schroeder 85

second coming 65- 67

Second Coming 65

sign of the cross 386

single-seeing 319, 320

Somebody 288, 289, 294, 307-309, 323

Sophia 170-173

Stevenson 158, 260

T

Temple 10, 21-23, 125, 126, 248

Teresa 118, 119, 154

The Inclusive Bible 25, 127, 307

theism 14, 155, 156

theistic 40, 155, 162, 176

theosis 132, 185, 190, 194, 196, 208

three basic perspectives 9, 11, 25, 26

Three Faces of God 1, 2, 7, 12, 25, 27, 212, 224, 311, 382, 385-387
three perspectives 9, 209
Tillich 39, 207
tongues 235, 236, 253
Torah 10, 21-23, 33, 125, 126
transforming friendship 96, 117, 118, 124
transpersonal 8, 41, 45, 48, 52, 53, 58, 61, 62, 84, 85, 87, 89, 91, 157, 158, 238
Trinitarian 3, 7, 30, 74, 95
Trinity 3-7, 11, 12, 22, 25, 29, 32, 41, 59, 70, 71, 75, 95, 183, 213, 333, 359

U

undead 296, 297
Underhill 82, 321, 328, 329

V

visions 55, 77, 78, 130, 139, 154, 159, 160, 167, 168, 220, 221, 232, 238, 239, 243, 245, 251, 258, 263, 329, 344, 351, 352

W

Weatherhead 119, 135, 136
Welcoming Prayer 309
Wilber vii, 8, 83, 85, 137, 152, 160, 161, 250, 257, 262, 267, 298, 315, 316, 331
Wolf 262, 295, 300
Wright 21, 22, 48, 125, 126, 314

Y

YHWH 22, 32-34, 73, 106, 230